Duty, Honor, Country

and

Wisconsin

Salute
To Ben
Bunzel from
all of us at the
C.K. Pier Civil
War Camp — we look
after our vets and
current servicemen
and women,

Tom Mueller

Tom Mueller
10-14-13

First published by Dog Ear Publishing
4010 W. 86th Street, Ste H
Indianapolis, IN 46268
www.dogearpublishing.net

ISBN: 978-1-4575-2164-5

This book is printed on acid-free paper.

Printed in the United States of America

Also by Tom Mueller

The Wisconsin 3,800

Heart of the Century 1949 to 1951

Building the Bridges to Victory

This book is dedicated to all those who gave their last full measure, particularly my relatives – Pvt. Martin Miller in Normandy in 1944 and Army Specialist 4 David Hellenbrand in Vietnam in 1968.

On the cover

Starting from the top, the men on the cover are

Moritz Ganser, who served in the Civil War from 1864 to 1865

Emil Dallmann, killed in World War I in 1918

Charles Fidler, MIA in World War II in 1942

Mitchell Red Cloud, killed in Korea in 1950 and a Medal of Honor recipient

Paul Derby, MIA in Vietnam in 1968

David Johnson, killed in Afghanistan in 2012

Table of Contents

WISCONSIN'S MILITARY SERVICE

Military Action	Number Served	Number Killed
Civil War	91,379[1]	12,216
Spanish-American War	5,469	134[2]
Mexican Border Service	4,168	NA
World War I	122,215	3,932
World War II	332,200	8,390
Korean Conflict	132,000	729
Vietnam	165,400	1,239
Lebanon/Grenada	400	1
Panama	520	1
Operations Desert Shield/Desert Storm	10,400	11
Somalia	426	2
Bosnia/Kosovo	678	NA
Iraq and Afghanistan Theaters of Operations since September 11, 2001	31,830	116[3]

Note: Includes Wisconsin residents who served on active duty during declared wars and officially designated periods of hostilities.

NA – Not available.

[1]Total includes some who enlisted more than once. The net number of soldiers recruited in Wisconsin was about 80,000.

[2]Casualties only from Wisconsin 1st, 2nd, 3rd and 4th Regiments. No details available for Wisconsin residents serving in federal units.

[3]Includes one killed in attack on Pentagon on September 11, 2001.

Sources: U.S. Veterans Administration; U.S. Department of Defense; and Wisconsin Department of Veterans Affairs, departmental data, June 20, 2011.

Introduction

Across its span of 165 years of history, the sons and daughters of Wisconsin have given their lives for the nation – in Tennessee and Georgia and Virginia and other states in the Civil War; in Europe and Russia in two world wars; in the Pacific and the Burma-India-China theater in World War II; in Korea; in Vietnam and adjoining countries; in the Persian Gulf, in Iraq and in Afghanistan.

This is their story. This is Duty, Honor, Country and Wisconsin.

Nearly 27,000 men and women from Wisconsin have made the Ultimate Sacrifice in the nation's wars, according to the state Department of Veterans Affairs.[1] They are represented in this book by several dozen people spanning from Kenosha to Bayfield to Marshfield, and from Mayville to Madison to Green Bay to Sauk City / Prairie du Sac, and from Eau Claire to Laona to Ettrick to Medford to Dousman and Milwaukee.

Most have not been written about since their deaths, and those obituaries did not have the context of the battle in which a soldier fell.

Among many others, readers of this book will meet the four men whose names are on the VFW and American Legion posts in Oak Creek in Milwaukee County, several from Oak Creek who were killed or died of disease in the Civil War, and a World War I man sent to fight in Russia in an anti-Bolshevik effort who was killed there as the war continued nearly two months after the Armistice.

They also will meet two dozen men killed in World War II; two lost in Korea in the disastrous month of November 1950 – one who received the Medal of Honor and another whose body was not identified until 62 years later. Readers also will meet all the 37 Wisconsin MIAs in Vietnam, the seven women killed in Iraq and Afghanistan plus two Dodge County men in Afghanistan in the final years of that war.

In more than a few cases in World War I, World War II and in Iraq, those in this book who made the Ultimate Sacrifice were serving in the Wisconsin National Guard, the 32nd Division – the Red Arrow. They were in

---

[1] Wisconsin Blue Book 2011-2012, http://legis.wisconsin.gov/lrb/bb/11bb/Stats_Military.pdf, p. 764.

1

World War I, World War II and in Iraq.[2] Many in the book from World War II, including those in the Red Arrow, are buried overseas or are on MIA walls, particularly in Manila. That cemetery has a total of 1,035 Wisconsin servicemen; overall there are 17,201 bodies and 36,285 names on its MIA walls.

While all those who are featured in this book deserve to have their photo included (but in some prominent cases, not even a VFW or Legion post had the photo of a man it honors), a line had to be drawn at some point just for purposes of feasibility when the book discusses several dozen people. So generally, those who are first or early in a chapter will be pictured. And, Vietnam MIAs whose photos were extremely difficult for anyone to obtain today also are being used.[3]

Similarly, it would have been impossible to try to find family of each and every person discussed in this book, and it would have become hopelessly repetitive for the reader. So there is a blend of cases where family was found and interviewed, including the chapter on the Oak Creek men whose names are on the city's American Legion and VFW posts. Those people serve as examples of families who received the horrible news from overseas.

Finding the context of battles from 150 years ago, nearly 100 years ago and a half-century ago is easier than it would seem, because the Civil War and World War I have been documented in books and state histories almost as well as the ubiquitous works of World War II. So were Korea and Vietnam.

Beyond all those who made the Ultimate Sacrifice, the state says nearly 900,000 from Wisconsin have served in conflicts from the Civil War to the present day.[4]

This book features seven Civil War soldiers who became Wisconsin governor and interviews more than three dozen male and female veterans of World War II, Korea, Vietnam, the Persian Gulf War, Iraq and Afghanistan. They were not prodded to talk in-depth about the worst days of their lives,

---

[2] http://www.32nd-division.org/history/32hist.htm

[3] The author helped Vietnam veteran Jeff Dentice of Muskego obtain missing photos, and his website proudly displays every one of the 37. See them at http://www.war-veterans.org/Wi37.htm, and listen to its song about veterans and MIAs. Dentice and Tom Mueller helped update the Vietnam Wall website, which now has every one of the 37 – see http://www.vvmf.org/thewall

[4] Wisconsin Blue Book 2011-2012, http://legis.wisconsin.gov/lrb/bb/11bb/Stats_Military.pdf, p. 764.

because that has been done by other writers, including two excellent recent books about Wisconsin veterans of Korea and Vietnam.[5]

Instead, this book gathers the simple facts of where they were, how young they were (so many were 19 and 20) and what their job was along with what their unit's job was – and lets them keep talking. Many had unheralded but vital jobs, such as a man who worked on a floating aircraft repair shop in World War II, a train engineer in India in that war and a submarine crewman in the Vietnam War. The vets also were invited to tell us what we should remember about their work and their era.

Those who are honored and interviewed in this book – as the Ultimate Sacrifice or as a vet – were selected with an eye toward geographical balance and balance among the Navy, Army, Marines and Air Force.[6] But the research went way beyond that – some accounts were developed when coming across as little as one sentence in a book and then playing a hunch by checking a name in the database of overseas burials and MIAs at www.abmc.gov, for example. This is an excellent and very searchable resource, all built around what state a service member was from.

Appendix 1 is about how a certain future well-known entertainer was an 18-year-old infantryman who encountered a concentration camp in Germany when it was liberated at the end of April 1945. It is one such example of a solitary sentence in a book leading to deeper research and very enlightening results.

Other story angles were developed when several VFW and American Legion posts across Wisconsin were asked for basic information about the people whose names are honored on their posts. A few posts eagerly took up this question, but unfortunately many others in the state ignored that question and thus missed an opportunity to see that those who made the Ultimate Sacrifice from their community were honored here. One post had lost track

---

[5] "Wisconsin Korean War Stories," by Sarah A. Larsen and Jennifer M. Miller (2008), and "Wisconsin Vietnam War Stories," by the same authors (2010). Both books also are documentaries on Wisconsin Public Television.

[6] Tom Mueller's book "The Wisconsin 3,800" (2009) also featured a Merchant Marine who was the first Wisconsinite to die in World War II, being lost on March 29, 1940, long before Pearl Harbor. Charles Coffey is buried in Tunisia. That book also profiled two Coast Guard men killed in that war, and examined the overall role of those two maritime services.

of where one of its honorees was buried, because so many of its founders have died out. The author quickly solved the case, to the post's thanks, and it sent flowers to his grave in Manila.

Similarly, some vets who were asked to participate in this book readily responded briefly and in person where they were and when, but balked at further contact with the author. That was their prerogative. But other men and women readily agreed to tell their stories.

One man wearing a Vietnam vet hat at a large event honoring veterans of all wars thanked the author for asking and for embarking on the project on behalf of veterans in general, but added that he just did not care to "remember again" what he had gone through. Others seemed to not want any spotlight to be put on them.

All in all, roughly one vet agreed to be interviewed for every three who were contacted in person, on the phone or via email.

During all of this, the author rechecked the record of his distant relative who was killed in Vietnam in 1968 and was very surprised to learn he had been awarded a posthumous Distinguished Service Cross, the second-highest medal that a soldier can receive. I salute him here: Army Specialist 4 David Hellenbrand of Janesville, 21, was killed Dec. 1, 1968, near Bien Hoa, Vietnam. He was in B Company, 18th Regiment, of the 1st Infantry Division.

Hellenbrand received the DSC for "extraordinary heroism" for "exceptionally valorous actions on 1 December 1968 as point man for his company during a reconnaissance-in-force mission southeast of Phouc Vinh. While breaking a trail through the thick jungle, Specialist Hellenbrand spotted three North Vietnamese soldiers in a bunker who were preparing to ambush his unit. He immediately shouted a warning to the other men and assaulted the entrenched Communists, firing his rifle as he advanced. The withering enemy fire mortally wounded him, but he managed to crawl to an opening in the bunker and threw a grenade inside, killing the three hostile soldiers and destroying the fortification. Because of his quickness and courage, he saved many of his comrades from injury or death."[7]

Hellenbrand's mother and the author's mother were first cousins; thus the soldier and the author are second cousins and had the same great-grandparents.

---

[7] http://militarytimes.com/citations-medals-awards/search.php?medal=2

No one from the Spanish-American war is included in this book, because of the conflict's very short length. The USS Maine exploded in the harbor at Havana, Cuba, on Feb. 15, 1898, and Congress declared war on April 21. The war ended less than four months later. The state Blue Book[8] says 5,469 Wisconsin men were in the war and that 134 were killed, but notes that those men were "only from Wisconsin 1st, 2nd, 3rd and 4th Regiments. No details available for Wisconsin residents serving in federal units."

One Wisconsinite in the Spanish-American war earned the Medal of Honor – Army Pvt. Oscar Brookins of Byron in Fond du Lac County, according to the Wisconsin Veterans Museum.[9] Brookins was two weeks short of age 29 when, on July 1, 1898, while serving with Company C, 17th U.S. Infantry, "in action at El Caney, Cuba ... (he) gallantly assisted in the rescue of the wounded from in front of the lines and under heavy fire from the enemy."[10]

The Veterans Museum list that includes Brookins also says there were seven Wisconsin recipients of the Medal of Honor for the Frontier Wars, which were against native Americans, from 1865 to 1891, and one for the Philippine-American war, earned in 1899. There were others awarded for service during the Boxer Rebellion in China in 1900 and the Mexican Border Campaign between 1914 and 1917.

The reader will see in multiple chapters the fine work of the Wisconsin Historical Society and the Pentagon's Defense Prisoner of War / Missing Personnel Office.

The Historical Society has worked seemingly forever to catalog Wisconsin's story, and is thanked for putting so much of it on its website (http://www.wisconsinhistory.org/).Its material was particularly helpful in the Civil War chapters, and was checked multiple times to see what it had for other chapters. Ditto the Wisconsin Veterans Museum, (http://wisvetsmuseum.com/).

---

[8] Wisconsin Blue Book 2011-2012, http://legis.wisconsin.gov/lrb/bb/11bb/Stats_Military.pdf, p. 764.

[9] http://www.wisvetsmuseum.com/researchers/military/Honors_Memorials/?ID=58

[10] http://www.militarytimes.com/citations-medals-awards/recipient.php?recipientid=2489. Some references, including the one at that site, have him as Brookin. The Wisconsin Veterans Museum has him as Brookins. He died in 1938 and is buried in Ohio. His gravestone, spells his name as Brookins.

And as the months went on, I helped each of those organizations if I saw something that needed correcting and when I wished to offer material. My earlier books and years of my newspaper stories written at the Milwaukee Sentinel are in the archives of the Veterans Museum.

The Pentagon office is able to make a few identifications a month, based on DNA and bone fragments of men lost in Vietnam, Korea, multiple countries of World War II and in the Cold War.[11] Its mottoes are "Keeping the Promise," "Fulfill their Trust" and "No One Left Behind." It notes that more than 83,000 Americans are missing from wars and that "hundreds of Defense Department men and women – both military and civilian – work in organizations around the world as part of DoD's personnel recovery and personnel accounting communities. They are all dedicated to the single mission of finding and bringing our missing personnel home. The mission requires expertise in archival research, intelligence collection and analysis, field investigations and recoveries, and scientific analysis."

This book's chapter on the Korean War will feature one MIA identified by that office in September 2012 – Pfc. Arthur Hopfensperger of Appleton, who was killed in November 1950.

I salute the work of the Historical Society, the Veterans Museum, the Pentagon office, the Wisconsin men and women who fell, and especially all the veterans. So does Wisconsin.

Tom Mueller

Oak Creek, Wis.

August 2013

The author also thanks Catherine Breitenbucher of Whitefish Bay, who edited segments of this book and corrected more than a few problems.

---

[11] http://www.dtic.mil/dpmo/

Chapter 1
The patriotic DNA of one community, part 1

This chapter and the next chapter discuss the men from a typical city who made the Ultimate Sacrifice, and that city's devotion to Duty, Honor, Country and Wisconsin throughout history.

The city is Oak Creek, a Milwaukee suburb, and it has paid its dues in the American story with the deaths of its sons in the Civil War, World War I, World War II and in Vietnam.

With this in-depth look at Oak Creek,[1] it is hoped that all in Wisconsin will better understand the stories that are right there in their own communities, and that they will act to preserve them in depth for future generations.

The names of those who made the Ultimate Sacrifice are revered, but in Oak Creek and elsewhere, the more decades that have passed, fewer and fewer remember much about them, particularly as the soldiers' families move away or die out. The same goes for what battle they were in, beyond the country and the date. The time is NOW for communities to act to record their own detailed stories of those who paid the price. This chapter will feature family interviews, telegrams and letters, plus information about the battles and days involved from books and websites.

At Oak Creek's Oelschlaeger-Dallmann American Legion Post 434, commander Jim Oswald, who spent six years in the Wisconsin National Guard, says: "For a parent to lose a loved one in time of war has to be terrible … we honor these brave men and women." He also says, "I truly am humbled and honored to serve the veterans that gave so many sacrifices and time to our United States of America either in peacetime or time of war."

Joseph Maniscalco, commander of Oak Creek's Meyer-Dziedzic VFW Post 8482, says the mission is "to recognize those that gave their all for their country."

It is important "for everybody to really think about what our veterans have given. They're the real patriots," says Maniscalco, who was in the Army in Vietnam in 1966 and 1967.

---

[1] The four men in this chapter originally were profiled by author Tom Mueller in 2011 in a series on www.oakcreekpatch.com. The stories have been revised and updated for this book.

Oak Creek Marine Pfc. James Meyer (above left) and Marine Pfc. Mark Dziedzic were killed within a month of each other in early 1968 in Vietnam. Their Ultimate Sacrifice followed in the footsteps of Army Sgt. Emil Dallmann (upper right), killed in World War I, and Army Pfc. Frederick Oelschlaeger in World War II. The names of Meyer and Dziedzic are honored on the VFW post in Oak Creek; the names of Oelschlaeger and Dallmann are on the city's American Legion post.

A year after Maniscalco left Vietnam, Oak Creek, then a town of less than 14,000, received a double shock of news from the other side of the world.

Like other cities in Wisconsin, it had lost a few men in World War I and World War II. It had escaped the loss of a son in Korea, a war that ended in a ceasefire two years before Oak Creek Township became a city in 1955.

It also had escaped losses in Vietnam in the first few years of American involvement, but the Grim Reaper caught up with a vengeance in 1968 when two local Marines were killed in the span of less than a month.

Their names – Marine Corps Pfc. James Fredrick Meyer Jr. and Marine Pfc. Mark Dziedzic – are carried on the city's VFW post. Oak Creek's American Legion post has names from World War II and World War I.

The four names are seen in the units' flags and color guards in the Fourth of July parade and at memorial events like Veterans Day in what today is a city of 35,000, far more than double what it had in 1968. They are major parts of the community's patriotic DNA, but while their names are familiar, the stories behind their names are far less known. Until now.

Vietnam

James Fredrick Meyer Jr., 19, arrived in South Vietnam on Dec. 31, 1967. He was dead only a few weeks later.

Meyer was killed Feb. 17, 1968, in Quang Tri Province, which is along the Demilitarized Zone.[2] This was during the Tet offensive of the North Vietnamese and Viet Cong, which had begun Jan. 30 and featured shocking attacks in more than 100 cities and towns, including a brief penetration of the U.S. Embassy in Saigon.

Meyer was in L Company, 1st Regiment, 1st Marine Division, III Marine Amphibious Force. He was a rifleman.

The Meyer family had moved from Milwaukee to a home on South Shepard Avenue off of East Rawson as James started at Oak Creek High School, from which he graduated in 1966.

The family had lived in Fort Atkinson, Wis., in Kentucky and then on 27th Street in Milwaukee before the move to Oak Creek. A decade or so after James was killed, it moved to Racine.

The Marine had two siblings: David, 8 at the time of his death, and Sharon Gaulke, who was 25, had three children and was living in Hales Corners.

"Jimmy was a fun-loving, happy-go-lucky brother," says Gaulke, now of Milwaukee, who had two more children after James' death and now has nine grandchildren. "He liked to tell jokes, and he loved sports. He was a wonderful brother. I couldn't ask for more. He was so kind-hearted and so full of life; a neat guy; a gorgeous guy."

David says his brother had a passion for cars, owning a dark blue Pontiac Tempest and a tan Volkswagen with a sunroof. They would ride together all over town, and often went to the State Fair to make a beeline for the Mousetrap ride, a kind of rollercoaster. "He showed me how to throw the

---

[2] The size of Quang Tri Province is 1,832 square miles, a little bigger than Rhode Island.

football and baseball. I miss him still," said David, who was in fourth grade at Edgewood Elementary School when the news from Vietnam arrived.

James also was an Explorer Scout and had oodles of merit badges, David says. And he worked with his father as an electroplater at Murray Metal Plating in Milwaukee.

He spent a year or so at the University of Wisconsin – Milwaukee, where he was reunited with a friend from middle school. Jon Lenichek. posted a remembrance message to Meyer on the website of the Vietnam Veterans Memorial in 2008, and discussed it via email.

"I knew Jim as a classmate and friend (albeit not my closest friend) from eighth grade into high school (Pulaski in Milwaukee). He was the only one of us who made the freshman football team, as I recall. A number of us stayed in touch even after he moved to Oak Creek, and then reconnected at UWM in fall 1966. I saw him pretty regularly while we both were there as freshmen, and continued to write after he enlisted. Jim was very funny and a riot to be around. Not exactly the model serious student, but certainly not a goof-off either."

The message that Lenichek posted was that he still had the last letter he sent to Meyer – returned unopened by the Marines because Meyer was KIA when it was received.

"I have no idea what my last letter says," Lenichek says now. "I have never opened it, and could not. It would be like opening his grave. For years I kept it framed in my office at work, and anytime I thought I was having a miserable day, I just looked up and realized what a skate my life had been."

While at UWM, Meyer knew he inevitably would be drafted, so he enlisted in the Marines. David says his brother won a coveted award in boot camp for being the best in his unit, called the Blues Winner Honor Man. He had hoped to get into a special training program, but the Marines being selected for it had much more than James' one year of college, and James lost out.

"He was very proud" of being a Marine, Gaulke says. "You could see he was learning from the experience." But in a final visit home before shipping out for Vietnam, "He was uneasy and had a sense of ill-boding," she adds.

David says the Marine had been based near the ancient city of Hue and the Perfume River, and was one of two men who had the task of providing cover fire for an evacuation helicopter. The copter got hit and those on it were rescued, but the extra time needed for the covering fire proved fatal to James and the other Marine. Gaulke tells a different version, about Meyer being on point and the first to be shot. "We were told that because he got shot, the rest of them could scatter and survive. They wrote us a letter saying that."

Tet was the lunar new year, a time when both sides usually observed a truce. The Communists broke it in 1968. As one history summarizes it: "On the Tet holiday, Viet Cong units surge into action over the length and breadth of South Vietnam. In more than 100 cities and towns, shock attacks by Viet Cong sapper-commandos are followed by wave after wave of supporting troops. By the end of the city battles, 37,000 Viet Cong troops deployed for Tet have been killed."[3] The offensive lasted through the end of March, and in terms of losses to the Communists, "Tet is nothing less than a catastrophe. But for the Americans, who lost 2,500 men, it is a serious blow to public support."

The deep division in the United States over the war before and especially after Tet "was an awful experience to those fragile young men," Gaulke says. "I was very torn for years, and angry. I'm not angry now. The worst thing was that we did not honor the veterans until much later. They deserved to be treated with respect. It broke my heart."

The searchable database of the Vietnam Veterans Memorial[4] shows 50 other men were killed the same day as Meyer. It could not readily be determined who was the Marine that David says killed with Meyer, but another WIsconsin Marine in his unit was killed the same day – Pfc. Kenneth Wayne Radonski of Milwaukee, who was in Headquarters and Service Company. Meyer was in Company L.

Gaulke's daughter Tracy has been to the Vietnam Wall in Washington, D.C., and "couldn't believe there were so many names (more than 58,200). They at first couldn't find my brother," who is on Panel 39E, Line 75.

Meyer is buried in Forest Hill Memorial Park, Oak Creek, with his mother, Zada, who died in 1986, and father, James Sr., who died in 1979.

David Meyer enlisted in the Marines in 1976, finishing in 1982 in the Reserves. His brother's service was in the back of his mind – "at the time I enlisted, I probably didn't think so, but there was a kind of 'if Jimmy can do it, I can.'"

James Meyer was the first from Oak Creek to die in Vietnam, and the community quickly mobilized to help the family. Gaulke says there was "a

---

[3] "Battlefield: Vietnam" at www.pbs.org/battlefieldvietnam/index.html
[4] www.thewall-usa.com/

huge, huge, huge procession for his funeral" from the Molthen-Bell Funeral Home in downtown South Milwaukee, with total support from the American Legion post for anything the family needed, and of course from the Marine Corps.

The city soon went through it again; again another Marine in the same Quang Tri Province. That was Pfc. Mark Dziedzic.

One of his brothers, Marine Lance Cpl. Chuck Dziedzic, who had been in Vietnam since November 1967 as a mortarman, was sitting at an ammo dump playing pinochle with a couple other Marines when he heard his name being called and the words, "Someone is here to visit you."

"As soon as I turned around to look, I saw the chaplain, with crosses on his collar, and I knew what had happened." Chuck says. The Navy chaplain, whom he had never seen before, had been sent out to inform Chuck and take him away for bereavement leave.

"They said 'get your stuff,' and we jumped on a truck and went back to Da Nang. I don't think I had time to say goodbye to half the guys I was serving with. I never saw them again," because he served out his tour stateside, then was in a different unit in his next tour in Vietnam.

Mark, 21, was the oldest Dziedzic (pronounced JAY-jick); Chuck was No. 3. The family's No. 2 child, Jeff, also had been a Marine in Vietnam, but his tour already had ended. Mark was born on July 12, 1946, and Jeff exactly one year and one day later.

Back in Oak Creek, when a pair of stone-faced Marines appeared at her home, Ella Mae Dziedzic knew that the news would not be good. She merely asked, "Which one?" – who the news was about: Jeff or Mark.

The bad news was about Mark, son of Robert and Ella Mae Dziedzic who lived on South Burrell Street, just off South Howell Avenue and south of East Ryan Road. The family was seven boys and two girls.

Mark was killed on March 16, 1968, in the final weeks of Tet. He was in H Company, 4th Marine Regiment, 3rd Marine Division.

The family's No. 7 child, Paula, was 9 at the time and tells what happened: "Two gentlemen in uniform walked up the driveway. My Mom was ironing and everything was blocking the front door, so she told them to go around to the other side of the house.

"After she broke down and cried, she called my Dad to come home," says Paula, whose last name is now Lewandowski and is a mother and grandmother, and still lives in Oak Creek. Her Dad was the body shop manager for an auto dealer on South 27th Street in Milwaukee.

Mark had gone to what is now the University of Wisconsin – La Crosse for one year, then went into the Marines. Jeff had become a Marine immediately after high school, and returned to Oak Creek after his Vietnam tour ended – only a few days before Mark shipped out for Vietnam. Chuck was in boot camp at Camp Pendleton in California at the same time Mark was, but had arrived there about five weeks later. Then they both were in Vietnam.

Mark had spent his summers doing work on some of the many farms in Oak Creek, and became very strong from pitching hay bales. He outplayed his small size of 5 foot 9 and 165 pounds, Chuck says, and was an all-conference halfback and a linebacker at Oak Creek High School, which won the Parkland Conference football title in his senior year. He also was a starter on the basketball team.

He wore No. 22, just like his father had in high school, and his brothers later wore the same number.

"He was a tough kid. What he lacked in size, he made up for in being tough," Chuck says.

The growing family had moved to Oak Creek from South 13 Street in Milwaukee, where it had lived with grandparents in what was getting to be a very crowded house.

"I was in the fourth grade when we moved," Jeff says. "We were happy being out in the country. My brothers and I would go out an explore the woods and where the ponds might be. We would go out in the cornfield and roast some ears right there. And we would go for crayfish under the bridge on South Shepard Avenue right where East Middle School is today."

Jeff says Mark wanted to be a history teacher, but after one year of college decided he did not want to borrow money for his education, planning to use his veterans' benefits when he got out.

Chuck says Mark originally signed up for the Navy, "but for some reason he changed his mind and decided to join the Marine Corps in March 1967. Maybe he felt it was more patriotic at the time," when the war was not yet as deeply unpopular as it would become.

Mark graduated in 1964 from Oak Creek High School, where his portrait and that of Meyer are the largest in a display case of pictures of military veterans and current service members who have attended the school.

Hundreds of teens and staffers pass the display every hour on their way to class, but to one person who worked there for nearly two decades – Lewandowski, a school aide – it has a Semper Fi meaning.

"I walk by his photo every day and say 'good morning' to my brother. How can you not? I would feel guilty if I didn't."

However, "When I hear 'Taps,' I can't even listen to it," Lewandowski says. "And my older sister fainted in the cemetery during 'Taps' and the gun salute." The Marine is buried in Holy Sepulchre Cemetery in Cudahy.

One other Wisconsin Marine in the same company as Dziedzic was killed with him – Pfc. Dennis Zwirchitz, 20, of Abbotsford in Clark County, west of Wausau, who received the Silver Star. A third Marine killed at the same spot on the same day was Sgt. David Simmons of Michigan, who was in an attached tank battalion.

The website www.virtualwall.org lists those two deaths on Dziedzic's page, and vice versa. It also has this account from the Marines' Command Chronology for March 16: "Hotel Company made heavy contact while successfully extracting an eight-man recon patrol which earlier made contact with a large enemy force at YD 261659, the fortified village of Vinh Quan Ha. Twenty-one enemy were killed while friendly losses were three KIA …"

A search at the database of the Vietnam Veterans Memorial[5] shows 45 other men were killed the same day as Dziedzic and the two other Marines.

The Tet offensive was smashed after weeks of difficult fighting. Marines were under siege / attack for 77 days – until April 8 – at Khe Sanh in Quang Tri Province and in pitched battles at Hue, like Meyer was in, some of the worst fighting of the entire war. There was a high cost in blood, and an even higher cost in domestic public perception and opinion.

It soon became known that Army Gen. William Westmoreland, commander in South Vietnam, had requested 200,000 additional troops on top of more than a half-million already there,[6] a stunningly depressing turn of events to a nation that often had been told there was light around the corner but now was learning how bad things were and that Westmoreland wanted a 40 percent increase in the number of men. Protests on college campuses across the nation grew and grew and became uglier and uglier; President Lyn-

---

[5] www.thewall-usa.com

[6] http://www.history.com/topics/william-westmoreland

don B. Johnson nearly was defeated in the March 12 New Hampshire Democratic primary by upstart Sen. Eugene McCarthy and withdrew from the presidential race on March 31, two weeks after Dziedzic was killed.

Before the war would finally end in South Vietnam's surrender in April 1975, three more Oak Creek men would be killed[7]: Army Cpl. Severiano Rios, on April 2, 1970; Army Sgt. Peter Michael Vanderweg, July 25, 1970, and Army Warrant Officer Glenn Edward Nowakowski, July 22, 1972.

Lewandowski says she cannot help but wonder what the dynamics of her family would have been if Mark Dziedzic had come home from Vietnam. There were nine kids, but then there were eight – meaning a birthday that would not come again, a wedding, extra grandchildren, etc. And because he was the oldest, he likely would have been first to be in all of these major events.

"I miss my brother every day," Jeff Dziedzic says. "He's the only big brother I ever had." Before Mark was killed, Jeff had been wounded slightly in the left hand by shrapnel, and he has a Purple Heart, but "the mental injury that you get from going to war stays with you forever. I feel guilty that I came back and he didn't."

Even before Meyer and Dziedzic were lost, the city had a very close call with death in the war when Army Specialist 4 Gary Wetzel was severely wounded, losing his left arm, on Jan. 8, 1968. Wetzel was in the 173rd Assault Helicopter Company and the door gunner of a helicopter that had come to a landing zone and then was trapped by heavy fire. What he did next earned him the Medal of Honor. The citation[8] said

> **Wetzel was going to the aid of his aircraft commander when he was blown into a rice paddy and critically wounded by two enemy rockets that exploded just inches from his location. Although bleeding profusely due to the loss of his left arm and severe wounds to his right arm, chest, and left leg ... Wetzel staggered back to his original position in his gun-well and took the enemy forces under fire. His machine gun was the only weapon placing effective fire on the enemy at that time.**

---

[7] http://www.virtualwall.org/istate/istatwi.htm

[8] http://www.war-veterans.org/Wetzel.htm

Through a resolve that overcame the shock and intolerable pain of his injuries, (he) remained in his position until he had eliminated the automatic weapons emplacement that had been inflicting heavy casualties on the American troops and preventing them from moving against this strong enemy force.

Refusing to attend to his extensive wounds, he attempted to return to the aid of his aircraft commander but passed out from the loss of blood. Regaining consciousness, he persisted in his efforts to drag himself to the aid of his fellow crewmen.

After an agonizing effort he came to the side of a crew-chief who was attempting to drag the wounded aircraft commander to the safety of a nearby dike. Unswerving in his devotion to his fellow man, Specialist Fourth Class Wetzel assisted his crew chief even though he lost consciousness once again during this action.

World War I

Oak Creek's Emil Dallmann died more than 90 years ago, but family members from a generation down the road look at his picture and readily see that their own grandchildren share some of his facial traits.

Dallmann, 22, a sergeant in Company H in the 39th Regiment in the Army's 4th Infantry Division, was killed in France on Oct. 10, 1918, in the last month of World War I. He died in giant fighting known as the second phase of the Meuse-Argonne offensive by the American Expeditionary Force. More than 1.2 million Americans were involved in that battle.

Franz Dallmann and his wife, Emilie Oldenburg, ran a 40-acre farm, on East Oakwood Road and east of the railroad tracks, which was sold in the 1950s and became a subdivision. Franz was born in 1837 in Pomerania in Germany and had two previous wives. One of the many children and stepchildren on the family tree also had been named Emil, a son of Franz and his first wife. That child died in a fire in South Dakota along with a brother.

Franz and Emilie Oldenburg had seven children of their own. Emil Dallmann the soldier was No. 5.

"He resembled my uncle Ernst," says Janet Johnson of Milwaukee, one of his many nieces. A nephew, the late Bob Dallmann, bore a strong resem-

16

blance to the soldier, too, according to Mildred Dallmann, his wife. Mildred says Emil's nose, eyes and hair color are evident in some of her grandchildren, and that his gentle features also were carried by her husband – "they were mad at him in the Army because he needed to shave only once a week."

The Dallmann farm had a postal address of Rural Route 1, South Milwaukee, and Emil is listed as being from that city in the 1925 book "Wisconsin's Gold Star List: Soldiers, Sailors, Marines, and Nurses from the Badger State Who Died in the Federal Service During the World War."[9] The listing also spells his name with one "N," a mistake that often still happens today, family members say.

The family received this Western Union telegram from the Army on Dec. 1, 1918, several weeks after Emil was killed: "Deeply regret to inform you that Sergeant Emil Dallmann infantry is officially reported as killed in action October fourteenth." Later correspondence amended that to Oct. 10, but the Gold Star book retained the later date.

Months later, on May 23, 1919, the family received a letter from Capt. R.W. Norton of Dallmann's 39th Regiment saying the American Red Cross had provided this description of what happened to the Doughboy (again misspelling his name; it also was wrong on his temporary grave in France):

> **During the early phase of the attack, Sergeant Dallman saw an enemy machine gun crew set its gun into a position which meant practical death for an entire platoon. Running with a squad of three others in the direction of the machine gun, it was seen to be impossible to reach the gun before it got into action.**
>
> **Sergeant Dallman dropped to one knee and fired into the crew, killing one. The machine gun opened fire. Sergeant Dallman was killed instantly, as was the remainder of the squad. ...**
>
> **In previous actions Sergeant Dallman had distinguished himself greatly, coming from a private to a sergeant in the first two engagements and won a reputation which was second to none.**

The letter does not give a specific location other than in the Argonne in eastern France, but the Gold Star book puts the site as Norroy, St. Thibault.

---

9 http://www.accessgenealogy.com/worldwarone/wisconsin/

Dallmann is mentioned by name in a recent article in the Quarterly Journal of Military History[10]. The article by Alfred S. Bradford Jr. is entitled, "Killing Machines at Meuse-Argonne, 1918." The article is based on a narration of fighting by the 39th Regiment in late September 1918 by the author's uncle, Lt. Francis (Bud) Bradford, of Appleton.

The lieutenant's account says Bradford and Dallmann's

H Company went into the first lines with a smash. By 9 we had advanced two kilos (kilometers) under terrific shrapnel, high explosive, and machine gun fire mixed plentifully with gas …. I can hear those bullets yet! I put on my mask. Inside of five minutes I had completely lost my bearings. We took off our gas masks and got through somehow.

We passed a high railroad before I realized that I was way in the lead of the regiment. Just at that moment a German machine gun opened on our right flank and another in our front, at 700 yards. To charge them across the open would have been suicide; to stay where we were on the nose of the hill, worse. We were partly concealed in brown weeds about a foot high.

I didn't pull any hero stuff. I ordered a withdrawal 100 paces to the railroad track to reorganize. We started, but just then the Boche artillery got our range and the heavens opened. Machine gun bullets were coming as thick as holes in player piano (music rolls). One got me in the right foot. I turned to (First Sgt. Emil) Dallman(n) and said, "Get the men back; I'm hit." Then all the bells in the land broke loose – I grabbed my head with my hand; blood poured down my face and blinded me. I lay there for several moments betting on whether I was dead or alive.

A bullet had gone through the middle of my tin derby. After I got the blood from my eyes, I wrote the captain a message of our predicament and turned to the runner on my left. He was sure hugging the ground. I hit him with a stone. He didn't move. He was dead. I turned to the man on my right. He was lying on his side and I saw him hit twice more.

---

[10] www.historynet.com/killing-machines-at-meuse-argonne-1918.htm

Bradford eventually crawled to safety, and his men had thought he was dead because of the hole in his helmet.

The Allied offensive came in the region of the Meuse River and the Argonne forest, and marked by far by heaviest American losses in the war. The Americans were in the fighting from April 1918 to the Armistice on Nov. 11 of that year.

The first phase of the offensive began Sept. 26 and ended Oct. 3. The second phase began the next day. For Oct 4, 5 and 6, Dallmann's "4th Division, attempting to scale the Cunel Heights on the far right of the attack, gained scarcely a mile, and were still overlooked by the Germans on the Heights above. Right across the line the same story was told: unparalleled resistance, very heavy casualties, little or no advance," according to the 2000 book "The Doughboys."[11]

One ordinary American Doughboy became famous right in that area two days before Dallmann was killed: Alvin York of the 82nd Division. He received the Medal of Honor for his actions of Oct. 8, with the citation saying: "After his platoon had suffered heavy casualties and the other noncommissioned officers had become casualties, Cpl. York assumed command. Fearlessly leading seven men, he charged with great daring a machine gun nest which was pouring deadly and incessant fire upon his platoon. In this heroic feat the machine gun nest was taken, together with four officers and 128 men and several guns."[12]

On Sept. 26, the Allies fired 1.842 million artillery rounds, and 853,000 the next day. The rate then "fell" to between 200,000 and 491,000 per day, and on Oct. 10 it was 244,000.[13]

Dallmann first was buried near the battlefield, and at his family's request his body was returned to the United States, arriving in December 1921. He and his parents are buried in Oakwood Rest Cemetery in the 200 block of West Oakwood Road, very close to the road. This time, the spelling on his tombstone was correct, with two Ns.

Those who remained behind in France were reinterred at the Meuse-Argonne American Cemetery and Memorial, where there are 14,246 graves

---

[11] "The Doughboys," by Gary Mead (2000), p. 313-314.

[12] http://militarytimes.com/citations-medals-awards/recipient.php?recipientid=134

[13] "The Doughboys," p. 323.

and 954 names on the MIA wall. A total of 381 are from Wisconsin, according to the American Battle Monuments Commission, whose website of www.abmc.gov has a searchable database.

Dallmann's nephew Bob Dallmann was a combat engineer in World War II in France (in the same general region where Emil had been killed), Belgium, Holland and Germany. Bob served as commander of the Oelschlaeger-Dallmann Legion post in the 1950s, and Mildred also was president of the auxiliary. They then lived in several other states.

World War II

Oak Creek Army Pfc. Frederick Oelschlaeger was killed July 16, 1944, on New Guinea amid a series of fierce battles near the jungle villages of Afua and Aitape and the Driniumor River. He was in the 127th Regiment of the Army's 32nd Infantry Division, and is buried in the Philippines.

Oelschlaeger was born Aug. 6, 1919, so his death came about two weeks before his 25th birthday.

The family had lived in Milwaukee and moved to the Town of Oak Creek in 1933, buying a 20-acre farm on East Oak Street up the hill from South Howell Avenue. Frederick was the first child, followed by Gordon, Audrey and Dan. The father, Fred, was of Luxembourg descent and was an engineer at the Lakeside power plant in St. Francis. The mother was Sophie.

Dan Oelschlaeger was 17 years younger than Frederick and always called his brother Fritz. Fritz called him Joe and when he came home on leave, "he'd throw me up in the air and catch me. He was 6-foot-2 or 3, a big guy." The Fritz and Joe show, complete with giggles and hoots and thrills, was far better than any carnival ride.

Dan was 8 when the fateful telegram arrived. Like the Dziedzic family from the Vietnam War earlier in this chapter, the Oelschlaegers were not sure whether it would involve Frederick or Gordon, who was a Marine in the invasion of Saipan, which had begun a month earlier. "My Dad was a pretty tough dude, but he sat on the sofa and put his head in his hands and was crying," says Dan, who still lives in Oak Creek. Dan had never seen his father cry before.

The memorial service was Aug. 19 at St. Stephen's Roman Catholic Church at its original site on South Howell, in an area that everyone then knew as New Coeln.

A newspaper article said it was the "first World War II Memorial Requiem High Mass" at St. Stephen's.

The pastor, Father C.J. Eschweiler, built his sermon around the Biblical verse, "No greater love hath any man than he who giveth his life for his friend." The story said "he emphasized that Frederick was the first to volunteer when his country was in danger, that he was the first of his congregation to meet death in action, and likewise the first of the Town of Oak Creek."

A newspaper story the day before the funeral gave Oelschlaeger's background: He was a graduate of Green Lawn School and of Bay View High School. "He was employed on the John Ballbach farm at the time of his enlistment … in the Wisconsin National Guard Sept. 26, 1940."

Ballbach ran a large dairy farm on what is now the south campus of Milwaukee Area Technical College.

The story said Oelschlaeger "went overseas May 27, 1942. He was twice hospitalized for injuries sustained in action, but each time returned to duty. He had expected to be home on furlough in a short time."

Oelschlaeger's 32nd Division, Wisconsin's famed Red Arrow, had started fighting at Buna, New Guinea, in September 1942 and was so depleted by jungle diseases and geographical and weather challenges, plus the Japanese, that it was out of action for nearly a year, based in Australia as it was refurbished and revitalized. It returned to combat at Saidor in New Guinea in the first days of 1944. Then came Aitape.

The official history of the division[14] said the hamlet of Afua "changed hands several times, and South Force (Oelschlaeger's group) engaged in over a week of complicated fighting, made particularly difficult by the broken jungle-covered terrain, the lack of roads, the inaccurate maps, and the mixing of units. … South Force's casualties between 13 and 31 July were 106 killed, 386 wounded, 18 missing, 426 evacuated because of illness."

Three men earned the Medal of Honor during the period, including one for actions on the very day that Oelschlaeger was killed and another in Oelschlaeger's regiment.

Second Lt. Dale Eldon Christensen of the 112th Cavalry, a unit fighting as part of the same large force that Oelschlaeger was in, was posthumously

---

[14] "The 32nd Infantry Division in World War II," by Maj. Gen. H.W. Blakeley, (1957), p. 164.

awarded the Medal of Honor for several examples of heroic leadership from July 16 to 19. "On July 16, his platoon engaged in a savage firefight in which much damage was caused by one enemy machine gun effectively placed. Second Lt. Christensen ordered his men to remain under cover, crept forward under fire, and at a range of 15 yards put the gun out of action with hand gernades," the medal citation said.[15] There were many more days of fighting, and Christensen was killed on Aug. 4.

Christensen, from Iowa, was 24 and is buried in Manila, the Philippines, in the same section, Plot A, of the cemetery where Oelschlaeger is.

A member of Oelschlaeger's 127th Regiment, Pvt. Donald Lobaugh of Pennsylvania, received the Medal of Honor less than a week after Oelschlaeger was killed. On July 22, "the enemy emplaced a machine gun, protected by the fire of rifles and automatic weapons, which blocked the only route over which the platoon could move," according to the medal citation. "Lobaugh volunteered to attempt to destroy this weapon, even though in order to reach it he would be forced to work his way about 30 yards over ground devoid of cover. When partway across this open space he threw a hand grenade," but took fire and was wounded.[16] Lobaugh, 19, died in the attack and is buried in his home state.

In late August, six weeks after Oelschlaeger was killed, his family received a general letter from Father Edward Connolly, chaplain of his regiment. "Of all the sorrows and crosses that may befall us in this life, to suffer the loss of a near and dear one is perhaps the greatest," Connolly said. "… In his unit your dear one was admired and respected by his fellow soldiers. He was a good soldier; a brave and courageous soldier. He has left us with a shining example, and we will long remember him and the cause for which he died."

Oelschlaeger was in Company K, commanded by Capt. George M. Ficklen. In a letter to the family on Sept. 1, 1944, Ficklen said: "I know that I speak for all the officers and men who knew him, when I say that he was highly regarded by all. We will long remember Frederick, and his outstanding performance in combat. I trust that he now rests in peace, free from the trials and tribulations of mortal man …."

---

[15] http://www.iowahistory.org/museum/exhibits/medal-of-honor/christensen_d_wwii/index.htm

[16] http://www.32nd-division.org/history/moh/32moh.html

As more and more of its World War II members died, the Oelschlaeger-Dallmann American Legion post lost track of where Oelschlaeger was buried. It knew he was a World War II vet and of course his picture was in a place of honor, but beyond that there was no information – until author Tom Mueller tracked it down for the post.

"We knew where (Emil) Dallmann was buried in Oak Creek, but in recent years, there was no one left who knew anything about Oelschlaeger or where he was buried," says James (Ozzie) Oswald, post commander. "On his own time and energy, Tom Mueller did research and found that Oelschlaeger is buried in Manila. He arranged for us to send flowers to the grave and compiled short biographies and listings, and we put them under the pictures of Dallmann and Oelschlaeger at our post.

"We owe Tom many thanks and gratitude for his research for these two soldiers and also the two men whose names are on the Veterans of Foreign Wars post, which shares part of our facility."

Chapter 2
The patriotic DNA of one community, part 2

Nine decades before Oak Creek even became a city, dozens of its young men served in the Civil War, being killed or wounded in battle or dying of diseases in faraway places like Tennessee, Georgia and Virginia.[1]

In August 1862, the largest group of soldiers left their homes in Oak Creek Township, which was the southeastern part of Milwaukee County. Two would make the Ultimate Sacrifice in Tennessee only four months later, and seven more would be wounded in the same battle, one case eventually proving fatal.

The youngest Oak Creek soldier to die in the entire war was 17, according to the few records that are available. The oldest was age 43; one of that man's sons served in the famed Iron Brigade and was wounded three times.

Oak Creek Township consisted of modern-day Oak Creek and South Milwaukee. White pioneers had arrived in the late 1830s and 1840s, at a time when Native Americans hunted and fished in the area. Wisconsin became a state in 1848, South Milwaukee incorporated as a village in 1892 and as a city a few years later, and Oak Creek did not become a city until 1955.

A total of 38 men from the township served in Company K of the 24th Wisconsin Volunteer Infantry, according to "Wisconsin Volunteers, War of the Rebellion, 1861-1865," an invaluable research book that has been put on the Internet by the Wisconsin Historical Society.[2]

The dead included two cousins – Frederick Fowle of Company K, in 1863 of wounds received in the Battle of Stones River in Tennessee, and Royal Fowle, an artilleryman in another unit who died of disease in 1864 in Louisville, Ky. Disease was an equal-opportunity killer of Union soldiers and Confederates in the war; both armies lost more men to illness than in battle.[3]

---

[1] The soldiers in this chapter originally were featured in a five-part series by Tom Mueller in 2011 on www.oakcreekpatch.com. The material has been substantially revised and updated for this book.

[2] www.wisconsinhistory.org/roster. It is quoted throughout this chapter, referred to as the book of volunteers or the Wisconsin roster.

[3] "2,000 Questions and Answers About the Civil War," by Webb Garrison (1992), p. 166.

This is the wedding photo of veteran Henry Schumacher and Elisabeth Schulte, eight years after the Civil War. It is one of the few photos of a young veteran from the Town of Oak Creek that exist today. Schulte's soldier brother had died of illness during the war.

Frederick was the son of Frederick Fowle Sr. and Electra Rawson, while Royal was the son of John Fowle Jr. and Lavina Fowle, according to Judy Balestrieri, a descendant of the Fowle clan and a mainstay of the South Milwaukee Historical Society. They were grandsons of John Fowle Sr., who was one of the first pioneers of the area and built two sawmills on the waterway that was named Oak Creek.[4]

Other Oak Creek men in Company K included Edward and Kendrick Day, and John and Adam Hafer, plus several pairs from Milwaukee. Edward Day's letters, preserved by the South Milwaukee historical group,[5] show that Kendrick was his brother, but it is lost to history precisely how the others were related.

Beyond the 24th Wisconsin, other men from Oak Creek served mainly in the 1st Wisconsin Volunteer Infantry Regiment and the 35th Regiment,

---

[4] The soldiers' uncle, Horace Fowle (son of John Sr. and Sarah Dibley Fowle), built a Queen Anne Victorian home in 1892 that today is the widely known clubhouse at the golf course in Grant Park along Lake Michigan.

[5] The soldier letters that are quoted briefly in this chapter all are in the archives of the South Milwaukee Historical Society.

according to the Wisconsin Historical Society, although a few also were in other units.

More than 80,000 men from Wisconsin served in the war, a remarkable number from a place that had a population of only 775,000 and had been a state for only 13 years.[6] More than 12,000 died in battle, from wounds or from rampant illnesses.

First major battle – at Stones River, Tenn.

The first battle deaths of soldiers from Oak Creek Township came on Dec. 31, 1862, at Stones River near Murfreesboro in central Tennessee. Nine were killed or wounded; that was 25 percent of the three dozen Oak Creek men in Company K of the 24th Wisconsin. Their battle zone of thousands of troops came to be known as the Slaughter Pen.

Pvt. Henry Pfaff was killed. So was Pvt. August Gage. Cpl. Frederick Fowle was wounded, discharged because of those wounds in March, and died at home two months after that.

The bloody roll call continued: Pvt. August Wrase was wounded. Pvt. Matthew Stevens, wounded. Pvt. Peter Hohner, wounded. Pvt. Horace Baldwin, wounded. Cpl. Edward Day, wounded. Pvt. John Gitter, wounded.

The death of Pfaff, 23, from artillery fire is graphically described in "The 24th Wisconsin Infantry in the Civil War," a book by William J.K. Beaudot.

"Just as a soldier in Company K arose, 'a shell came crashing toward us striking a man about 20 (paces) from me in the forehead, taking the top of his head completely off & scattering his brains in all directions,'" the book says. That account was from a lieutenant Greene. The book also quotes Edwin Parsons, lieutenant of Company K who later became its captain, as saying the shot also "scattered the dirt and stones over me so that I thought at first I was struck."[7]

---

[6] "Wisconsin in the Civil War," by Frank L. Klement (1997, 2001). Slightly higher numbers are in the state Blue Book at http://legis.wisconsin.gov/lrb/bb/11bb/Stats_Military.pdf, p. 764.

[7] "The 24th Wisconsin Infantry in the Civil War," p. 146-147.

Pfaff's name is spelled as Pfuff in the book of Wisconsin volunteers. While it is invaluable, that roster contains many spelling errors, either as outright typos; mistakes in transcribing handwriting; because families changed their own names over the decades; and because of Americanization of some names by the military. (The latter happened in the case of the great-great uncle of the author of this book, whose name appears in the roster as Ganzer when it actually was Ganser.)

Another Oak Creek man killed at Stones River, Pvt. August Gage, also is listed in the index of the roster as Augustus Gotsch. It is not known why, although a non-German census-taker or military enlistment recorder possibly would hear someone with a strong German accent giving a name that sounded like "Gage."

Nancy Dzidzan, a retired teacher, used census and genealogical records to research Gage and other soldiers from Oak Creek Township as a volunteer project for the archives of the Oak Creek Historical Society.[8]

Dzidzan found that August Gage was born about 1819, so he was 43 when killed at Stones River, which is quite old for a soldier. He was a wagon maker in Oak Creek, something that would have been in great demand in the Union Army as it transported huge amounts of supplies and armaments on many fronts in many states.

Gage and Pfaff are buried on their battlefield, in the Stones River National Cemetery, according to its searchable database at http://www.stonesrivernc.org/. Pfaff's grave is N-5409 but the database does not give a grave number for Gage. The cemetery has more than 6,000 Union graves from Stones River and other nearby battles. About 1,300 from the other side are buried in the Confederate Circle at the Evergreen Cemetery in Murfreesboro.

The most seriously wounded man from Oak Creek at Stones River was Frederick Fowle, 19, who died of those injuries on May 21, 1863, back in Wisconsin. He was discharged March 18, according to the Wisconsin roster, which does not report his death.

Fowle is buried in the cemetery of First Congregational United Church of Christ on North Chicago Avenue in South Milwaukee. He has an updated

---

[8] All references to census records in this chapter are to material collected by Dzidzan and graciously shared with the author.

government tombstone because so many stones from that era eroded badly over the decades and half-centuries.

Dzidzan found records in the South Milwaukee Historical Society that said his original tombstone bore this inscription: "We hold thy memory dear and blest our thoughts at thee. Thy life was nobly given for God and liberty."

Those are stirring words, but there was nothing romantic about it: In addition to the total of 3,000 Union and Confederate dead, many of the 16,000 wounded lay on the battlefield for days before getting help and medical treatment. Many on both sides were begging for water, and the night was pierced by moans and calls for help. About one-third of the men in the battle were killed or wounded, according to a history by the National Park Service.[9]

Six days before the battle, Cpl. Edward Day had written a letter home on Christmas Day 1862, and said:

> **We have got a new brigade general and I suppose he wants us to drill as well as other brigades. His name is Sill, and you may see accounts of Sills Brigade.**
>
> **The order is that we have 3 days cooked rations in our haversacks ready to march in the morning. Probably we move farther south and more than likely shall stand a good chance of getting into a fight as there is no doubt but what the enemy are in force not a great ways from us.**

That fight came fast. Day would be wounded and taken prisoner. The general he referred to was Brig. Gen. Joshua Sill, brigade commander for the 24th Wisconsin and three other regiments. He was killed in the battle, and a staff member, Lt. John Mitchell of Milwaukee, reported:[10]

> **I came across the brigade adjutant; he had just seen the general's horse galloping to the rear (with no one in the saddle). In our search for Sill we almost stumbled over his prostrate body. A bullet had penetrated his brain; he had tumbled from his horse without even a friendly arm to ease his fall. He lay unconscious and alone, bubbling out his last breaths**

---

[9] http://www.nps.gov/stri/historyculture/battle0.htm

[10] "No Better Place to Die: The Battle of Stones River," by Peter Cozzens (1990), p. 113.

through the blood that thickly flowed over his fair face and silky beard. … This scene and its dread surroundings horrified me with war.

Mitchell later started a family, and his oldest son, born in 1879, was Billy Mitchell, of aviation fame. Fort Sill, Okla., is named for the fallen general.

In addition to Sill, the other two brigade commanders were killed or mortally wounded in the Slaughter Pen area at Stones River, marking an unusual circumstance of high-level losses. All three served under Brig. Gen. Philip Sheridan in the 3rd Division of the Army of the Cumberland.

Although the worst day was Dec. 31, the Stones River fighting lasted until Jan. 3, 1863, when the Confederates under Gen. Braxton Bragg retreated. This battle was only three months after the carnage at Antietam in Maryland and days after a shocking and bloody Union loss at Fredericksburg, Va., so it was a very trying time for the Union Army.

Despite all the difficulties, on New Year's Day, President Abraham Lincoln issued the Emancipation Proclamation. Lincoln had been planning his action to free slaves for months, and in September 1862 had said it would come Jan. 1.

So the deaths of the Oak Creek men and the 3,000 other Union and Confederate dead at Stones River make a particularly striking juxtaposition in history.

What was the goal of the war? Ending the rebellion. What was the moral reason for the war? Slavery, although historians always discuss a wide range of deep differences between North and South. In fact, there are many caveats to the proclamation itself, such as freeing slaves only in the South, not in slave-holding border states.

Lincoln proclaimed that slaves "shall be then, thenceforward, and forever free," and ended his executive order by saying: "And upon this act, sincerely believed to be an act of justice, warranted by the Constitution upon military necessity, I invoke the considerate judgment of mankind and the gracious favor of Almighty God." He would utter equally stirring words 11 months later at Gettysburg, "that we here highly resolve that these dead shall not have died in vain."

Besides Frederick Fowle, three of the Oak Creek men at Stones River were so seriously wounded that they were discharged – termed "mustered out" in that era – from the military. August Wrase was discharged March 28, three months after the battle, followed three days later by Matthew Stevens, whose rank is not listed in the Wisconsin roster book. Peter Hohner was discharged July 14 because of disability.

The other Oak Creek wounded at Stones River remained in the regiment and fought in more battles, in two cases being wounded again. Here are their listings in the book of volunteers:

– Horace Baldwin recovered to a degree and was in later action, but was transferred on Nov. 1, 1863, to the Veteran Reserve Corps, which was a place for partially disabled and infirm soldiers to perform light duty. He remained there for the rest of the war and was mustered out three months after Appomattox.

– Edward Day, who wrote the letter on Christmas, wounded and taken prisoner, was wounded again at Franklin, Tenn., in 1864. He made it to the end of the war and was mustered out June 10, 1865.

– John Gitter, whose name also is given as Gutter in the roster, was wounded again at Adairsville, Ga., on May 17, 1864, but he also made it to mustering-out on the same date as Day.

Another Oak Creek man in Company K had been Pvt. George Howes, who did not even make it to Stones River before he suffered from disease that would prove to be fatal. He was born in 1841, so he was 21 or 22 when he died.

Howes became ill during the regiment's movement from Louisville, Ky., to Nashville, Tenn. The 24th Wisconsin had a small role in the battle of Perryville, Ky., on Oct. 8, and moved to Nashville between Oct. 16 and Nov. 7. Howes spent time in a hospital and was so ill that he was discharged on Feb. 11, 1863. He died Feb. 27, and is buried in the same cemetery in South Milwaukee as Frederick Fowle.

The cemetery is right off the main drag of South Milwaukee, but the Dairy Queen in that area near the entrance to Grant Park is much more prominent and draws more traffic.

One neighborhood in the war

When a driver on the main street of Oak Creek, South Howell Avenue, turns onto East Rawson Avenue and heads toward Lake Michigan, there is small hill and an assortment of houses on the passenger side of the vehicle.

On the driver's side of the car are abundant open spaces and the occasional business a little more than a mile from the north-south runway of Mitchell International Airport.

In 1863, people in this same area would have been driving their horses and wagons past township farms that had sons away in the Civil War – the Schumacher farm, the Schulte farm, the Verhaalen farm (which would be spelled Verhalen on the 1876 plat map) and most likely others.

George Verhaalen, whose family owned land on the south side of the road in what is now the 500 block of East Rawson, was a private in the 24th Wisconsin Infantry, enlisting Aug. 21, 1862.

A little over a year after Verhaalen left for the war, two other men from the neighborhood, Henry Schumacher and Peter Schulte, enlisted in Company B of the 35th Wisconsin Infantry Regiment on Dec. 8, 1863. Schumacher was a corporal and Schulte a private. For some reason the book of volunteers lists them as being from Milwaukee, but they were Oak Creek all the way – Schulte lived one farm east of Verhaalen, and Schumacher lived across the road in what is now the 1100 block of East Rawson.

"George Verhaalen was born in Till-Moyland, Rhineland, in Prussia, on April 14, 1841," says Dean Collins of Brookfield, his great-grandson. "He came to America at age 13, arriving in New York and ending up in Oak Creek Township. His father, Peter, bought land on May 31, 1854."

Verhaalen was an apprentice for a local blacksmith and was 21 when he enlisted. He was not injured in the 24th Wisconsin's first battle, at Stones River, but was wounded and taken prisoner nine months later in the epic battle at Chickamauga, Ga., on Sept. 20, 1863.

He was shipped to Richmond, Va., the Confederate capital, probably to a prison known as Belle Island, but at some point "dug a hole underneath a stockade with a frying pan and escaped," Collins reports. "On the way out, he and another POW killed a Confederate picket. He returned to Union lines in Knoxville, Tenn."

Collins grew up hearing Verhaalen's story frequently recounted by an aunt. "I don't know what kind of wound he sustained, but it must have been serious since he was detached from the 24th Wisconsin and assigned to the Ambulance Corps." Injured or ill soldiers who still were able to work usually were put into such units.

Despite the aunt's love of telling the family history, Collins has no photo of the soldier at any stage of life, and did not know exactly where Verhaalen lived in Oak Creek until being contacted for this book. Nor did Collins know that Sgt. Byron Covalt of Oak Creek said in a letter to home a month after the Chickamauga battle that Verhaalen was "reported killed." Here is some of Covalt's account of the battle (he uses a play on the word Confederacy, meaning con-thieve-racy):[11]

> **We fought for two days against greatly superior numbers (or the papers say against the southern contheiveracy) and gained what we fought for and the rebels lost what they fought for, or rather did not get what they fought for.**
>
> **We wanted to get into Chattanooga and so did the rebels; we got there and the rebels did not. ... The right commenced about 13 miles from Chattanooga and Monday morning we had fell back on the right to within six miles of Chattanooga so you see that we were not so badly whipped in the two days fight as we might have been.**
>
> **The 24th lost about 105 men on Sunday. ... Co. K lost five men. George Verhaalen who used to work for Mr. Carey is reported killed. The other two are strangers to you. One John Colar used to live in Town (of) Lake a few years ago. Val Wentworth was wounded slightly in the shoulder and Bernard Stolenwark from the Howel Road was the other one. The balance of the Creek boys, Ed Day, Fred Stearns, Sanford Grover and (last and least of all) myself came out safe and sound.**

Verhaalen and Stollenwert (as that man's gravestone says) had not come back from the battle and so Covart assumed they were killed. Actually, Verhaalen was wounded and taken prisoner, according to the Wisconsin roster book. So was Stollenwert.

Both would return to action and make it through the war, being discharged two months after Appomattox.

Verhaalen spent most of the rest of his life in Saukville. "George's house is still standing on the village square, at 283 E. Green Bay Ave.," Dean Collins says. "He was the village blacksmith and also a carriage maker." When Verhaalen died on July 10, 1879, he had a daughter, Petronella, who was only 10 months old – she was Collins' grandmother. Verhaalen is buried in Saukville.

---

[11] This letter is in the archives of the South Milwaukee Historical Society.

Stollenwert is buried in a little cemetery one mile south of the Rawson Avenue neighborhood of Verhaalen, Schumacher and Schulte, on South Howell Avenue by The Gables apartments and across the street a little north of Culver's. Dozens and dozens of cars pass by this cemetery every hour, far more than go through the busy Rawson Avenue neighborhood. Stollenwert's tall white stone is clearly visible from the northbound lanes on Howell. His family's farm was on the west side of Howell, stretching two miles from Drexel Boulevard to what is now the heart of Oak Creek, at Puetz Road and Howell.

Stollenwert was born Nov. 18, 1837, in Bickerath, Prussia, according to a long family genealogy that is on the Internet.[12] So he was nearly four years older than Verhaalen and age 24 when he enlisted in Company K in 1862. Stollenwert's gravestone has nothing about when he died, nor does the genealogy.

One neighbor of Verhaalen, Henry Schumacher, was from Dunstekoven in Rhineland in what became Germany. He was 11 months old when his family emigrated via Amsterdam to America in early 1845, according to a family history assembled by Pete Schumacher of Oak Creek – Henry was his great-great uncle (brother of Pete's great-grandfather). This was three years before Wisconsin became a state. Henry's father, Johann (Joseph), was 38 and his mother, Anna Maria, was 35. There were four older siblings.

Joseph Schumacher bought 40 acres of land on the north side of Rawson from a land speculator, Martin Otis Walker. This was across the road and a little to the east of the Verhaalen and Schulte lands.

Henry Schumacher was 19 when he enlisted at the end of 1863.

Neighbor Peter Schulte went into the 35th Regiment the same day as Schumacher, but would be dead in 10 months – from disease on Sept. 21, 1864, in Chicago, according to the Wisconsin book of volunteers. Dysentery, pneumonia, typhoid and malaria were ailments that soldiers commonly picked up in the South. Overall, the 35th Regiment lost only two enlisted men and zero officers in battle but 274 – three officers and 271 enlisted like Schulte – to disease.

In the spring and summer of 1864, the 35th passed through or was stationed briefly at several spots in Louisiana and then at St. Charles, Ark.,

---

[12] http://boards.ancestry.com/localities.northam.usa.states.wisconsin.counties. milwaukee/236.422/mb.ashx

before returning to Louisiana in August. This is the period in which Schulte likely became ill.

In October, the 35th was part of a brigade that fought at Simsport, La., and other sites. In February 1865, it began its work in the drive against Mobile, Ala., the siege of Spanish Fort there, and the capture of Fort Blakely. In March, in the final weeks of the war, Schumacher was injured while building log defenses known as breastworks at Spanish Fort, which guarded Mobile Bay.

"Henry's pension papers name his disabilities as 'ruptures of both sides,'" Pete Schumacher says. "The circumstances of the injury are described as 'The first disability above named was incurred at or near Mobile in the state of Ala. on or about the 24th day of March year of 1865 under the following circumstances: by carrying material (logs) for the purpose of making breastworks.' The battle of Spanish Fort coincides with this date."

In March 1865, Union forces were moving toward Mobile from two directions. Spanish Fort and Spanish Bluffs controlled one of the main water approaches to Mobile, and the Confederates had built massive fortifications and deployed equally formidable artillery batteries there. Union forces of Maj. Gen. E.R.S. Canby laid siege to Spanish Fort for 12 days, outnumbering the Confederates by a ratio of 15 to 1.[13] "The battle began on March 27, 1865, and continued to escalate as Union troops encircled the land approaches to the Confederate fortifications, digging siege works and placing artillery," a history of the battle says. That is the type of work in which Schumacher was injured.

Spanish Fort became an incorporated city in 1993, and its website[14] says, "Breastworks from the Civil War still remain throughout our area and the residential subdivisions."

Schumacher soon recovered from his injuries and stayed with the regiment until it was mustered out nearly a year after Appomattox.

When he returned home, he and his brother William already had purchased additional land beyond the family's original 40 acres. In 1873 Henry married Elisabeth Schulte, the sister of his Civil War colleague Peter who had died of disease, and built a home at 1108 E. Rawson Ave., very close to his

---

[13] www.exploresouthernhistory.com

[14] http://cityofspanishfort.com/

family's original home and using some of the original timbers. In 1878, their father sold half his farm to Henry and half to William.

William Schumacher also stayed in the neighborhood to find his bride, Magdalena Bautz. He bought her family's farm and established the Schumacher Pickle Factory on land that now is occupied by Milwaukee County's Runway Dog Exercise Area, 1214 E. Rawson, and Gastrau's Golf Center, 1300 E. Rawson.

Henry Schumacher died March 10, 1912, and is buried in St. Joseph's Cemetery on Howell Avenue south of College Avenue, about a mile north of his farm. It is not known where Peter Schulte is buried.

A string of other losses

Beyond Stones River and Chickamauga, other Town of Oak Creek men fell at famous sites and at sites that are lesser known, plus from the many diseases. Two privates, John Moore and Engelhardt Fink, died in the same week on widely separated battlefields.

Moore, 20, of the 24th Regiment like so many others in this chapter, was killed on May 14, 1864, in fighting at Resaca in northwestern Georgia, part of the Union drive on Atlanta. Moore is buried with his parents in the cemetery of First Congregational United Church of Christ in South Milwaukee, along with some colleagues discussed earlier in this chapter. Moore's gravestone gives his birthdate of May 1, 1844, so he had just turned 20.

Cpl. Edward Day wrote about this sad loss in a letter home a few weeks after the battle (the spellings in the next paragraphs are the originals).

Poor Johney Moore has gon. He was a good boy. Everyone in the Co. thought a good deal of John, he was always cheerful and full of fun, always ready to do any duty he was asked to do. ... He was a brave boy and did not know what it was to be afraid but the poor boy fell fighting bravely. Was shot through the head and was killed instantly. He probably never knew what hurt him.

We put his name and regiment on a board and laid it upon his body and the detail that buried the dead probably put it up at the head of his grave. I tried to get permission to go myself but I could not go. The Major sayd that the inspector on our brigade

staff say that there would be arrangements made for burying the dead, so I could not go. The Rebs evacuated the next night after Johney was killed and we had to march in persuit early in the morning.

Moore's death is described in "The 24th Wisconsin Infantry in the Civil War," the same book that reported Henry Pfaff's death.

> Men went down under the whining lead missiles and shrieking iron shrapnel. One of Capt. (Edwin) Parsons' and the regiment's personal favorites, little Johnny Moore, was shot through the forehead, dead even before his body crumbled into the mud.

> The lad from Oak Creek, a farming community south of the city (Milwaukee), had a countenance as youthful as McArthur's, and he had always done his duty without complaint; "his loss was much deplored," said a new soldier. "He was a noble little fellow and died like a hero in the thickest of the fight," Parsons said.[15]

Four days before the loss of Moore, Pvt. Engelhardt Fink became MIA near Spotsylvania, Va., only a few days after the Battle of the Wilderness near the same area.

The Wilderness ranks as one of the most vicious of the war. At one spot that came to be known as Bloody Angle, an oak tree with a circumference of 22 inches was felled from the sheer amount of musket balls and other shots fired into it. A piece of the trunk still is on display at the National Museum of American History of the Smithsonian Institution in Washington, D.C. It was not the only tree felled by rifle fire, either.

That Fink was MIA in such a carnage was not a surprise. "I estimate 8,000 were killed outright over the two-week period," Donald Pfanz, staff historian of the Fredericksburg and Spotsylvania County Battlefields Memorial of the National Park Service, said via email. "Most of the dead were later taken to Fredericksburg National Cemetery for burial. Seven out of eight soldiers buried in that cemetery are unidentified. ... we can estimate that there

---

[15] "The 24th Wisconsin Infantry in the Civil War," p. 296-297. Parsons' reference to McArthur is to Arthur McArthur of the 24th, who was age 18 when he earned the Medal of Honor at Mission Ridge, Tenn., six months earlier. He wound up as colonel of the regiment and often was referred to as "the boy colonel."

were 7,000 unknown dead at Wilderness and Spotsylvania. That's just for Union soldiers."

Census records show Fink was born in 1843, so he was 20 or 21 when he died. His father's name was recorded as Engelhard in the census, and his mother as Catharine. Their farm was south of College Avenue and west of North Chicago Avenue. The soldier was No. 3 in his family behind Mary and Henry, and ahead of Jacob, Ellen, Luessa and Simon, according to the census.

Fink's unit was part of the 3rd Brigade of the 1st Division of the VI Army Corps. Maj. Gen. John Sedgwick, commander of that corps, was killed on May 9 by a sharpshooter, only seconds after famously saying, "They couldn't hit an elephant at this distance."

Fink had enlisted April 21, 1861, only nine days after the start of the war, as throngs of eager and patriotic young men answered the call of President Abraham Lincoln and Wisconsin Gov. Alexander Randall for volunteer forces. Fink was in Company C of the 5th Wisconsin Volunteer Infantry Regiment.

That regiment's long battle record over the next years included Antietam, the two battles at Fredericksburg, Va., and then Gettysburg. Later came the Wilderness, and finally Fink's number came up at nearby Spotsylvania.

In other battle deaths, another Oak Creek soldier, Pvt. Frederic Stearns, Company K, 24th Wisconsin, was fatally wounded at Mission Ridge, Tenn. Stearns died of the wounds four months after the battle, on March 16, 1864, in nearby Chattanooga, Tenn. He is buried in the Chattanooga National Cemetery, according to the database of the U.S. Department of Veterans Affairs.[16] The cemetery has nearly 13,000 Civil War burials, including 4,189 as unknowns.

At Mission Ridge, Company K was very close to the group of other 24th Wisconsin men that included Arthur McArthur – father of Gen. Douglas MacArthur of World War II fame and both Korean War fame and infamy (Douglas inserted an "A" in the family's last name).

The brief citation for his Medal of Honor said McArthur "seized the colors of his regiment at a critical moment and planted them on the captured works on the crest of Missionary Ridge,"[17] a steep cliff littered with fallen

---

[16] http://gravelocator.cem.va.gov/j2ee/servlet/NGL_v1

[17] http://www.homeofheroes.com/moh/citations_1862_cwh/macarthur_arthur.html

trees. McArthur wrote this citation himself in applying for the medal in 1890 after discovering that officers were eligible for the honor, not just enlisted men. He provided plenty of testimonials for the action, including support from Parsons, commander of Stearns and the many other Oak Creek men in Company K.

One of the main people quoted about the climb in William J.K. Beaudot's book was Parsons, the same man who described the killing of Oak Creek's Henry Pfaff earlier in this chapter and of John Moore. "Arthur was magnificent. He seems to be afraid of nothing. He'd fight a pack of tigers in a jungle," Parsons said.[18]

Other reports said McArthur had rallied the men with cries of "On, Wisconsin!" while scaling the cliffs.

The Fowle clan of what is now South Milwaukee, which had suffered the loss of Frederick on May 21, 1863, lost another son, Royal, on Jan. 14, 1864. Royal, who was only age 17, was in Company B of the 1st Regiment, Wisconsin Heavy Artillery. He is buried in the same South Milwaukee cemetery as his cousin.

Royal enlisted Aug. 17, 1863. Battery B was organized at Milwaukee and went to Fort Terrell at Murfreesboro, Tenn., where it remained until January 1864, the time of Royal's death. Murfreesboro had been where Frederick suffered the wounds that proved fatal within a few months.

In the entire war, the 1st Wisconsin Heavy Artillery lost four enlisted men and two officers to battle injuries, and far more to disease – two officers and 77 enlisted like Royal Fowle.

Heavy Artillery units included huge siege guns and huge mortars; not the conventional field artillery cannons that are seen in many photos. Heavy artillery usually was on seacoasts and at garrisons, such as Fort Terrell.

Two other Oak Creek men died of disease – Pvt. Andrew Galagher, Company K, on Feb. 10, 1864, in Louisville, Ky., and John Puffenroth, Company K, on July 26, 1864, in Madison, Ind. Puffenroth's rank is not listed in the Wisconsin roster.

The story of August Gage, killed at Stones RIver and discussed earlier in this chapter, did not end there.

---

[18] "The 24th Wisconsin Infantry in the Civil War," p. 267

He had four children in the 1860 census, led by Leo Gotsch – his name was on the Wisconsin roster only with that last name, not two ways like his father – who was 18.

Leo enlisted on June 1, 1861, less than two months into the war, and was in Company F of the 6th Wisconsin Volunteer Infantry Regiment, which became part of the famed Iron Brigade and which did some of the heaviest fighting of the entire war. According to the Wisconsin roster, he was a sergeant and was wounded three times: in September 1862, on June 18, 1864, and on March 31, 1865, in the closing days of the war. The regiment fought in those periods at Antitetam; the siege of Petersburg, Va., and the campaign around Appomattox.

Leo died in 1911 and is buried in Franklin, in the little Painesville cemetery at South 27th Street and West Ryan Road. His grave is about two dozen feet from the busy Highway 100 and the stone is in bad need of leveling.

With the war in its final year, Sgt. Byron Covalt of Company K wrote home from near Atlanta on Aug. 30, 1864:

This is the most miserable country that I ever was in, and I would like to know how a good country looks, for if I live a year I except to come home, and I wish to be prepared a little before I get there.

But Covalt would be dead in three months, killed at Franklin, Tenn., on Nov. 30. At Franklin, only 189 on the Union side were killed, but 1,750 Confederates died, by some estimates.[19] Six Confederate generals were killed outright or mortally wounded.

---

[19] http://www.civilwar.org/battlefields/franklin.html and http://www.civilwar.org/battlefields/franklin/franklin-history-articles/franklincartwright.html

Chapter 3
7 Civil War soldiers who became governor

The seven soldiers in this chapter fought at big places like Bull Run, Gettysburg, Vicksburg, Atlanta, in Louisiana and at South Mountain in Maryland, plus many other points in between. Some were infantry; some were cavalry. Some were wounded, including an amputation; some were taken prisoner. Most were officers, including a major general. Some were in the same regiment at the same time; others were in the same unit at different times.

And all seven of them later became governor of Wisconsin.

This is the story of Lucius Fairchild, of Cadwallader Washburn, of Jeremiah Rusk, of William Dempster Hoard, of George Peck, of William Upham and of Edward Scofield.

Fairchild was the first to become governor, holding office from 1866 to 1872, back in the days when gubernatorial elections were in odd-numbered years, not the even ones. That was changed in 1882. Scofield, who was a soldier in a Pennsylvania unit, was the last governor who was a Civil War veteran, serving from 1897 to 1901, being succeeded by Robert M. LaFollette Sr., who was only age 5 when the war began in April 1861.

In between the governorships of Washburn and Rusk (both of whom have northwestern Wisconsin counties named for them), there were three governors who were not war veterans – from 1874 to 1882.

Fairchild and Upham both were in the 2nd Wisconsin Volunteer Infantry Regiment, part of the famed Iron Brigade. Upham was wounded and taken prisoner at Bull Run in Virginia in July 1861 and was out of the war; Fairchild lost his left arm at Gettysburg in 1863. Hoard served in the 4th Wisconsin Infantry in Louisiana, but was discharged because of illness; after it was turned into the 4th Wisconsin Cavalry, one of its new members was Peck.

Here are the stories of these soldiers / governors, in the order that they served as governor. For decades, the Wisconsin Historical Society has done a diligent and thorough job of compiling and posting information about dozens of political figures and other leaders, and is quoted often in this chapter.[1]

---

[1] The Historical Society's main search page is http://www.wisconsinhistory. org/dictionary/. This chapter will rarely use the full citation page for a particular figure, because that URL gets very long, such as this for Jeremiah Rusk: http://www.wisconsinhistory.org/dictionary/index.asp?action=view&term_id=2710 &term_type_id=1&term_type_text=People&letter=R

Edward Scofield was a 19-year-old in a Pennsylvania regiment in the Civil War, and was the last of the seven Wisconsin governors who were veterans of the conflict. He left office in 1901. This photo is from an Oconto County history project at www.rootsweb.ancestry. com/~wioconto/scofield.htm

Lucius Fairchild, who lost his left arm at Gettysburg, was the first Civil War veteran to become Wisconsin governor. Wisconsin Historical Society, WHS-6601

Col. / Gov. Lucius Fairchild

Col. Lucius Fairchild of Madison was shot on the first day at Gettysburg. Only four months later, he would be elected secretary of state of Wisconsin at the age of 31, having been put on the ballot by Republicans as a war hero.

When the war began at Fort Sumter, S.C., in 1861, Fairchild, age 29, jumped at the chance to enlist, and was elected captain by the troops. He advanced quickly from there, and became colonel of the 2nd Wisconsin. Two years later, the 2nd Wisconsin had only about one-third of its original men; the rest were killed, wounded (like Upham), discharged because of illness, etc.[2]

---

[2] "Those Damned Black Hats!" by Lance J. Herdegen (2008) p. 57.

Approaching the top of McPherson's Ridge at Gettysburg on July 1, 1863, the 2nd ran smack into Confederate forces. "Charge, men, I mean charge!" Fairchild shouted amid the din.[3]

Fairchild's biography, "The Empty Sleeve," takes it from there:[4]

The next few minutes were an unbelievable horror. Confederate infantry had their muskets trained on the rise, wiping out almost a third of the 2nd Wisconsin with their fusillade. Lucius staggered among the dead, the maimed, and the defiantly alive; his left arm shattered above the elbow by a Rebel musket ball. Two of his men supported him until they found a stretcher.

At this moment, a Union staff officer came galloping by shouting that (Maj.) Gen. John Reynolds, the I Corps Commander, had been killed.

Reynolds, who was behind the 2nd Wisconsin, was shot off his horse and was one of the highest-ranking officers to fall at Gettysburg. Reynolds not only was corps commander, but also was in command of the entire left wing of the Army of the Potomac (I, III, and XI Corps and First Division, Cavalry Corps). The 2nd Wisconsin and the rest of the Iron Brigade made up the 1st Brigade of the 1st Division of I Corps.

"The Empty Sleeve," Fairchild's story, continues: "To Lucius such details were vague recollections in the agony of pain which followed the bone-splintering shock."[5]. He was given a large dose or morphine and taken into the town of Gettysburg (population about 2,400) for treatment. This was in the home of Rev. Charles F. Schaeffer, chief of the Lutheran Theological Seminary there.

The 2nd Wisconsin's surgeon, Andrew Ward, arrived and amputated the left arm above the elbow, and when Fairchild woke up, "he looked at his bandaged stump. Tears coursed down his face as he groaned, 'Thank God! I still have one left.'"[6]

---

[3] "Those Damed Black Hats!" p. 92.

[4] "The Empty Sleeve: A Biography of Lucius Fairchild," by Sam Ross (1964), p. 48-49.

[5] "The Empty Sleeve," p. 49

[6] "The Empty Sleeve," p. 49.

Like at Bull Run a year and a half earlier, the 2nd Wisconsin again took a severe blow. It started at Gettysburg with 273 troops and when the battle ended a few days later, had only 40 who still could fight.[7]

Less than two months later, on Aug. 28, the Republican state convention was held in Milwaukee to select candidates for the November election. The Madison and Milwaukee machines of the GOP could not agree on whom to run for secretary of state, a position that in those days was considered a steppingstone to the job of governor. A Milwaukee delegate rose and proclaimed there was a soldier "who has lost blood" and "who, though heretofore a member of the Democratic party, is now ready to give up all party consideration for his country."[8] Fairchild considered the offer to be a choice of duty over old friendships in his original party, "The Empty Sleeve" adds.

He was nominated, accepted the nod and was elected.

Two years later, in 1865, Fairchild stepped up to run for the higher office when GOP Gov. James Taylor Lewis did not seek a second term. Fairchild drew support from a combination of Republicans and war-supporting Democrats[9] to pull 55 percent of the vote in defeating a Democrat, Brig. Gen. Harrison Hobart of the 4th Wisconsin Infantry and the 21st Wisconsin. Hobart had been in several battles and was held at Libby Prison at Richmond, Va., until escaping with 108 other men in February 1864 and going back into the war in Georgia.

Fairchild was re-elected in 1867 and 1869. He was the first three-term governor of Wisconsin in its young existence. After the last term, Fairchild left office at age 40 and then held diplomatic posts in three European countries, including ambassador to Spain. In 1887, when he was age 55, he was national commander of the Grand Army of the Republic, the veterans' organization that had more than 400,000 members in that era, and charged into battle again – against President Grover Cleveland.

Cleveland had ordered that all captured Confederate battle flags in the care of the secretary of war be returned to their original states. This was after staff of the War Department found them decaying in the agency's attic, and staff knew that battle flags of Union units held by the War Department

---

[7] "The Empty Sleeve," p. 50.

[8] "The Empty Sleeve," p. 55.

[9] "The History of WIsconsin: Volume II," by Richard Current (1976), p. 407-408.

already had been returned to those states. Fairchild learned of the order about Southern flags while at a GAR local meeting in Harlem in New York City.

"The Empty Sleeve" reports: "Trembling with anger, the one-armed commander stood before them, an Avenging Angel. Under the thick white eyebrows his blue eyes blazed with outraged fury. In an atmosphere charged with emotion he thundered, 'May God palsy the hand that wrote the order! May God palsy the brain that conceived it! And may God palsy the tongue that dictated it!' ... (The flags) 'were intended,' he cried, 'to be kept in the archives of the nation as mementoes of hard-won fields of battle. ... the trophies won at such a fearful sacrifice of blood.'"[10]

Such words about the commander in chief of the United States from the commander in chief of the GAR, which consisted of soldiers who had sworn allegiance to the president of the United States during their service, touched off a storm of protest from the public. That GAR audience on that particular night was a red-meat crowd, and Fairchild fed off its angry energy.

Plenty of other old soldiers were equally enraged. Northern governors sent telegrams calling the president's order "an insult to the heroic dead" and senators were "deeply saddened."[11] But In the following days and weeks, GAR leaders urged Fairchild not to press the matter. Fairchild later said his comments were "the bitter words the Good Lord put into my mouth."[12]

Another of the many colorful aspects of Fairchild's life is that a few months after Gettysburg, he asked for the return of his arm, which Rev. Schaeffer's family had buried in a tin box in their garden. Two books have passages:

While his stump was healing in the months after the battle, he was bothered by phantom pain from the elbow, forearm, wrist and hand of his missing arm. Troubled by an itch, he would absently scratch "only to find nothing there." The missing arm, he told friends and family, was "tired of being so constantly in the same position."

Acting on a superstition that such discomfort was caused when an amputated limb was (buried) cramped or cooked, he had friends at Gettysburg disinter the tin box containing his

---

[10] "The Empty Sleeve," p. 207.

[11] "An Honest President: The Life and Presidencies of Grover Cleveland," by Paul H. Jeffers (2000), p. 167.

[12] "The Empty Sleeve," p. 208.

arm from the garden near by the Lutheran Seminary Building and sent to him by express. The pain gradually disappeared and Fairchild later admitted he was never sure whether the relief came from natural healing or the rearrangement of his amputated left arm.[13]

Fairchild died in 1896 at age 64 and was buried with his amputated arm at Forest Hill Cemetery in Madison.[14]

Maj. Gen. / Gov. Cadwallader Colden Washburn

Cadwallader Colden Washburn served three terms in the U.S. House before the war began, then became a colonel, brigadier general and major general. But in 1864 when Confederate cavalry raided Memphis, Tenn., seeking to seize him and two other generals, he fled (or was evacuated by his men) into the night wearing only his nightshirt. The Confederates seized his uniform but sent it back later.

A short, one-way street in downtown Memphis bears the sign "General Washburn's Escape Alley" because of the bizarre event involving the Wisconsinite.

After the war, Washburn served two more terms in the House and was governor of Wisconsin for one term, but was defeated in his bid for re-election. He also was an industrial empire builder and founder of what became General Mills, a name that many people see every morning on their box of cereal. "Few people of his generation had as much influence on Wisconsin history," says his biographical page on the website of the Wisconsin Historical Society.

Washburn was born in Maine and arrived in Mineral Point, Wis., in 1842, the year he turned 24, from time in Davenport, Iowa and Rock Island, Ill. He was a lawyer, founded a bank, and was a Republican member of the U.S. House from 1855 to 1861.

Six months after the war started, Washburn, who was living in La Crosse, was appointed by Gov. Alexander Randall as colonel of the 2nd

---

13 "Those Damned Black Hats!" p. 240; "The Empty Sleeve," p. 52-53.

14 "Those Damned Black Hats!" p. 300.

Wisconsin Cavalry, on Oct. 10, 1861. Washburn was age 43; the 2nd Cav served first in Missouri and Arkansas.

Washburn was elevated to brigadier general on July 16, 1862, then to major general at the end of November of that year, one of the top people under U.S. Grant. He led all cavalry units – including his old 2nd Wisconsin Cav – in the XIII Corps at Vicksburg, Miss., before the 1863 siege, and then as the commander of the detached XVI Corps before the Vicksburg surrender in July 1863.[15]

The next month, Washburn led 16,000 men in support of the Red River Expedition in Louisiana and Texas. He spent most of 1864 and the spring of 1865 in command at Memphis and Vicksburg. And the direct dangers of war fell directly in his lap on Aug. 21, 1864.

The story is this, as told in a biography of Confederate Gen. Nathan Bedford Forrest: One raider rode his horse directly into a hotel where Maj. Gen. Stephen Hurlbut had been staying, but that general was actually at another place. Another, Brig. Gen. Ralph Buckland, was awakened and jumped out of his window and ran to a nearby barracks to start forming resistance. Another Confederate group headed for the Union Street headquarters of Washburn, who fled in his nightclothes to Fort Pickering, a half-mile away – "without having given any command as to what should be done by our troops," a subordinate later officially complained. His unceremonious exit from his quarters is said to have prompted Hurlbut to make one of the wittier remarks of the war: "They removed me from command because I couldn't keep Forrest out of West Tennessee, and now Washburn can't keep him out of his own bedroom!" [16]

No substantial biography of Washburn could be found at several Internet and Wisconsin library sites. A comprehensive 2005 article on his career in the Wisconsin Magazine of History[17] devotes exactly two paragraphs to the nightshirt story and Hurlbut's criticism. And a 1925 book about Washburn and his two brothers contains a letter from Cadwallader to Elihu saying "We

---

[15] http://www.civilwarhome.com/vicksburgorgunion.htm

[16] "Nathan Bedford Forrest: A Biography," by Jack Hurst (1993), p. 213.

[17] Kelsey, Albert V.B. (2005). "CC Washburn: The Evolution of a Flour Baron," Wisconsin Magazine of History. Volume 88, No. 4, summer. p.38-51. http://content.wisconsinhistory.org/cdm/ref/collection/wmh/id/42729

had a big (thing) here on Sunday morning and ran a very narrow escape; indeed it was almost a miracle that I was not either killed or captured. One main drive of the expedition was to catch me."[18]

The Rebel raiders penetrated Memphis about 4 a.m. and the action petered out by 9 a.m. A total of 22 Confederates and 15 Union soldiers were killed, and the Confederates seized about 600 prisoners, including 200 civilians or infirm soldiers. The raiders also attacked Irving Block Prison, where about 500 Confederates were held, but that attack failed. The raiders snuck out of the city in groups of two or three.[19]

The biography of Forrest continues the story:[20]

> **Forrest, under a flag of truce, first proposed that all his prisoners be exchanged for others Washburn held. When Washburn claimed to have no such authority, Forrest said that since they had been captured in nightclothes and Washburn wouldn't exchange them, humanity dictated that the Union general send out suitable attire for them to wear matching southward.**
>
> **After receiving the demanded clothes, Forrest used a similar argument to persuade Washburn to send these prisoners two wagonloads of food – which he then shared with his hungry troopers. During negotiations for these unusual gifts, he sent Washburn the general's own uniform, which had been captured .... Washburn graciously responded by conveying to Forrest enough 'gray cloth with buttons and lace to make Forrest and his staff full uniforms.'**

In addition to the "Escape Alley," there is a building called the historic Washburn building in downtown Memphis, at 60 S. Main St., that was being leased out for condos in 2013.[21]

After the war, Washburn went back to the U.S. House, serving from 1867 to 1871. He was elected governor in the fall of 1871 and served from 1872 to 1874, defeated for re-election by Democrat William Taylor.

---

[18] "Israel, Elihu and Cadwallader Washburn: A Chapter in America Biography," by Gaillard Hunt (1925), p. 347.

[19] "Nathan Bedford Forrest: A Biography," p. 214.

[20] Nathan Bedford Forrest: A Biography," p. 214

[21] http://www.thewashburn.com/

He had a home and estate in Madison – "he built a handsome house at the city's edge, which he appropriately named Edgewood."[22] When he left Madison, he donated Edgewood Villa to the Dominican Sisters, who moved their St. Regina Academy from downtown Madison to Edgewood. The name endures today as Edgewood High School and College. The Villa building burned down in 1895 but was rebuilt. The building that everyone passing by on Monroe Street knows as Edgewood was built in 1927.[23]

Washburn had been building his business interests ever since the war ended. Before the war, he had opened his first flour mill in Minneapolis, Minn., which became known as General Mills. The corporation tells its story:

Critics didn't understand Cadwallader C. Washburn's vision.

They said demand for flour from Midwestern spring wheat would never match what Washburn's company could supply. He didn't see it that way.

Washburn formed the Minneapolis Milling Company in 1856 to lease power rights to mill operators, and 10 years later he built his first flour mill near the falls of St. Anthony on the Mississippi River in Minneapolis.

Despite continued criticism, he built a second, even larger facility in 1874. ...

In 1880, Washburn and (partner John) Crosby entered their finest flours in competition at the first International Millers' Exhibition in Cincinnati, Ohio, winning the gold, silver and bronze medals, and establishing the Washburn Crosby Company's flour as the best in the world.

Soon after, the company changed the name of its finest flour to Gold Medal flour, which is still the No. 1 flour brand in America today.[24]

Washburn County in extreme northwestern Wisconsin is named for this Civil War veteran and governor. The county was created in 1883, a decade

---

[22] "Israel, Elihu and Cadwallader Washburn: A Chapter in America Biography," (1925), p. 383.

[23] http://www.edgewood.k12.wi.us/about/index.php?category_id=3625

[24] http://www.generalmills.com/Company/History/Beginnings.aspx

after Washburn left office and one year after his death at age 64, out of a piece of Burnett County. Shell Lake is the seat of Washburn County.

3 non-veterans

Succeeding Washburn as governor was Taylor, who had turned 41 the year the war began, and was not a veteran. Taylor was governor from 1874 to 1876. He was succeeded by Republican Harrison Ludington, who had turned 49 in 1861, and was governor for one term. In 1878, Republican William E. Smith took office and served two terms. Smith had turned 37 in 1861.

Then came the ascendance of a string of five more Civil War veterans as governor.

Big. Gen. / Gov. Jeremiah M. Rusk

Jeremiah M. Rusk, of Viroqua, was a leader in the 25th Wisconsin Volunteer Infantry Regiment, starting out as a 32-year-old major on July 22, 1862, when it was organized, and ending as a brevet (temporary) brigadier general from March 13, 1865, and onward. He is listed in the "Roster of Wisconsin Volunteers, War of the Rebellion, 1861-1865," as a lieutenant colonel.[25]

Rusk was wounded on June 15, 1864, at Kennesaw Mountain in Georgia, in the prelude to the big battle there two weeks later and the larger battle for Atlanta. It evidently was a minor wound because the roster does not say he was out of action, and Rusk did not discuss it in a long speech to his fellow regimental veterans 22 years after the war that will be quoted a few paragraphs from now.

He was elevated to command of the regiment five weeks after being wounded, when Col. Milton Montgomery of Sparta was shot on July 22 and taken prisoner. Montgomery's right arm was amputated. This was the biggest day of the battle for Atlanta. On the same day, Maj. Gen. James Birdseye

---

[25] www.wisconsinhistory.org/roster It is quoted throughout this chapter, referred to as the book of volunteers or the Wisconsin roster.

McPherson, the top Union commander of the Army of the Tennessee, was killed by a small group of Confederate soldiers who surprised him and his staff while on their horses; he was the second-highest Union officer to die in the entire war.

Months later, the 25th was at Vicksburg, where it was one of the 48 regiments and batteries in Cadwallader Washburn's corps. Rusk became a lieutenant colonel in August 1863, a month after the Confederates surrendered there.

More than two decades after the war, on June 9, 1887, Rusk spoke to a reunion of his regiment, giving a step-by-step recitation of its service. The speech was printed in the Wisconsin State Journal, and he said the 25th, in "every trying position in which it was placed, it did its duty. It was composed of patriotic men who cheerfully took up the burdens and dangers of war that the Union might be preserved. Their patriotism and valor are a part of the history of the war. I have no greater pride than to be able to say that I was a member of that regiment."[26]

Rusk gave this speech while serving as Republican governor from 1882 to 1889 (he had been elected to the U.S. House in 1870, 1872 and 1874). His term as governor came amid labor disturbances nationally, and Milwaukee would be no exception.

On May 5, 1886, things took a deadly turn when throngs of Polish immigrants seeking the eight-hour day marched on the Milwaukee Iron Co. rolling mill in the Bay View area on Milwaukee's South Side. They were confronted by state militia, called up by Rusk at the urging of executives of various industries. "Rusk's orders were: Should the rioters ... attempt to seek an entrance, 'fight 'em.'"[27] Another account quotes him as saying, "Fire on them."[28]

Maj. George Traeumer led the militia and gave the fateful order. "The approaching men were not visibly armed with anything other than sticks and stones. They apparently had no firearms and no shots were fired by them. Traeumer did not wait to learn their intent" and ordered his troops to fire.[29]

---

[26] http://www.wisconsinhistory.org/wlhba/articleView.asp?pg=1&orderby=&id=5394&pn=1&key=&cy=

[27] "The History of Wisconsin: Volume III," by Richard C. Nesbit (1985), p. 397 and 399-404.

[28] "The Making of Milwaukee," by John Gurda (1999), p. 154.

[29] "The History of Wisconsin: Volume III," p. 402-403.

Seven people were killed in the incident, and a historical marker stands on the quiet site today – near South Superior Street and East Russell Avenue – with the title of "Bay View's Rolling Mill." The marker does not discuss how many were wounded, although Wisconsin historian Richard Nesbit's book quotes newspaper reports as saying eight or 10.[30]

It was a turbulent time in America. The Bay View incident occurred one day after the Haymarket Square disturbance in Chicago when a bomb was thrown at police trying to break up a labor demonstration. Seven policemen were killed, along with four other people, and scores were injured.

"The majority of the state press was unreservedly favorable to Gov. Rusk's prompt action, which was assumed to have saved Milwaukee from total anarchy," Nesbit writes, and a coroner's jury found the shootings to be justified.[31]

However, unions denounced it as "overzealous, unjustifiable and damnable," and others viewed it as what Milwaukee historian John Gurda calls "chilling evidence that industrial property was valued more highly than industrial workers."[32]

Rusk was re-elected six months later, 46 percent to 40 percent for Democrat Gilbert Motier Woodward in a four-man race.[33] He did not seek another term after that and was appointed by Republican President Benjamin Harrison in 1889 as the nation's first secretary of agriculture (another man held the office briefly at the end of the presidency of Grover Cleveland, but did not receive approval by the full Senate).

Rusk County in northwestern Wisconsin is named for the governor, who died at age 63 in 1893, although it originally was named for land entrepreneur James Gates when it was established in 1901. That was changed to honor Rusk in 1905.[34] The county seat is Ladysmith, and the county area originally was part of Chippewa County.

---

[30] "The History of Wisconsin: Volume III," p. 403.

[31] "The History of Wisconsin: Volume III," p. 404

[32] "The Making of Milwaukee," p. 156.

[33] These and other election results in this chapter come from http://www.ourcampaigns.com, which has performed the noble task of putting 150-year-old vote tallies online.

[34] "The History of WIsconsin: Volume IV," by John D. Buenker (1998), p. 72.

Pvt. / Gov. William Dempster Hoard

This future giant of the dairy industry was a Republican who was elected governor in 1888, succeeding Rusk.

Hoard was a New York native who came to Wisconsin in 1857. In 1861, when the Civil War began, he was age 24 and his residence was Lake MIlls, and he enlisted on May 23 of that year. He is listed as a musician (no military rank) with the 4th Wisconsin Volunteer Infantry, one of 25 musicians listed in the Wisconsin roster of volunteers for the unit.[35]

"He played the fiddle and taught singing to students through his church," Kori Oberle, director of the Hoard Historical Museum in Fort Atkinson, told the author of this book.

But after a year in the Army, Hoard was discharged because of medical disabilities on June 25, 1862. This was shortly after the 4th Regiment occupied New Orleans and proceeded inland to Baton Rouge. Many soldiers from Wisconsin were adversely affected by Louisiana water and other regional illnesses such as swamp fever and malaria.

Hoard went home to New York to recover, and two years later, on Sept. 9, 1864, he enlisted in Battery A of the 1st New York Light Artillery as a private.[36] During his time, the unit was based at several cities in Pennsylvania.[37] Hoard was mustered out two months after Lee's surrender at Appomattox, on June 28, 1865.

After the war and Hoard's service in the New York artillery unit ended, he returned to Wisconsin and launched the Jefferson County Union newspaper in Lake Mills, moving it to Fort Atkinson three years later.

Hoard's original 4th Wisconsin kept fighting in Louisiana and was part of the siege of the Mississippi River city of Port Hudson, which surrendered on July 9, 1863, a few days after the end of the more-famous siege of Vicksburg, Miss., a city that was 132 miles up-stream – but far longer via the winding river. Then the 4th was turned into cavalry because the Union Army decided such a mobile force was needed in the area – and one of the replacement soldiers would be George Peck, who would oust him as governor.

His true love was dairying. "A pioneer in the promotion of scientific dairy farming and the 'special purpose dairy cow,' Hoard was instrumental in

---

[35] http://www.wisconsinhistory.org/roster

[36] http://dmna.ny.gov/historic/reghist/civil/rosters/Artillery/1stArtCW_Roster.pdf

[37] http://www.civilwararchive.com/Unreghst/unnyart2.htm#bata

organizing county dairymen's associations, and in 1872 helped establish the Wisconsin Dairyman's Association," the Wisconsin Historical Society says.[38] "… Hoard advocated tuberculin tests for dairy cows and was one of the first men in Wisconsin to recognize the value of alfalfa and the silo for use in cattle feeding. He was instrumental in persuading the railroads to provide special low-rate refrigeration service to New York, and thus aided in greatly expanding the Wisconsin dairy market."

Hoard lived to the age of 82, dying in 1918.

2nd. Lt. / Gov. George W. Peck

George W. Peck was 20 when the Civil War started. He worked in newspapers, including the production of the Whitewater Register and the Jefferson County Republican (as half-owner) before and after the war. Then he rose to popular acclaim as a humorist who published several books, most of them built around a young imp, Bad Boy.

What a background to go into politics with!!!

Peck was elected mayor of Milwaukee in the spring of 1890, but quickly set his sights on Madison. That November, he ousted Hoard as governor amid an outcry over a new law aimed at immigrants, which "specified that children could only go to parochial schools located in their public school district. It also required that all schools, public and private, conduct classes in English,"[39] according to the Wisconsin Historical Society.

Peck's gubernatorial victory was "one of the most dramatic routs in Wisconsin's political history,"[40] the Historical Society says. He got 52 percent and the incumbent Hoard 43 percent. Peck was the only Democratic governor of the state between 1876 and 1933.[41] He won a second term as governor in 1892 but the next time, was soundly defeated by fellow war veteran William Upham, a Republican. Peck tried one more time in 1904, at age 64, but lost the election to Robert M. LaFollette Sr., who earned his third term.

---

[38] http://www.wisconsinhistory.org/dictionary/

[39] http://www.wisconsinhistory.org/turningpoints/tp-031/?action=more_essay

[40] "The Making of Milwaukee," p. 197.

[41] "The History of Wisconsin: Volume IV," p. 408.

Peck had published one book in 1890, but then not again until 1899, evidently so he could devote full, serious attention to the political world.

In the war years, Peck's home was Delavan, according to the Wisconsin roster of volunteers, and he enlisted on Dec. 29, 1863. He began as a private and ended as a second lieutenant. His war memoir, published three years before his foray into politics, is a compilation of columns and the title reflects his tongue-in-cheek approach: "How Private George W. Peck Put Down the Rebellion, or the Funny Experiences of a Raw Recruit."[42]

The unnamed chaplain of the unit is the foil for many of Peck's tales. One chapter is devoted to Peck overseeing the construction of a wooden bridge, which was put up one mile away from where it was supposed to be, but heroically completed by the deadline. His general arrives to inspect it and exclaims: "Where is the corporal, the star idiot, who built that bridge?"[43] Peck's exhausted team took it down in record time and put it up where it was supposed to be, and he visited the span a few years after the war.

Peck also discusses once being so ill that his ever-prepared and caring friends brought a coffin to the hospital to immediately put him into.

However, there are some serious moments in the book.

Peck says he ran into a group of rebels after overseeing a funeral for a black cook and that after other Union cavalry arrived to help, there was shooting. Soon,

> **there was sorrow, for three or four boys in blue had been killed in an ambush, and the rebels had got away across a bayou. As I rode up on my mule ... I saw the three soldiers of my regiment lying dead under a tree, two others were wounded and had bandages around their heads, and for the first time since I had been a soldier, I realized the war was not a picnic. I could not keep my eyes off the faces of my dead comrades, the best and bravest boys in the regiment, boys who always got to the front when there was a skirmish.[44]**

More of Peck's serious accounts will be in the next chapter of this book, which will feature one of Peck's colleagues in the 4th Cavalry, Cpl. Moritz

---

[42] "How Private George W. Peck Put Down the Rebellion, Or the Funny Experiences of a Raw Recruit," by George Peck (1887).

[43] "How Private George W. Peck Put Down the Rebellion ...," p. 148.

[44] "How Private George W. Peck Put Down the Rebellion ...," p. 70.

Ganser of Roxbury. Both arrived in Company L, which was a group of replacements.

After the war and before politics, Peck established the "Peck's Sun" newspaper in La Crosse and moved it to Milwaukee a few years later. It was known for humorous sketches, and in 1883 he published the book "Peck's Bad Boy and His Pa."

The Bad Boy perpetually hangs out at a food store and swipes goodies while telling stories about his family, especially his father. For example, one tale involved how a male friend of the Bad Boy dressed up as a girl and and encountered Pa, who courted her in a way, saying his wife had died 14 years ago. Somehow Bad Boy brought his mother to the scene, and "Pa was just leaning down to kiss my chum when Ma couldn't stand it any longer, and she went right around in front of them and she grabbed my chum by the hair and it all came off, hat and all … and Ma she turned to Pa and he turned pale …"[45]

At the end of the story, Pa "said I was at the bottom of the whole bizness, and he locked me up, and said I was enough to paralyze a saint. I told him through the key-hole that a saint that had any sense ought to tell a boy from a girl, and then he throwed a chair at me through the transom."

Two movies were based on the book. The silent film "Peck's Bad Boy" came out in 1921, starring Jackie Coogan, who decades later portrayed Uncle Fester on TV's "The Addams Family." That film came out five years after Peck's death at age 75. The 1934 remake of the movie starred Jackie Cooper, who was 11.

Cpl. / Gov. William H. Upham

William H. Upham of Racine was three weeks shy of age 20 when the war began in 1861. Little more than three months later, he was wounded at the first battle of Bull Run (also called Manassas), then taken prisoner when Confederates seized the church that was serving as a temporary hospital. He was released from prison camps in Richmond, Va., the Confederate capital, and soon was commissioned by President Abraham Lincoln to West Point.

Three decades later, Upham was Wisconsin governor, from 1895 to 1897.

---

[45] "Peck's Bad Boy and His Pa," by George Peck (1958 version), p. 71-75.

Upham was born in Massachusetts and lived in Michigan before coming to WIsconsin in 1853. He was a corporal in F Company of the 2nd Wisconsin, while future Gov. Lucius Fairchild was colonel of the regiment.

The 2nd Wisconsin was part of what would go down in Civil War lore as the Iron Brigade. The 2nd, and other units in the Iron Brigade, had not yet earned that name when the first Bull Run came on July 21, 1861. It would be more than a year later, just before the second Bull Run battle, when Gen. George McClellan would exclaim of these members of his army, "they must be made of iron."

Upham described his wound in a letter to his family in Racine: "The ball that struck me went in the lower part of the left side of the neck and came out by the backbone four inches down the back. It was a very narrow escape for me. Had the ball varied a quarter of an inch from where it entered, it would have struck some of the large veins in the neck and I should have probably bled to death before I could have got help."[46]

His son, Bill Jr. was born in 1916, the year when his father turned 75. Bill heard many war stories while sitting on his Dad's lap. "He … was left for dead. It was three days without any medical treatment." Another soldier, thinking Upham was dead, tried to take the wounded man's shoes. Upham stopped the thief by summoning the strength to gasp, '"hope to wear those shoes one day."[47] About 12 days later, he was taken to Richmond, Va., as a prisoner of war. Seven months later, Upham was exchanged, paroled and returned to Washington. He met with President Lincoln and "the president asked him to take off his shirt in order to see the wound. We always say that he was the first Upham to lose his shirt to the president."

Lincoln appointed him to West Point, and he graduated as a second lieutenant in 1866. He became a lumberman in Marshfield and established other businesses there.

After serving one term and being succeeded by fellow Republican Edward Scofield, Upham went back to Marshfield and running the Upham Manufacturing Co. He died in 1924 at the age of 83.[48]

---

[46] "If This Is War," by Alan D. Gaff (1991), p. 267.

[47] http://www.suvcw-wi.org/trueSons.html. This is an article by Steve Michaels, who was Wisconsin department commander and then national commander-in-chief of Sons of Union Veterans of the Civil War, the successor to the GAR. Bill Upham Jr. of Milwaukee, who died in 2009, was a member of the Sons.

[48] When William Jr. died at the age of 93 in 2009, he was the last remaining Wisconsin son of a Union veteran.

Capt. / Gov. Edward Scofield

The final Wisconsin governor who was a Civil War veteran served into the new century, 40 years after Fort Sumter. Edward Scofield was governor from 1897 to 1901, and was the only governor who spent his entire service in another state's unit – the 11th Pennsylvania Reserves, which became the 40th Pennsylvania Volunteers.

He had just turned 19 when the war broke out. The regiment was mustered into U.S. service on June 29, 1861, and served to June 1864, fighting at such places as Antietam, Fredericksburg, Va., Gettysburg and the Wilderness.[49]

Scofield, who had risen to captain during the long months, was captured during the Battle of the Wilderness – which was fought May 5-7, 1864 – and held for 10 months.

In 1868 he moved to Wisconsin and then Oconto, and eventually started his own lumber business. He was a Republican and tried to get the nomination for governor in 1894, but it went to Upham. He tried again and won in 1896, then was re-elected two years later with 60 percent of the vote, the biggest margin in three decades.

Over the years in Oconto, Scofield (who died in 1925) told his war story.[50]

His first promotion, to the office of lieutenant, came as a result of exceptional heroism at the battle of Fredericksburg. The story is told that the Confederates placed timed shells before their outworks so as to blow up when the Union troops were charging into their earthworks. The order to charge came at daylight.

With a yell the troops under the command of acting Lt. Scofield dashed toward the enemy in the face of a withering fire. When they arrived near the Confederate earthworks, the timed bombs exploded, tearing great gaps in the ranks. But

---

[49] http://www.civilwararchive.com/Unreghst/unpainf1.htm#11thres

[50] http://www.rootsweb.ancestry.com/~wioconto/civilwarrecords.htm. This gives the service of several Oconto County residents; the account on Scofield is researched and written by Ron Renquin.

they forged ahead, climbing over the bodies of dead and dying comrades until they were in the midst of the rebels' earthworks. ... Desperate and bloody encounters followed fast upon each other.

... Then came Gettysburg. Here Lt. Scofield again distinguished himself and in recognition of his service was made captain. Then followed the desperate fighting of the Battle of Wilderness which took the lives of two-thirds of the members of the famous Pennsylvania (unit) .... Here the forces of the South executed a brilliant military maneuver and captured 2,500 Union troops in a mass. ...

Imprisonment conditions in the Southern stockades were intolerable. Once Capt. Scofield escaped for a short time, hid in swamps and woods, lived on what negroes were able to smuggle to him. But he was recaptured and thrown into a dungeon as punishment. He was transferred from camp to camp. One period of his imprisonment was served in Andersonville Prison, where the barbarous treatment accorded prisoners cannot be depicted even in the imagination.

Shortly before the close of the war he was exchanged with many other prisoners. The long period of exposure, hardship, and starvation had left him thin, haggard, weighing only 96 pounds. Be he wished to see the conflict through to the end and enlisted as a substitute for a drafted man.

Scofield died in 1925 at the age of 82.

Wartime governor drowned near the battlefield

As of 2013, there have been 45 governors of Wisconsin. This chapter has detailed the seven soldiers who became governor, but it cannot overlook the devoted civilian service of the four who were in office during the war and thus spent much of their time forming, equipping and supplying Wisconsin regiments.

That makes a total of 11 governors who were deeply involved in the war, meaning that even as of today, nearly one-quarter of WIsconsin governors had direct ties to the Civil War. The war thus left a major footprint on Wisconsin political history.[51]

The story of one incumbent is an incredibly sad case: Gov. Louis Harvey made a trip to Tennessee immediately after the Battle of Shiloh (April 6 and 7, 1862), to deliver supplies to the legions of wounded Wisconsin soldiers. Harvey, 41, a Republican, had just taken office three months earlier, succeeding fellow Republican Alexander Randall. Harvey had served as secretary of state from 1860 to 1862.

Two days before Harvey's death, the Manitowoc Herald[52] had reported:

There were probably five or six Wisconsin regiments in the battle of Pittsburg (Landing; soon renamed Shiloh). As soon as Gov. Harvey ascertained the fact, he telegraphed to the Chamber of Commerce in Milwaukee, to Janesville and Beloit, appealing for the citizens of those cities to furnish immediately such surgical materials as could be gathered and forwarded to this city.

The Milwaukee Chamber of Commerce, on receipt of the telegraph at noon on Wednesday, voted at once $200, to bear the expenses of Drs. Wolcott and Bartlett, the best surgeons in the city, and of sending the desired articles. Gen. E.H. Brodhead, a prominent gentleman of the same city, accompanies them to assist in their humane mission.

The Chicago Tribune of Friday, gives the following particulars of the progress of this humane undertaking: "Gov. Harvey and Commissary General Wadsworth arrived last evening at the Tremont, where they were met by the Milwaukee delegation, and tomorrow morning the whole party, consisting of the governor, his secretary, Gen. Brodhead, and nine

---

[51] The Civil War, with seven future governors in the fight, left an even bigger mark that World War II – six Wisconsin governors were soldiers or sailors – Walter Kohler in the Navy, Gaylord Nelson in the Army on Okinawa, John Reynolds in the Army, Warren Knowles in the Navy at D-Day, Patrick Lucey in the Army and Lee Dreyfus in the Navy. During the war, the state's governors were Julius Heil and Walter Goodman.

[52] This article was posted in May 2012 on the website of the Wisconsin Civil War Sesquicentennial Commission, www.civilwarwisconsin.com

surgeons leave on the Illinois Central railroad for their destination, taking with them 90 boxes of hospital supplies for the
wounded Wisconsin soldiers."

When we consider that these abundant supplies were
raised within less than 24 hours, by the three cities that were
here mentioned, and by the people of Madison, we can but
accord honor to the prompt benevolence which is thus manifested, and of the energy and humanity of Gov. Harvey. The
Illinois Central, with its usual patriotism, carries the surgical
material free. If the state authorities everywhere took as good
care of their volunteers as those of Wisconsin do of theirs,
there will be little neglect to complain of. All honor to them.

The rest of the story comes from the book "Wisconsin in the War of the
Rebellion; A History of All Regiments and Batteries" by William DeLoss
Love, published in 1866 and digitized by the Wisconsin Historical Society.[53]

On Saturday morning, April 19th, Gov. Harvey bade
farewell to the soldiers at Pittsburg Landing, and went down to
Savannah (Tenn.) 10 miles below, on the Tennessee River. It
was not expected to take a steamer for Cairo (Tenn.) until the
next morning, and some of the company had retired for the
night, on board the (steamboat) Dunleith, lying at the wharf.

But at 10 in the evening the Minnehaha (steamboat) hove
in sight, the party were aroused, and Gov. Harvey, with others,
took position near the edge and fore part of the Dunleith
awaiting the opportunity to pass to the approaching boat. As
the bow of the Minnehaha rounded close to the party on the
Dunleith, the governor stepped back on one side, either for
convenience or to get beyond harm, and the night being dark
and rainy, and the timber of the boat slippery, by some misstep
he fell between the two steamers.

Dr. Wilson, of Sharon, being near, immediately reached
down his cane, which the governor grasped with so much force
as to pull it from his hands. Dr. Clark, of Racine, jumped in
the water, made himself fast to the Minnehaha and thrust his

---

body in the direction of the governor, who, he thinks, once almost reached him, but the current was too strong; the drowning man, it is supposed, was drawn under a flat-boat just below, and when his life was despaired of, Dr. Wolcott and Gen. Brodhead, of Milwaukee, and others of the party, made diligent and long search to recover the body of the lost one, but in vain, until some children found it 65 miles below.

Harvey's body was found 14 days later in the rain-swollen, swiftly moving river.

Wisconsin was shocked at the sudden loss of its top elected official. One newspaper story began this way: "A great calamity has befallen the State in the death of Gov. L.P. Harvey, one of her best men, and certainly her best Governor. He lost his life while on an errand of mercy to Wisconsin's suffering sons, and a whole State is plunged into mourning."[54]

Harvey was succeeded as governor by Edward Salomon. In November 1862, Salomon became a lightning rod when he called out troops to halt riots in Ozaukee County over the draft instituted by Lincoln. He did not get the GOP nomination, which went to James T. Lewis, who won the 1863 election over Democrat Henry Palmer. Lewis took office in 1864, serving one term and being succeeded by war veteran Lucius Fairchild of the GOP.

The first wartime governor, Republican Alexander Randall, mentioned earlier, led the charge in organizing and equipping the first Wisconsin volunteer regiments after the call by President Lincoln. Randall's name is constantly in the news in Madison all year and during football season everywhere else because of Camp Randall Stadium. That area was named Camp Randall when Wisconsin soldiers by the tens of thousands trained there for the war. A landmark of Madison, the Camp Randall Memorial Arch, is on the east end of the property, fronting on Randall Avenue.

Randall was governor from 1858 to 1862 and did not run again, succeeded by Harvey.

---

54 http://content.wisconsinhistory.org/cdm4/document.php?CISOROOT=/quiner &CISOPTR=27785&CISOSHOW=27732

4 U.S. senators were veterans

Four Civil War veterans – all officers – later served as U.S. senator from Wisconsin, in an era when senators were elected by legislatures, not directly by the people.

The first was John Coit Spooner, who had come to Madison from Indiana two years before the war and was 18 at the time of Fort Sumter. He enlisted on May 13, 1864, in the 40th Wisconsin Volunteer Regiment, which saw service in the defense of Memphis, Tenn. It helped to repulse a raid by Confederate forces of Maj. Gen. Nathan Bedford Forrest on Aug. 21. As reported earlier in this chapter, one of the goals of the raid was to abduct three generals, including Maj. Gen. Cadwallader Washburn, future governor of WIsconsin.

The 40th Regiment's enlistment term expired in September, and Spooner mustered out. But at the end of February 1865, he was back in the military, as captain of Company A of the 50th Wisconsin Regiment. That group was organized in March and April, and sent to Missouri right after the war ended. It was mustered out in June.

Spooner, a Republican, was in the Senate from 1885 to 1891 and again from 1897 to 1907, when he resigned.

Democrat William F. Vilas, whose last name is very recognizable in Madison today, was a senator from 1891 to 1897. Vilas was 20 when the war began and was in the 23rd Volunteer Regiment as captain of Company A; organized on Aug. 14, 1862. He was promoted to major the following February and lieutenant colonel a month after that. Vilas commanded the regiment at Vicksburg, Miss., then in the siege of Jackson, Miss. He resigned on Aug. 29, 1863.

Vilas was postmaster general of the United States from 1885 to 1888, appointed by President Grover Cleveland.

Forty years after the war, Vilas and his wife, Anna, gave land to Madison for its landmark Vilas Park. The Henry Vilas Zoo's history says: "From 1905 through 1910, the Vilas family donated an additional $42,000 for improvements, and public donations of $10,000 were raised for the enlargement and improvement of the park. The park was named in memory of the Vilases' son, Henry, who died at a young age due to complications from diabetes. In 1911, the first animal exhibits were created, representing the start of the Henry Vilas Zoo. In what has proved to be a defining and truly visionary move, the Vilas family stipulated that the park always be admission-free."[55]

John Mitchell, a Democrat, was in the Senate from 1893 to 1899. He was from the prominent Milwaukee banking family and would become the father of Gen. Billy Mitchell of aviation fame. When the war began, John Mitchell was 18, and on Aug. 16, 1862, he enlisted in Company K of the 24th Wisconsin and was a second lieutenant. He was promoted to first lieutenant on Jan. 17, 1863, soon after the unit's first major battle, at Stones River, Tenn. He left the Union Army on Sept. 1, 1863, three weeks before the bloody battle of Chickamauga.

Joseph Very Quarles, a Republican from Kenosha, was in the Senate from 1899 to 1905. At the time of Fort Sumter he was 17. He served only briefly, from May 20, 1864, to September of that year, and was first lieutenant of Company C of the 39th Wisconsin Regiment.

The regiment was mustered in on June 3, 1864, and mustered out on Sept. 22. It had garrison, railroad guard and picket duty around Memphis, Tenn., and, along with the regiment of Spooner, repulsed the Confederate raid on Memphis Aug. 21.

The 17th Amendment to the U.S. Constitution provided for direct election of senators. Wisconsin ratified it on Feb. 18, 1913, and by April 13, the required three-fourths of the states had ratified.

---

[55] https://www.vilaszoo.org/guests/index.php?category_id=490

Chapter 4
One Wisconsin man in the Civil War

This is author Tom Mueller's story about how he discovered he had a relative in the Civil War and then worked to track down the soldier's story. This also is the story of tens of thousands of other Wisconsin men.

After doing this research about his little-known relative, Mueller soon joined the Sons of Union Veterans of the Civil War and is an officer in C.K. Pier Badger Camp #1 in Milwaukee and in the Wisconsin department of the group.

We all have learned about the Civil War in school, books, movies and television specials.

But these lessons mean a lot more if you, the unsuspecting reader, discover that you had a long-lost relative in the war of 1861 to 1865. You owe it to his memory to track down what happened – it is three, four and five generations later, and your work will mean a lot for current and future generations of your family.

If elements of your family tree were in America as of 1855 or so, someone may well have been in the epic conflict.

Here is the story of one such man and how I did the tracking. He is my great-great uncle (the great-uncle of my father and the uncle of my grandmother). She was age 3 when he died in 1895 and thus perhaps never even knew about his service. Her father was the soldier's brother, three years younger.

I decided to check into a little picture of Moritz Ganser that was in a 1970s family genealogy with the caption of "Civil War" but zero details.

Finding Ganser's record was not overly hard. The Wisconsin Historical Society and the Wisconsin Veterans Museum have put online the roster of the state's soldiers, "Wisconsin Volunteers, War of the Rebellion, 1861-1865."[1] It showed what his unit was, and taking that to the Goggle quickly found that a book had been written about Ganser's regiment; the book has a website and his photo is available.

But be advised that your relative's name may be spelled differently either via an error or otherwise. Moritz's name was spelled wrong both ways on the book

---

[1] www.wisconsinhistory.org/roster

Cpl. Moritz Ganser of Roxbury posed for this photo against a painted backdrop. He was in the Civil War from 1864 to 1865. The sword is kept today by his grandchildren and great-grandchildren in Alberta, Canada.

website (as Mority Ganzer) and wrong one way in the state record (as Ganzer), but in both places there was no mistaking his hometown of tiny Roxbury, Wis.

The rest of this chapter was accomplished by more-traditional methods: Poke around on the Web for the regiment's history and its battles, get related books, and there you go.

Moritz Ganser served in the war in 1864 and 1865, when his 4th Wisconsin Cavalry Regiment was stationed in or "visiting" Louisiana, Mississippi, Alabama, Georgia and Texas as part of the Army of the Gulf. Most Northerners may not even know there was Civil War fighting in Louisiana, because we hear so much about the battles at Gettysburg, Bull Run, Fredericksburg, Chancellorsville, Shiloh, etc.

This chapter particularly relies on two books, "A History of the 4th Wisconsin Infantry and Cavalry in the Civil War,"[2] which runs 570 pages, and

[2] By Michael Martin (2006)

"How Private George W. Peck Put Down the Rebellion, or the Funny Experiences of a Raw Recruit."[3]

Moritz was a corporal when he enlisted and a sergeant when he went out. He was born Aug. 10, 1836, so he was ages 27 to 29 in the war.

He had come to the United States from Niederprum, Germany, in 1854 at the age of 18, along with his brother John and many other members of the family, including their parents, John and Anna. A short account written by his grandson Ray Ganser says Moritz later joined tens of thousands of people in the gold rush in the Cariboo District of British Columbia, which at the time was known as the Northwest Territories, before coming home and enlisting in the Civil War in 1864. The Cariboo rush was between 1860 and 1863, focused around what became the boom town of Barkerville.[4]

In the Wisconsin roster that repeatedly has been mentioned in the Civil War chapters of this book, Moritz's last name was spelled as Ganzer, with a Z, presumably because that is the way it sounded or some Army clerk was not very meticulous or "Americanized" it. The spelling of his name also varied in his official military record – in the form that he filled out when enlisting, he signed his name as Maurice, apparently because the person filling out the form also had done it that way. And eight of the Army's 10 handwritten pay records have him as Gauser, but they were corrected each time to Ganser.

He had hazel eyes, dark hair, a fair complexion and was 5 feet, 11½ inches tall,[5] and his profession was farming, according to the Muster and Descriptive Rolls of Wisconsin Regiments, on microfilm at the Civil War Museum in Kenosha.

The 4th Wisconsin Infantry Regiment had been organized in July 1861. It briefly fought in Maryland before being sent on ships to New Orleans, where it was part of an invading force that forced the city to surrender in April 1862 with hardly any fighting. The 4th often was stationed around Baton Rouge, La., and its major action was being part of the force that attacked, then besieged Port Hudson, La., on the Mississippi River.

---

[3] By George Peck (1887). Peck became Wisconsin governor, and his story was told in the previous chapter of this book.

[4] www.thecanadianencyclopedia.com and www.bcheritage.ca/cariboo

[5] Those are strong family genes, because the author of this book has the exact same hair, complexion and height.

The Confederates at Port Hudson surrendered July 9, 1863, a few days after Gen. U.S. Grant forced the surrender of Vicksburg, Miss., and the two actions opened the river on a permanent basis for the rest of the war. This period also saw the victory at Gettysburg of July 3,1863, and marked a turning point in the war.[6]

But that was all before Ganser arrived, and while the regiment was still infantry.

On Sept. 1, 1863, in the relatively quiet period after the fall of Port Hudson, the War Department ordered the 4th Wisconsin to be converted into a cavalry regiment because the war in Louisiana was changing from large battles and sieges into smaller conflicts, and the mobility of cavalry was needed.

Michael Martin, who wrote the regiment's history, says: "The change marked a profound shift in the type of service the regiment would perform during the remainder of the war. No longer would the Badgers be called upon to assault an entrenched enemy on foot. Instead, the Wisconsin soldiers would be assigned the arduous and lonely task of picketing and patrolling the primary approaches to Baton Rouge. The 'new' enemy would include both regular and (guerrilla) soldiers and the engagements would be short, sharp and often lethal ....."[6]

In one such mission, on May 3, 1864, Col. Frederick Boardman, regimental commander, was shot and killed at a place on the Comite River east of Baton Rouge where Confederates had burned a bridge. "The enemy, who were waiting in the line of woods across the river, unleashed a volley" and Boardman was hit in the mouth, killed instantly."[8]

This occurred about two months before Ganser arrived in Louisiana.

Ganser was in Company L and enlisted on March 9, 1864. The 4th Regiment was adding two companies – Moritz's L and Company M – essentially as replacements for those killed in the earlier fighting or who fell victim to sunstroke or diseases such as malaria and typhoid, and the more-usual pneumonia and dysentery.

---

[6] "Receding Tide: Vicksburg and Gettysburg, the Campaigns That Changed the Civil War," by Ed Bearss (2010).

[7] "A History of the 4th Wisconsin Infantry and Cavalry in the Civil War," p. 213.

[8] "A History of the 4th Wisconsin Infantry and Cavalry in the Civil War," p. 252.

He reached the regiment in Baton Rouge, La., on June 27, 1864, according to his record in the National Archives and the Muster Roll. Ganser soon was transferred to E and remained there for the rest of the war.

Ray Ganser's account says "he was disabled at Baton Rouge, La., on Aug. 10, 1864." The Muster record refers to Moritz being ill and in the hospital and then on sick furlough, both in November of that year.

The Muster record credits Ganser with participation in combat actions at the Comite Bridge in Louisiana in August and at Liberty, Miss., in November. On March 1, 1865, he was promoted to sergeant.

Here is a list of where the 4th Cavalry was stationed or in action during the time of Ganser's service. In some raids, only a few companies of the regiment participated, while other groups were elsewhere.[9]

– **Baton Rouge, La., June 16, 1864.**

– **Plaquemine, La., June 28.**

– **Ordered to Morganza, La., June 29, and duty there until Aug. 9.**

– **Plaquemine, La., Aug. 6.**

– **Moved to Baton Rouge, Aug. 9.**

– **Near Bayou Letsworth, La., Aug. 11.**

– **Expedition to Clinton, La., Aug. 25 to 29.**

– **Olive Branch, Comite River and Clinton, La., Aug. 25.**

– **Expedition to Clinton, Greensburg and Camp Moore, Oct. 5 to 9.**

– **Expedition from Baton Rouge to Brookhaven, Miss., and skirmishes, Nov. 14 to 21.**

– **Liberty Creek, Miss., Nov. 15.**

– **Jackson, Miss., Nov. 21.**

– **Davidson Expedition to Mobile & Ohio Railroad and Pascagoula Bay, Miss., Nov. 27 to Dec. 13.**

– **At Baton Rouge, La., until April 1865.**

---

9 http://www.civilwararchive.com/Unreghst/unwicav.htm#4thcav and from the website 4th Wisconsin Volunteers www.hughesfamilies.com/fourth/index.cfm

– Mobile, Ala., campaign, April 1865.[10]

– Capture of Mobile, April 12, 1865.

– March through Alabama to Georgia and to Vicksburg, Miss., April 18 to June 5, 1865.

– Moved to Shreveport, La., June 26 to July 2, 1865.

– March to San Antonio, Texas, July 8 to Aug. 3, and duty in that state until October 1865. The regiment's mission was to prevent smuggling of weapons across the Rio Grande, defend the border from attacks by groups based in Mexico, prevent Confederates from going to Mexico to regroup, protect the area against Indian attacks, etc. Company E was based at Laredo, Texas.[11]

One of Ganser's fellow new arrivals in Company L in 1864 was Pvt. George Peck, who was born in 1840, four years after Ganser. Peck had arrived in Louisiana on Dec. 29, 1863, a few months before Ganser, went on to become a lieutenant in Company E on Aug. 22, 1865, the day Ganser's service ended, and then was governor of Wisconsin from 1891 to 1895, as was reported in the previous chapter of this book.

When Peck made it home he wrote a humorous series of newspaper columns that became an 1887 book that has been republished in recent years.

The book itself does not give Peck's regiment, but the dates and general places of service (Peck rarely gives names of towns) match up with Ganser's, and the Milwaukee Public Library summary of the book says he was in a replacement company in the 4th Wisconsin. Thus, the kind of things that Peck saw and felt are likely what Moritz saw and felt.

Peck described one raid conducted by the regiment.[12]

As we neared the town it was just light enough to see. The advance captured the (rebel) picket post without a shot being fired, and moved right into town, followed by the regiment, and we actually rode right into the camp of the boys in gray,

---

[10] Miller, Francis Trevelyan (1957). "The Cavalry: The Photographic History of the Civil War," by Francis Trevelyan Miller (1957). This book gives great context of being in a cavalry unit, particularly the sheer number of horseshoers and veterinarians employed.

[11] "A History of the 4th Wisconsin Infantry and Cavalry in the Civil War," p. 349; and http://museum.dva.state.wi.us/Res_CWRegiments.asp).

[12] "How Private George W. Peck Put Down the Rebellion ...," p. 95.

and woke them up by firing. They scattered, coatless and shirt-less, firing as they ran, and in five minutes they were all cap-tured, killed, gone out of town, or were hiding in the buildings. Then began the conflagration (fires set by the cav-alry). Immense buildings, filled with goods, or bales of cotton, were fired, and soon the black smoke and falling walls made a scene that was enough to set a recruit crazy.

Here is Peck's report of a bigger battle:[13]

We went off towards the fighting, then right down by our own cannon and formed in line behind the infantry, that was at work with the enemy, the artillery firing over our heads at the Confederates in the woods. The noise was so loud that one could not hear his neighbor speak; but above it all came a bugle note, and glancing to the left, another cavalry regiment, and another, formed on our left.

Another bugle note, and to the right another cavalry reg-iment formed, and for half a mile there was a line of horsemen, deafened by the noise, waiting the command of some man, through a bugle. If the rebels had time to notice those four reg-iments of cavalry, fresh and ready for a gallop, they must have known that it was a good time to get away.

Finally, our artillery ceased firing and it seemed still as death, except for the rattling of infantry in front of us. ... As we neared the place where our infantry had been stationed, it was necessary to break up a little to pass the dead and wounded without riding over them.

... All idea of being sorry for the enemy, all charity, all hope that the war might close before any more men were killed, was gone. After looking in the upturned faces of our dead and wounded on the field, the more of the enemy that were killed the better. It is thus that war makes men brutal .... The next 10 minutes was the nearest thing to hell that I have ever experienced, and it seemed as though my face must look like that of a fiend. I felt like one.

(The enemy was) so near that you could see their counte-nances, their eyes. Some of them were mounted, others were on

---

[13] "How Private George W. Peck Put Down the Rebellion ...," p. 224-226.

foot, some on artillery caissons, all full of fight. It did not take long to exhaust (shooting with) the revolvers, and then the sabers began to come out, and the horrible word "charge," came from a thousand throats, and every soldier yelled like a Comanche Indian .....

Sabers whacked, horses ran, and everybody yelled....Many of our men were killed and wounded, and many of theirs were treated the same way. Those who could get away, got, and those we passed without happening to hit them, were prisoners, because the infantry followed and took them back to the rear.

Although Peck does not give a date or place for this, it certainly was a big enough encounter that the entire regiment was involved; thus it may have been the Comite River in Louisiana or Liberty, Miss.; events that Ganser's record says he was in.

While Moritz was discharged on Aug. 22, 1865, the regiment remained in existence until May 28, 1866, when it was mustered out at Brownsville, Texas. Peck was mustered out on that day.

In all, the regiment lost 11 officers and 106 men in combat or other action, plus three officers and 311 dead to disease. Losing more men to disease than to combat was not at all unusual in the war.[14]

Some of Moritz's colleagues from during his time in E Company are buried at the National Cemetery at Baton Rouge, La., including Pvt. Francis Duvall of Sun Prairie, who was killed on Aug. 6, 1864 (the list of where the regiment was based or fought shows this would have been near Plaquemine), and two men who died of disease: Pvt. Christian Reehl (also spelled Riehl) of Milwaukee, July 7, 1864; and Sgt. Barton Whipple of Bradford (in Rock County), Sept. 17, 1864. The cemetery also has several others from L Company who died of disease.[15]

Ganser came home to Wisconsin and in 1866 married Barbara Classen, 13 years younger. He died unexpectedly in his sleep on Jan. 1, 1895, at the age of 58 and is buried in St. Norbert's Cemetery in Roxbury. His three youngest children were 6, 4 and 2 when he died.

---

[14] http://museum.dva.state.wi.us/Res_CWRegiments.asp
[15] "A History of the 4th Wisconsin Infantry and Cavalry in the Civil War," p. 413-415

Chapter 5
Dying in World War I – in Russia, weeks after Nov. 11, 1918

Pvt. Frank Mueller went off to World War I in the 339th Infantry Regiment, and his last name is familiar to everyone in Marshfield today because it is enshrined on the city's Mueller-Hintz VFW Post 1866.

His story, however, is not: Mueller was killed in Russia on Dec. 30, 1918, seven weeks after the Armistice that ended the Great War.

That's right: Mueller died in combat in Russia. Seven weeks after the Armistice. So did 2nd Lt. Carl H. Berger of Mayville, killed one day after Mueller, and so did a few other Wisconsin men, from wounds or illness.

Many other Wisconsin men fought in Russia in the 339th Regiment of the 85th Infantry Division, including Lt. John Cudahy, son of Patrick Cudahy of meatpacking fame in Cudahy, Wis.

The fact that President Woodrow Wilson ever sent about 5,000 troops to north Russia, as did Britain and other major allies – into the frozen, forested, marshy area a few hundred miles below the Arctic Circle and east of Finland – is rarely discussed today. But the story of what is called the Polar Bear regiment is readily found in comprehensive books about World War I, and especially in the 2000 book "When Hell Froze Over: The Secret War Between the U.S. and Russia at the Top of the World!" by E.M. Halliday.[16]

A major reason that was given for the Allied foray into Russia was to protect extensive amounts of weapons and supplies that had been shipped to that country and destined for the Eastern Front of World War I; after the Bolsheviks took over in November 1917, they declared the war had ended on their front.

The mission also was designed to allow the 120,000 Czech Legion troops who were in Russia to get out and then be put back into the war on

---

[16] Halliday also wrote versions in 1958 and 1960, originally entitled "The Ignorant Armies." The book is highly recommended reading, but has no footnotes as to where his substantial bits of information came from. Halliday worked with some veterans of the excursion when he was an Army correspondent in World War II. Halliday kept researching while he was a university teacher of literature and history, and as a senior editor of American Heritage magazine for 16 years.

The Marshfield Times newspaper reported the death in Russia of a local soldier, Pvt. Frank Mueller, on its front page on Feb. 5, 1919. His death came several weeks after the armistice that ended World War I in Europe, but an American regiment remained in combat in Russia.

field

ostoffice, Marshfield, Wis., Under Act of 1875

sin, Wednesday, February 5, 1!

LOSES HIS LIFE IN BATTLE IN RUSSIA

Frank Mueller, Jr., Killed in Action at Archangel, - Russia.

Frank Mueller, Washington avenue received a war department message Friday which stated that his son Frank Mueller, Jr., had been killed in action in the fighting in Russia. This news came as a surprise to the relatives coming two months after the signing of the armistice. The family received a letter from him Monday in which he stated that he spent Thanksgiving day in the trenches This letter was sent from Archangel a seaport in Russia. Private Mueller

the Western Front. They had been sent to help Moscow attack Germany (and later were stationed along the Trans-Siberian railway line and ordered into prisoner camps, and also sometimes were in combat against the Bolsheviks).

The above are complex issues that are perhaps oversimplified here, but it also is evident that another factor was vehement opposition, particularly by the British, to what would become known as Communism, even to the extent of intruding in another nation's internal affairs.

The American force wound up in that country's fighting between the Bolsheviks and the White Russians and others who had overthrown the czar in early 1917 but in turn were ousted by the "Bolos" in November of that year.

Mueller, Berger and their 339th Regiment were in the American North Russia Expeditionary Force, which arrived in the White Sea port city of Archangel (the Russian word is Arkhangelsk) in September 1918 and soon was in combat. A total of 13 other nations also sent forces into Russia, led by Britain, Canada, France and Japan (which sent its forces to the Far East). About 8,000 other Americans went to Vladivostok in Siberia on the Sea of Japan – the Army's 27th and 31st Infantry Regiments – but there was no major fighting there other than against the brutal weather.

Mueller, 28, was in E Company of the 339th Regiment. His company lieutenant was Berger, 27, and both were killed in an attack against Bolshevik forces near Kodish, Russia. It is not known what the current name of Kodish is; maps of the area focus more on Archangel than on anything smaller in the forests; a Google search for "Russia current name for Kodish near Archangel" finds only the World War I articles.

The vast majority of Mueller and Berger's regiment was from Michigan and had trained at Camp Custer between Battle Creek and Kalamazoo. Many records have been put online by the "Detroit's Own" Polar Bear Memorial Association; and a history by the group, written by Mike Grobbel, president, says:

On July 22, 1918, the men of the U.S. Army's 85th Division boarded troop ships in New York City and set sail to join the Great War. Thirteen days later, they docked in Liverpool, England ... for additional training prior to heading for France – or so they thought.

Gen. John J. Pershing, the commander of all American forces in Europe, had just received the Allied intervention directive from President Wilson and decided to change the orders for the 339th Infantry Regiment (and its attached units), the 1st Battalion of the 310th Engineers, the 337th Field Hospital and the 337th Ambulance Company. Instead of continuing to the Western Front with the rest of their 85th Division counterparts, these units were designated to be re-equipped and re-trained before joining the British and French Allies in Archangel as the American Expeditionary Force North Russia.[17]

Archangel is on the White Sea, which is a body of water on the Barents Sea, which is part of the Arctic Ocean. The population is more than 300,000 today.

So why were American troops going into Russia? What were the forces of other countries doing there?

"... Following the March 17 revolution (against the czar), which established the Provisional Government, and the revolution of October, which brought the Bolsheviks to power, Russia was no longer a dependable ally for the British and French,"[18] World War I author Gary Mead writes. "On 12 February 1918 the Bolsheviks declared that Russia would no longer continue

---

[17] http://pbma.grobbel.org/westriding/polar_bear_news.htm Accessed February 2013. The website has dozens of articles, citations and lists. Particularly good is a collection of diaries, at http://pbma.grobbel.org/polarbearstories.htm

[18] "The Doughboys," by Gary Mead (2000), p. 270.

the war against the Central Powers (Germany). Russia's collapse signified a huge disaster for the Allies, who almost overnight lost some 12 million Russian soldiers fighting in their cause," and nearly a million German soldiers now could be moved to the Western Front.

Wilson was lobbied feverishly by the British and French, who among other things noted that if Allied forces were in Russia, there still could be an Eastern Front. Wilson finally relented in July 1918.[19]

"President Wilson's decision to join this expedition was one of his most ill-judged moves, and cast a pall over U.S.-Russian relations for many years to come."[20]

Along with being a policy morass, the scene in Russia was even more severe weather-wise and combat-wise than the trench warfare of France and Belgium – a snowy quagmire with temperatures often 30 degrees below zero or worse. "Most of the doughboys who went to Russia survived, but many were traumatized by the climate, the living conditions, and the almost complete inability to tell who was the enemy, who was the friend," Mead says. "Although the Allies ended (the period as) bitter enemies of the Bolsheviks, confusingly enough they also occasionally fought alongside some elements of the Bolshevik forces" vs. Germans and Finland, under an agreement signed in July 1918 in Murmansk.[21]

In Mayville, the local newspaper had reported in a short story on Oct. 18, 1918, that Berger had sent his wife a letter from Archangel saying "conditions in Russia are more terrible than we can imagine. He states that the Russian people look upon the Americans from the land of promise and thinks that after the war there will be extensive migration to America."

Berger was in The Mayville News again on Jan. 9, 1919, with the story reporting his death.[22] The one-column story did not give a date of death, which was Dec. 31. The story noted that he had a two-week-old baby son when he departed for Europe, and began:

The sad news was received here Sunday morning that Lt. Carl H. Berger had been killed in action in Russia. The news

---

[19] "Woodrow Wilson," by August Heckscher (1991), p. 463-465; 476.

[20] "The Doughboys," p. 270.

[21] "The Doughboys," p. 271.

[22] These articles were tracked down by the Dodge County Pionier newspaper, descendant of the Mayville publication, and the Mayville Historical Society.

of his death and burial came in the form of a cable message, from Lt. Alfred Kliefoth who is also stationed in Russia....

Lt. Berger, who was born at Oshkosh May 17, 1891, was a native of Milwaukee. He graduated from W. Div. High School, then Milwaukee Normal School (a forerunner of UW – Milwaukee) and the University of Wisconsin (in Madison). He was a member of the Alpha Sigma Phi and Honorary Phi Beta Kappa. For a time he was employed by the Harley-Davidson Motor Co. and later served for two years as instructor of the public school at Mayville.

He went from the University of Wisconsin to the first officers' training camp at Fort Sheridan, where he won his commission. He was stationed at Camp Custer until last July, when his regiment was sent overseas.

Lt. Berger was prominent in debating, dramatic and literary activities through his high school, normal school and university careers. He will always be remembered here for his pleasant, interesting way of arranging affairs, as music director, etc.

Lt. Berger was married to Miss Adele Thielke of this city on Sept. 29, 1917. Mrs. Berger lived at Battle Creek (Mich.) with her husband until last July, when he left for overseas. A son, Carl H. Jr., was born two weeks before Lt. Berger left the port of embarkation.

To the north, Mueller's death was reported on the front page of The Marshfield Times on Wednesday, Feb. 5, under the headline of "Loses His Life in Battle in Russia." The story said the family had been notified a few days earlier; that was about four weeks after Berger's family got its own bad news. As in Mayville, this newspaper had no date of death. Here is the story in its entirety:

Frank Mueller, Washington Avenue, received a war department message Friday which stated that his son, Frank Mueller Jr., had been killed in action in the fighting in Russia.

This news came as a surprise to the relatives, coming two months after the signing of the armistice. The family received a letter from him Monday in which he stated that he spent Thanksgiving Day in the trenches. This letter was sent from Archangel, a seaport in Russia.

Pvt. Mueller left with the Wood County contingent the 23rd of May, 1918, and reported at Camp Grant (at Rockford, Ill.). He was called home the 25th of May by the death of his mother.

This is the first soldier from this vicinity to lose his life in the fighting in Russia.

Pvt. Mueller was born Aug. 1, 1890 .... He leaves to mourn his noble sacrifice, besides his father, four sisters, three of whom are sisters at the Sacred Heart convent in this city, and Miss Anna Mueller of Milwaukee; and three brothers, Henry, who was recently discharged from service, and is now employed as baker at the Wright bakery; Joseph and George, also of this city.

Berger's body was returned home in November 1919, but Mueller's was not returned until 1930. Possibly that was because Berger was an officer and Mueller a private; possibly they had been buried in different locations because of where they fell (Berger had been taken a field hospital). Berger's funeral was Nov. 21, 1919, and the Mayville weekly paper ran this story on Nov. 27 (the first name of the general in it cannot readily be determined today):

The military funeral of Lt. Carl Berger was one of the most impressive Mayville has ever seen. The remains had arrived here Thursday evening, having been among the hundreds that were returned from Russian soil, where our heroes fell in battle, which great cortege made such a deep impression on the people at New York and again at Milwaukee, from which so many were sent to their home towns.

Lt. Berger's remains were accompanied here by Brig. Gen. Davison and were met at the station by many friends and relatives. Gen. Davison had asked the war department for permission to accompany the remains of Lt. Berger, when he heard that he was to be shipped to Dodge County. The general is a former Dodge County boy, having been born on a farm in the Town of Chester, and is a brother of Dist. Atty. Chas M. Davison of Beaver Dam.

Even the weather Friday was funereal in harmony with the sad day. But the mist and rain did not deter great crowds of people from gathering at the H.J. Thielke residence, where the casket reposed on the large veranda and was draped with a large flag – the flag for which Lt. Berger fought and fell.

The casket was further surrounded by beautiful floral tributes from friends of the family. On the casket a small floral piece held its touching message "To Daddy," from the only little son of the soldier thus honored. The other pieces on it were a beautiful star of hope and a cluster of largest white chrysanthemums, with long graceful petals. Among the other offerings one fashioned like an American flag had been sent by his comrades here.

Mr. L.S. Keeley, who for several years was associated with Mr. Berger in his school work here, delivered the impressive eulogy. He gave an interesting review of Mr. Berger's life, from his childhood at Oshkosh through his school days at Milwaukee and his university career at Madison, which he terminated to answer the call to arms.

Mr. Keeley's eloquent and patriotic address was followed by a wonderful song "The Lord Is My Shepherd." It was sung by Mrs. Arnold Berger, concert singer of Milwaukee and instructor at Lawrence Conservatory of Music in Appleton.

When the casket was carried out to the hearse, it passed between two long lines of our soldier boys, who stood at attention as their dead comrade was borne past them on the way to his final resting place. Arno Deitze, adjutant of the Bonau-Whereatt (American Legion Post),[23] was captain for the day and the boys (almost 60) were in their khaki uniform. It was a sight that will not be forgotten by any who witnessed it.

Our young veterans then headed the long cortege on its way to Graceland Cemetery. They were followed by the ladies

---

[23] The post was named for two Mayville men killed in World War I on successive days – Pfc. Frank W. Bonau, 27, and Pfc. Walter Ira Whereat, 21. Bonau was with the 127th Infantry of the 32nd Division, the WIsconsin Red Arrow, and was MIA on Aug. 2, 1918. Whereat was in the 107th Field Signal Battalion of the Red Arrow and was killed on Aug. 3. Bonau is on the MIA wall at the Aisne-Marne American Cemetery at Belleau, France; Whereatt is buried at the Oise-Aisne American Cemetery in Fere-en-Tardenois.

of the Relief Corps, the Commercial Club and the students of the high school.

At the cemetery the two columns of soldiers again saluted as Lt. Berger was carried to the flower-decked grave that soon received him. Six of his friends from Milwaukee and Madison were the pallbearers. He was followed to his last resting place by his young widow, his only brother, Arnold, his parents, Mr. and Mrs. Berger of Milwaukee, other relatives and many friends.

A prayer was read by Carl Owen, chaplain of the local post of the American Legion, and the Owen quartet rendered several fine songs.

The close of the service was a bugle call by B. Bernard, answered in the distance by Rich Garling.

A decade later, there was some brief confusion as to whether it actually was Berger's body that was returned to Mayville. The Mayville paper said on Oct. 16, 1929, that a Milwaukee paper had reported Berger's body was being returned "from its resting place in the Shenkhurst region on the Dvina River in Siberia." That was straightened out in an article a month later that said the local American Legion commander had received a letter stating that two men named Carl H. Berger had been killed in Russia – the one from Company E and another from the regimental Supply Company. The paper said:

Lt. Bradley Taylor, of Rhinelander, in a letter to his friend, Atty. E.A. Kletzien of this city, relates the story of Berger's death. Near Archangel, Russia, two detachments of American soldiers were moving up to attack a body of Bolshevicks. A road had to be crossed, before reaching the trench where the Russians were situated, and machine gun fire was sweeping the area. The American soldiers were crawling across the road, and Berger's men had reached the other side. Taylor's force was still on the farther side of the road, when Taylor heard someone exclaim: "They've got Berger."

As soon as the Russian force had been driven back, Taylor hurried to his friend Berger's side, and had him taken to a hospital. It was found that a mushroom bullet had torn away part of the back of his head, and although life was still present in his body, the physicians at the field hospital could not save Berger's life and he died shortly after arriving there.

During the time Taylor's force was located near Archangel, he made several visits to Berger's grave. When the question arose as to the identity of the body buried here (Mayville) in 1919, Mr. Kletzien wrote to Taylor, asking him for details, and received the reply that there could be no question that the body sent here 10 years ago actually is that of Carl Berger.

Mueller's body was not returned by the Russians until February 1930, according to the Marshfield VFW post's history.[24]

"A military funeral was held, and it was conducted by 40 members of the Burns Post 388, VFW, of Wausau, who drove to Marshfield to conduct the service in minus-20-degree weather," the history says. "Following the service, local veterans obtained information from Wausau about starting a post here." The Marshfield post was organized in July of that year. Its building today is on West Depot Street.

According to the history, "The names of Marshfield residents killed in the Spanish American and First World Wars were placed in a hat, and the third and sixth names picked would be used as the post's title. ... The third name picked from the hat was Frank Mueller and the sixth was Fred Hintz." Hintz was a corporal in the 127th Infantry Regiment of the Red Arrow. He was killed on Oct. 7, 1918, and is buried in the Meuse-Argonne American Cemetery in France.

Of the 30 charter members of the Marshfield post, 29 had received the Purple Heart for wounds in World War I, the history says.

Here is how the Polar Bear Memorial Association describes the weeks of various battles in which Mueller and Berger fought (then this chapter will zero in on the fateful late December battle in Kodish):

With the Allies adopting a defensive posture and settling in for the winter, the Bolshevik leaders were inclined to become more aggressive. By now, they had realized the true size of the Allied interventionist forces and having seen how they were deployed, they rightly felt that nature, time and numbers were

---

[24] The Polar Bear Memorial Association in Michigan also said the majority of bodies in that area were not returned until 1930. A total of 56 of the Michigan men lost in the 339th Regiment and the attached units such as the engineers are buried in a special plot in White Chapel Cemetery in Troy, Mich., arranged around a monument of a polar bear. It was dedicated May 30, 1930.

on their side. In addition to (the village of) Toulgas, during November the Bolos also attacked Allied forces at Verst 445 (a distance marker) on the Railroad Front (Nov. 4), Kodish (Nov. 5-8) and Ust Padenga (Nov. 29). The Bolos were unsuccessful in their efforts only at Verst 445 and they continued to pressure the forces along the Dvina River Front.

In an effort to relieve that pressure, Gen. (British Maj. Gen. Sir Edmund) Ironside approved a plan for a late December series of coordinated attacks along the Railroad Front with the objective of taking the town of Plesetskaya. French soldiers on snowshoes would depart from Obozerskaya and hike through the deep snow to make a rear attack on Emtsa. At the same time, the forces at Verst 445 would break through and fight their way down the railroad to Emtsa. The Onega Force would make a diversionary move up the Onega River towards Plesetskaya and K Company would retake Kodish from the Bolos and with the help of a White Russian and British Force that would prevent a Bolo retreat, they would then all continue southwest towards Plesetskaya.

The "railroad push", as it was known, was scheduled for Dec. 29-30 but word leaked to the Bolos when a group of White Russians deserted from Verst 445 and the Bolos immediately stepped up their artillery attacks in the area. The French were slowed to a crawl by the very deep snow and were exhausted and out of action before they ever got close to Emtsa.

The Onega Force was stalled by a Bolo counterattack and despite the successful retaking of Kodish, the White Russian and British force failed to take their objective and the Bolshevik forces were able to retreat from Kodish towards their stronghold in Plesetskaya.[25]

Mueller and Berger's Company E, plus Company K, plus a machine gun platoon and a mortar section, were the main attacking force at Kodish. The Americans had halted north of the town after the fighting in the fall and were holed up in blockhouses built by the 310th Engineers.

---

[25] http://pbma.grobbel.org/westriding/polar_bear_news.htm

In the middle of the night on Dec. 29-30, a lieutenant named Baker led the E and K troops across the Emtsa River in temperatures of more than 20 below zero. The attack began, but ...

"Any notion that Kodish was going to be easily taken was soon destroyed, however," Halliday writes. "The road leading into the town was still in enemy possession, and as Baker and his men attempted to work down it they were met by a fusillade from Soviet rifles and machine guns. They took again to the woods, and a long-drawn-out battle began. ... Companies E and K got the distinct impression that they were capturing the Soviet position without aid from their allies. When it was all over, a good deal later, they found out what the trouble was: Both the White Russians and the British had let them down" by not carrying out their parts of the attack plan.[26]

Not only that, "but it was apparent that the strength of the enemy had been underestimated. It was not merely a matter of numbers, although on that score the proportion was fearfully one-sided: 450 Americans actually dislodged more than 2,000 Soviet soldiers from Kodish and its surrounding defenses,"[27] but the Russian fighting skill was far better than it was a few months earlier. The Americans seized Kodish, but then "were subjected to a disadvantage which earlier had been a problem for the Reds: Kodish was in a hollow, with hills on three sides, and it consequently was more easily attacked than defended."

It thus was far more dangerous to hold Kodish than to seize it in the first place. Mueller, Berger and five other men were killed, most of them after the city fell and not in the earlier attack that seized it.

Overall, it was futility in capital letters. "From a strictly military point of view, the operation on the Kodish front at the very end of 1918 was a puny affair .... A few hundred Americans went out into the snow and the darkness and took an insignificant Russian village, held it for a while, and gave it up again to the enemy," Halliday writes.

"A few dozen were wounded and frostbitten; only seven were killed outright in action. But as if the eerie northern light by which it was fought somehow had revealed truths about the battle which otherwise would have been obscure, the men who struggled in the snow at Kodish saw it as a star epitome of the whole north Russian fiasco. The knowledge of the armistice was still fresh in their minds, and it was becoming ever more clear that whatever

---

[26] "When Hell Froze Over," p. 141-142.

[27] "When Hell Froze Over," p. 143.

it was they were fighting for had nothing to do with 'the War,'"[28] by which he means World War I, which had ended.

Another of those killed on Dec. 30 was Sgt. Michael Kenney, of Company K of the 339th and from Detroit. His nephew, John Evangelist Walsh, wrote a long article about the ordeal in Russia for the Wisconsin Magazine of History in the Winter 2001-2002 issue.[29] Although Kenney had no Wisconsin tie and the article did not mention Mueller or Berger, it said there were "a few hundred from Wisconsin"[30] in the regiment. The article also had a sidebar featuring photos of several men from the state in the 339th in the snowy depths of Russia.

One member of Mueller and Berger's Company E, 1st Sgt. George E. Comstock of Detroit, was awarded the Distinguished Service Cross for his rescue actions of Dec. 30 and 31 at Kodish. A good amount of what he went through most likely was experienced by Mueller and Berger, too. The medal citation said Comstock "went forward 200 yards in advance of our lines and guided back a man who had been blinded by shellfire and was stumbling around in full view of the enemy, who were sniping at him. On two other occasions he went forward in advance of our lines, exposing himself to heavy enemy fire, and returned with a wounded man."[31]

Comstock survived that fighting and the entire ordeal.

Besides Mueller and Berger, here are the other Wisconsin dead from the 339th Regiment in the entire Polar Bear Expedition, including the site of the death if listed:[32]

---

[28] "When Hell Froze Over," p. 147-148.

[29] "The Strange, Sad Death of Sergeant Kenney: A Personal History of Heroism and Loss During America's Russian Intervention of 1918-19," by John Evangelist Walsh. Wisconsin Magazine of History, Volume 85, No. 2, Winter 2001-2002, p. 2-14. At http://www.wisconsinhistory.org/wmh/pdf/wmh_winter01_walsh.pdf One of the sidebars to the article is, "Wisconsin in the Midnight War."

[30] "The Strange, Sad Death of Sergeant Kenney," p. 5.

[31] http://www.homeofheroes.com/members/02_DSC/citatons/02_interim-dsc/dsc_06russia_american.html

[32] This list uses information both from http://pbma.grobbel.org/polarbearhonor roll.htm and the "Wisconsin Gold Star List Soldiers, Sailors Marines and Nurses Casualties," an official 1925 book that is online at http://www.accessgenealogy. com/worldwarone/wisconsin/ and is searchable by county. The book also is at http://content.wisconsinhistory.org/cdm4/document.php?CISOROOT=/tp&CISO PTR=54449&CISOSHOW=54230

– Pvt. Ferdinand Passow, 23, of Mosinee, Co. D, died of pneumonia Sept. 11, 1918.

– 2nd Lt. Marcus T. Casey, 26, of New Richmond, Co. C, died of pneumonia at Seminvokia, Russia, Sept. 16, 1918.

– Pvt. Adolph Schumann, 25, of Milwaukee, Co. C, killed in action Nov. 13, 1918.

– 1st Lt. Francis W. Cuff, 36, of Hawkins in Rusk County, Co. C, killed in action Nov. 29, 1918 at Trogimovskaya, Russia.

– Pvt. Sebastiano Lencione, 28, of Whitewater, Co. A, died of wounds Jan. 22, 1919.

– Pvt. Andrew J. Kulwicki, 29, of Milwaukee, Co. K, died of pneumonia Jan. 28, 1919.

– 1st Lt. Edmund R. Collins, 28, of Racine, Co. H, died of wounds March 24, 1919 at Archangel, Russia.

One other Wisconsin man who was in the fighting in Russia was John Cudahy, a member of the meat-packing family. He was a lieutenant in Company B of the 339th, and was candid both in describing the fighting and the haziness of the mission. He was 38 and a lawyer before going into the Army.

"Week follows week, and November goes by, and December, and no word comes from the War Department" about going home now that the war in Europe was officially over, Cudahy said. "No word comes and the soldier is left to think that he has been abandoned by his country and left to rot on the barren snow wastes of Arctic Russia."[33]

Col. George Stewart, commander of the 339th Regiment, sounded his frustration and that of his troops in this cable to the War Department three days after the historic peace date of Nov. 11: "Men of this command have performed most excellent service under the most trying climactic conditions of cold, snow, wet and miry marshes. ... Allies have not been received with the hospitality the object of this expedition warranted. ... The original object ... no longer exists. The winter port of Archangel will be practicable for navigation 20 to 30 days longer and then closes until June. My inference is plain. Immediate consideration requested."[34]

DeWitt C. Poole, the American charge d'affairs at Archangel, told the troops on Thanksgiving: "You men want to know what you are doing here. You are protecting one spot in Russia from the sanguinary bedlam of Bolshevism; you are keeping safe one spot where the real progressives of the Russian revolution (the first one of 1917, not the Bolshevik one) may begin to lay the foundation of the great free Russian state which is to come."[35]

---

[32] "When Hell Froze Over," p. 18.

[33] "When Hell Froze Over," p. 126.

[34] "When Hell Froze Over," p. 127.

That did not seem to have much to do with World War I.

Poole added, "Don't think you are forgotten. Washington knows what you are doing, what you are up against. You may be sure that the president has thought of you and in good time will tell you and the rest of us what he expects each to do in order to hold steady the light of our forward-looking democracy."

But more battles for the regiment were to come soon.

As author E.M. Halliday put it, pressure began to build from families of the forgotten soldiers in Russia, that "their young men were fighting in an undeclared war for undeclared reasons months after the armistice. Protest meetings were held in various places in Michigan, and Congress was made acutely aware that something seemed to be rotten in north Russia."[35]

Overall, Cudahy described Russia as "a cluster of dirty huts, dominated by the severe white church, and encircling all, fields and fields of spotless snows; Russia, terrible in the grasp of devastating Arctic cold; the squalor and fulsome filth of the villages; ... Russia, her dread mystery, and that intangible quality of melodrama that throngs the air, and lingers in the air, persistently haunts the spirit, and is as consciously perceptible as the dirty villages, the white church and the grief-laden skies."[36]

After the 339th finally were pulled out of Russia in June 1919, Cudahy said: "When the last battalion set sail from Archangel, not a soldier knew, no, not even vaguely, why he had fought or why he was going now, and why his comrades were left behind – so many of them beneath the wooden crosses."[37]

Cudahy served from 1933 to 1940 as U.S. ambassador to Poland, Ireland, Belgium and Luxembourg.

---

[35] "When Hell Froze Over," p. 252.

[36] "When Hell Froze Over," p. 171.

[37] "When Hell Froze Over," p. 270.

Chapter 6

One Wisconsinite got highest honor in World War I

A total of 122,215 soldiers from Wisconsin fought in World War I as part of the American Expeditionary Force, and 3,932 made the Ultimate Sacrifice.[1]

Exactly one earned the Medal of Honor.

Oct. 8, 1918, came during the heart of the Meuse-Argonne offensive a wave of battles in which 26,277 Americans were killed and 95,786 wounded, by one count.[2] It finally ended with the armistice on Nov. 11.

What Pvt. Clayton Kirk Slack did on Oct. 8 earned him the Medal of Honor. Some accounts say he was the only Wisconsin recipient; other accounts say there was a second; others say the medal also went to two other men who had been born in the state but who had moved elsewhere before going into the Army. The research for this book agrees with the first figure of this paragraph – Slack was the only current Wisconsin resident. A second man had an official address in Milwaukee as of a decade earlier, but his medal is credited to New Jersey and so evidently he was there for some time.

Slack, 22, of the Plover area, was a member of Company D of the 124th Machine Gun Battalion in the Army's 33rd Infantry Division, battling near Consenvoye, France, which is in the Lorraine region.

The Medal of Honor citation saluted Slack for "extraordinary heroism …. Observing German soldiers under cover 50 yards away on the left flank, Pvt. Slack, upon his own initiative, rushed them with his rifle and, single-handed, captured 10 prisoners and two heavy-type machine-guns, thus saving his company and neighboring organizations from heavy casualties."[3]

Slack died in 1976 at the age of 80 and is buried at Arlington National Cemetery in Virginia.

---

[1] http://legis.wisconsin.gov/lrb/bb/11bb/Stats_Military.pdf, page 764

[2] http://www.worldwar1.com/dbc/bigshow.htm Also see a summary of the battle at http://www.historynet.com/meuse-argonne-offensive-of-world-war-i.htm

[3] http://www.arlingtoncemetery.net/ckslack.htm and http://projects.militarytimes.com/citations-medals-awards/recipient.php?recipientid=511

Army Pvt. Clayton Slack of the Plover area received the Medal of Honor for actions on Oct. 8, 1918.

Slack is honored on a web page of Eau Claire County history[4] because he ran a resort for many years near Hayward, about 110 miles away. It tells more about his life:

> A few years later, Slack embarked on a more profitable career. Starting in February 1925, Slack went into show business, presenting a military show in theaters in 42 states. Dressed in his old Army uniform with all 13 medals prominently displayed, Slack showed four different military films of World War I and the two German machine guns he captured.
>
> ... Later years of his life were spent at his resort in the Hayward area, but Slack still took an interest in military and foreign affairs. This included some fairly scathing remarks on the Vietnam War, an event that Slack termed "the biggest blunder this country ever made. "I wouldn't go myself today, if I were a young man," Slack said in an interview during the war.

The Meuse-Argonne offensive ran from late September to the Armistice in November and involved 1.2 million Americans.[5] Slack's 124th Machine Gun Battalion was part of the 66th Infantry Brigade in the 33rd Division. This is the battalion's action report for the period in which Slack received the Medal of Honor:

> Company remained in position until Oct. 8, when it was withdrawn for operations on east side of Meuse (River). As the result of hard work the night of Oct. 7, this company placed 12 guns in position about Forges, and on the morning of 8th opened fire on Chaume Wood.

---

4 http://www.usgennet.org/usa/wi/county/eauclaire/history/ourstory/vol5/medal. html Accessed February 2013.

5 "The Doughboys," by Gary Mead (2000), p. 176.

On the 9th, moved to trenches southeast of Consenvoye, and at 6:45 on the morning of the 10th moved forward … through Consenvoye and Chaume Wood, delivering effective fire from northern edge of latter wood upon enemy machine gun positions and bodies of the enemy fleeing over the edge of the ridge.

The next move forward, to the top of the opposite ridge, was under extremely heavy gunfire from front and flanks, resulting in heavy casualties and loss of four guns. Nevertheless … delivered fire which silenced several enemy snipers and put to flight parties of the enemy assembling on the extreme right for counterattack. The enemy launched a counterattack on the afternoon of the 11th, which the guns of this company quickly stopped.[6]

Slack is the only Wisconsinite who received the Medal of Honor in this war, by one count.[7] But the Wisconsin Veterans Museum says there were two[8] – Slack and John Otto Siegel – and a Memorial Day article on May 30,1955, in the Milwaukee Sentinel says there were a total of four recipients who been born in Wisconsin, Slack and Siegel included.[9]

Siegel was a 28-year-old Navy boatswain's mate second class who was serving on the USS Mohawk, a tugboat based at Norfolk, Va. He earned the medal on Nov. 1, 1918, and the government listing has him as being from New Jersey – meaning he lived there when the medal was awarded. Had he felt deeply connected to Milwaukee, he no doubt would have had it credited to Wisconsin.

The citation described what happened: "For extraordinary heroism while serving on board the Mohawk in performing a rescue mission aboard

[6] http://genealogytrails.com/ill/mclean/mil_wwi_124machinegunbattalion.html. The original battalion was heavily men from McLean County, Ill., just as the original division was the Illinois National Guard before being bulked up with new men for the war. This summary of service is from a 1921 compilation, "McLean County, Illinois, in the World War, 1917-1918;" by Edward E. Pierson & Jacob Louis Hasbrouck. Accessed June 2012.

[7] http://www.homeofheroes.com/moh/states/wi.html

[8] http://www.wisvetsmuseum.com/researchers/military/Honors_Memorials/?ID=58

[9] http://news.google.com/newspapers?nid=1368&dat=19550530&id=Q21QAAA AIBAJ&sjid=chAEAAAAIBAJ&pg=7204,4454352. Accessed February 2013.

the Hjeltenaes (this was a five-mast sailing ship), which was in flames on 1 November 1918. Going aboard the blazing vessel, Siegel rescued two men from the crew's quarters and went back the third time. Immediately after he had entered the crew's quarters, a steam pipe over the door burst, making it impossible for him to escape. Siegel was overcome with smoke and fell to the deck, being finally rescued by some of the crew of the Mohawk who carried him out and rendered first aid."[10] The citation does not say exactly where this happened.

Siegel died in 1943 in Gary, Ind., and is buried there. A short biographical item at Find a Grave tells more of his story[11] but also leaves several questions when it is read closely. Nevertheless, it does fill some holes. The Find a Grave item says it was written "with the help of Siegel's grandson Robert William Stefanski Sr.," without saying where the man lives.

It says Siegel was born in 1892 in Germany and then lived in Canada. "By 1903 Julius was living in Milwaukee and still working as an architect. By 1905 John and his mother are also with Julius in Milwaukee. By 1910 John has joined the Navy and is listed as an "ordinary seaman" working onboard the USS Virginia which was docked at Hampton Roads, Va., in 1909 for modifications. He also shows up living at the same address as his father Julius N. Siegel at 418 12th St." in Milwaukee.

That sounds like Milwaukee is just the home of record, and that Siegel already was gone from Milwaukee at least nine years before his Medal of Honor incident. In 1910 he would have turned 18.

This item says the incident happened "in the Norfolk Naval Shipyard," so that goes further than the medal citation did. Some Navy tugboats based in the United States had been sent to Europe to do work during the war.

The other two Wisconsin-connected recipients of the Medal of Honor are Deming Bronson, born in Rhinelander, and Charles Whittlesey, born in Florence. The 1955 article says Slack was living in Hayward. This chapter now reviews each.

A 2001 movie was made about Whittlesey, entitled "The Lost Battalion." Whittlesey, an Army major, was born in 1884, and his family moved in 1894 from Florence to Pittsfield, Mass. He got a law degree from Williams

---

10 http://www.homeofheroes.com/moh/citations_1918_wwi/siegel.html

11 http://www.findagrave.com/cgi-bin/fg.cgi?page=gr&GRid=58991422

College in Pittsfield and was 34 when he earned the Medal of Honor for actions from Oct. 2 to 7, 1918, northeast of Binarville, France, in the Argonne Forest. This was the same Meuse-Argonne offensive in which Slack earned his medal. Whittlesey was in the 308th Regiment of the Army's 77th Infantry Division.

The citation says:[12]

Although cut off for five days from the remainder of his division, Maj. Whittlesey maintained his position, which he had reached under orders received for an advance, and held his command, consisting originally of 46 officers and men of the 308th Infantry and of Company K of the 307th Infantry, together in the face of superior numbers of the enemy during the five days.

Maj. Whittlesey and his command were thus cut off, and no rations or other supplies reached him, in spite of determined efforts which were made by his division. On the fourth day, Maj. Whittlesey received from the enemy a written proposition to surrender, which he treated with contempt, although he was at the time out of rations and had suffered a loss of about 50 percent in killed and wounded of his command and was surrounded by the enemy.

An extensive account at "Doughboy Center: The Story of the American Expeditionary Forces,"[13] says that on Oct. 2, there were 550 American troops in this area, and at the end of the ordeal, there were only 194 alive and unwounded. There was heavy German fire of all kinds, plus mistaken fire from Allied forces, and the only means of communication out of this area was via homing pigeons. The troops had to take "dressings from dead men to use on the wounded, among many of whom gangrene had already set in."[14]

Airplanes made history's first airdrop of supplies on Oct. 6, but much of it missed the target. The 50th Aero Squadron's DH.4 (De Havilland) biplane bomber was piloted by 1st Lt. Harold E. Goettler, accompanied by observer 2nd Lt. Erwin R. Bleckley of the field artillery. Later that day, German ground fire shot them down on their second mission to help the battalion.

---

[12] http://www.homeofheroes.com/moh/citations_1918_wwi/whittlesey.html

[13] http://www.worldwar1.com/dbc/whitt.htm

[14] "The Doughboys," p. 315.

Goettler and Bleckley were killed, and were posthumously awarded Medals of Honor.[15] Later, another air-drop team from the 50th spotted the Lost Battalion, Whittlesey's group, and it finally was rescued Oct. 7.

"Early on Oct. 7, before the relieving Allied troops arrived, the German commanding officer who surrounded the Americans sent a letter to Whittlesey via an American prisoner requesting his battalion's surrender. Whittlesey and George McMurtry, his second-in-command, refused to acknowledge this request and even pulled in the white panels (being) used to signal Allied planes for fear the Germans would mistake them for surrender flags. It was widely reported in the American press that Whittlesey had responded 'Go to Hell!' immediately upon reading the letter. He later denied having made the statement, suggesting that no reply was necessary."[16]

All of that is perfect fodder for the movies, particularly dramatizing the surrender refusal, and it was told in the 2001 film "The Lost Battalion."[17] RIck Schroder was the star, portraying Whittlesey.

Three years after the war, in November 1921, Whittlesey committed suicide by jumping off a ship that was en route from New York to Havana, Cuba. Only two weeks earlier, on Armistice Day / Veterans Day, he and other Medal of Honor recipients had been honorary pallbearers in Washington, D.C., where solemn ceremonies led by President Warren Harding dedicated the Tomb of the Unknown Soldier at Arlington National Cemetery. The unknown was unearthed from a cemetery on the battlefield and brought to Washington with the same solemnity that other Allies had conducted for their honored unknown, and the same outpouring of grief, respect and national catharsis. The New York Times said in reporting Whittlesey's death that he had been "deeply affected by the ceremonies."[18]

The account at the Doughboy Center tells of his death: "On Nov. 26, after having stayed up late drinking and talking with other passengers, Whittlesey walked to the rail of the ship and jumped overboard. None of his friends or relatives had known about his travel plans and were thus disbelieving when the

---

[15] http://www.usaww1.com/50th-Aero-Squadron-Harold-Goettler-Erwin-Bleckley-Remicourt.php4

[16] http://www.worldwar1.com/dbc/whitt.htm

[17] http://prweb0.voicenet.com/~lpadilla/lostbn.html

[18] "Unknown Soldiers: The Story of the Missing of the First World War," by Neil Hanson (2005), p. 352.

news arrived from the captain of the ship that Whittlesey had been lost at sea and that he had left behind letters to those close to him ...

"Some believed that his suicide was caused by feelings of guilt: the possibility that he had given incorrect coordinates to the 'Pocket', thereby causing friendly fire, or having refused to surrender to the Germans, leading to increased loss among his men. Others believed that it was his modesty and inability to adjust to the life of a hero that caused the depression that eventually ended his life."[19]

Another Medal of Honor recipient, Deming Bronson, was a first lieutenant in Company H of the 364th Regiment of the Army's 91st Infantry Division. He was age 24 when he earned the medal on Sept. 26-27, 1918, near Eclisfontaine, France, during the same Meuse-Argonne offensive in which Whittlesey and Slack were cited for heroism. He was born in Rhinelander and had entered service at Seattle, Wash.; other research shows he had a football career with the University of Washington in Seattle and thus was not living in Wisconsin as an adult.

The medal citation details how Bronson was wounded three times in two days:[20]

> **On the morning of 26 September, during the advance of the 364th Infantry, 1st Lt. Bronson was struck by an exploding enemy hand grenade, receiving deep cuts on his face and the back of his head. He nevertheless participated in the action which resulted in the capture of an enemy dugout from which a great number of prisoners were taken.**
>
> **This was effected with difficulty and under extremely hazardous conditions because it was necessary to advance without the advantage of cover and, from an exposed position, throw hand grenades and phosphorous bombs to compel the enemy to surrender.**
>
> **On the afternoon of the same day, he was painfully wounded in the left arm by an enemy rifle bullet, and after receiving first aid treatment he was directed to the rear. Disregarding these instructions, 1st Lt. Bronson remained on duty**

---

[19] http://www.worldwar1.com/dbc/whitt.htm

[20] http://www.homeofheroes.com/moh/citations_1918_wwi/bronson.html

with his company through the night although suffering from severe pain and shock.

On the morning of 27 September, his regiment resumed its attack, the object being the village of Eclisfontaine. Company H ... was left in support of the attacking line, Company E being in the line. He gallantly joined that company in spite of his wounds and engaged with it in the capture of the village. After the capture he remained with Company E and participated with it in the capture of an enemy machine gun, he himself killing the enemy gunner.

Shortly after this encounter the company was compelled to retire due to the heavy enemy artillery barrage. ... 1st Lt. Bronson, who was the last man to leave the advanced position, was again wounded in both arms by an enemy high-explosive shell. He was then assisted to cover by another officer who applied first aid. Although bleeding profusely and faint from the loss of blood, 1st Lt. Bronson remained with the survivors of the company throughout the night of the second day, refusing to go to the rear for treatment. His conspicuous gallantry and spirit of self-sacrifice were a source of great inspiration to the members of the entire command.

Bronson died in 1957 at the age of 62, and, like Slack, is buried in Arlington National Cemetery.[21]

On Veterans Day in 2009, the University of Washington in Seattle dedicated a campus monument to its eight alumni who earned the Medal of Honor in the nation's wars.[22] Its statement said Bronson was a forestry major and a football player for the Huskies from 1912 to 1916 (it is not evident how he was there for five seasons, but perhaps football players were redshirted in that era, too). The Huskies won the Pacific Coast Conference title in his senior year, with a record of 6-0-1 and a conference mark of 3-0-1.[23] The tie was 0-0 against Oregon. The team never lost a game from 1912 to 1916; the season records were 6-0, 7-0, 6-0-1, 7-0 and 6-0-1.

---

[21] http://www.arlingtoncemetery.net/demingbr.htm

[22] http://www.washington.edu/news/archive/id/51839

[23] http://grfx.cstv.com/photos/schools/wash/sports/m-footbl/auto_pdf/2011-12/misc_non_event/FB_Record_Book.pdf, p. 185. This is the school's annual media guide.

This chapter now takes a look at some other World War I deaths of Wisconsin soldiers, in notable incidents and in cases where VFW and American Legion posts are named for soldiers from the Great War.

Death after the Armistice

Army Pvt. Carl Nilson, who was killed on Armistice Day, Nov. 11, 1918, is pictured in this photo that is part of his gravestone. He is buried at Kings Valley Lutheran Church near Osseo.

The Great War finally slogged to an end at 11 a.m. on the 11th day of the 11th month of 1918. But not before a substantial last bloodletting, and one man – Pvt. Carl Nilson of Hale in Trempealeau County a few miles south of Osseo – possibly died AFTER 11 a.m. when the fighting kept going in one small area.

Nilson, 29, whose family later began spelling its name as Nelson, was in the 356th Regiment of the Army's 89th Infantry Division. His tombstone at Kings Valley Lutheran Church four miles south of Osseo has his picture and says he was in Company K and in the Meuse River battles. Osseo is home of the Carl Nelson American Legion Post 324.

Nilson's grand-nephew, Ron Nelson of Amherst, N.H., says there are two versions of his death: "One of his commanders wrote a letter saying he died that morning when a shell landed near him. Family folklore says he was was shot in the afternoon of Nov. 11 well after the armistice due to his unit being forward and engaged with the enemy."

It is a fact that Nilson's regiment was fighting AFTER the Armistice time. Gary Mead's book "The Doughboys" has this passage: "Right up to the last minute Francis Jordan of Company H (because Nilson was in Company K, he would have been very close by) ... was in the thick of the fighting. The 356th was officially the last to be informed of the Armistice and in fact kept firing until midday, an hour after the official ceasefire. In the early hours of 11 November Jordan's unit was ordered, along with many others, to cross the Meuse by means of some flimsy bridges. It was a senseless order which needlessly cost the lives of many doughboys, but regimental colonels and battalion majors were too insecure in their positions to do anything else but keep the pressure on right to the end; anything else meant their career was forever blighted."[24]

Jordan was wounded by a machine gun in the left hand, and that gun also killed a first sergeant and a sergeant.

Here is an account of these hours from the official history of the 89th Division:[25]

> **At 8:30 hours information was received … from the Corps that an armistice would go into effect at 11:00 hours, and that fire should cease at that time. Word was immediately sent out by all available means of liaison, including officer couriers, to the front-line battalions. Artillery was directed to cease firing at 10:45, in order to avoid mistakes and violations of the armistice.**
>
> **The terms of the armistice, or the letter of instructions giving the warning as to the approaching armistice, was not received at the Division P.C. until about 10:30 hours.**
>
> **Since the division had been in the line a considerable period without proper bathing facilities and since it was realized that if the enemy were permitted to remain in Stenay, our troops would be deprived of the billets and the probable bathing facilities there, instructions were immediately sent to the infantry commander at Laneuville to push directly and take Stenay, not waiting for any any assistance of support of the 90th Division.**
>
> **There has been considerable discussion over the matter of taking this town. It is well-established that troops of this division entered the town from Laneuville and occupied its northern portion about 10 a.m. These troops stated they met practically no resistance and found no Americans in the town. The enemy, however, had patrols in the near vicinity which were encountered near Cervisy.**
>
> **Not being thoroughly familiar with terms of the armistice, the division commander directed that our troops**

---

[24] "The Doughboys," p. 336.

[25] http://www.usgennet.org/usa/mo/county/stlouis/89thdivision/89th-history-39.jpg. The very thorough site devoted to the 89th Division is http://www.usgennet.org/usa/mo/county/stlouis/89thdivision/89th-history.htm

push forward until the enemy was actually encountered; that the enemy would not be fired upon unless he attacked; that hostilities must cease, but that any terrain that might be of military value to us and which had been abandoned by the enemy would be taken and would be occupied. It was intended to complete the operation by occupying the heights east of the river between Stenay and Moulins. The enemy, however, was found to be in Inor and in Cervisy. Moreover, orders were later received not to advance beyond the line held at 11:00 hours, and these orders were enforced.

The German High Command made an official complaint that the American troops on the Stenay-Beaumont Road had not ceased attacking at 11:00 hours but continued their advance.

On Dec. 11, the Osseo News reported Nilson's death and spelled his last name as Nelson, but the story about it coming after the Armistice began was not reported, and evidently did not become known until later.

The story said "He left Whitehall for service on April 26, 1918, and spent two weeks in Camp Grant and then he went to Kansas and on June 6 left for France. It will be seen that his training took a remarkably short time and he was found to be a capable soldier. The last letter received from him was Oct. 23. He was the third of a family of 11 children and leaves his mother and father (Mr. and Mrs. August Alstad), two sisters and eight brothers, all at home except Harry, who also is in France. Carl was a bright, capable, strong and likable young man, a hard and thorough worker, and will be sadly missed in the home as well as other circles."

Nelson was far from alone in being a Wisconsin man killed on the last day.

The history of the Red Arrow says "the Roll of Honor of the 32nd Division contains the names of many of its soldiers who were killed in action on 11 November 1918. In the evening of the Armistice Day, (Maj. Gen. William) Haan, in a letter to his wife, wrote: 'This morning we resumed the attack at 6:30 which we had stopped last night after dark. At 7 we received orders to stop the battle. That was some job too. We got it stopped entirely at 10:45, just 15 minutes before the armistice went into effect. One of my chaplains was killed at 10:40. Hard luck!'"[26]

---

[26] http://www.32nd-division.org/history/ww1/32-ww1a.html#Meuse-Argonne

The history lists 16 Red Arrow men as being killed on the last morning. If their counties or cities are listed here, they were found on the Wisconsin Gold Star list of war deaths.[27] Other information comes from the American Battle Monuments Commission, which runs overseas cemeteries. Here are the names:

– Pvt. Guiseppe Basta, Co. B, 121st Machine Gun Battalion, killed in action. He was from Connecticut and is buried at Meuse-Argonne American Cemetery at Romagne, France.

– Cpl. Wilfred W. Barlow, Co. B, 127th Infantry, KIA.

– Pvt. Willie Blevins, Co. A, 128th Infantry, KIA.

– Pvt. Robert Blanford, Co. A, 128th Infantry, KIA.

– Musician 3rd Class Gaylord A. Bradley, HQ Co., 128th Infantry, died of wounds. He was 22 and from Mauston. However, the Wisconsin Gold Star list and www.abmc.gov say he died on Oct. 7. Bradley is buried in the Meuse-Argonne Cemetery.

– Sgt. Ralph B. Clemens, Battery A, 322nd Field Artillery, KIA.

– First Lt. William F. Davitt, Chaplain, 125th Infantry, KIA. This no doubt is the chaplain in the general's letter. He was a Roman Catholic priest and he had been a football star at College of the Holy Cross in Worcester, Mass., before being ordained in the Diocese of Springfield, Mass. An article in the sports area of Holy Cross' website[28] says: "About 90 minutes before the Armistice began, Davitt brought to his commanding officer an American flag that he had carried in his bedroll through the war. It was to be raised at 11 o'clock in celebration of the war's end. As he was re-crossing the clearing to return to his field office, the Germans sent one last shell over the lines. A piece of shrapnel killed Davitt instantly, and, so, he became the last American officer to die in World War I."

– Pvt. Glenn S. Frederickson, HQ Co., 127th Inf., KIA.

– Pvt. Thomas L. Foley, Co. H, 128th Infantry, died of wounds.

– Pfc. Roscoe Hawkins, Co. L, 127th Infantry, died of wounds.

– Pvt. Henry P. Harper, Co. A, 128th Infantry, KIA. He was from Arkansas and is buried in the Meuse-Argonne Cemetery.

– Pvt. George Henniger, 128th Infantry, died of wounds.

– Pvt. James McDonald, Co. D, 128th Infantry, died of wounds. He was from Illinois and is buried in the Meuse-Argonne Cemetery.

– Pfc. Wayman J. McGregor, Co. M, 127th Infantry, KIA. He was from Abrams in Oconto County. He is buried in the Meuse-Argonne Cemetery.

– Cpl. Hugh P. Minehan, Co. M, 127th Infantry, KIA. He was from Montana and is buried in the Meuse-Argonne Cemetery.

---

[27] "Wisconsin Gold Star List Soldiers, Sailors Marines and Nurses Casualties," an official 1925 book that is online at http://www.accessgenealogy.com/worldwar one/wisconsin/ and is searchable by county. It will be referred to in this chapter as the Gold Star list. The book also is online at the Wisconsin Historical Society. It is best to go to Google to find that, because the URL is http://content.wisconsinhistory.org/cdm4/document.php?CISOROOT=/tp&CISOPTR=54449&CISOSHOW=542 30 Some information also is at http://pbma.grobbel.org/

[28] http://www.goholycross.com/sports/m-footbl/spec-rel/082307aab.html

– Sgt. Otto Perlick, Co. H, 128th Infantry, KIA. He was from Michigan and is buried in the Meuse-Argonne Cemetery.

There are 381 soldiers from Wisconsin buried in the Meuse-Argonne Cemetery or on its MIA wall. Of those, a total of six are from Nov. 10 and one (McGregor) from Nov. 11. The cemetery has the largest number of dead Americans from any war in Europe – 14,246 burials and 954 names on the MIA wall. It is located east of the village of Romagne-sous-Montfaucon (Meuse), France, which is 26 miles northwest of Verdun.

The MIA wall includes those from the U.S. expedition to northern Russia in 1918 to 1919, as reported in the previous chapter.

If a soldier is not in www.abmc.gov, the database of overseas burials and MIAs, his body was returned to the United States.

One more Wisconsin man who died in this time was essentially a neighbor of Nilson and was in his same 356th Regiment – Pvt. Olaf Thompson, 31, who was killed one day before the Armistice.

The Thompson-Red Cloud VFW Post 1959 in Black River Falls says he was the son of Mr. and Mrs. Ole E. Thompson. However, the state's Gold Star list has him as being from Vilas County, and given his age he probably was working there. The website devoted to the 89th Division in World War I says he was from Black River Falls and was in Company M of the 356th Regiment.[29]

The distance between Nilson's Osseo and Thompson's area near Black River Falls is less than 30 miles.

The second name on the Black River Falls VFW post is Mitchell Red Cloud, who was killed in Korea in November 1950 and earned the Medal of Honor. He is discussed later in this book.

Deaths in a torpedoing

More than a dozen Wisconsin men – most of them in the 107th Supply Train of the Wisconsin Red Arrow 32nd Infantry Division – were among the 210 dead when a German submarine torpedoed the troop ship SS Tuscania off the Scottish isle of Islay on Feb. 5, 1918.

---

[29] http://www.usgennet.org/usa/mo/county/stlouis/89thdead412.gif

Four are MIA; two are listed on the Tablets of the Missing at the Brookwood American Cemetery in England and two more on the Tablets of the Missing at the Suresnes American Cemetery in France. It is not evident why they are honored at different locations.

The four are Cpl. Arthur C. Junker of Kenosha and Sgt. Benjamin H. Brown, 24, of Barron[30], both honored at Suresnes, and Pvt. Alcide Carollo (spelled "Cor-ollo" on the Wisconsin Gold Star list), 18, of Lohrville in Waushara County and Cpl. William B. Spencer, 20, of New London, both honored at Brookwood.

The Red Arrow's history [31] says a total of 13 members were killed; but no names are given. A comprehensive website devoted to the sinking, "Tuscania, an American History," shows the Wisconsin toll was 17.[32]

The Tuscania was a passenger liner carrying 2,013 troops heading into the war and a crew of 384. Islay is the southernmost of the Inner Hebrides island. Here is an account of the sinking:[33]

... the convoy was sighted seven miles north of the Rathilin Island lighthouse by the German submarine UB-77 under the command of Lt. Cmdr. Wilhelm Meyer. At 5:40 p.m. he fired two torpedoes at the Tuscania, the first of which missed, the second scoring a direct hit.

By 7 p.m. all the ship's lifeboats had been launched, but about 1,350 men remained on board. The convoy's escorting (eight British) destroyers assisted in removing these, but were hampered by the continuing presence of the UB-77 in the area.

---

[30] Brown already was a father. Local newspaper stories from that period and information about him is at http://www.findagrave.com/cgi-bin/fg.cgi?page=gr&GRid=7063722

[31] http://www.32nd-division.org/history/ww1/32-ww1.html

[32] http://freepages.history.rootsweb.ancestry.com/~carmita/hoyle/Americans.htm

[33] http://www.worldwar1.com/dbc/tuscania.htm. About 40 men from Kenosha survived, according to a research project by Frank and Michelle Laycock lists them at http://www.rootsweb.ancestry.com/~wikenosh/tuscania.htm A long account of the sinking, by Leo V. Zimmermann of Milwaukee, who was the historian of the Natonal Tuscania Survivors Association, is at http://freepages.history. rootsweb.ancestry.com/~carmita/Novus_Fabula_02/zimmermann02.htm. This site was created by Steven Schwartz of Renton, Wash., grandson of injured passenger George Edward Schwartz of the 20th Engineers.

The Tuscania finally sank at 10 p.m., over four hours after being struck ....

The Tuscania was the first ship carrying American troops to be sunk in the war, and public opinion in the USA regarded its loss as an outrage. In 1920 the American Red Cross erected a monument on the Isle of Islay, where many of the victims had been buried before their transfer that year to the American War Cemetery at Brookwood (England) or to their homeland.

The four MIAs were named in previous paragraphs. Thirteen Wisconsin men whose bodies were returned home are:

– Pvt. Homer Llewellyn Anderson, 22, Cumberland, 107th Supply Train.

– Pvt. Russell Bennett, 19, Plainfield, 107th Supply Train.

– Pvt. Raymond Butler, 19, New Richmond, 20th Engineers.

– Pvt. Alvin Collins, not found on Wisconsin Gold Star list but listed as Wisconsin in the Tuscania website list.

– Pvt. Arthur Harvey, 19, of Chippewa Falls, 107th Supply Train.

– Sgt. James Hawley, 22, Neenah, sanitary squad.

– Quartermaster Sgt. Otis Hutchins, 22, Whitehall, 107th Supply Train.

– Cpl. Claire Metzenbauer, of Chippewa Falls, 107th Supply Train.

– Cpl. Clifford Norris, New London, 107th Supply Train.

– Pvt. James Schleiss, 32, Rice Lake, 20th Engineers.

– Pvt. Charles E. Swanson, not found on Wisconsin Gold Star list but listed as Wisconsin in the Tuscania website list.

– Pvt. George Reinhardt, 23, Jefferson, 20th Engineers.

– Pvt. Earl Odear Weisenberger, 25, Chippewa Falls, 107th Supply Train.

May 1918 battles

World War I began in 1914 but the United States did not declare war until April 1917. It then took many months for the American Expeditionary Force to be organized, equipped, trained and transported to Europe. Americans did not become heavily involved in the fighting until the middle of 1918.

Two Wisconsin men killed in some of those first battles were Pfc. Frederick Vergenz of Waukesha and Pvt. James Burns of Wausau, both in the 28th Regiment of the Army's 1st Infantry Division. The division was the first American unit to arrive in France.

Vergenz, 21, was in Company H and was killed May 27, 1918, at Cantigny, France, according the history of the Soat-Vergenz VFW Post 721 in Waukesha. Local newspapers on June 25 reported the death of the son of Mr. and Mrs. Fred Vergenz, 810 Arcadian Ave., a member of Waukesha's Reformed Church.

Vergenz is buried in Plot C, Row 10, Grave 13 at the Somme American Cemetery at Bony, France. There are 47 men from Wisconsin buried there or on the MIA wall; overall the cemetery has 1,844 bodies and 333 on its MIA wall. Vergenz is the only Wisconsin man there from May 27, but nine others are from the next day and seven from May 29.

The VFW post is named for the first to die from Waukesha (Vergenz) and for the city's first man to enlist in World War I (Robert Soat, who would be killed in July; see the next section of this chapter).

One day after Vergenz was killed, so was Burns, of Wausau. The Wisconsin Gold Star list does not give Burns' company in the 28th Regiment. Burns was 26 and is buried at home.

The fighting at Cantigny was one part of what became known as the third battle of the Aisne (a river), which ran from May 27 to June 5. About 27,500 Americans were in that battle.

July 1918 battles

Wausau and Waukesha again shared a sad linkage in another major battle, the Aisne-Marne, two months later.

Two privates first class died of wounds in this month – Robert Soat, 20, of Waukesha, on July 21 and John Burns, 19, of Wausau, two days later. A history by the Waukesha post says he was in Company H of the 128th Regiment of the Red Arrow, but the Wisconsin Gold Star list has him in the 28th Regiment, which was in the 1st Division like Vergenz and James Burns (that is a one-keystroke typing error by someone).

Soat was wounded three days earlier (July 18), and the Gold Star list does not give the date of Burns' injuries.

Burns is the brother of James Burns from the previous section of this chapter, and died less than two months after his sibling. Wausau VFW Post 388 is named the Burns Post in honor of the brothers.

The post's history[34] says they were "the sons of Mr. and Mrs. Patrick Burns ... These parents also had another son wounded in action. He was Patrick Burns Jr., and was a member, and later post commander (the boys' mother was the first president of the post's auxiliary). The post arranged for and took part in the funeral of the Burns brothers on April 4, 1921. It was the largest funeral of Wausau's history and the entire city (attended). An eloquent sermon by Rev. Father O'Toole of St. James Catholic Church preceded the burial in Pine Grove Cemetery."

Little more than a week after the deaths of Soat and James Burns, Lt. Marion Cranefield of Madison was killed July 31 in Grimpettes Woods near Roncheres, according to VFW Post 1318 in Madison, which is named for Cranefield. He was 28 and was a platoon leader in Company G of the 127th Regiment of the Red Arrow.

The Red Arrow's history says it had been moving from duty in the Alsace "bound for a different sector of the front ... The division had suffered 440 losses from all causes, including: killed, one officer and 39 men; severely wounded, three officers and 79 men; slightly wounded, nine officers and 211 men; gassed, seven officers and 67 men; died of wounds, one officer and 15 men; taken prisoner, eight (and eight German prisoners were captured).[35]

But then came much larger fighting. "The 32nd Division received its baptism of fire (first major offensive action) at 1430 hrs on 30 July 1918 when the 127th Infantry went over the top and followed a rolling barrage into the Bois des Grimpettes. ... During the night the Germans launched a counterattack from the Bois de Meuniere and a bayonet melee raged for hours in the dark, tangled woods, until the attacking force was finally routed."[36]

The Madison post's history says Cranefield was "urging his men forward though severely wounded. He was killed by a head wound during this battle."[37]

The history also says his father was Frederic and mother was Laura, and the family lived at 304 N. Orchard St., a neighborhood that today is taken up by buildings at the University of Wisconsin – Madison.

---

[34] http://www.vfw388.com/VfwPostHistory.htm

[35] http://www.32nd-division.org/history/ww1/32-ww1.html#Aisne-Marne

[36] http://www.32nd-division.org/history/ww1/32-ww1.html#Aisne-Marne

[37] http://myvfw.org/wi/post1318/post-information/

The history continues: "In the September 1918 issue of Wisconsin Horticulture, editor Frederic Cranefield eulogizes his son in part, 'His blood cries, not for vengeance but for justice, and in the name of all those who sacrificed sons I ask that you do not falter in your determination that this Beast among nations (Germany) be forever rendered impotent to overturn civilization. ... (the killed men) believed that 'the right is more precious than peace', and each made of 'his breast the bulwark and his blood the moat.'"

Cranefield is buried in Forest Hill Cemetery in Madison. The Aisne-Marne battle lasted from July 18 to Aug. 6 and included 270,000 Americans.[38]

Les Terribles

Much mention has been made in this chapter about individual men in the Wisconsin Red Arrow who made the Ultimate Sacrifice in its various regiments and other components.

It arrived in France in May 1918 and got its moniker in August in the Alsace. Its history says: "When this fight first started, (Maj. Gen. Jean F.L. Piarron) de Mondesir, the 38th French Corps commander, under whose orders the 32nd was serving at the time, went to the front to see how the Americans were conducting the battle. After he personally observed the 32nd clearing the Germans out of their powerful positions with regularity and determination, he exclaimed 'Oui, Oui, Les soldats terrible, tres bien, tres bien!' (French Gen. Charles) Mangin heard of it and referred to the 32nd Division as 'Les Terribles' when he asked for the division to join his famous 10th French Army of shock troops north of Soissons. He later made the nickname official when he incorporated it in his citation for their terrific punch at Juvigny."[39]

It served six months in combat until the Armistice, with only 10 days out of the line. It battled in three big offensives – the Aisne-Marne, Oise-Aisne and Meuse-Argonne. It had nearly 14,000 dead and wounded from all causes, including 2,660 killed in action.[40]

---

[38] "The Doughboys," p. 176.

[39]   http://web.archive.org/web/20090225021010/http://www.32nd-division.org/history/ww1/32-ww1.html#Alsace

[40] "The 32nd Division in the World War (1920), p. 296.

The 32nd was mainly composed of Michigan and Wisconsin National Guard units. The individual units were:[41]

– 32nd Division Headquarters, under Maj. Gen. James "Galloping Jim" Parker, commanding.

– 63rd Brigade Headquarters, under Brig. Gen. Louis C. Covell (formerly commanding officer of the 1st Michigan Brigade). This brigade was made up of the 125th Infantry Regiment, led by Col. John B. Boucher; 126th Regiment, Col. Joseph P. Westnedge, and 120th Machine Gun Battalion, under Maj. David E. Cleary (former commanding officer of 3rd Battalion, 31st Michigan Infantry)

– 64th Brigade Headquarters, under Brig. Gen. Charles R. Boardman (former commanding officer of 1st Wisconsin Brigade). This brigade was made up of the 127th Infantry Regiment under Col. Wilbur M. Lee (formerly commander of 2nd Wisconsin Infantry); 128th Infantry Regiment under Col. John Turner (formerly CO of 3rd Wisconsin Infantry), and 121st Machine Gun Battalion, led by Maj. Frank H. Fowler (formerly CO of 1st Battalion, 3rd Wisconsin Infantry).

– 119th Machine Gun Battalion, under Maj. Percy C. Atkinson (formerly commander of a battalion of the 6th Wisconsin Infantry).

– 107th Engineer Regiment, Col. P. S. Bond, U.S. Army.

– 107th Field Signal Battalion, Maj. William Mitchell Lewis (formerly CO of 1st Wisconsin Signal Battalion)

– 32nd Military Police Company

– 57th Field Artillery Brigade, Brig. Gen. William G. Haan, U.S. Army. The brigade was made up of the 119th Field Artillery Regiment, under Maj. Chester B. McCormick; 120th Field Artillery Regiment, Col. Carl Penner (formerly CO of 1st Wisconsin Cavalry), 121st Field Artillery Regiment, under Col. Philip C. Westfahl (formerly CO of 1st Wisconsin Field Artillery);107th Trench Mortar Battery and 107th Mobile Ordinance Repair Shop

– 107th Train Headquarters, led by Col. Robert B. McCoy (formerly CO of 4th Wisconsin Infantry). This group was composed by the 107th Supply Train (discussed in the Tuscania part of this chapter); 107th Sanitary Train; 107th Ammunition Train; 107th Engineer Train, and 107th Motor Supply Truck Unit.

---

[41] http://web.archive.org/web/20090212113937/http://www.32nd-division.org/history/ww1/32ww1org.html

Chapter 7
World War II in Europe

This chapter will explore the deaths of several Army men killed in Europe in World War II during the push by millions of Americans and other Allied forces, along with bomber missions based out of north Africa. Some of their names are on VFW or American Legion posts along with another name from World War II; in those cases the other man is covered later this book.

January 1944
Army Pfc. Norbert Elffors, Laona
and Pvt. Theodore Pederson, Ettrick
– killed in sinking of British hospital ship

Pfc. Norbert Elffors and Pvt. Theodore Pederson were wounded in the first day or two of the Allied invasion at Anzio, then were evacuated to the safety of a British hospital ship for surgery and more treatment in north Africa.

But German planes soon attacked and sank the ship, and the two Wisconsin soldier / patients were killed. This was on Jan. 24, 1944.

Elffors, 25, was in the 30th Regiment of the Army's 3rd Infantry Division, and is memorialized on the Cook-Elffors VFW Post 6823 in Laona, which is in Forest County. His name is sometimes spelled as Elfors. Pederson, 32, was in the 540th Engineer Regiment, and his name is on the Runnestrand-Pederson American Legion Post 354 in Ettrick in Trempealeau County. The post says he was born on Dec. 15, 1911.

Ettrick and Laona are about 230 miles apart, but share an identical background when it comes to Pederson and Elffors, and they both are among the 3,095 names on the Tablets of the Missing at the Sicily-Rome American Cemetery at Nettuno, Italy. The two posts were not aware of their connection until the author of this book discovered the tie.

Elffors' record shows he received a Bronze Star and a Purple Heart with Oak Leaf Clusters, meaning he was wounded earlier in the war, before the injury at Anzio.

Army Pfc. Norbert Elffors was wounded at Anzio and taken away on a British hospital ship. But he was killed when the Luftwaffe attacked and sank the ship.

Pederson also was wounded twice, because he too has the Purple Heart with Oak Leaf Clusters.

The British ship was the HMHS (His Majesty's Hospital Ship) St. David. The sinking of a medical vessel is one of the most shocking accounts in a war that was full of shocking accounts. It was not the first case of a supposedly safe hospital ship under the Geneva Convention being attacked – the British ship HMHS Newfoundland had been damaged by bombs the previous September, also off the coast of Italy. American nurse Ruth Hindman, who will be quoted here, went through each of the attacks.

The Allied invasion of Anzio began Jan. 22. The St. David entered Anzio's harbor the next day carrying British doctors, nurses, sailors and an American orthopedic specialty group, led by Maj. John Adams, a surgeon. Seventy-eight wounded from the first day of the invasion were brought to the ship,[1] went through triage and surgery began. Then the battle came to their very doorstep.

"Adams' team was in the midst of their first surgery when the ship's public address system announced that German planes had begun bombing the port of Anzio, Anzio harbor and the beaches where the Allies were digging in to make their bridgehead more secure. Air-raid alarms continued all afternoon and the St. David, only half a mile offshore, was assaulted by low-flying German planes and their exploding bombs, and antiaircraft fire from American and British warships,"[2] Evelyn Monahan and Rosemary Neidel-Greenlee write in a history of American nurses in Europe and north Africa.

---

[1] "And If I Perish: Frontline U.S. Army Nurses in World War II," by Evelyn M. Monahan and Rosemary Neidel-Greenlee (2003), p. 241.

[2] "And If I Perish: Frontline U.S. Army Nurses in World War II," p. 242.

Because of the attacks, the St. David and the two other hospital ships sailed 20 miles out to sea to continue round-the-clock surgery during the night, each fully lighted and clearly marked under the Geneva Convention, and keeping five miles from each other and 20 miles away from actual warships. The St. David returned to Anzio the next day, but the weather was too rough to pick up any new patients. Air battles continued all day, and the ships again left for the night. As one account tells it:

> At 2000, a loud explosion and a violent rocking awakened cabin mates Ruth Hindman and (another American nurse) Anna Bess Berret. "We had gone to sleep with our cabin lights on," Hindman remembered. "When we opened our eyes, it was in total darkness."
>
> … They left to head up to the deck, and "we were surrounded by the deafening noise of things crashing and people screaming."
>
> Through the passageways, they could see patients who were able to walk making their way toward the upper decks, while the more severely wounded were being carried up.
>
> Hindman encountered surgeon Adams, who was climbing down a ladder to medical wards on the lower deck, not up to safety. Hindman remembered Adams' last words to her: 'I have to check on a couple of patients to make sure they get out.'[3]

Adams, of the 2nd Surgical Group, never was seen again. He is on the MIA wall at the Sicily-Rome Cemetery, just like Elffors and Pederson. He received the Distinguished Service Cross for his action – "for conspicuous gallantry and intrepidity in action against a hostile force. … His unquestionable valor in close combat is in keeping with the highest traditions of the military service and reflects great credit upon himself, his unit, and the United States Army," the citation said.[4]

The two nurses finally got up to the deck and found a scene of pandemonium. "Suddenly, there was a loud crunching sound. Hindman looked up and saw the ship's mast rolling toward them. Several people screamed and someone yelled for everyone to jump. 'In a matter of seconds, I found myself

---

[3] "And If I Perish: Frontline U.S. Army Nurses in World War II," p. 243-244.

[4] http://ameddregiment.amedd.army.mil/dsc/wwii/wwii_ad.html

under water. … There was a strong jolt as my head ran into something hard and I began to feel the ship's suction pulling me down again. … I told myself that I was a goner.' … (But then suddenly) her downward motion stopped, and without warning, the ship's suction released her and she was shooting upward like a bullet. …"[5]

She latched onto a floating piece of wood. "… we used the plank as a makeshift raft for two patients who were in the water near us. Another joined us and we three held onto the planks and took turns waving the flashlight one of the officers had with him."[6] Two hours later, the group was rescued from the icy water by another hospital ship.

Accounts differ on the final toll on the St. David. Monahan and Neidel-Greenlee say 25, including 15 American patients (Elffors and Pederson being two).[7] A history of the Army Nurse Corps says there were 130 survivors who were rescued by the damaged British hospital ship Leinster.[8] That would mean 96 dead, based on the number of people on the St. David when it sailed, but it is possible that other ships picked up other people. A third account says 55 were killed.[9] The St. David's captain, Evan William Owen, went down with the ship.

Hindman gave these additional details at some point in The Daily Telegraph in London:[10]

We did our best with the wounded. Fortunately a good proportion of them were walking casualties. It all seemed one confused rush, and then the ship began to heel over, and we were told to jump for it.

… The whole of the time from the bomb hitting our ship to the time we had to jump into the water was only four minutes – it seemed much longer. I felt myself being sucked down

---

[5] "And If I Perish: Frontline U.S. Army Nurses in World War II," p. 244.

[6] "And If I Perish: Frontline U.S. Army Nurses in World War II," p. 244.

[7] "And If I Perish: Frontline U.S. Army Nurses in World War II," p. 245-246.

[8] http://www.history.army.mil/books/wwii/72-14/72-14.HTM and the same numbers are at http://members.iinet.net.au/~gduncan/maritime-2b.html

[9] http://www.roll-of-honour.com/Ships/HMHSStDavid.html

[10] http://www.thewarillustrated.info/175/i-was-there-the-nazis-bombed-and-sank-our-hospital-ship.asp

under the ship. I struggled and came up twice, and each time something hit me on the head. The third time I was luckier.

Elffors' 3rd Division had fought on Sicily starting in July 1943 and was part of the invading force at Salerno in September 1943 before being pulled out, put on ships and sent up the coast to land again at Anzio.[11] Pederson's engineer regiment was in charge of organizing and controlling the pace of landings at Anzio, and also had been at Salerno.[12]

By the end of the first day at Anzio, the Allies had landed more than 36,000 men and 3,000 vehicles, with 13 men killed and 97 wounded.[13]

Elffors went into the Army on Nov. 2, 1942, via Milwaukee, according to his record at the National Archives.[14] He had four years of high school and was single. The Archives does not have a soldier's record if his computer punch card was flawed in some way; Pederson is one such case.

Like the American surgeon Adams, a British doctor died while trying to save patients on the ship. "Capt. Jenkin Robert Oswald Thompson organized parties to transfer the patients from his ward to safety on another ship. However, one injured patient remained trapped below decks. Thompson refused to leave the ship and returned to make further efforts to free his trapped patient," and was never seen again, one account says.[15]

Thompson was awarded the George Cross Medal of Honour for Civilian Bravery for actions between May 1940 and his last day. He had served on the HM Hospital Carriers Paris and Dunkirk in the fighting on Sicily. The George Cross was named for the British monarch, King George VI.[16]

---

11 http://www.jrtc-polk.army.mil/4-10/2-30_History.html and http://www.warfoto.com/3rdsocietyHistory.htm

12 "Fatal Decision: Anzio and the Battle for Rome," by Carlo D'Este (1991), p. 114, and http://www.6thcorpscombatengineers.com/540th.htm

13 "Fatal Decision: Anzio and the Battle for Rome," p. 123.

14 http://aad.archives.gov/aad/fielded-search.jsp?dt=893&tf=F&cat=WR26&bc=s

15 http://www.stephen-stratford.co.uk/brookwood.htm

16 http://theoldcoot.blogspot.com/2011/02/george-cross-j-r-o-thompson.html and http://www.findagrave.com/cgi-bin/fg.cgi?page=gr&GSob=c&GSmpid=46780914&GRid=8479523&l

Four months before the sinking of the St. David, the British ship HMHS Newfoundland, carrying British and American doctors and nurses, arrived off of Salerno on Sept. 12, nine days after the Allied invasion there.

Its reception was "hundreds of individual black puffs of smoke. Monahan and Neidel-Greenlee write: "The German artillery was shooting at vessels in the gulf, and the battleships and destroyers were shooting back. ... Every few minutes, a shell would fly past the Newfoundland, land in the blue-gray water, and send a white fountain of spray 12 to 15 feet into the air. ... Suddenly, a German plane swooped down over the Newfoundland and a high, whistling sound filled the air, followed by an explosion and a tall waterspout just to the starboard side of the ship. The German pilot had released a bomb and it had narrowly missed ...."[17]

The ship and two other hospital ships were ordered back to sea. "The nurses felt safe, protected by the red crosses and Hague Conventions (other wartime rules), as the hospital ships floated through the night lit up like three giant Christmas trees. ... (The next morning), a loud explosion rocked the Newfoundland. In flagrant violation of the Hague Conventions, a German plane had bombed the hospital ship" and it was on fire.[18]

American nurse Lt. Ruth Fischer said, "We had to hurry as we saw and heard the flames crackling away. We barely got up the steps when they collapsed. Then came a problem ... there were only two lifeboats that we could use; all the others were burning. ... Some nurses jumped into the lifeboats and others of us had to get down the rope net. If they (the hospital ship St. Andrew, which also would be near the St. David) hadn't sent their lifeboats to our assistance, we would all have gone down, as we were packed in like sardines."[19]

Six British nurses were killed in that bombing, along with other medical personnel. Four American nurses were wounded.[20] The ship was damaged so heavily that the Allies sunk the hulk.

Hospital ships had been operating under a policy in which "information regarding their sailings and routes was routinely radioed to the enemy, and ...

---

[17] "And If I Perish: Frontline U.S. Army Nurses in World War II," p. 185.

[18] "And If I Perish: Frontline U.S. Army Nurses in World War II," p. 185-187.

[19] "And If I Perish: Frontline U.S. Army Nurses in World War II," p. 188-189.

[20] http://www.history.army.mil/books/wwii/72-14/72-14.HTM

ships bore easily distinguishable and unique markings. ... the special markings gave the nurses, medical personnel and ship's crew a strong sense of security, despite traveling through a combat zone," Monahan and Neidel-Greenlee write. "That promise of safety also led hospital ships to sail in a straight line rather than in the zigzag pattern used by all other vessels at sea."[21]

Besides Elffors and Pederson, another American killed on the St. David was Pvt. Leo Patton of Pennsylvania, who like Elffors was in the 3rd Division but in a different regiment – the 15th.[22] He also is on the Tablets of the Missing at the cemetery at Nettuno. Patton was born in 1924, so he was age 19 or 20.

August 1943
Army Air Forces Staff Sgt. Frederick Durand, Gile in Iron County
and Army Air Forces 2nd Lt. Paul Singer, Milwaukee County
– B-24 bombers in a heavy month of combat

This is the story of two Wisconsin men who were on shot-up, crippled, failing planes of the 44th Bomber Group in missions over Romania and Italy during August 1943.

Most of the men on the B-24 bombers made it out – the first plane had to ditch at sea and the crew of the second plane was ordered to bail out. Some were rescued; others were taken prisoner and later escaped.

But a few crew members did not make it safely out of these two bombers. They included Army Air Forces Staff Sgt. Frederick Durand of Gile in Iron County, who was the tail turret gunner on one plane, and 2nd Lt. Paul Singer of Milwaukee, the navigator on the other plane.

Durand is MIA from Aug. 1, 1943, in the daring raid on oil production facilities at Ploesti, Romania, a daring attack that shocked the world but took a heavy toll in American lives. He was in the 67th Squadron of the 44th

---

[21] "And If I Perish: Frontline U.S. Army Nurses in World War II," p. 181.

[22] http://dsf.chesco.org/heroes/PattonL/patton_l.htm

Bomber Group, and is on the Tablets of the Missing at the Sicily-Rome American Cemetery at Nettuno, Italy. Durand received the Distinguished Service Cross, Air Medal with two Oak Leaf Clusters, and Purple Heart.

The DSC citation said Durand "acquitted himself with great skill as his aircraft flew through one of the most heavily defended areas of Europe. When the plane ... was severely damaged he continued on, in the face of almost insurmountable odds. Over the blazing target, Staff Sgt. Durand, with heroic calm and unflinching loyalty, remained steadfast by his guns until he was killed by enemy fire. The personal courage and devotion to duty ... at the cost of his life exemplified the highest traditions of the military service ...."[23]

Durand's enlistment record at the National Archives[24] shows he was born in 1922, so he was 20 or 21 when he was killed.

Singer was in the 506th Squadron of the 44th Bomber Group. He was killed Aug. 16, 1943, in an attack on airfields and railroad yards at Foggia in southeastern Italy. He is buried at the same cemetery where Durand is on the MIA Wall. Singer was awarded the Air Medal and Purple Heart.

Singer's enlistment record at the National Archives shows he was born in 1918, so he was 24 or 25. He had four years of high school, as did Durand. Singer enlisted in May 1942; Durand in March 1941.

The two attacks by the 44th Bomber Group – known as the Flying Eight Balls – were flown out of Benina Main airfield in Libya, 15 miles east of Benghazi.

Bomb squadrons kept meticulous records compared to the daily havoc of men in action in an infantry division, battalion or company. An airplane crew had a defined number of men checked in for the mission and on each plane, and what happened was collected in the mission debriefing. Thus the stories of the deaths of Durand and Singer are readily available[25] in a 454-page report compiled over the years by Will Lundy, a ground crewman in the 67th Squadron.

---

[23] http://www.homeofheroes.com/members/02_DSC/citatons/03_wwii-dsc/aaf_ d.html. However, the pilot's account of Durand's death has different details. It runs later in this segment.

[24] http://aad.archives.gov/aad/fielded-search.jsp?dt=893&tf=F&cat=WR26&bc=sl

[25] "44th Bomb Group Roll of Honor and Casualties," at http://www. 8thair-force.com/44thbg/lundyroh.pdf The 44th Bomb Group's highly detailed site is http://www.8thairforce.com/44thbg/

The pilot of Durand's plane was 1st Lt. Reginald Carpenter. His plane, crippled by flak over Ploesti and by attacking Messerschmitts, made it out over Mediterranean Sea, but had to ditch. Carpenter was rescued and returned to duty, as did the navigator, bombardier, engineer and left wing gunner. The co-pilot was wounded and taken to the hospital, as was the radio operator.

Like Durand, the right wing gunner was killed – Staff Sgt. Walter Brown of Cooper, Texas. Like Durand, he is on the MIA wall at the Sicily-Rome Cemetery.

Here is what happened:[26]

Lt. Carpenter's aircraft suffered considerable damage over the target and several men were wounded. They were losing gasoline from a severed gas line, and then they encountered an enemy air attack as they approached the sea. An Me (Messerschmitt) 109 had attacked other stragglers and, coming off one attack on them, managed to get in a shot at Carpenter, knocking out another engine.

But they continued on out over the sea, losing altitude due to the loss of two engines now. Finally, a third ran out of gas and stopped. The pilots managed to start it again for a few minutes, but only long enough for them to feather all propellers – and they prepared to ditch.

They hit the water easily the first time, but the plane glanced off of it and hit again some distance away. The ditching tore off the rear fuselage section just aft of the wing. All nine crew members were in the nose section as per instructions. Seven men got out of the plane and released the two life rafts.

Neither Walter L. Brown nor Fred Durand got clear of the sinking ship. They drowned when it went down.

Pilot Carpenter, however, reported the two "were crushed on the flight deck when the top turret tore loose from the fuselage and they were unable to escape."[27]

---

[26] http://www.8thairforce.com/44thbg/lundyroh.pdf, p. 95-96.

[27] http://www.8thairforce.com/44thbg/lundyroh.pdf, p. 96. Carpenter also told this story on page 212-213 of "Ploesti: The Great Ground-Air Battle of 1 August 1943, by James Dugan and Carroll Stewart (1962, 1998).

As for Singer's bombing mission, the 44th's history says: "Just 15 days after the horrors of Ploesti, the 44th BG was to suffer another devastating blow. This was the mission to the airfields of Foggia. On previous flights into that territory the missions were "milk runs," but this day proved far from that. Seven planes failed to return; two of them in Singer's 506th Squadron.[28]

Singer's plane was named Southern Comfort, and the pilot was 1st Lt. Horace Austin. The pilot wound up being captured and held as a POW, but later escaped. So did six of the other crew. One POW stayed in custody. Singer, the navigator, was killed, along with bombardier 2nd Lt. Sheldon Finder of Chicago.

The Bomber Group's history says:

> **Fifteen minutes after bombing the target, this aircraft pulled out of formation and lost altitude under continued attack by enemy aircraft. From three to 10 chutes were observed before the aircraft itself was seen to explode in the bomb bay section and crash. Both No. 2 and No. 3 engines had been on fire.**

> **Sgt. Charles J. Warth, hatch gunner, had these comments: "We came in sight of our target (at 20,000 feet) and saw something else – half of the German Luftwaffe were waiting for us. In just a very few minutes you would have thought the gates of Hell were open, as there were a bunch of us trying to get in – both American and German. Southern Comfort took an uncountable number of direct hits from the German fighters who were coming at us from every o'clock position. I know we shot down at least three of them, and very possibly more. ...**

> **"Shortly, we heard the bail-out klaxon sound, three of our engines were shut down or on fire; the bomb bay was a blazing inferno, and we in the rear of the plane were completely cut off from the pilot and the rest of the crew forward. I made it from the tail turret to the camera hatch, turned around and saw the door to the bomb bay vaporize in flame!**

> **"... The sky for many miles around was a mass of aircraft – some on fire, some still pressing attacks, others trying**

---

[28] http://www.8thairforce.com/44thbg/lundyroh.pdf, p. 106.

their best to fight them off, and everywhere patches of white chutes! ..."

Lts. Singer and Finder never reached the ground alive. Both of their bodies were found later by the Germans who reported that their parachutes were flak and bullet-ridden, and failed to open properly.[29]

The history also reports that "co-pilot Andrew Fabiny said that soon after he got out of the plane and was floating down in his chute, he saw Lt. Singer pass quite close to him, but his parachute was damaged and was only partly open. Sgt. Lee explained that Lt. Finder did not parachute" because he was severely wounded.[30]

Singer and Finder are buried at the Sicily-Rome Cemetery.

A radio operator in another plane said in the history that Singer had a premonition before the mission: "The navigator on the Austin crew, a guy named Singer, had tried to get out of going on this mission – he said that he was afraid of flying today. But they made him go anyway."[31]

1944 and 1945
The Dutch love their liberators

In early 1945, before World War II even ended, people in the Netherlands began a formal program to provide eternal care for the graves of their Liberators. It continues strongly today.

Grave adoption is a core element of Dutch patriotism. The Dutch people adopt individual graves of American soldiers, honoring the man's birthday and Memorial Day, plus tending them at other times of the year. There also is a strong program in nearby Belgium.

People in the Margraten area adopt graves at the Netherlands American Cemetery to show they are "grateful because they helped us get our freedom back," says one of them, John Vervoort.

---

29 http://www.8thairforce.com/44thbg/lundyroh.pdf, p. 115-116.

30 http://www.8thairforce.com/44thbg/lundyroh.pdf, p. 116.

31 http://www.8thairforce.com/44thbg/lundyroh.pdf, p. 120.

The Dutch organization that organizes adoptions says that soon after the Battle of the Bulge, "a couple of Margraten citizens started to plan the first activities which eventually led to the tradition of adopting American graves. This group became known as the Civilian Committee of Margraten. The adoption tradition was passed on from generation to generation. ... These adopters visit the respective grave on a frequent basis, placing flowers at special days in the year, symbolically "standing in" for the American families of soldiers who can no longer visit or are not able to visit the grave of their loved ones. [32]

In Belgium, a ceremony in September 2011 featured more than 300 people adopting graves of Americans.

"Part of the reason we do this is to get the younger generation involved," said Michel Duchene, 62, of Liege, president of an association of retired Belgian Army NCOs, Cercle Royal le Briscard. The organization co-sponsors the event and has been providing certificates to the grave-adopting volunteers since 1991. "And we do this also because of our tendency to forget," Duchene said.[33]

This chapter tells the stories of six of the Wisconsin soldiers.

Work on the stories dates back to the mid-1980s, when the Wisconsin Veterans of Foreign Wars referred John Vervoort's request for information to the author of this book, who at the time was the world and national news editor of the Milwaukee Sentinel newspaper. Tom Mueller's research resulted in a story about Pfc. Dennis Venne of Tomahawk and Milwaukee, who was in the 36th Tank Battalion of the 8th Armored Division and died of wounds on April 4, 1945.

Venne is buried at Margraten. Overall, it has 8,301 graves and 1,722 names on its Tablets of the Missing. There are 208 from Wisconsin.

Belgium has two American cemeteries – Ardennes and Henri-Chapelle. Ardennes has 5,323 graves and 462 names on the MIA wall; Henri-Chapelle has 7,992 and 450. There are 224 from Wisconsin at Henri-Chapelle and 111 at Ardennes.

In the decades since Mueller wrote the story about Venne and Vervoort, the author has helped a few other Dutchmen find information

---

[32] http://www.fallennotforgotten.nl/

[33] http://www.army.mil/article/66380/Belgians_honor_American_WWII_liberators

about the serviceman whose grave they adopted, and photos. The men in this chapter are from a variety of units – ranging from the two segments of the 8th Armored to the 89th Infantry to the 28th Infantry to the 3rd Armored to the 83rd Infantry – and thus form a microcosm of the ground war in Europe. These six deaths range from November 1944 to April 1945.

Army Pfc. Hans Bergmayr's photo was placed in a floral decoration on his grave in the Netherlands after author Tom Mueller located the photo at the soldier's parish in Milwaukee. Dutchman Bart van der Sterren adopted Bergmayr's grave but always wanted to know what the soldier looked like. The photo at the right was taken three years before he found out.

• **Pfc. Hans Bergmayr, Milwaukee, February 1945:** Bart van der Sterren, of Schinveld in The Netherlands, adopted the grave of Milwaukee's Hans Bergmayr, who was from the St. Francis of Assisi Roman Catholic parish on North 4th Street.

Bergmayr, 20, who was in Company B of the 49th Infantry Battalion of the 8th Armored, was killed on Feb. 26, 1945, when he stepped on a mine

25 yards outside van der Sterren's hometown of Posterholt, the Dutchman's research found.

Trying to track down Bergmayr's story, van der Sterren turned to message boards on the Internet, and the pleas were answered by Laura Phillips of Inverness, Fla., and Mueller, of Oak Creek, Wis. Phillips found that Bergmayr's original church was St. Francis; Mueller found it had a website and asked whether in the 1940s it had compiled a list of those killed. Office manager Bernice Valentin found it had run several times in the church's anniversary books, and Mueller then continued his research amid dusty boxes at the church. He got the photo, emailed it to van der Sterren, and within days it was on Bergmayr's grave along with a floral arrangement.

Van der Sterren is in his mid-40s and adopted the grave in 2007, going four years without knowing what the soldier looked like.

Phillips had used a Milwaukee friend to find a story in the Milwaukee Journal of March 14, 1945, accompanied by photos of Bergmayr and 11 other men recently killed in the war. It said his memorial service would be March 24 at St. Francis, gave his original address of 2224 N. 7th St. and said he was a graduate of Boys' Tech High School in 1943 and was the class salutatorian, entering the Army one month later. He had been born in Germany, it added.

Bergmayr's house was a few blocks north and west of the parish and it still stands today.

The 8th Armored landed in France on Jan. 5, and two weeks later fought in the area of the Saar and Moselle Rivers. Six days later, it moved north to the area around Maastricht, Holland, to join the massive attack toward the Rhine River. The history of the unit says the division crossed the Roer River on Feb. 27, exactly one day after Bergmayr died, and assisted the 35th and 84th Infantry Divisions in their push eastward, taking Tetelrath, Oberkruchten, Rheinberg and Ossenberg.[34]

• **Pfc. Wayne Clark, Mosinee and Waupaca, April 1945:** Another Dutchman, Jo Winkens of the town of Vaals, adopted the grave of Pfc. Wayne Clark of the 354th Regiment in the 89th Infantry Division, who was killed on April 9, 1945. The grave, like that of Bergmayr, is at Margraten.

---

[34] http://www.8th-armored.org/division/8history.htm and http://www.8th-armored .org/index.htm

Clark, 26, was a native of Mosinee and Waupaca.

Winkens turned to Mueller for help. Mueller turned to the Marathon County Library, which found that the front page of the Wausau Daily Record-Herald of April 28 had a five-paragraph story about Clark. It said he was killed in Germany and that his wife, Beatrice, was living at 202 Grand Ave. in Wausau. Clark was the son of Mrs. Frank Shobutte of Mosinee, it added, and reported his division had gone overseas Dec. 26, 1944. So he was dead barely four months later.

The story said he had been living in Waupaca when drafted in May 1944 and had been a truck driver in Clintonville. He had attended grade school in Mosinee and high school in Waupaca, and had been married in Shawano in 1940 to the former Beatrice McCabe. He had four children.

But Clark's name (and that of his sister, Delia Green, who the story said was living with Beatrice) are very common, and so obtaining a photo for Winkens is a mission not yet accomplished. The library could not locate any later newspaper story about his memorial service. The Waupaca Area Public Library said high school yearbooks had been halted during the Depression and so there was not one for 1937, his presumed year of graduation.

Winkens is in his 50s. "Vaals has a population of 10,000 souls and is located in the extreme southeast of the province Limburg in the Netherlands, at the foothills of the Ardennes-Eifel range," he says. "Vaals is the place where the borders of Germany, Belgium and the Netherlands cross at a so called 'triple country-point.' Well-known cities in the neighborhood are the famous German emperor city Aachen and the Belgium cities of Malmedy and Verviers, known for its important part in The Battle of the Bulge."

The 89th had crossed the Rhine in March, and its history[35] of the days in which Clark died says:

> **On April 4, the Division CP closed at Nesselroden, beside the Dresden-Frankfort autobahn. The 89th was the easternmost United States infantry division, and one of the closest to the Russians. (VE was little more than a month away) ...**
>
> **By April 9 (the day Clark was killed), the division was along the general line Waltershausen-Friedrichroda. The 354th (Clark's regiment) continued to screen the division front from**

---

[35] http://www.89infdivww2.org/combat/centraleu.htm

Ohrdruf southeast to Wolfis. Companies E and G moved against Crawinkel and were forced to withdraw in face of strong fire from the wooded heights west of the town. The next morning, planes dropped 500-pound bombs on the town and the ground attack was resumed shortly after noon."

• **Pfc. Vincent Popielarski, Milwaukee, November 1944:** Michel Liegeois of Landgraaf, Holland, was seeking to adopt a grave at Margraten and, in November 2011, was able to add one in nearby Belgium. The grave was that of Pfc. Vincent Popielarski of Milwaukee, and it was adopted at the suggestion of Mueller, who had included that soldier in his 2009 book "The Wisconsin 3,800" and thus already had a photo and a family contact to provide to Liegeois.

Given that the Dutchmen search for years to find information and a photo, this one was very easy.

Popielarski was in the 36th Armored Infantry Regiment, 3rd Armored Division. He was killed Nov. 17, 1944, three months after his younger brother Andy had died in Normandy in the same Army infantry regiment and on the same date (Aug. 1) as Tom Mueller's uncle.[36] Vincent was age 29 and is buried in the Henri-Chapelle American Cemetery in Belgium

Liegeois is in his 50s. He told Mueller, "As kids we grew up with the stories our parents and grandparents told us about the WWII period. We frequently visited the cemeteries and somehow I was always interested in the stories behind the names on the graves."

Vincent had a 2-year-old daughter, who now is Toni McMasters of Berlin, Wis., and she was near tears, out of happiness and pride, by news of the grave adoption. "He seems like a very nice man and I am so grateful that you gave us the opportunity," she told Mueller after exchanging emails with Liegeois. "I told him about the Packers and he went online to find more info, so I sent him a Packers shirt."

McMasters said that when she got married in 1963, she had her Uncle Eddie Popielarski, the only one of the three brothers who came home from

---

[36] The story of the Popielarski brothers and Mueller's uncle, Pvt. Martin Miller, was told in "The WIsconsin 3,800," by Tom Mueller (2009). Miller, age 24, is buried at St. James, France, and Andy, 20, at Omaha Beach. Mueller does not know of any French adoption program like the ones in the Netherlands and Belgium. Over the years, he has sent information about his uncle to the cemetery director and the mayor of St. James.

the war, march her up the church aisle. She still has the hope chest that her father gave her mother when they got engaged.

Edward Popielarski was the last of his entire family to die, and his nieces and nephews do not remember what unit he was in.

The 3rd Armored, known as the Spearhead, had seen considerable action in Normandy, and four months later, Vincent was killed near the city of Aachen, Germany. The division had besieged and captured Aachen in only a few days in late October, and was in what its history calls "the grinding Stolberg stalemate" for the next two months.

Pfc. Dennis Venne, Tomahawk and Milwaukee, April 1945: Dutchman John Vervoort of Eijsden was the one whose letter seeking information about Pfc. Dennis Venne made its way to the Milwaukee Sentinel in 1985.[37]

Venne, age 34, was in the 2nd Platoon of Company D, 36th Tank Battalion, 8th Armored Division, the same division that Bergmayr was in. Venne was wounded in early March and died April 4, a month before VE Day. He is buried at Margraten, about 12 miles from Vervoort's home.

Venne was a native of Tomahawk who moved to Milwaukee in 1942 because of abundant wartime factory work. He tried three times to enlist in the Army, only to be rejected because of physical problems, including poor eyesight, missing teeth and foot trouble. But late in the war, manpower needs became more acute and he finally was accepted for service in 1944.

Vervoort rendezvoused with Tom Mueller at the grave in 1988 while Mueller was on a newspaper exchange in Germany, and said he loves the cemetery because it is such a peaceful place. He eagerly recounted many facts about it that he had learned in his visits, and hosted Mueller for dinner at his house, then came to Milwaukee a few years later to meet Venne's relatives and see Mueller again.

Irene Bielinski of Milwaukee, Venne's sister, said in the 1985 newspaper story that she was touched by Vervoort's efforts. She said the only thing her family knew about Venne's death was from a letter that her father received from a lieutenant who was wounded at the same time. It said "his tank took a direct hit ... while they were running for cover, they caught shrapnel fire."

---

[37] Mueller, Tom (1985). Dutchman seeks out fallen GI's kin. Milwaukee Sentinel, Dec. 12, page 1, Part 3. Used with permission of Milwaukee Journal Sentinel.

Vervoort also was in touch with the 8th Armored, and this information is posted in Venne's area at the Dutch adoption website about the fighting on March 5, 1945:[38]

> The blood-red clouds in the sky that greeted the sun on the morning of Monday 5 March 1945 were a forecast of the shedding of the blood of men of the 36th who were to die that day on German soil.   The tankers were to meet an overwhelming force …. The 36th Tank Battalion, as a part of Combat Command B, was attached to the 35th Infantry Division with the mission of moving forward, seizing Lintfort and Rheinberg and then, if ordered, to seize the bridge across the Rhine at Wesel. Their G-2 information was that there was only minor opposition to be expected; that there were only three self-propelled weapons, one anti-tank gun, no tanks and about 300 disorganized and demoralized soldiers on this side of the Rhine. That information, they were to learn soon, was "all wet."
>
> D Company, the M24 light tank company of the 36th, commanded by Capt. Arthur C. Erdmann, moved over Kamperbruck to an attack position southeast of Alterspan Wood. The M24 tanks moved with no prior reconnaissance, and had no idea of what was ahead.
>
> Enemy guns engaged the company but were speedily knocked out. Receiving fire from anti-tank guns, small arms, mortars and artillery, the company nevertheless moved forward and after the third assault, three tanks, later knocked out, entered Rheinberg. … Dennis' (this is Venne) tank took a direct hit. When dismounting their tank, the crew was hit by shrapnel. Dennis was severely wounded in his back. 2nd Platoon leader Lt. Ryan, who later wrote a letter to the family of Dennis, lost his right arm in one of the blasts. Dennis and the lieutenant were captured and brought to the St. Joseph hospital in Apeldoorn, The Netherlands.

The official Web site compiled by veterans of the 8th Armored[39] says that on March 5, "heavy fighting in and around Rheinberg resulted in 199

---

[38] http://www.fallennotforgotten.nl/

[39] www.8th-armored.org/division/8histmar.htm

casualties and the loss of 41 tanks while the Germans suffered 350 men killed and 512 taken prisoner."

Pfc. William Simon, Middleton area, November 1944: An unnamed Dutchman has adopted the name of Pfc. William L. Simon of Dane County, who is on the MIA wall at Margraten. The organization that oversees the adoptions says it cannot give out the name without permission, and no adoptee has written to Mueller after he inquired about Simon – in fact, the message about privacy was sent by Liegeois, and that is how he came to adopt the grave of Vincent Popielarski in Belgium at the author's suggestion.

Mueller's father was a member of the VFW, and the closest post was the William (Sonny) Simon Post 8216 in Middleton. Simon was in the 109th Regiment of the 28th Infantry Division, and was lost on Nov. 5, 1944, during the ill-fated battle of the Hurtgen Forest. He was 20.

Simon received a Bronze Star. His military plaque-type headstone is attached to the civilian stone of his parents, George and Margaret, in St. Bernard Parish Cemetery in Middleton. The parish was founded in 1889 as a mission parish of St. Peter's in Ashton.[40]

Multiple authors[41] have called the Hurtgen one of the dumbest attacks ever because the forest easily could have been bypassed, and faulted the generals all the way up to Supreme ETO Commander Dwight D. Eisenhower. Cecil B. Currey wrote an entire book about it and called it a "waste, misuse and destruction of literally thousands of United States soldiers in futile and unnecessary assaults."[42] Gen. James M. Gavin, who on D-Day had parachuted into Normandy in command of the 82nd Airborne, passed through the Hurtgen in the spring of 1945 and was sickened at the sight of dozens of American corpses that had not yet been removed, months after the disaster. He said "it was a battle that should not have been fought."[43]

The Hurtgen was about 50 to 70 square miles in area and was densely packed with fir trees, which "interlocked their lower limbs at less than two

---

[40] http://www.stbmidd.org/OurParish/ParishHistory.aspx

[41] Cecil B. Currey, "Follow Me and Die," (1984), Stephen Ambrose, "Citizen Soldiers: The U.S. Army From Normandy Beaches to the Bulge to the Surrender of Germany, (1997) and Stephen W. Sears, Eyewitness to World War II (1991).

[42] "Follow Me and Die," p. 45.

[43] "Eyewitness to World War II," p. 274.

meters, so everyone had to stoop all the time."[44] It was a nest of German fortified positions. Artillery fire caused not only a rain of metal, but a rain of wood splinters. There was little in the way of roads. And it had rained for weeks, and did not stop. It sleeted. It got colder by the day. Losses were so heavy that some new men were brought up in the morning and taken out dead the next day.

Pfc. Leo Jutrzonka, West Allis, February 1945: He was a member of the 330th Regiment in the 83rd Infantry Division. Jutrzonka, 20, died on Feb. 25, 1945, and is buried at Margraten.

Jo Smeets of Holland submitted a family record to the Dutch website: "He was the third-youngest son of a family with 14 children; three daughters and 11 sons. His father, Stephen, was originally from Poland and was an interpreter but maintained a farm. He passed away on 1 February 1941. His mother was also from Poland and she had to raise her large family on her own after Stephen's death. Leo worked at his father's farm before he entered the Army." [45]

Jutrzonka was killed one day before Bergmayr, from earlier in this story and from a different division.

The 83rd had fought in Normandy starting two weeks after D-Day, then battled in Brittany, the Hurtgen Forest and the Battle of the Bulge. It is not readily known whether he was in all of that, or like many soldiers was a replacement at some point.[46] When Jutrzonka was killed, the 83rd Division's command post was at Schaufenberg, Germany, starting Feb. 22 and Hasselsweiler starting Feb. 28.[47]

The 83rd Spearhead, the division's newspaper, in its edition dated Feb. 24, one day before Jutrzonka was killed, had this for the main headline in what obviously was the calm before another storm: "Mickey Rooney Makes Personal Tour of 83rd; Visits Each Regiment."[48] But before that, the 83rd had

---

[44] "Citizen Soldiers," p. 167.

[45] http://www.fallennotforgotten.nl/ under "Stories"

[46] http://83rdinfdivdocs.org/documents/330th/various/The_Story_of_the_330th_across_Europe.pdf

[47] http://www.history.army.mil/documents/ETO-OB/83ID-ETO.htm and http://www.lonesentry.com/unithistory/thunderbolt/index.html

[48] http://83rdinfdivdocs.org/documents/newspapers/83rd_Spearhead_February_24_1945.pdf and http://83rdinfdivdocs.org/documents/newspapers/83rd_Spearhead_February_3_1945.pdf

been in the thick of the Battle of the Bulge, and its top headline proclaimed in the Feb. 3 edition: "83rd Hits Nazis in Bulge," with a deck headline of, "Advance 20,000 Yards Through Ardennes; Doughboys Buck Bitter Cold and Waist-High Snowdrifts to KO Panzer Thrust."

September 1944
Army Pfc. James Cramer, Prairie du Sac
– Moselle River in France

James Cramer graduated from high school in 1943, and his next class was not in a classroom – it was in World War II. Like a good many 1943 grads, he never returned.

Cramer, 19, of Prairie du Sac, a private first class, was killed on Sept. 13, 1944, in a major battle near the Moselle River in eastern France while with the 10th Regiment of the 5th Infantry Division.

Cramer is buried at the Lorraine American Cemetery near St. Avold, France. He had graduated barely a year earlier from Prairie du Sac High School, and his name is on the Lachmund-Cramer VFW Post 7694 in his hometown (the other, Edwin Lachmund, is in Chapter 9).

Cramer was killed in the third day of a five-day battle, and a history of the division says the area was declared "secure by Sept. 15 but the casualties were exceptionally high, 1,400 of the Red Devils (nickname of the 5th Division) were killed or wounded in the Moselle bridgehead operation."[49]

The history says his 10th Regiment had crossed the Moselle "near Arnaville and, joined by the 1st and 3rd Battalions of the 11th (Regiment), spent five days overcoming the worst thrown at them by a fanatical enemy."

This was two months after the 5th Division arrived in France, where it was part of the Allied Breakout from Normandy starting at the end of July. It was commanded by Maj. Gen. S. Leroy Irwin and served in Gen. George Patton's Third Army. The autumn fighting went through several World War I battle sites such as Verdun and was all part of an effort to soon attack the large city of Metz, France, which would fall in late November. The city guarded the fortified German Siegfried line.

---

[49] http://www.ranger95.com/divisions/5th_ID_WWII.html

As of the end of August, "In 27 days the 5th Division had covered 700 miles. It was now preparing to enter Germany. However, presently at Verdun, all forward advance was halted due to having run out of supplies. The Third Army's rapid drive across France had outrun its supply lines. A resupply of ammunition and especially gasoline for the vehicles was received on Sept. 6, allowing the Third Army to continue its drive eastward. However, the lull in the activities during this short period, enabled the Germans to halt their flight, stop and prepare a strong defensive line on the east side of the Moselle River."[50] Here is an account from the day of Cramer's death:[51]

A cold, driving rain began during the night of 12-13 September. By daylight the little bridgehead across the Moselle River was a morass of mud boding no good for the assembled armor and adding to the discomforts of the battle-weary infantry. The infantrymen, who had seen little sleep for three days and four nights, were nonetheless grateful for a surcease from the fierce enemy counterblows. Both the 1st and 2d Battalions, 10th Infantry, atop Hills 370, 369, and 386, had been reduced to 50 percent of their original strength, and battle fatigue had become a serious problem ....

At about 0900 on 13 September a platoon of light tanks of Company D, 735th Tank Battalion, with one 105-mm. assault gun and one 81-mm. mortar attached, and the 5th Reconnaissance Troop crossed into the bridgehead to patrol south along the east bank of the river. No sooner had they headed south than they were stopped by intense enemy shellfire.

Later in the morning the 1st Battalion, 10th Infantry, sent a small foot patrol toward the troublesome south-flank town of Arry. By 1100 the patrol's report was back, indicating promise for a drive to enlarge the bridgehead to the southeast:

---

[50] http://www.ranger95.com/divisions/5th_ID_WWII.html. The 5th Division is mentioned briefly in other accounts of this period in the weeks before Cramer's death – in "Citizen Soldiers," by Stephen E. Ambrose (1997), p. 114-117; "The Duel for France 1944," by Martin Blumenson (1963) and "August 1944: The Campaign for France," by Robert A. Miller (1988).

[51] http://www.ibiblio.org/hyperwar/USA/USA-SS-Three/USA-SS-Three-I-4.html

In Arry the riflemen had found only dead Germans and four enemy tanks, all knocked out; the town had been abandoned. ...

Information compiled for Cramer's Lorraine Cemetery says that on Sept. 21, a week after Cramer was killed, his Third Army and the American Seventh Army "linked up near Epinal, extending the Allied front line from the North Sea to the Swiss border."[52] This was a force of millions of men, including 91 Allied army divisions. Gen. Dwight Eisenhower commanded 4.5 million overall, including air forces.[53]

But at a very high price – there are 431 men from Cramer's 10th Regiment buried in Epinal and other American cemeteries in Europe, or their names are on MIA walls there. Those include Cramer and 12 others from Sept. 13; one of those is Sgt. Emmett J. Reilly of Fond du Lac County. If a soldier's body was brought back to the United States at his family's request after the war, he is not in the database at www.abmc.gov, so the numbers of deaths are higher. At Epinal overall, there are 5,255 buried and 424 on the MIA wall; 137 are from Wisconsin.

Cramer was the son of James D. and Elsie M. Cramer of 747 Seventh St. in Prairie du Sac.

John Gillespie of the VFW post, who provided the information about him, lives at that very address today. He says: "I bought my restored Victorian home from Judy Miller in 2002. She and her husband bought it from the Cramer family in 1994, which occupied it for more than 70 years until Elsie, James Cramer's mother, had to be put in a nursing home. I was quite surprised to see my address listed on the wall in the VFW (as Cramer's home) when I joined. Quite a coincidence."

December 1944
Army Technician 5th Class Carlyle Klossner, Medford – Battle of the Bulge

Army Technician 5th Class Carlyle J. Klossner of Medford was in the heart of the Battle of the Bulge, part of the VIII Corps, whose commander was based at the start of the battle in the soon-to-be-famous strategic town of Bastogne, Belgium.

---

[52] http://www.abmc.gov/publications/VisitorBrochures/Lorraine_Brochure.pdf

[53] "Victory in Europe," by Charles B. MacDonald (1973, 2007), p.477.

Klossner was in the 635th Antiaircraft Artillery Battalion, Automatic Weapons, which was part of the corps.

The .50-caliber quadruple machine guns of such automatic antiaircraft batteries – including the 635th and the two similar battalions in the VIII Corps, plus other battalions in the other corps in the battle – were important to the panicked and weapons-short American forces during the surprise German attack and advance.

Klossner, 23, was killed on Dec. 26, 1944, the very day that American forces punched through to relieve their besieged colleagues in Bastogne. The Bulge had begun Dec. 16 and finally ended on Jan. 25, with Dec. 26 considered the turning point.[54] He is buried at the Luxembourg American Cemetery in that country, in Plot H, Row 11, Grave 62.

Klossner's name is on VFW Post 5729 in Medford, the Klossner-Dietzler Post. The story of Marine Sylvester Dietzler, killed on Iwo Jima, is told in Chapter 9 of this book.

Klossner had four years of high school and enlisted on Aug. 10, 1940, in the Coast Artillery Corps. His record has "Enlistment for the Panama Canal Department" in the category of "term of enlistment."[55] He was born in Milwaukee on April 7, 1921, according to the Medford post, which also says that in January 1942, Klossner was in the first convoy that sailed for duty in Iceland and England.

The VIII Corps was led by Maj. Gen. Troy Middleton, and included Klossner's unit plus two other antiaircraft automatic weapons battalions – the 467th and 778th.[56] However, that was at the end of the battle, and no table of organization is easily found for the start. Presuming that Klossner's 635th was in VIII Corps throughout the battle, it would have been attached at some point, as needed, to one of the bigger components of the corps: the 9th Armored Division, 11th Armored, 17th Airborne, 28th Infantry, 87th Infantry or 101st Airborne.

---

[54] "The Ardennes: Battle of the Bulge," by Hugh M. Cole (undated); http://www.secondworldwarhistory.com/battle-of-the-bulge.asp and http://www.army.mil/botb/

[55] http://aad.archives.gov/aad/fielded-search.jsp?dt=893&tf=F&cat=WR26&bc=sl

[56] "A Time for Trumpets: the Untold Story of the Battle of the Bulge," by Charles B. MacDonald (1985), p. 637-639.

What definitely is known is that on Dec. 16, VIII Corps and its three divisions occupied a front of 85 miles, "a distance approximately three times that normally assigned an equivalent defending force by U.S. service school teaching and tactical doctrine."[57]

Middleton was based in Bastogne itself until being ordered out on Dec. 19 and leaving the next day. He was replaced there by 101st Airborne Brig. Gen. Anthony McAuliffe, who famously responded "Nuts" to a German demand for surrender on Dec. 22.

The weapons of the antiaircraft units were important in staving off the Germans. Although the examples that follow do not involve Klossner's particular unit, here are some reports of what these antiaircraft men did, arranged in chronological order:

• On the first day of the battle, "Company C of the 447th Antiaircraft Artillery Battalion used its quad mount machine guns to chop down the infantry following behind" German tanks.[58]

• As Bastogne was imperiled on Dec. 19, American losses in infantry and tank units were "horrendous ... and a company of the 447th Antiaircraft Artillery Battalion was also virtually erased."[59]. And as Americans tried to escape from the town of Wiltz, "the leading half-track hit a mine (planted in the road), it blew up. The driver of the next vehicle, a half-track of the 447th ... its quad-50s blazing, drove deliberately into the minefield; that half-track, too, went up in a deafening explosion, but it got rid of the mines. As the paratroopers fled, the sacrifice made by the men in the half-track provided a safe path for the vehicles that followed."[60]

• "On Dec. 23, "the 390th Antiaircraft Artillery Automatic Weapons Battalion, moving close behind the infantry point, blasted at wood lines, hedges, haystacks and farm buildings. Their .50-caliber machine guns and the 37-mm. cannon mounted on half-tracks pinned the German infantry

---

57 "The Ardennes: Battle of the Bulge," p. 56. This book has two full chapters on plight of the VIII Corps, pages 294-329. But Klossner's small unit is not mentioned.

58 "The Ardennes: Battle of the Bulge," p. 202 and p. 464. This also is described briefly in "A Time for Trumpets: the Untold Story of the Battle of the Bulge," p. 354.

59 "A Time for Trumpets: the Untold Story of the Battle of the Bulge," p. 286-297

60 "A Time for Trumpets: the Untold Story of the Battle of the Bulge," p. 304.

down until supporting artillery could be brought to bear, then shifted to a new position before the German gunners could get on target."[61]

• Around Bastogne, "When the enemy infantry formed to join their tanks in an assault … they came directly under the eyes of Battery B of the 796th Antiaircraft Artillery Battalion, whose .50-caliber 'meat choppers' quickly ended this threat."

Standard weapons in automatic weapons antiaircraft artillery units were the M1 40mm Bofors-designed gun, and the M51 or M55 quad-mount .50 caliber machine gun, according to a comprehensive article on artillery and antiaircraft weapons by Rich Anderson at militaryhistoryonline.com. The history says antiaircraft battalions "were classified as mobile (that is, towed), or SP (utilizing halftrack-mounted guns, the M16, a quad .50 caliber mounting, and the M15, a combination mounting twin water-cooled .50 caliber and a single 37mm), or semi-mobile (with a reduced number of prime movers, designed for the defense of static installations)."

The article adds: "Normally, an AAA automatic weapons battalion was attached to each division, SP if attached to an armored division, and mobile if attached to an infantry division."

These antiaircraft artillery soldiers fought as infantry, too – in the Bulge, "a volunteer squad of seven noncoms from Battery A, 482nd Antiaircraft Artillery Battalion, made the assault with Tommy guns and hand grenades" on a large group of Germans in a house.[62]

Klossner is one of 143 soldiers from Wisconsin buried in Luxembourg or on the MIA wall there. The most famous grave in the cemetery is that of Patton, who died Dec. 21, 1945, after a vehicle crash in Germany and wished to be buried among his men. Overall, the cemetery has 5,076 bodies and 371 names on its MIA wall.

The only other man from Klossner's antiaircraft battalion who is buried overseas, and thus in the www.abmc.gov database, is Pvt. Edward Wallis of Connecticut, who was killed Dec. 19 and is buried at the Henri-Chapelle American Cemetery in Belgium.

---

[61] "The Ardennes: Battle of the Bulge," p. 522-523.
[62] "The Ardennes: Battle of the Bulge," p. 236.

Chapter 8
Pacific and China-Burma-India; Army and Air Forces

This chapter focuses on Army and Army Air Forces men who made the Ultimate Sacrifice in the Pacific and the China-Burma-India theater in World War II.

Their ranks range from a private first class to a brigadier general. Some were infantry; some were pilots; one was a VIP passenger on a plane.

January 1944
Army Pfc. John Wagner, Milwaukee
– Distinguished Service Cross and KIA at Saidor, Papua New Guinea

Pfc. John Wagner was killed in only his third day of combat as a replacement for the legions of men who had been killed months earlier in the 32nd Infantry Division, the Red Arrow. He earned a Distinguished Service Cross for what he did.

Wagner later was one of the servicemen saluted in a religious comic strip, in a nine-panel story entitled "The True Story of Hero Pfc. John Wagner."

The strip, which apparently ran in the Catholic Herald Citizen, the newspaper of the Milwaukee Archdiocese, noted he was from the Basilica of St. Josaphat and had him saying "Jesus, help me! Blessed Mother, pray for me" as he lay dying. The last frame had a desk-bound officer saying, "Wagner gave his life in one of the most heroic actions in combat of which I have personal knowledge."

Wagner, 22, a member of the 126th Regiment in the Red Arrow, was killed on Jan. 4, 1944, near Saidor in the jungles of New Guinea, a strategically important Pacific island that is north of Australia and is bigger than Texas.

The Red Arrow had launched an amphibious landing at Saidor two days earlier, after being out of action for nearly a year because of all its losses to

This serious comic strip about the heroism of Army Pfc. John Wagner of Milwaukee ran at some point in 1950 or 1961, presumably in the Catholic Herald Citizen, given its mention of his parish and his prayers. It likely was part of a national series about Roman Catholic war heroes. The strip was taped into a family scrapbook.

fighting, disease, jungle conditions and the like in its battles in Papua New Guinea, the eastern half of the island of New Guinea. That fighting ended in early 1943, and the 32nd was sent to Australia for substantial replacements and training. Saidor marked its return to combat.

Joni Rohde of New Berlin knew very little about her Uncle John's ordeals and heroism other than the fact he was killed in the Pacific. Then her father, Chester, who was a Marine on Okinawa and a Purple Heart recipient, died in 1992 at the age of 66. Her brother came across a shoebox of material about John Wagner, including the comic strip, newspaper clips, photos and letters. A family friend, Brian D. McManus of Wind Lake, researched the background and found that Wagner was mentioned in some accounts of the 32nd Division.

Rohde says her uncle worked at the A & P grocery warehouse and attended St. Josaphat's on West Lincoln Avenue; their house was at 2428 S. 5th Place. The family consisted of John, Chester, six other siblings and their mother, Mary.

Wagner entered the Army on Oct. 20, 1942, according to records at the National Archives.[1] He was single with a grammar-school education, and his occupation was classified as "packing, filling, labeling, marking, bottling and related occupations."

The landing at Saidor by 9,000 members of the Red Arrow began Jan. 2, 1944. Capt. William Fleischer of Wagner's 126th Regiment described the fighting in his diary:

> **4 January. … A Company K patrol (this included Wagner) was dispatched to Cape Iris, crossing the swift Mot River to get there. It carried one SCR-284 radio for hourly reports to 3rd Battalion, but it never worked at all. This patrol ran into five enemy at Teteri and killed one and dispersed the rest. Near Bilau village this patrol signaled the LCMs (landing craft, mechanized) offshore which were bringing up their packs, extra rations and additional ammunition, to come on in. But as the LCMs closed in on the beach they came under enemy machine gun fire from the bush. They opened up return fire with two caliber .50 MGs. But they didn't fire on the Japanese, but at (our) patrol. By good luck their aim was poor and no one was hit.   At 1430 about 30 Japanese armed with rifles and two light MGs attacked this patrol. The enemy staged a banzai bayonet charge but our patrol met it with automatic weapons fire and killed three and drove the rest back. The Company K patrol lost one killed (that was Wagner). It withdrew to the east bank of the Mot, killing two more Japanese on the way. Total casualties for this day were one killed, five wounded.[2]**

The medal citation honored Wagner for "extraordinary heroism … (his) patrol was attacked in a banzai charge by Japanese forces. Remaining behind, he provided covering fire that allowed his patrol to withdraw, sacrificing his

---

[1] http://aad.archives.gov/aad/fielded-search.jsp?dt=893&tf=F&cat=WR26&bc=sl

[2] http://www.32nd-division.org/history/ww2/32ww2-6.html#Saidor

own life to save the lives of his comrades. Pfc. Wagner's intrepid actions, personal bravery and zealous devotion to duty at the cost of his life, exemplify the highest traditions of the military forces of the United States and reflect great credit upon himself, the 32d Infantry Division, and the United States Army."[3]

Rohde says the box of her father's belongings was handed down by her grandmother but did not include the DSC itself, and that she has no idea where it is.

The illustrated strip – which, like all such pieces, oversimplified and idealized his case while still giving the essentials – proclaimed: "Rising to his feet, fully exposing himself to the enemy, Wagner poured 120 rounds of ammunition point blank at the charging Japs" and his "heroic action enabled the rest of the patrol to get back to headquarters with their information."

In researching this chapter, it first was thought that the strip had run in the Milwaukee Journal or Milwaukee Sentinel, given the amount of resources that it would have taken to draw it. However, a look at Sunday editions of both papers in various months of various years in the late 1940s and throughout the 1950s yielded nothing like it for any solider; much less Wagner. It was thought something like this would run only on a Sunday. Such items were standard fare for young boys' reading in the 1950s and 1960s, and many a movie being run endlessly on television in that era.

An important clue then came on the back side of the comic, which Rohde carefully peeled out of the album. There was a headline – not in the type font that was used by the Journal, but looking very much like the Sentinel – that said, "Father Hubbard to Tell About Yanks in Alaska," in a speech at Marquette University High School in Milwaukee "on Sunday, April 16."

April 16 was a Sunday only in 1950 and 1961 (it would have come again in 1956, but that was a leap year). Father Bernard Hubbard, a noted Alaska missionary, died in 1962, a fact easily found via Google. The short on the reverse side of the cartoon did not say anything about Alaska being a new state, which it became in 1959. That would point to 1950 for when the strip ran.

The reverse side of the cartoon also had various pieces of a long story about a Catholic saint, Stephen Harding, who died in the year 1134, the last

---

[3] http://www.homeofheroes.com/members/02_DSC/citatons/03_wwii-dsc/army_w.html

paragraph said. And it had a two-column ad for a store named Reels, 207 E. Wisconsin Ave., that had the main caption of "Spring Fantasy," featuring a woman in a dress and a blazer.

Given the saintly content of the Wagner strip itself, the news short and an article about a saint who lived more than 800 years ago, it was deduced that the strip ran in the Catholic Herald Citizen, and probably was part of a syndicated series featuring Catholic war heroes from around the country.

The Catholic Herald was consulted, and Managing Editor Maryangela Roman agreed with the above logic – the headline fonts and paper width matched the Herald, and it had content like that over the years, including a syndicated strip called "The Fighting Chaplain," she said.

Author Tom Mueller then went to the Archdiocesan offices to search microfilm and bound volumes – and could not find the Wagner strip.

Editions of the newspaper were searched for February, March and April of 1950 and 1961. No luck. However, the page size of the strip and the headline fonts on the back of it, along with the saintly content, all were staples of the paper. The advertising formats also were the same, although nothing from the Reels fashion store or vendors who had bought one-column ads when the Wagner strip ran was found again.

If the cartoon ran in a national publication, the reverse side of it would not have had a short about a speech in Milwaukee or ads for Milwaukee stores and vendors. St. Josaphat parish theoretically could have produced something about one of its members, but only with a huge amount of labor and expense.

In that era and extending decades afterwards, there was a comic book called "Treasure Chest of Fun & Fact,: distributed in parochial schools.[4] The drawings of its strip are much the same as the item about Wagner, but its page size was far too narrow – space only for two panels across, and the panels all were the same size in the many issues that were checked. The Wagner strip had panels of varying widths.

And so where the strip about John Wagner ran remains a mystery of sorts. What is not a mystery is what John Wagner did.

Wagner is buried in the Manila American Cemetery in the Philippines, in Plot L, Row 15, Grave 110. The rest of his colleagues in the Red Arrow

---

[4] http://archives.lib.cua.edu/findingaid/treasurechest.cfm

fought in New Guinea at Aitape, Biak and Morotai before lengthy campaigns in the Philippines, where many more would die, including some who are featured in this book.

At some point, Wagner's parents received a handwritten letter from Johnny B. Wax, commanding officer of Company K. It had no date, no location and no rank for Wax, and he was not necessarily the commanding officer on Jan. 4; deaths, wounds and other attrition regularly change the rosters of all units, infantry in particular. It was not known what happened to Capt. Fleischer, who wrote the diary item quoted earlier in this chapter. The four-paragraph note no doubt was a template that also was sent with minor changes to other families.

Wax said in very neat penmanship that "John served so courageously (and) I wish to express my sincere sorrow and deepest sympathy at the loss of your loving son."

"Human expressions of condolence seem woefully inadequate. You can well be proud of John who sacrificed his life for his country. ... John was a courageous and fearless soldier, a leader and a boy, who was loved by all in the company. The loss to you and to us is something that cannot easily be replaced. One consolation is that John suffered none in his last hours. His death was almost instantaneous."

Joni Rohde says all of this makes her "feel sad. Because I didn't really know much about him. And then of course proud." She adds: "Looking back I am touched by the number of letters my grandmother received from the American legion, his chaplain, his commanding officer, among others, and, of course, from General MacArthur. It must have warmed her heart to know that so many people actually took the time to write her and convey their sympathy."

Her father did not discuss his Marine service much other than that on Okinawa, "a Japanese woman had a hand grenade under her dress. My Dad was a private guy about his feelings on anything," Rohde says.

She does remember "seeing 'the box' when I was a child and studying Japan in school. My Dad brought out the box and showed me a couple of the small Japanese flags, some pictures of him in his uniform and gave me some of the Japanese currency to take to school. He never showed me anything else."

March 1945
Army Staff Sgt. Walter Milling, West Allis – killed on Luzon in the Philippines and especially remembered in one woman's heart

Walter Milling never came home from combat in the Philippines, but he has never left the heart of the woman who would have married him.

Milling, 22, of West Allis, was killed on March 16, 1945, on the Villa Verde Trail near Mount Imugan on Luzon, the main island in the Philippines. He was a staff sergeant in the 128th Regiment of the Red Arrow and is buried in Manila, 8,000 miles from home.

"He died from sniper fire on Luzon," says Jeanne Anderson Gruel, who lived a few blocks away from Milling and now lives in Waukesha. "I wanted to die, too, when I lost him. Time gave me a choice of finding a way to go on. I gave myself <u>one year</u> to find a reason to live. Just before that year ended I met a man who <u>needed</u> me, and I married him and stayed with him for 57 years until his death. We had two children. ... After all this, I still miss Wally."

And so do many war brides who quickly became widows, and even more women who were fiancées or what are called today "significant others" like Gruel was. Their hearts still are heavy at the thought. So Milling's story is also their story.

Gruel was the seventh of eight kids in her family. The Andersons and the Millings attended the same church, First Lutheran at South 74th and West Lapham Streets, and Wally was a friend of her older brother Leonard. When he came to Leonard's house, he soon also made a connection with Jeanne, nearly five years younger. Early on, "we did the dishes together and then I arranged to meet him at the library. ... I sang in the choir and was the soloist at West Allis Central High School, and he loved to hear me sing."

She added: "I knew he was going to come home and marry me, from what his letters said. He had told his mother." And he was very caring to her younger sister when the girl was ill – "he carried her in from the car so tenderly. He would have made a good father."

The fatal wound was not Milling's first wound. Gruel said he had one that took a week or two to recover from. He earned a Purple Heart with Oak Leaf Clusters, awarded for two wounds.

Milling lived in the 1400 block of South 72nd Street. He was born on April 4, 1922, so he was two weeks from his 23rd birthday when he was killed.

He enlisted on Oct. 19, 1942. He had two years of high school and his civilian occupation is listed in Army enlistment records as "semiskilled chauffeurs and drivers, bus, taxi, truck and tractor" in his record at the National Archives.[5] Gruel remembers that he was driving a truck between two cities for a factory in West Allis; a trip long enough that he would send her a letter during the trek.

The Red Arrow started fighting on Luzon, the biggest Philippine island (roughly the size of Colorado), on Jan. 30, 1945, about six weeks before Milling was killed. Here are some key parts of the division history in that period, with minor editing in order to flow smoothly:[6]

> **By Feb. 2 ... the division's zone of advance was now in a northeasterly direction astride the Villa Verde Trail. Originally a foot and carabao (water buffalo) path pioneered in the 1880s by a Spanish priest named Juan Villa Verde, this trail leads from the Lingayen Gulf area over the Caraballo Mountains to the lush Cagayan Valley of northeast Luzon. ... most of the rest of the trail was simply a footpath over a 4,800-foot high Salacsac Pass to Imugan, where it joined the road to Santa Fe. ...**
>
> **The Sixth Army commander, Lt. Gen. Walter Krueger, described the situation: "The enemy had made good use of the terrain, which, with its sharp ridges and deep ravines, was ideally adapted for defense. He had dug innumerable caves, had provided defense positions on the reverse slopes of the ridges and had established excellent observation stations that permitted him to use his artillery to best advantage. Repeated personal observation convinced me that the advance along the Villa Verde Trail would prove to be costly and slow."**
>
> **... The enemy's main defenses were (finally and with great difficulty) reached early in March. They were generally astride Villa Verde Trail about four miles west of Imugan, and covered the passes.**

---

[5] http://aad.archives.gov/aad/fielded-search.jsp?dt=893&tf=F&cat=WR26&bc=sl

[6] http://www.32nd-division.org/history/ww2/32ww2-11.html

Krueger described it again: "The terrain in this area was much worse than any which the Division had so far encountered. Hills with nearly perpendicular slopes and deep, precipitous ravines made all movements exceedingly difficult."

Another account describes the situation one day before Milling was killed: "On 15 March the 2d Battalion, 128th Infantry, attached to the 127th Infantry, also started up the trail from Valdez. After it reached a point a mile southwest of Imugan ... 128th was stopped cold – the Japanese were prepared for just such maneuvers."[7]

On March 27, a week and a half after Milling died, Col. John A. Hettinger of Kansas, commander of Milling's 128th Regiment, was killed in action. Hettinger "was reconnoitering the front when the Japanese spotted his jeep. The vehicle was immediately caught in an artillery barrage. The colonel and his driver made it to a foxhole. Seconds later, however, the foxhole took a direct hit and Hettinger was killed."[8]

Milling is buried in the Manila American Cemetery.

Joe Tadych took his motorcycle out for a spin while home on leave in Manitowoc in 1942 or 1943. Tadych, a second lieutenant, was the pilot of a C-46A cargo plane that crashed in China in 1945, and is MIA.

---

[7] http://www.ibiblio.org/hyperwar/USA/USA-P-Triumph/USA-P-Triumph-26.html
[8] http://www.historynet.com/world-war-ii-the-us-32nd-infantry-division-battle-to-control-the-villa-verde-trail.htm

March 1945
Army Air Forces 2nd Lt. Joseph Tadych, Manitowoc – pilot MIA in China while flying the 'Hump'

Every day in a seldom-featured zone of World War II, hundreds of American planes flew "the Hump" from India over Burma to China, lumbering over the Himalayas with gasoline, vital supplies and weapons for American airbases in China and for the Chinese troops of Chiang Kai-Shek.

The mountainous and atmospheric conditions on the 500-mile flight were very challenging and the mechanical issues were even worse. Sometimes the pilots flew three roundtrips a day. And for many months, Japanese Zeroes lay in wait. Nearly 600 planes did not make it to their destination; crashing in India, Burma or China. More than 1,000 aviators were killed;[9] the bodies of hundreds have not been recovered.

"The amount of materiel flown over the Himalayas was a logistical achievement unparalleled at the time," the Pentagon says.[10]

One of those lost was Army Air Forces 2nd Lt. Joseph Tadych of Manitowoc, 26, pilot of a cargo plane that was lost on March 13, 1945, in rugged terrain in China near the border with Burma. The crew issued mayday calls for more than an hour before it crashed. Tadych, 26, was in the 1333rd Army Air Force Base Unit and is on the MIA wall at the Manila American Cemetery in the Philippines.

Tadych's C-46A plane was carrying supplies from Chabua, India, to Kunming, the capital of Yunnan Province in southwest China. It developed several mechanical difficulties and crashed about 10 miles inside China from the border of Burma. The two other men on his plane also were killed.

By the end of the war, there were 13 airbases in India and six in China. The China-Burma-India Hump Pilots Association put out three books over the years for its alumni, who were in bomber groups, fighter units, various air

---

[9] "China-Burma-India," by Don Moser, (1978), p. 80. A good overview of the units in the theater is at http://www.cbi-history.com/part_x.html And many photos are at http://cbi-theater.home.comcast.net/~cbi-theater/menu/cbi_home_detail.html

[10] http://www.dtic.mil/dpmo/news/news_releases/2011/release_mease.pdf

commands, weather and photographic organizations, liaison pilots and air commandos.[11]

The Hump flying was especially necessary because the Japanese had seized the Burmese capital of Rangoon and other significant cities, and so land routes from India were out of the question, even if they could navigate the nearly impossible terrain. The Ledo Road was hacked out of the mountainous jungle, finally opening in January 1945. But there still was a huge need for the Hump flights like Tadych's fatal mission two months later.

An official accident report tracked down by researcher Brian D. McManus of Wind Lake, Wis., for a friend who is a relative of Tadych listed the cargo on the fateful flight as engineering mortar, shovel points, cab panels, and transmissions; the cargo totaled 8,940 pounds. The plane was named Stork. The report continued:

> **The plane departed Chabua Army Air Force Base on pre-designated route "Easy" at 1156 hours, headed for Kunming, China. Two hours later, the plane issued a mayday call, and requested a check of its location from the Chabua base. The mayday calls lasted for more than an hour, until 1512.**
>
> **The last plotted position was 85 miles from Myitkyina, which is in northern Burma (and had been seized in 1944 after months of fighting by the Chinese and by the Allies). All airfields in the vicinity of the last known position were notified of the plane's trouble.**
>
> **Army Air Forces investigators determined that the plane experienced a probable loss of one or both engines due to carburetor icing, or mechanical failure due to extreme turbulence.**

Three months later, on June 12 (this was two months before the war ended), the wreckage of the plane was found in Yunnan Province of China, about 25 miles west of the city of Baoshan. Three unidentified bodies were located with the wreckage and buried by a "ground party," the report said.

The report does not specify the nationalities of those in the ground party. It is a mystery how three bodies were buried in 1945, because today

---

[11] "China-Burma-India," p. 82. A list of codenames for bases and other facilities is on page 50 of "China-Burma-India Hump Pilots Association (1992)." The group's description of all the people who flew the route is on p. 9.

one crewman is buried in Hawaii, while Tadych and the other crewman are recorded as MIA.

Jerome Zelenka of Milwaukee, a veteran of the China-Burma-India theater, says the ground crews "probably were Chinese natives in the area. Nobody in their right mind would have gone out there because of the danger of getting lost or being annihilated by the Chinese." Zelenka was a sergeant who was based in India in 1945 and 1946, in Delhi, Karachi (which now is Pakistan) and Calcutta. He worked in the Army Airways Communications System.

The crash site was visited again after the war, apparently by American graves registration personnel or other American troops, but the report does not say exactly whom. The report says one – repeat, one – body was recovered.

Tadych's co-pilot was 2nd Lt. William E. Carroll of Harris County, Texas, which is Houston. He is on the MIA wall at Manila. The radioman was Pfc. John D. Moore Jr., 24, of Hughes County in central Oklahoma. He is buried at the National Memorial Cemetery of the Pacific, known as the Punchbowl, in Honolulu, Hawaii.[12]

Two weeks after the crash, Tadych's hometown paper, the Manitowoc Herald-Times, ran news about several local boys on page 10 of the March 28 paper. There was an item about the memorial mass for a soldier killed in Germany, and a roundup with the reported death of another soldier in Europe, then Tadych being MIA and another man missing in Germany. Plus a fifth man who was missing in France since Nov. 30 now being classified a prisoner. Tadych's parents were Joseph and Clare, and they lived at 1815 Marshall St. The article said:

> **In the ferrying command, Lt. Tadych is a veteran of over four years service. A graduate of Lincoln High School with the Class of 1936, he was a member of the football and swimming teams. As an aviation student he was trained at Mitchell Field,**

---

[12] http://gravelocator.cem.va.gov/index.html shows Pfc. John D. Moore Jr., killed on March 13, 1945. He is buried in Section P, Site 1030. More information on the Tadych plane and other crashes is at http://www.aviationarchaeology.com/src/AARmonthly/Mar1945O.htm and http://aviation-safety.net/database/record.php?id=19450319-2

N.Y., and received his coveted silver wings of the AAF at Spence Field, Ga.

His first foreign assignment was to Africa, where he remained two years. He came back to the United States on a leave, and six months later was sent to Italy. After a brief period spent in the States again, he went to the India-Burma theater.

His brother, 1st Lt. Reinhardt Tadych, has been in the air forces on the western front (which means Europe), and at present is on ground duty.

The only other Wisconsin man in Tadych's 1333rd who is buried overseas or MIA and thus in the database at www.abmc.gov is Cpl. Alvin P. Palecek of Winnebago County. He was lost on Jan. 6, 1945, and is on the MIA wall in Manila. He was born in 1922 and thus was age 22 or 23. Three other men in the 1333rd were killed the same date as Palecek, so it is likely that most or all of them were on the same plane.

A private organization named MIA Recoveries[13] specializes in locating and recovering U.S. airmen lost in India and Burma. The organization is run by Clayton Kuhles of Prescott, Ariz., who says he had never heard of the Hump flights until 2002, when visiting the area, and it quickly became his passion.[14] He seeks donations and says the average expedition costs $15,000.[15]

Kuhles' site has reports about various missing aircraft that he has reached and documented. He says a case that successfully led to identifications started with his finding of wreckage in October 2003.[16] The debris was found near Latti, India, in Arunachal Pradesh state. He found human remains and turned them over to the Pentagon's Joint POW / MIA Accounting Command.

That C-87 Liberator Express plane crashed April 24, 1943, on a flight from Yangkai, China, to Chabua, India. Three of the five people on the plane

---

[13] http://www.miarecoveries.org/index.html

[14] http://www.miarecoveries.org/pdf/c-87_41-23696-site-report.pdf He tells his own story after the specifics of this particular crash and investigation.

[15] http://www.miarecoveries.org/historical_background.html

[16] http://www.miarecoveries.org/reports.html

were indeed identified by the Pentagon and those IDs were announced to the public in 2011 and 2012 after families decided on memorials and disposition of the remains.

The three were the pilot, Capt. Jennings H. Mease Sr. of the 77th Squadron, 22nd Ferry Group; co-pilot, 2nd Lt. Samuel Lunday, and flight engineer, Pvt. Mervyn E. Sims.

The identification of Sims was announced first, on April 11, 2011, and the Pentagon described that flight: "Prior to takeoff a ground crew determined the aircraft had sufficient fuel for the six-hour flight to the air base on other side of the Himalayas in Chabua, India. Once cleared for takeoff there was no further communication between the aircrew and airfield operators. Army Officials launched a search effort when the plane did not arrive at the destination."[17]

Apparently referring to Kuhles, it said "an American citizen in Burma" reported the discovery of the wreckage to U.S. officials in 2003 and "he was detained by Burmese officials when he attempted to leave the country with human remains and artifacts from the site. The remains and materials were handed over to officials at the U.S. Embassy in Rangoon." So Kuhles apparently found these remains in Burma, or he found them in India very close to the border and then crossed into Burma. The Pentagon announcement said he found them "112 miles east of Chabua."

Kuhles gave a eulogy at Sims' memorial service on April 22, 2011, in Petaluma, Calif.[18]

Kuhles does not discuss any expeditions inside China, where Tadych's plane crashed. But the United States has been able to make some progress with Burma, India and China over the decades, depending on the overall state of their relations.[19]

With China, in August 2012, the Defense POW / Missing Personnel Office reported on the status of its discussions involving MIAs from World War II, the Korean War and the Cold War. It said the Joint POW / MIA Accounting Command "met with China's Ministry of Foreign Affairs to propose operations for FY 2012 and FY 2013. The Ministry of Foreign Affairs approved an investigative mission on two WW II aircraft crash sites in Shanxi Province" in

[17] http://www.dtic.mil/dpmo/news/news_releases/2011/release_sims.pdf

[18] http://www.miarecoveries.org/pdf/Memorial-Service-Pfc-Mervyn-E-Sims.pdf

[19] http://www.dtic.mil/dpmo/news/factsheets/documents/burma_factsheet.pdf

eastern China, far from where Tadych went down. And in May 2012, U.S. officials "met with Chinese military archivists in Beijing to sign a new technical arrangement to cooperate for another three years on sharing information about American military personnel missing in conflicts with China."[20]

The statement, however, focuses mostly on the Korean War and the Cold War, not cases involving the China-Burma-India theater of World War II.

June 1942
Army Air Forces Staff Sgt. Edmund Kolonka, South Milwaukee
– Bataan Death March and died as POW

Edmund Joseph Kolonka survived the Bataan Death March, but died a few weeks later at Cabanatuan, one of the prison camps where thousands of Americans wound up.

Kolonka, 24, of South Milwaukee, was a staff sergeant in the 27th Bomber Group and died on June 22, 1942. His last birthday was Feb. 8, during the dogged but futile resistance on the Bataan Peninsula against the Japanese invasion that had begun in December and amid severe shortages of food and ammunition that grew worse every day.

Gen. Douglas MacArthur and some brass and enlisted personnel were evacuated to safety in Australia on PT boats and submarines from the rocky fortress island of Corregidor. On April 9, 1942, Gen. Edward P. King surrendered American forces on Bataan in the largest capitulation of American troops in history.[21] Then came the Death March of 12,000 Americans and more than 60,000 Filipinos; they went about 80 miles to Camp O'Donnell and then shipment to other prisons.

Hundreds of Americans and even more Filipinos died in the march – Japanese brutality plus the deliberate lack of water supplies and food were among the biggest factors.

---

[20] Both quotes are from http://www.dtic.mil/dpmo/news/factsheets/documents/china_factsheet.pdf. The joint command has a comprehensive website at http://www.jpac.pacom.mil/ and issues frequent press releases about its current searches.

[21] http://www.history.com/this-day-in-history/us-surrenders-in-bataan

The march took about five days and went from Mariveles to San Fernando, where the prisoners were shoved onto extremely overcrowded trains with even worse conditions than the march. The prisoners first were taken to Camp O'Donnell. Then some were loaded onto trucks to the Cabanatuan prison camp, which was even more overcrowded and lacking in food, medicine and, particularly, in humane treatment. Others were taken other prisons or put on overcrowded ships and moved to Japan to provide slave labor.[22] Ernest Norquist, father of future Milwaukee Mayor John Norquist, was in the Death March and at Camp O'Donnell, then on a ship to Japan.[23]

The ships were called hellships because they were extremely overcrowded with men already in very poor physical condition; dumped into holds with little ventilation and less food. Then they were subject to U.S. submarine and aerial attacks because they were Japanese shipping at a time of war. Many also were carrying war cargo.[24]

---

[22] The story of the Death March is told in many books and, in particular, at http://www.eyewitnesstohistory.com/bataandeathmarch.htm; http://history1900s.about.com/od/worldwarii/qt/Bataan-Death-March.htm; http://philippine-defenders.lib.wv.us/html/bataan.htmll and http://www.tragedyof bataan.com, which is the site for a PBS documentary in 2012.

[23] http://www.wisvetsmuseum.com/collections/oral_history/transcriptions/N/Norquist,Ernest%20_OH%20195_.pdf.

[24] The ships were the subject of a fine book by Gregory Michno, "Death on the Hellships: Prisoners at Sea in the Pacific War," published in 2001. Author Tom Mueller calculated that the worst day for Wisconsin in the war likely was Oct. 24, 1944, when an American submarine sunk the hellship Arisan Maru with 1,782 POWs aboard. There were 49 Wisconsin men killed that day, the majority of whom were from the Bataan Death March, given that they were from units that were based in the Philippines when the war started. The ship was torpedoed because it was enemy shipping. The Battle of Leyte Gulf also was going on that day, and the aircraft carrier Princeton was hit by one Japanese bomb that caused a later explosion, killing 108 on the carrier plus 233 on the cruiser USS Birmingham, which was alongside helping to fight fires. See http://www.history.navy.mil/photos/events/wwii-pac/leyteglf/cvl23-12.htm and the 1972 book "Leyte Gulf: The Death of the Princeton," by Edwin P. Hoyt. The list of MIAs from Oct. 24 appeared in Mueller's book "The Wisconsin 3,800," and there were 14 Navy men on it – five that later research showed were on the Birmingham, whose list of dead can be found by searching at http://www.navylog.org/Portals/0/tabid/76/default.aspx

A fellow member of Kolonka's 27th Bomb Group was mess hall sergeant James Drake of Alabama. The unit had trained to fly the A-24 Dauntless, a dive bomber. The men first arrived in Manila via ship on Thanksgiving, Nov. 20, 1941, but the separate ship carrying their planes was diverted to Australia in the first days of the war.[25] Drake's story continues:

Without aircraft, the 27th Bomb Group became "flying infantry" and was issued weapons and ammunition. Drake was given a Browning Automatic Rifle and all the ammo he could carry.

... Drake's outfit, now designated the 27th Provisional Infantry Battalion, was moved to the Bataan Peninsula, where they engaged the enemy. Many of his friends and acquaintances were killed in the heavy fighting. As months went by, all hope of relief was lost.

(Drake became a captive the day of the surrender) near the town of Mariveles, at the extreme southern end of the Bataan Peninsula. Uncertain of what lay ahead, he and hundreds of others were herded into a field and told to sit. They were given no food or water.

... The men were force-marched 90 miles north toward a large holding camp. They were already weak from short rations before their ordeal began, and it only got worse. Some were suffering from dysentery. They were given little or no water or food for days at a time. Stragglers were not tolerated and most were shot or bayoneted. Drake recalls anyone who fell was not allowed to get up. The unfortunate man was killed and thrown to the side of the road.

After interminable days of being herded along like animals, Drake's assemblage of comrades arrived at Camp O'Donnell. This was only the first of five different camps Drake would occupy over the next 41 months of captivity,

---

25 The history of the 27th is at http://www.ozatwar.com/27bg.htm and says, "The commanding officer, Col. John H. Davies, and 20 pilots were flown to Australia to get their aircraft and only got as far as Java because of the deteriorating situation in the Philippines."

starvation, mistreatment and torture. He spent time in Cabanat-uan, the largest camp in the Philippines. During his ordeal, he would contract beriberi, and temporarily lose his eyesight.[26]

At Cabanatuan, one account says, "many ultimately ended up in 'Zero Ward' – so named because should one land there, his chances of leaving alive were zero …. The Japanese did issue some antitoxin when a diphtheria epidemic threatened their own personnel, but otherwise they remained largely indifferent to the prisoners' suffering. 'Buried 52 today,' read one of (American Steve) Mell-nik's late June diary entries. 'Camp is gloomy morgue. Dead men lie on streets until noon.' (American Jack) Hawkins recalled bulldozers aiding in the disposal of corpses, but most of the (burial) details remained dependent on human labor.[27] Hawkins and Mellnik would wind up at Davao, and would be in a group that escaped and told the world of the horrors that were going on.

Another account tells it: "Isolated from other cases, the patients in Zero Ward were a study in collective misery: naked, skeletal, sprawled on a wooden floor. They were covered in feces and coated with vomit; their bodies twitched with bluebottle flies. They had no blankets, and initially there was no water for them unless it was collected from rooftops or ditches. … Some couldn't make it to the latrines, 50 to 100 yards away; others died in the grass or expired beneath the barracks."[28]

Every day at Camp O'Donnell, and presumably at Cabanatuan where Kolonka was, this was the burial routine: " 'Then you would take the dog tag, if they had one, and put it in their mouth for burial and cover them up.' Then there was no ceremony, no prayers, just corpse after corpse, sometimes 20 or 30, little more than bones and skulls, the remnants of men who had fought for a common cause thrown together in a common pit."[29]

---

[27] http://www.costoffreedom.org/Bataan_Death_March.html. Another vivid account of the Death March brutality and time at Camp O'Donnell is by James Bol-lich, who was assigned to the 16th Bomb Squadron in Kolonka's 27th Bomb Group. It is at http://www.af.mil/news/story.asp?id=123308539. However, Bollich did not get sent to Cabanatuan.

[28] "Escape From Davao: The Forgotten Story of the Most Daring Prison Break of the Pacific War," by John D. Lukacs, p. 97.

[29] Conduct Under Fire: Four American Doctors and Their Fight for Life as Prisoners of the Japanese," by John Glusman (2005), p. 257.

[30] "Escape From Davao," p. 79.

Bodies in prison camp cemeteries were exhumed after the war, and Kolonka was brought home to Holy Sepulcher Cemetery in Cudahy. His name is on the Van Eimeren-Kolonka American Legion Post 27 in South Milwaukee, next to the city's library.

The other name on the South Milwaukee post is from World War I: Pvt. Everhart John Van Eimeren, who was in the 120th Field Artillery of Wisconsin's 32nd Red Arrow Division and was killed in France on Aug. 29, 1918. He was 19. The post says he was killed near Juvigny, France;[31] the list of Wisconsin deaths[32] says he died at Tartiers.

April 1944
Army Air Forces 1st Lt. Raymond Zenner, Milwaukee
– B-24 pilot on Pacific islands

Raymond Zenner was in multiple hairy missions as the pilot of a B-24 bomber in the far-flung islands of the far Pacific, but his number came up on April 2, 1944, and he was killed while bombing a Japanese base in the Caroline Islands. Reports say a crippled B-24 veered into the path of his plane and both went down, killing all their crews; 19 men were listed.

Zenner, 26, a native of Milwaukee whose family had started out in Medford, was a first lieutenant in the 394th Bomber Squadron of the 5th Bomber Group. His name is on the MIA wall at the Manila American Cemetery in the Philippines.

He was awarded the Air Medal with three Oak Leaf Clusters, meaning he had been honored four times. The Air Medal is awarded to any person who "shall have distinguished himself by meritorious achievement while participating in aerial flight."[33]

The Carolines are a widely scattered of 500 small islands, north of and east of the Philippines. Today, some of the islands are in the nation called the

---

Federated States of Micronesia and others are in the country named the Republic of Palau. Both are tiny but send athletes to the Olympics.

A combat chronology of the Army Air Forces gives this for April 2: "31 B-24s fly a strike against Dublon Island, Truk Atoll, causing considerable damage to the warehouse and dock areas; the bombers claim 30-plus fighters downed; four B-24s were lost."[34] The toll for enemy fighters probably means a combination of those destroyed on the ground plus shot down by gunners on the bombers.

Truk is known today as Chuuk and is part of Micronesia.

Marcia Dalsky of Wausau contacted author Tom Mueller in 2009 after reading of his work "The Wisconsin 3,800," about those from the state buried overseas or MIA. She wanted to tell him about her Uncle Raymond, the last of the nine children of Peter and Margaret Zenner. In 2012, at the author's request, she dug up some newspaper clips about him.

Zenner graduated from Messmer High School in Milwaukee in 1935 and when he enlisted in 1940, his photo appeared in the Milwaukee Journal under the headline, "Milwaukee's 1000th Army Recruit." The caption noted that the city "has been the district Army recruiting headquarters for less than four months," and Zenner's home address was given as 4244 W. Capitol Drive. Also in the picture was Lt. Col. James A. Summersett, the district recruiting officer.

Zenner and his picture would appear in several more short articles. One was when he graduated from the Gulf Coast training center as a pilot. The mugshots of several other Milwaukeeans appeared with Zenner, and the caption said his address was 4447 N. Hopkins St.

Later, in late 1943 or 1944, he was in the paper again, under a dateline of "Somewhere in the South Pacific," in an article generated by the Army Air Forces about the vital role of navigators in a nighttime raid at Rabaul. Such articles often appeared in Stars and Stripes and then were sent to the hometown paper, eager for news of local men and women. "So far as I was concerned, it was strictly a fine job by my navigator," Zenner was quoted as saying. The story said he was 26, so this between his birthday in September 1943 and his death in early April. The story called him a "powerfully built Army pilot of one of the Liberators," and said 11 B-24 bombers had been in the raid.

---

[34] http://paul.rutgers.edu/~mcgrew/wwii/usaf/html/Apr.44.html

Zenner added: "I couldn't see on the way up, and when I got there i was too busy trying to dodge Jap searchlights to see." The story called it their toughest mission to date, except for the one before it – "a daylight task over Kavieng, New Ireland (an island in Papua New Guinea). The plane was well shot-up on that occasion, during an hour and 10 minute battle with Zeroes. Large chunks of metal were ripped out of the plane by 20mm cannon shells and two members of the crew were wounded slightly."

The article also quoted the navigator, "quiet" 2nd Lt. Boyer Westover, and the bombardier, 2nd Lt. Ralph Smalley. They would die along with Zenner, as will be seen a few paragraphs from now.

Another newspaper story, one paragraph with Zenner's photo, said four Japanese planes had pounced on his bomber in one raid, and that the waist gunner shot one down and the tail gunner damaged another.

Soon, Zenner's photo ran again – under the headline of "War Casualty Names Listed." Five other hometown boys who made the Ultimate Sacrifice elsewhere in the war also had their mugshots in the Milwaukee paper on that day.

Dalsky said Zenner loved flying with his older brother. Then he joined the Army Air Corps and took his training at a Chanute Field in Illinois, where he was a mechanic instructor. He then decided to train to be a pilot, and earned his wings in March 1943. Dalsky added: "In a letter dated Oct. 16, 1943, he wrote from California: 'I'm getting my (air) ship and crew fully equipped there for our trip across the ocean. We have our own B-24 and we named her Homesick Angel."

Many air units have detailed records of their service on the Internet, including specifics of each plane in each mission and its crewmen. Zenner's unit is not one of them. However, one item that was found via Google was this exchange in 2010 on a forum devoted to the Army Air Forces about what happened to Zenner's plane – a midair collision with another B-24 that had been hit by extensive fire and was out of control:[35]

"Looking for the crew information on aircraft 42-73142 flown by 1st Lt. Raymond H. Zenner when it crashed on 2 April 1944 and on aircraft 42-73150 flown by 1st Lt. Theodore A. Rauh, crashed same date. Looking for crew names, positions, status. Thanks in advance for any information." This message was sent by Randy Watkins of Dupo, Ill.

---

[35] http://forum.armyairforces.com/m194839-print.aspx

The question received a detailed answer from someone named Rich (no last name) of St. Louis: "I've been working on these two crews since September when a pilot that flew this mission to Truk told me that Rauh's plane was struck by AA and collided with Zenner's plane. Both went down and no chutes were seen. These were both 394th Squadron / 5th Bomb Group planes / crews."

Rich continued: "I have a copy of a letter from the chaplain of American Legion Post 1168 in Friendship, N.Y. written about seven years ago that lists the crew of Zenner's plane as:

"First Lt. Raymond H. Zenner, 2nd Lt. Donald F. Michael, Staff Sgt. Alexander N. Colovos, Tech Sgt. Marvin B. Ericson, 1st Lt. Boyer Westover, Staff Sgt. Cornelius D. Murphy, 1st Lt. Ralph E. Smalley, Staff Sgt. Carl W. Prost, Tech Sgt. Raymond Belcher and Staff Sgt. Pascal Urgo.

"Zenner was the pilot, Michael was co-pilot, Smalley was bombardier so Westover had to be the navigator. Belcher was the engineer, which probably makes Ericson the radio operator as the other tech sergeant."

Except for Belcher, the names listed all have the same unit and death date at www.abmc.gov, the database of MIAs and foreign burials, and all are on the MIA wall in Manila. Belcher's date is given as Oct. 2, the same numeral as the crash but a far different month, and that probably is just an error, given the specificity in the message.

Rich lists the names on the other plane as:

"First Lt. Theodore A. Rauh, Tech Sgt. Harry P. Whitney, 1st Lt. Richard E. Wotring, Staff Sgt. Raymond C. Dixon, 1st Lt. John C. Smith, Staff Sgt. Russell H. McCarthy, 1st Lt. Travis L. Moore, Staff Sgt. Bernard J. McDonald and Tech Sgt. Richard M. Hager."[36]

In their listings at www.abmc.gov, most of the men on the two planes have Air Medals with multiple Oak Leaf Clusters, like Zenner. Rauh, the pilot of the stricken plane, had the Air Medal with three clusters, and was from Massachusetts.

A brief history of the 394th says Zenner's squadron served on the island of Fiji in its first overseas posting, "although in January and again in April-

---

[36] There is a photo of Westover along with unidentified officers of the 394th Squadron at https://www.facebook.com/media/set/?set=o.118022234918726 &type=3

June 1943, the unit operated from Espiritu Santo and Guadalcanal. Also sometime in 1943, the squadron began swapping its B-17s for the B-24 Liberator.

"From June 1943 through April 13, 1944, the 394th called Guadalcanal home, although from Feb. 28 to April 9, 1944 (just a few days after Zenner's death), the squadron called Munda, New Georgia, home. From Guadalcanal, the 394th ventured to Momote Airfield, Los Negros, in April 1944."[37]

Zenner's niece Dalsky concluded, "I last saw him in Milwaukee at the family home when he had a furlough before going overseas. I treasure a snapshot that was taken of the whole family, and we both were in it. ... I still miss him and still read his letters."

February 1945
Army Air Forces Brig. Gen. James Andersen, Racine
– plane disappeared

Brig. Gen. James Andersen had just finished a major and important task, overseeing creation of bases and runways for B-29s on the island of Guam.

On Feb. 25, 1945, the B-29 Superfortress flew its first combat missions from the airfields that Andersen had worked months to create. The very next day, Andersen, a 1926 West Point grad from Racine, and his boss, Army Air Forces Lt. Gen. Millard Harmon, left Guam on a flight to Hawaii to plan the next step of the war, including the atomic bomb.

Andersen and Harmon never arrived.

A C-87A-CF Liberator, serial number 41-24174, carrying them and eight other men vanished in clear weather sometime after its intermediate

---

[37] http://ranger95.com/airforce/combat_tng/394th_cts.html. More information about the overall 5th Bomb Group is at http://www.armyaircorpsmuseum.org/5th_Bombardment_Group.cfm. Information on Munda is at http://www.pacificwrecks.com/airfields/solomons/munda/index.html and Momote Airfield is at http://www.pacificwrecks.com/airfields/png/momote/index.html

stop at Kwajalein.[38] They are on the MIA wall at Honolulu. The aircraft was Harmon's command plane, a converted B-24.

Andersen was 41 and had been promoted to brigadier general only a month earlier; he was the highest-ranking Army / Army Air Forces officer from Wisconsin to be lost in World War II.[39]

Andersen and Harmon had been headed for a meeting to help plan the next step in the Pacific war, the invasion of Japan, but they also had been let in on a top secret: the forthcoming atomic bomb. That is according to Maj. Gen. Leslie Groves, leader of the Manhattan Project, and they were some of the few Air Force brass to know.

How much they were told is up to speculation, because Groves says his main rule always was that people should be told only what was vital for them to know, not the entire picture. That was especially true among those planning early stages of the project and building plutonium and uranium processing plants, and working at them, and in 1945 Air Force personnel and crews were busy creating special, isolated facilities on the island of Tinian and training for the historic flight. They would have known it was some sort of super bomb weighing far more than any other and requiring substantial new procedures, according to other parts of Groves' history of the project.[40]

Groves says he had to get approval from Army Chief of Staff George Marshall, a top adviser to President Franklin D. Roosevelt, to inform Harmon "and two of his staff about our plans" because the bombing would be conducted from that area. Harmon, 57, was a three-star general and commander of Army Air Forces, Pacific Ocean Area. He also was deputy commander of the 20th Air Force, whose leader was Gen. Henry "Hap" Arnold. Anderson was Harmon's chief of staff.[41]

---

[38] http://www.pacificwrecks.com/aircraft/b-24/41-24174.html

[39] Based on Tom Mueller's research in "The Wisconsin 3,800" (2009). The book dealt with MIAs and overseas burials, a comprehensive and solid database at www.abmc.gov. There is no central point to find burials in Wisconsin or the United States, but no name of any other top officer has surfaced from the Wisconsin Veterans Museum or elsewhere since Mueller published the book.

[40] "Now It Can Be Told," by Leslie Groves (1962).

[41] www.globalsecurity.org/military/facility/andersen.htm and http://www.af.mil/information/bios/bio.asp?bioID=10235 ⸱

Groves continues: "Unfortunately, soon after this, Harmon and the two staff officers disappeared in flight en route from Guam to Washington."[42] Groves does not name Andersen. The list of crew and passengers shows the next highest-ranking officer on the plane was Col. William Bell.[43]

Bomber Legends magazine ran a story in 2004 in which a Milwaukee native, Tech Sgt. Sam Maas, who usually was on Harmon's crew but was leaving on furlough on the day the flight departed, maintained he saw a mechanic repairing a gasoline-fueled heater just before the flight. Maas said he suggested a new heater rather than the repair, because that kind of heater was known to emit explosive gasoline vapors.[44]

The Racine Journal-Times newspaper reported on March 5, 1945, that the military said that when last heard from, the plane carrying Andersen and Harmon "reported ample fuel to complete the flight and was traveling in good weather over calm seas. When the plane failed to respond to communications ... all available naval ships and planes were dispatched to join the search."

Before Andersen set up the bases and other facilities on Guam, the B-29 already was flying from Saipan and Tinian; adding Guam allowed for huge raids – such as the infamous March 9-10 firebombing of Tokyo by 334 Superfortresses that killed more than 80,000 people. Each B-29 carried 1,520 firebombs.[45]

The Air Force built and maintained three airfields on Guam[46] – North Field, a B-29 facility (named for Andersen a few years later); Depot Field, a B-29 depot and maintenance base (later renamed Harmon Field in honor of

---

[42] "Now It Can Be Told: The Story of the Manhattan Project," p. 278-279.

[43] http://www.pacificwrecks.com/aircraft/b-24/41-24174.html. However, Bell is not listed among the MIAs at www.abmc.gov nor at the Pentagon's list at http://www.dtic.mil/dpmo/wwii/reports/. The pilot was Maj. Francis E. Savage, who is in both databases. Groves' book has several references to top scientists traveling incognito in military uniforms, so one wonders whether Bell actually was a private citizen.

[44] http://www.dmairfield.org/people/harmon_mf/Harmon_Disappearance_Article_Opt.pdf

[45] "Conduct Under Fire: Four American Doctors and Their Fight for Life as Prisoners of the Japanese 1941-1945," by John A. Glusman (2005), p. 376.

[46] www.globalsecurity.org/military/facility/andersen.htm

the lieutenant general but closed a few years after the war); and Northwest Field, a combined B-29 / fighter base.

Today, Andersen Air Force base is a centerpiece of American defenses in the Pacific.[47]

Andersen was born in Racine on May 10, 1904, and graduated from Racine High School in 1922, a few years before it was replaced by Washington Park High School. In the school yearbook, the Kipikawi, his name was given as Anderson, with an 'o.' He was senior class secretary, and the clever line by each graduate's photo said for him, "He's fickle – but who cares?" Page 97 lists him as associate editor of the Enicar magazine.

Andersen went to the U.S. Military Academy and graduated in 1926, ranking No. 37 out of 152 in his class, according to the records in the West Point Library.[48] That put him in the upper 25 percent of the class.

A newspaper story from 1937 reported Andersen's graduation from Air Corps Advanced Flying School at Kelly Field in Texas. It said their children were ages 8 and 2, and that they would be coming home to Racine to visit the family of his wife, nee Esther Hau, plus Andersen's brother, Morris, who lived on Roe Avenue, and sister, Mrs. Fred Hanson, who lived on Clarence Avenue. Andersen was a captain at that time.

One of Andersen's next career steps was as an instructor in the Department of Chemistry and Electricity at West Point, and the first director of Stewart Field, the new air training field at West Point. Until Stewart Field was established in 1942, all cadets trained at Kelly Field.

---

[47] http://www.andersen.af.mil/ and http://usmilitary.about.com/od/airforcebase-profiles/ss/Andersen.htm

[48] www.library.usma.edu/archives/special.asp

Chapter 9
Pacific; Navy and Marine Corps

This chapter explores some Navy and Marine men who made the Ultimate Sacrifice in the Pacific and the China-Burma-India theater in World War II. Some of their names are on VFW or American Legion posts along with another name from World War II; in those cases the other man is covered in another chapter of this book.

June 1942
Navy Aviation Machinist's Mate 1st Class Bruno Gaido, Milwaukee
– executed by Japanese in Battle of Midway

While the famous Battle of Midway saw dozens of torpedo bombers, dive bombers and fighter planes attacking, planes galore being shot down or ditching in the ocean and aircraft carriers being sunk, the death of one Wisconsin man jumps right off the page for its sheer barbarity.

Navy Aviation Machinist's Mate 1st Class Bruno Gaido of Milwaukee and his pilot were executed after their dive bomber ditched in the sea and they were picked up by a Japanese destroyer. Gaido was the gunner; his pilot was Ensign Frank O'Flaherty.

Author Craig Symonds tells what happened aboard the destroyer Makigumo: "After the Japanese interrogated the two Americans, they tied weights to their ankles and dropped them over the side."[1]

The execution was June 15, which was 11 days after the battle, so they endured days of abuse before being executed.

Gaido's plane was from the aircraft carrier USS Enterprise and presumably ran out of fuel, as did many in the battle, Symonds writes. When author Tom Mueller saw the sheer brazenness of this act while reading Symonds' book, he checked the two Navy names in the database of foreign burials and

---

[1] "The Battle of Midway," by Craig L. Symonds (2011), p. 313. Also http://www.cv6.org/company/pow.htm

Bruno Gaido of Milwaukee, a Navy aviation machinist's mate first class, was executed by the Japanese after being captured in the Battle of Midway. Weights were attached to the ankles of Gaido and his pilot, and they were pushed overboard. This photo comes from http://www.findagrave.com/cgi-bin/fg.cgi? page=gr&GRid=74715857

MIAs, www.abmc.gov, to see what their home states were. It showed Bruno Peter Gaido was from Wisconsin.

Further checking, in the Navy / Marine book of Wisconsin deaths in the war, showed Gaido lived at 3067 N. 2nd St., Milwaukee, and his next of kin was his father, John Gaido.[2]

Information at Find a Grave[3] and a message board there with a posting by Clair Gaido of Milwaukee, the sailor aviator's niece, fills out the Gaido story. Contacted via her email address at the message board, Clair reported he was age 22 and that his mother was Clementa.

Clementa died Aug. 9, 1942, soon after receiving word about her son's death. Clair says this was from "a broken heart." Clementa was age 61, according to Archdiocese of Milwaukee cemetery records.

Clair says Bruno had two brothers and several sisters – including her own father, Dominic, who was the youngest; Peter, Rena, Flora and Mary. One more sister died at the age of 2 or less.

"He was handsome and was considered quite a ladies' man. I was told on a couple of occasions that I have my uncle's smile, which of course dazzled the ladies," Clair says.

"Some of the records of him that I found, indicated his fellow sailors considered him the bravest man they knew. "I will say that my uncle's short life has provided me a wonderful source of how to live life with courage."

O'Flaherty, 24, was from Nevada. He and Gaido flew in Scouting Squadron 6 (VS-6) from the Enterprise.

Their plane went down in the heart of the battle on June 4. They were fished out of the water – it is not clear how long after, although one job of the ships that accompanied aircraft carriers of either nation was to look for downed pilots.

---

[2] http://www.accessgenealogy.com/navy/wisconsin/index.htm

[3] http://www.findagrave.com/cgi-bin/fg.cgi?page=gr&GRid=74715857

One account of the battle and their ordeal says they were in a division of SBD-3 Dauntless dive bombers led by Lt. Charles R. Ware. VS-6 had just successfully attacked the Japanese carrier Kaga. Ware and his gunner soon would be lost, as were most others in VS-6. The squadron's role and the gruesome fate of O'Flaherty and Gaido is described in a stirring but rah-rah war account:[4]

On the morning of 4 June 1942, Lt. Cmdr. C. Wade McClusky led 30 Dauntless SBD dive-bombers from the carrier USS Enterprise in an attack that destroyed the Japanese fleet carriers Akagi and Kaga. After he had made his own attack, and despite the sky over the Japanese carrier fleet now swarming with Zero fighters whose angry pilots were desperate to avenge the loss of Japan's two best carriers, Lt. Charles R. Ware delayed his own departure from the burning carriers.

His purpose was to rally to him the "rookie" pilots of his own division and any other inexperienced pilots who might need his experience and combat skills to lead them to safety. Despite heavy Zero attacks, Ware was able to collect and form up five SBDs into an ad hoc division.

Keeping his SBDs close to sea level to guard their unprotected bellies from the attacking Zeroes, Ware led his pilots on a south-east course away from the Japanese fleet. ... Because of Ware's skilled management of his division under sustained attack by the Zeroes, the only significant damage suffered by the six planes of his division was to the fuel tanks of Ensign Frank W. O'Flaherty's SBD. The loss of fuel was a calamity for O'Flaherty and his radio-gunner, Bruno P. Gaido, because all of the SBDs involved in the attack on Akagi and Kaga had been a long time in the air and were already low on fuel.

Once clear of the Japanese fighter screen, Ware led his division on a north-east course where he hoped to find USS Enterprise. However, on this day misfortune was dogging Lieutenant Ware and his small band of pilots. They were sighted by a strike group of Aichi Val dive-bombers and six

4   http://navy.togetherweserved.com/usn/servlet/tws.webapp.WebApp?cmd=ShadowBoxProfile&type=Person&ID=557720

escorting Zeroes from the surviving Japanese carrier Hiryu. ... Before the Zeroes reached them, O'Flaherty's tanks ran dry and he was forced to ditch in the sea. O'Flaherty and Gaido were last seen ... inflating and then scrambling aboard their life raft ...

Sadly, O'Flaherty and Gaido were spotted and fished from the sea by the crew of the Japanese destroyer Makigumo. After interrogation, and when it was clear that the Japanese had suffered a disastrous defeat in the Battle of Midway, O'Flaherty and Gaido were murdered by the angry and vindictive Japanese. The two unfortunate American airmen were bound with ropes, tied to weighted fuel cans, and then thrown overboard to drown.

Gaido was awarded only the Purple Heart, according to his listing at www.abmc.gov But O'Flaherty, his pilot, received a posthumous Navy Cross "for extraordinary heroism. ... Participating in a devastating assault against a Japanese invasion fleet, Ensign O'Flaherty, with fortitude and resolute devotion to duty, pressed home his attacks in the face of a formidable barrage of anti-aircraft fire and fierce fighter opposition. His gallant perseverance and utter disregard for his own personal safety were important contributing factors to the success achieved by our forces ...."[5]

The USS O'Flaherty, a destroyer escort, was named for the pilot, and launched on Dec. 14, 1943. Navy ships built during the war often were named for particular heroes.

Eight months later, the Makigumo hit a mine off of Guadalcanal in February 1943, although there were only three deaths and two missing. The rest of the crew, more than 200, were evacuated to another ship, and the Japanese scuttled the Makigumo with a torpedo.[6]

---

[5]   http://militarytimes.com/citations-medals-awards/recipient.php?recipientid=21433

[6] http://www.combinedfleet.com/makigu_t.htm

June 1942
Navy Electrician's Mate 3rd Class John W. Mehltretter, Dousman
– Torpedo plane crew in Battle of Midway

The story of the pivotal Battle of Midway had been made into multiple movies and books because it marked a turning point of World War II, seven months after Pearl Harbor.

One small detail of the battle is that five of the six pilots who flew into the battle from an airport on Midway island were killed, as were most of their crewmen – including Navy Electrician's Mate 3rd Class John W. Mehltretter Jr. of Dousman. Other torpedo planes flew into the battle from the carriers USS Hornet, Enterprise and Yorktown, and also were nearly wiped out.

Mehltretter was killed on June 4, 1942, in the heart of the battle. He was an electrician's mate third class and was the radioman / torpedo aimer / on the three-man plane.

Mehltretter, 22, received a Distinguished Flying Cross and is on the Tablets of the Missing at the Honolulu Memorial in Hawaii, along with his pilot and the third crewman. Their date of loss is listed as one year and one day later, according to Navy tradition. The Distinguished Flying Cross is given for "extraordinary heroism."

The pilot was Ensign Victor Alan Lewis of Massachusetts, who received the Navy Cross, which is one category below the Medal of Honor. The turret gunner was Aviation Metalsmith 3rd Class Nelson Leo Carr of Michigan.

The Wisconsin book of Navy and Marine deaths lists Mehltretter's next of kin as his father, John Mehltretter, of Dousman.[7]

The American Legion Post 405 in Dousman is named the Jones-Mehltretter-Ehrlich-Wagie Post, named for the Midway man plus men lost, in order, In World War I, Korea and Vietnam. The post reports that Mehltretter went by the name of Bill while growing up, because John Sr. was the village barber and well-known to all.

---

[7] http://www.accessgenealogy.com/navy/wisconsin/index.htm

Mehltretter's plane and five others flew out of Naval Air Station Midway because their aircraft were a new model, the Grumman TBF Avenger, and had not yet been landed on their aircraft carrier, the USS Hornet. The planes had arrived on Midway only three days earlier. Other pilots in the battle used Devastators, an older model.

Here is what Mehltretter's plane went through, according to the pilot's medal citation: "In the first attack against an enemy carrier of the Japanese invasion fleet, Ensign Lewis pressed home his attack in the face of withering fire from Japanese fighters and anti-aircraft forces. Because of events attendant upon the Battle of Midway, there can be no doubt that he gallantly gave up his life in the service of his country. His courage and utter disregard for his own personal safety were in keeping with the highest traditions of the United States Naval Service. He gallantly gave his life for his country."[8]

The medal website where Lewis' citation is posted is comprehensive, but does not have every such medal ever awarded – and has nothing for Mehltretter. The citation for him could not be found via Google, either, although he is listed as a crewman in many articles.

Lewis and the other five pilots had flown their new aircraft into Midway three days before the battle began. "All six pilots earned the Navy Cross, in addition to two enlisted members of their crews. Five of the six pilots received their awards posthumously after being listed as Missing in Action. The only survivor, Ensign Albert Earnest, earned two Navy Crosses at Midway, bringing the squadron (of six planes) total to nine awards (seven posthumously),"[9] one summary says.

Earnest, who was 25, and one of his crew, Radioman 3rd Class Harry Ferrier, wrote a magazine article in 1996 about their role, entitled "Avengers at Midway."[10]

... On the morning of 4 June at about 0600, a Marine officer rode up in a jeep, climbed up on (Lt. Langdon) Fieberling's wing and told him something ... Another Marine came over to my aircraft and shouted up to me, "Enemy forces at

---

[8] http://militarytimes.com/citations-medals-awards/recipient.php?recipientid=20028

[9] http://militarytimes.com/citations-medals-awards/recipient.php?recipientid=19836. The TBF is described at http://www.militaryfactory.com/aircraft/detail.asp?aircraft_id=300

[10] http://www.midway42.org/aa-reports/tbf-detach.pdf

320 degrees, 150 miles." We immediately started our engines and taxied out. ... Shortly after we joined up, (Seaman 1st Class Jay) Manning, my turret gunner, told me he could see firing from Midway. Just then, a Japanese aircraft made a pass at us but did not fire.

Suddenly, however, I saw a large force ahead of us, with at least two carriers. Almost instantaneously, Manning called that we were being attacked by enemy fighters. It quickly became obvious as they were all around us, so many that they seemed to be getting in each other's way. Manning fired the turret gun a number of times, but soon it fell silent.

Ferrier looked up to see why, and saw Manning hanging limp in the safety harness, obviously dead. As Ferrier said later, "Quite suddenly, I was a scared, mature old man at the age of 18."

As soon as we were attacked, we all opened our bomb bay doors, dove down to about 200 feet and headed for the nearest carrier. As scared as I was, I couldn't help but be amazed at the maneuverability of the Zeroes as they swarmed around us. Bullets were clanging off my armor plate and cannon shells began hitting the wings. Something flew through the canopy and hit me in the neck. There was blood everywhere; I don't remember it hurting.

We were still quite a way from the carrier when I lost elevator control, and the plane started gently down. It seemed obvious that I was going into the water, but I wanted to drop that torpedo. There was a Japanese destroyer or light cruiser to port, so I kicked the airplane around with rudder and ailerons and dropped the torpedo at it.

Somehow, Earnest's plane remained aloft. He had no compass, the hydraulic system was shot out, the bomb bay doors would not close, he could not lower his flaps and only one wheel could be put into position when landing. But he made it back to Midway. Manning was dead and Ferrier wounded.

Of the 51 torpedo planes that attacked the Japanese that day – 41 TBDs, six TBFs (Earnest's new kind of plane and Mehltretter's too) and four B-26s (bombers modified to drop torpedoes) – only four TBDs returned to their carrier, Enterprise, and two B-26s and one TBF returned to Midway. There were 26 surviving pilots and crewmen of the 120 who flew into battle, Earnest said.[11]

But the torpedo planes took up the attention of Japanese fighters, and ate up their fuel, too, and so American dive bombers were able to pounce. In a matter of minutes, three Japanese carriers were on fire and sinking, with another lost later the same day.[12]

In the end, the United States lost one carrier, the Yorktown, a destroyer and more than 100 planes. "But this was a small price to pay," historian C.L. Sulzberger concluded. "The Japanese Navy had forced a showdown with superior strength, and it was decisively beaten. Instead of threatening Hawaii and the West Coast, Japan suddenly found itself upon the defensive for the first time."[13]

Later in the war, future President George Herbert Walker Bush also was a torpedo bomber pilot on an aircraft carrier, the USS San Jacinto, and his TBM Avenger was shot down Sept. 2, 1944, as he was trying to bomb a radar station on the island of Chichi Jima. Both his crewmen were lost, and Bush was rescued by a submarine. He received the Distinguished Flying Cross, the same medal that Mehltretter received.

The other men honored on the name of the Legion post in Dousman are: Army Pvt. Ellis Jones of World War I, who died of pneumonia on Oct. 15, 1918; Korean War Sgt. Leland Ernest Ehrlich, 22, a Marine who is MIA since Dec. 7, 1950 (he received the Navy Cross); and Army Sgt. Dennis Richard Wagie, 22, who was killed in Vietnam on May 2, 1969. Wagie was

---

[11] http://www.midway42.org/aa-reports/tbf-detach.pdf

[12] "The Battle of Midway," by Craig L. Symonds (2011). This book is a detailed overview of the entire battle plus the unit-by-unit, moment-by-moment segments plus the strategic overview before, during and after.

[13] "The American Heritage Picture History of World War II," by C.L. Sulzberger (1966), p. 185. Also see http://www.secondworldwarhistory.com/battle-of-midway.asp. A comprehensive list of air crews at Midway is at http://www.centuryinter.net/midway/appendix/appendixfour_midway_airgoups.html Many photos are at http://www.history.navy.mil/photos/events/wwii-pac/midway/midway.htm All crewmen assigned to the Hornet, including Mehltretter, are honored at http://www.maritimequest.com/warship_directory/us_navy_pages/aircraft_carriers/hornet_cv_8/uss_hornet_cv8_roll_of_honor.htm

a field artillery repairman and was killed in what was classified a non-hostile death, ground casualty.[14]

Jimmy Doolittle's dramatic raid on Tokyo with B-25 Mitchell bombers had flown off the deck of the Hornet (Mehltretter's ship) on April 16, 1942, less than two months before Midway.

Seaman 2nd Class Charles Fidler of Milwaukee was killed when his Navy oiler was sunk six weeks after the attack on Pearl Harbor. The USS Neches was on its way to refuel a carrier task force, but was torpedoed only hours after leaving Oahu.

January 1942
Navy Seaman 2nd Class Charles Fidler, Milwaukee
– Ship sunk near Pearl Harbor

Six weeks after the attack at Pearl Harbor, the seas around Hawaii were treacherous for any ship, particularly an unescorted one.

The USS Neches, a Navy oiler, was less than 12 hours into its mission out of the heavily damaged base when a Japanese submarine torpedoed it on Jan. 23, 1942. The Neches was unescorted at the time, but was going

---

[14] http://www.accessgenealogy.com/scripts/data/database.cgi?file=Data&report=SingleArticle&ArticleID=0009771 for Jones; www.abmc.gov for Ehrlich; and http://www.virtualwall.org/dw/WagieDR01a.htm for Wagie.

to rendezvous with a destroyer and then proceed to provide refueling to the task force containing the aircraft carrier USS Lexington, which was then headed for an attack on Rabaul, New Britain.

The Neches sank little more than an hour later, and the death toll was 57, including Seaman 2nd Class Charles Fidler of Milwaukee. Fidler is on the MIA wall at the Honolulu Memorial in Hawaii, and his sacrifice is honored by VFW Post 9469, which has his name on it. The post now meets in the suburb of St. Francis, but was located on South Howell Avenue in Milwaukee for decades.

Charles Eugene Fidler's next of kin was his father, Frank Fidler, 5349 S. 9th St., Milwaukee, just north of Grange Avenue on what is now the western edge of the airport. Post Commander Phillip Shaw says that as a boy, Fidler was well-known in his neighborhood for riding around on bikes with his three best friends, all of whom went to war. Fidler was the only one who did not make it home.

The Neches' hull number was AO-5 and it was carrying 18 officers and 218 enlisted, the latter including 65 sailors on board for transport elsewhere. It was carrying 45,000 barrels of fuel oil, 8,700 barrels of diesel fuel and 100,000 gallons of gasoline.[15]

At 1540 local time on 22 January 1942, the tanker pulled out from Pearl Harbor. At 0310 the next morning, the Japanese submarine I-172 hit it with three torpedoes, the first of which was a dud. This was about 120 nautical miles west of Pearl Harbor.

R.D. White was a crewman on the Neches along with Fidler, and in 1997 wrote an account of the sinking.[16]

With as much of a load as she could carry, (the Neches) left Pearl alone about 5 in the afternoon heading west to refuel another task force. We were to meet an escort the next morning at sea. (About 3 a.m.), we had a torpedo hit just

---

[15] http://www.navsource.org/archives/09/19/19005h.htm The Navy and its followers have posted several photos of the Neches, most from the 1920s, at http://www.navsource.org/archives/09/19/19005.htm A discussion of Navy oilers in World War II can be found at http://www.ibiblio.org/hyperwar/USN/ships/ships-ao.html

[16] http://canisteo.freeservers.com/neches.htm

about midship, but it was a dud that did not explode. Next a torpedo on the starboard side hit on the stern, killing almost all of the crew aft and destroying our engine room.

At that time everyone knew that we were under attack by a Japanese submarine. I fell out of my bunk, grabbed my clothes under my arm, slid my shoes on and headed topside. On the Neches under the fo'c'sle (forecastle, immediately aft of the bow) was our carpenter shop where our life jackets were stored. One of the guys remembered that he had several hundred dollars in his locker that he had won at poker so he went below to get it. He never came back.

I was dressing and just finished tying the last belly band of the life jacket when the next torpedo hit just below us on the port side. The concussion was so strong that it knocked a lot of us off our feet and made us disoriented for a short time. I reported to my battle station on the bridge and was told to go abaft to the boat deck and help free all the lifeboats. Since we had no power for our wrenches, all we could do was to release all turnbuckles on the motor launches and hope that they would float clear after the ship sunk.

We did put four donut rafts over the side. While working with the lifeboats the Japanese sub surfaced and started firing at us with their deck gun. It was a real dark night; not even the moon was shining. All three of the shots the sub made you could hear the shells screaming as they went overhead.

The Neches had one 5-inch (gun) and one 3-inch on the port side that started firing as rapidly as they could, not knowing if we were doing any good or not, but just firing in the general direction of the sub. After three shots from the sub, we did not hear anything else.

The Neches was listing to the starboard and going down by the bow. The guns kept firing until they could not depress enough, then stopped firing. Most of the crew came abaft to where the lifeboats were and when the word was given to abandon ship they jumped in and swam for the life rafts. I was just about one of the last to leave the ship and when I did, all I had to do was just step off into the water (because the listing to that side was so great).

We were real lucky that the first torpedo was a dud, because there never was an oil leak or anything to cause a fire. If that first torpedo had exploded, we all would still be going up.

The Neches went down rather quickly. From the beginning to the end was just about an hour or less. Our luck still holding, we did recover all of our lifeboats that had floated after the ship sank. By a little after daylight, we were all in the lifeboats and out of the water. The captain (Cmdr. William Bartlett Fletcher Jr.) spoke to all of us and calmed us down and told us that the radio operator got off an SOS with our location and we should hear or see something before long. We were all worried that the Jap sub might reappear at any time, but it never did. A muster list was read to check who was present. During that time it was as quiet as a mouse. ...

After an hour or so a PBY sea plane came into sight. They saw us and dropped a smoke bomb and landed and loaded three injured men into the plane. After leaving us all of their cigarettes, candy bars and taking some pictures of us they took off for Pearl. About noon a destroyer (White does not give the name) came over the horizon and spotted us with no trouble. It turned out that they were the one that was going to be our escort to the task force we were going to refuel.

White's account is posted on a private website devoted to Navy oilers.[17] The Neches had a cargo capacity of 7,843 tons of fuel. It was built in 1919 at the Boston Navy Yard in Massachusetts and was launched on June 2, 1920.

Fletcher had been the captain of the oiler since March 10, 1941. He went on to other duties in which was awarded four medals: the Navy Distinguished Service Medal (for a range of efforts in the assaults on Bougainville and Guam), the SIlver Star (for actions in August 1942 off of Guadalcanal and in October in the Elice Islands), Bronze Star (in April 1943 in the

---

[17] http://canisteo.freeservers.com/ The host of the site is David Merrill, who served on the oiler USS Caniesto during the Cuban missile crisis.

Solomons) and Legion of Merit (for actions between July 1943 and August 1944).

The Japanese sub that sank the Neches was sunk 10 months later in fighting off of Guadalcanal.[18] On Nov. 3, 1942, "At 0510 (Zulu), the I-172 sends a short 'enemy vessels sighted' report. This is the last signal received from the I-172." On Nov. 27, it was reported as "presumed lost with all 91 hands off Guadalcanal. The cause of her loss remains unknown."

When the Japanese attacked Pearl Harbor, the Neches had been en route from San Diego with fuel, and arrived Dec. 10, 1941. "We went right past battleship row and everything was still smoking, the whole harbor was covered with oil," White said.

Before its fateful mission, the Neches had made one trip out of Pearl and refueled a task force. "That was the first and only time I ever saw a tanker refuel ships at sea," White said. "We refueled the Saratoga, an aircraft carrier, and some of her escort vessels. We could have two destroyers along side at the same time, one on the port and one on the starboard. I do remember that the Saratoga's flight deck did come down and strike the port bridge wing of the Neches because of rough seas, but it did not do much damage. The reason I remember is, that is where I stood lookout watches."

The Neches was the first Navy oiler lost during World War II, and its name lived on — as did the names of many Navy ships that were sunk — when another oiler, the USS Neches (AO-47), was commissioned on Sept. 16, 1942.

The other oilers that were sunk during World War II were the USS Pecos, by Japanese planes off of Java on March 1, 1942; USS Neosho, in the battle of Coral Sea in March 1942, USS Kanawha, hit by Japanese planes off of Guadalcanal in April 1943; and USS Mississinewa, torpedoed by a Japanese submarine at Ulithi in November 1944.[19]

---

[18] http://www.combinedfleet.com/I-172.htm

[19] http://canisteo.freeservers.com/missinewa.htm

March 1945
Marine Cpl. Sylvester Dietzler, Medford
– near the flag-raisers on Iwo Jima

Sylvester Leo Dietzler left Medford in 1943 to fight as a Marine, and two years later he was part of the invasion of Iwo Jima, where members of his very own battalion raised the two historic flags over Mount Suribachi on Feb. 23, 1945.

Suribachi is one of the most storied sites in Marine Corps history, and the second flag-raising event there is even more storied, because of the famous photograph. Dietzler's 28th Marine Regiment was battered on the beach the day of the Feb. 19 invasion and at such sites as Nishi Ridge on March 3 and Kitano Point in the closing days of the fighting.

Dietzler was in Company D, 2nd Battalion of the 28th Regiment, 5th Marine Division. The flag-raisers were in E Company of the same battalion.

The 21-year-old Marine corporal was killed on March 11, D-plus 20 in invasion lingo. At that time, Dietzler's regiment was closing in on Gen. Tadamichi Kuribayashi's final cave stronghold near Kitano Point at the cliffs at the northern edge of the island. Iwo Jima finally was declared "officially secured" on March 17, although substantial fighting continued several more days, with 1,724 more American dead and wounded.[20] The final message from Kuribayashi to his troops came March 21 (he likely committed suicide on March 25).

The epic invasion of the Sulfur Island was carried out by the 3rd, 4th and 5th Marine Divisions, along with hundreds of Navy ships and Army units. By the end, a total of 6,821 were dead.[21]

In Dietzler's 5th Division, the units were the 26th, 27th and 28th Regiments, plus the 13th Regiment Artillery. His regimental commander was Col. Harry Liversedge, and the 2nd Battalion leader was Lt. Col. Chandler

---

[20] "Iwo Jima: Legacy of Valor," by Bill Ross (1985), p. 329-330.

[21] "Iwo Jima: Legacy of Valor," plus http://www.eyewitnesstohistory.com/iwoflag.htm and http://marines.togetherweserved.com/usmc/servlet/tws.webapp.WebApp ?cmd= ShadowBoxProfile&type=Person&ID=163106

Johnson,[22] who had given his men the first flag to raise, but quickly ordered another group to find another flag because the first was going to be needed for historical purposes by the brass. The second flag was larger, and Associated Press photographer Joe Rosenthal took his famous shot when it was hoisted.

The six raisers of the second flag included Pharmacist's Mate 2nd Class John Bradley of Appleton and later Antigo, Wis. Bradley was wounded in both legs on March 11, the same day that Dietzler was killed, and evacuated from Iwo; Bradley would earn the Navy Cross for his actions that day under fire but his family did not know that until after he died in Antigo in 1994 at the age of 70, according to his son's book.[23]

Two leathernecks in Dietzler's 2nd Battalion earned the Medal of Honor posthumously on Iwo: Pvt. George Phillips (no company is given in the citation, but it would be D, E or F) on March 14, three days after Dietzler was killed, and Pfc. Donald J. Ruhl of Dietzler's E Company for actions between Feb. 19 and 21. Three men in other battalions of the the 28th Regiment also received the medal. And in one single day, March 3, in the fighting at Nishi Ridge, five Marines of the 5th Division earned the medal.

All in all, 2,416 men from the division were killed in action on Iwo Jima. A total of 6,860 were wounded.[24]

Before the ships came to take them away from Iwo on March 27, Marines went to the 5th Division cemetery, where Dietzler was newly buried, to attend memorial services. Jewish chaplain Lt. Roland B. Gittelsohn was one of the speakers, and eloquently painted in Gettysburg Address style why they fought:[25]

This is the grimmest, and surely the holiest, task we have faced since D-day (Feb. 19). Here before us lie the bodies of comrades and friends. Men who until yesterday or last week laughed with us, joked with us, trained with us. Men who were on the same ships with us, and went over the side with us as we

---

[22] Johnson would be killed by a mortar on March 3, eight days before Dietzler was killed.

[23] "Flags of Our Fathers," by James Bradley, son of the flag-raiser (2000), p. 240-241.

[24] http://www.ww2gyrene.org/spotlight5_awards.htm

[25] http://www.geocities.com/rbackstr2000/dead/dead.htm

prepared to hit the beaches of this island. Men who fought with us and feared with us.

Somewhere in this plot of ground there may lie the man who could have discovered the cure for cancer. Under one of these Christian crosses, or beneath a Jewish Star of David, there may rest now a man who was destined to be a great prophet to find the way, perhaps, for all to live in plenty, with poverty and hardship for none. Now they lie silently in this sacred soil, and we gather to consecrate this earth to their memory.

... Here lie officers and men, Negroes and whites, rich and poor together. Here no man prefers another because of his faith or despises him because of his color. Here there are no quotas of how many men from each group are admitted or allowed. Among these men there is no discrimination, no prejudices, no hatred. Theirs is the highest and purest democracy.

... This war has been fought by the common man; its fruits of peace must be enjoyed by the common man. We promise, by all that is sacred and holy, that your sons, the sons of miners and millers, the sons of farmers and workers, will inherit from your death the right to a living that is decent and secure.

VFW Post 5729 in Medford is the Klossner-Dietzler Post. The post's history says Dietzler also had been on Bougainville, which the Marines invaded on Nov. 1, 1943, and had been part of the 1st Marine Parachute Regiment. Such men had participated in beach raids as amphibious troops, and the parachutist battalion was disbanded in February 1944 because of many factors; no Marine parachuted into combat.[26]

Dietzler's parents were Robert and Catherine Dietzler; he was born in Medford on Dec. 16, 1923, and entered the Marines via Milwaukee on Feb. 3, 1943. He is buried in the Fort Snelling National Cemetery in Minneapolis, Minn., being interred there in July 1948.[27]

---

[26] http://www.ww2gyrene.org/spotlight5_5thmardiv.htm

[27] http://www.accessgenealogy.com/navy/wisconsin/d.htm and http://files.usgw archives.net/mn/hennepin/cemeteries/fortsnelling/ftsneldf.tx

November 1942
Navy Ensign Edwin Lachmund, Sauk City
– Iron Bottom Sound at Guadalcanal

The battle of Guadalcanal is well-known, but much of that notoriety comes from the grueling fighting waged by the Marines on land. While the travails of the Marines and the Cactus Air Force deserve to be legendary, so does the fact that so many American, Australian and Japanese ships were lost in four months of sea battles between Guadalcanal and Savo Island that the area became known as Iron Bottom Sound.

Both navies were striving to supply and rearm their troops on the island and bring in new forces. There were seven separate, large sea battles, with such names as the Battle of Savo Island and the Battle of Cape Esperance. The Japanese effort was dubbed the Tokyo Express; their route was dubbed the Slot.

Ensign Edwin Lachmund, 22, of Sauk City, was one of those killed when the destroyer USS Walke was torpedoed and sunk by a Japanese submarine and fire from ships on Nov. 15, 1942. This was named the Second Naval Battle of Guadalcanal; the first had come two nights earlier.

A total of 82 sailors, more than one-third of the total crew, were killed on the Walke, including its skipper, Cmdr. Thomas Fraser.

Lachmund's name is on the Lachmund-Cramer VFW Post 7694 in Prairie du Sac and on the Tablets of the Missing at the Manila American Cemetery in the Philippines. Lachmund's death date at www.abmc.gov, is Nov. 16, 1943, the traditional one year and one day after a Navy man disappears.

He was the son of Edwin and Lillian Lachmund, 717 Water St., Sauk City, and graduated in 1937 from Sauk City High School, according to John Gillespie of the post. The community's Village Hall is across the street from the Lachmund home. The home is a historic one in Sauk, because it was built in 1861 by Charles Halasz, founder of what became the Lachmund Lumber company. Lachmund family members lived in the house until it was sold in 1944, two years after Edwin died.[28]

---

[28] http://www.saukcity.net/vertical/sites/%7B4E3188F1-DD40-422F-A8CE-A991 AFA87553%7D/uploads/Walkers_and_Wheels_Guide.pdf

The Walke had served as one of the screens for the aircraft carrier USS Yorktown in attacks such as those at Makin and other atolls in late January 1942 and at Tulagi in May. She returned to San Francisco in August for refurbishing.

The Marines invaded Guadalcanal on Aug. 7, and the series of naval battles that made Iron Bottom Sound began Aug. 9. The naval battles were at night as the Japanese came down the Slot, and were marked by enormous bursts of star flares that turned things into noon, even more enormous explosions of ships, ships appearing out of nowhere, confusion about whose ship was whose, miscommunication and more. All while the imperiled Marines wondered, "Where is the Navy?"

After returning from San Francisco, the Walke joined three other destroyers in the carrier group of the USS Enterprise to the north. But in November they were ordered to accompany two battleships to the Guadalcanal zone because, researcher James D. Hornfischer notes, they were the four destroyers "that happened to have the most fuel."[29] The group was named Task Force 64, under Rear Adm. Willis Lee, and the battleships' power was needed at Guadalcanal in the wake of such severe Navy losses.

The Walke arrived one day before being sunk. Two of the other destroyers met the same fate; the fourth would be damaged.

On the fateful night, the Walke was leading the group of destroyers, which were followed by the battleships USS Washington and South Dakota. This was the scene:

> **Captain Fraser was working to set up a torpedo solution (preparation to fire at a Japanese destroyer) at a large target to starboard when the enemy fish arrived. One struck the Walke forward of the bridge, lifting the forward half of the ship "bodily out of the water," the action report read.**
>
> **As the destroyer crashed back into the sea without a bow forward of the bridge superstructure, one of the ship's magazines detonated and its explosion ruptured forward fuel oil tanks and tore holes in the superstructure decks. A few seconds later, several medium-caliber warheads (fired by surface ships)**

[29] "Neptune's Inferno: The U.S. Navy at Guadalcanal," by James D. Hornfischer (2001). This book has excellent research and battle descriptions. p. 337.

slammed into the ship, blowing away a swath of her forecastle and forward superstructure decking. ... The severed bow floated as the stern sank.[30]

Also lost that night were the destroyers Preston and Benham; the battleship South Dakota was damaged along with the fourth destroyer, the Gwin. The American death toll was 242. The Japanese lost a battleship and destroyer, and one of their heavy cruisers was damaged.[31] This was all two days after the Nov. 13 First Naval Battle of Guadalcanal, which had killed 1,439 Americans, the worst single day of the entire series of battles.

In that carnage, the Japanese torpedoed and crippled the light cruiser USS Juneau, and hours later it was torpedoed again, exploded and sank, killing nearly 700. Five of its crewmen were the Sullivan brothers of Waterloo, Iowa.

All in all, the Navy lost 5,041 men at Guadalcanal and the Marines and Army a total of 1,592.[32]

June 1944
Navy Motor Machinist's Mate 2nd Class Arnold Cook, Laona
– lost on submarine

Arnold Jerome Cook and other submariners who were lost in World War II are on "eternal patrol."

Cook and 83 other men were aboard the USS Herring when it was lost on June 1, 1944, in the Kuril Islands east of Russia and north of Japan. The sub was sunk by Japanese shore batteries after it had sunk two merchant ships moments earlier but then apparently ran aground, making it a sitting duck, essentially. The loss was the only time a sub had been sunk by shore batteries in the war, according to an account that will be quoted here.

---

[30] "Neptune's Inferno: The U.S. Navy at Guadalcanal," p. 357. More information about the battle is http://www.history.navy.mil/photos/events/wwii-pac/guadlcnl/guadlcnl.htm and http://destroyerhistory.org/goldplater/usswalke/

[31] "Neptune's Inferno: The U.S. Navy at Guadalcanal," p. 436.

[32] "Neptune's Inferno: The U.S. Navy at Guadalcanal," p. 437.

Cook was born July 15, 1922, so he was age 21, according to the VFW Post 6823 of Laona in Forest County, the Cook-Elffors Post.

Cook, a motor machinist's mate second class, and his crewmates[33] are on the Tablets of the Missing at the Honolulu Memorial in Hawaii. The death date for Cook by the American Battle Monuments Commission[34], which runs the memorial, is given as Jan. 17, 1946; the Navy usually lists such a date as one year after the sinking of a vessel, but this evidently was some sort of closing of the records a few months after Victory in Japan Day when no POWs from the sub were found.

The Defense Prisoner of War / Missing Personnel Office gives his date of loss as July 5, 1944, which is when the sub failed to arrive back at Midway as planned.[35]

Cook was the son of Mr. and Mrs. Robert James Cook of Route 1, Laona, according to the book of Wisconsin losses in the Navy and Marine Corps in the war.[36]

The Herring was built at Portsmouth Naval Shipyard in Maine and began World War II in the Atlantic, running four war patrols and then leaving its base in Scotland to go to Connecticut for refurbishing. It then was sent to Pearl Harbor, where it left for its next war patrol on Nov. 15, 1943.

Material about how many patrols Cook was on is not readily available. There are a few new sailors on any patrol of a submarine.

Here is the story of the Herring's last mission:[37]

On May 16, 1944, the Herring, captained by Lt. Cmdr. David Zabriskie Jr., departed Pearl Harbor on her eighth and final war patrol. On May 21, she topped off her fuel at Midway Island, and then headed for her assigned patrol area in the Kurile (another spelling for Kuril) Islands. On May 31, she kept a rendezvous with the (submarine) USS Barb to coordi-

---

[33] http://www.oneternalpatrol.com/uss-herring-233.htm

[34] www.abmc.gov

[35] http://www.dtic.mil/dpmo/wwii/reports/nav_m_c.htm

[36] http://www.accessgenealogy.com/navy/wisconsin/index.htm

[37] http://www.subsowespac.org/world_war_ii_submarines/uss_herring_ss_233.
shtml

nate patrol strategy. This would prove to be the last contact anyone would have with the Herring.

A few hours after parting ways, the Barb detected and began approaching an enemy convoy. Then she heard a distant depth-charge barrage and assumed the Herring had attacked the same convoy and was being counterattacked. Later, the Barb fished an enemy sailor out of the water who said the Herring had sunk an escort vessel (the frigate Ishigaki) from the convoy the Barb was tracking. The Barb eventually tracked, torpedoed, and sank two of the fleeing vessels .... The Herring had destroyed the third merchant, the freighter Hokuyo Maru.

The Herring failed to acknowledge receipt of orders dispatched to the Barb and her by ComSubPac (submarine command center) on June 4, 1944, directing them to stay clear of a restricted area during the Marianas Campaign. ComSubPac did not suspect the Herring had been lost until late in June. ... it was expected she would arrive at Midway by July 3 or 4, 1944. When she had not been heard from by July 13, 1944, the Herring was listed as presumed lost. ...

Japanese reports obtained after the war revealed that the Herring was sunk on June 1, 1944, two kilometers south of Point Tagan in the Kuriles, after sinking two merchant ships at anchor close to shore at Matsuwa To with torpedoes at 0742 hours.

The report stated the surfaced submarine appeared to have been damaged from running aground off Cape Tagan. In a counterattack made at 0756 hours, shore batteries scored two direct hits on the Herring's conning tower, and the gallant submarine went down with all hands. The Japanese report stated the sinking brought bubbles and foam to the surface; later a 15-mile-long heavy oil slick covered the surface. The Herring was the only U.S. submarine to be sunk by a shore battery during the war.

Chapter 10
2 who fell in Korea

This is the story of two Wisconsin men who made the Ultimate Sacrifice in Korea in November 1950 while battling waves of Chinese forces that were surging into the war. One soldier received the Medal of Honor; the other was MIA and his remains were not identified until nearly 62 years later.

The first soldier was Army Cpl. Mitchell Red Cloud Jr. of Merrillan in Jackson County, a member of the Ho-Chunk tribe.

Red Cloud, 26, was a member of Company E in the 19th Regiment of the 24th Infantry Division. During World War II, he was a Marine who fought on Guadalcanal and was wounded on Okinawa. He was discharged and then enlisted in the Army three years later, and was killed in Korea on Nov. 5, 1950, when he sacrificed himself to protect his unit from being overrun. Because of his Medal of Honor actions, Red Cloud is a major figure in Ho-Chunk tribal history and teachings, right alongside the legendary chiefs that were his ancestors on his grandmother's side.

The second soldier was Army Pfc. Arthur W. Hopfensperger, 18, of Appleton. He was in Company B of the 32nd Regiment, 7th Infantry Division, and was killed on Nov. 28, three weeks after Red Cloud.

Hopfensperger died in the chaos at the frozen Chosin Reservoir after China sent in hundreds of thousands of troops and dramatically changed the conflict from imminent United Nations victory into ignominious retreat. The two colonels who led Hopfensperger's large task force were killed. The three worst days of deaths for Wisconsin in the entire 1950-'53 war occurred in a single week, with Hopfensperger being one of 14 killed on Nov. 28.[1]

Hopfensperger was MIA and buried in a mass grave, which was all that troops could do during the massive turnabout amid the droves of Chinese

---

[1] "Heart of the Century: 1949 to 1951," by Tom Mueller (2010), p. 113-117. The worst day was 16 Wisconsin deaths on Dec. 2; Nov. 28 and 30 each had 14. Hopfensperger is listed on page 115 of the book. The Milwaukee Journal Sentinel's Meg Jones reported on Mueller's findings in a 60-year anniversary story at http://www.jsonline.com/news/wisconsin/111172614.html and interviewed some survivors of the Chosin Reservoir action plus other Korean War veterans.

Army Cpl. Mitchell Red Cloud Jr. (left) of Merrillan received the Medal of Honor after being killed in November 1950 in Korea, and Army Pfc. Arthur Hopfensperger of Appleton was killed a few weeks later. Both died battling waves of Chinese forces.

and severe cold. Remains recovered between 2002 and 2005 were identified as Hopfensperger's in October 2012 by the Defense Prisoner of War / Missing Personnel Office.[2] His remains were reburied in Appleton on Oct. 8, 2012.

While the Chinese were pouring into the war when Hopfensperger was lost, American forces had begun to encounter groups of them in late October 1950, a week or two before Red Cloud's death. Intelligence reports were sometimes wrong and sometimes right; assessment by Army brass usually was wrong and Gen. Douglas MacArthur and others were cockily talking about taking the war all the way to the Chinese border. The situation turned into an utter disaster for the United States.

The Medal of Honor citation[3] tells of Red Cloud's

conspicuous gallantry and intrepidity above and beyond the call of duty in action … against enemy aggressor forces at Chonghyon, Korea, on 5 November 1950.

From his position on the point of a ridge immediately in front of the company command post, Cpl. Red Cloud was the first to detect the approach of the Chinese Communist forces and (to) give the alarm as the enemy charged from a brush-covered area less than 100 feet from him.

---

2 http://www.dtic.mil/dpmo/news/news_releases/2012/release_hopfensperger.pdf The release identifies his home as "Outagamie," referring to his home county. Announcements are on the office's home page of http://www.dtic.mil/dpmo/ with a very-easy-to-use list for past years.

3 http://militarytimes.com/citations-medals-awards/recipient.php?recipientid=2411 Chonghyon is roughly halfway between the North Korean capital of Pyongyang and the China border, as can be seen at http://www.newstrackindia.com/information/locations /Korea-(North)/1242621-city-chonghyon.htm

Springing up, he delivered devastating point-blank automatic rifle fire into the advancing enemy. His accurate and intense fire checked this assault and gained time for the company to consolidate its defense. With utter fearlessness he maintained his firing position until severely wounded by enemy fire. Refusing assistance, he pulled himself to his feet and, wrapping his arm around a tree, continued his deadly fire again, until he was fatally wounded.

This heroic act stopped the enemy from overrunning his company's position and gained time for reorganization and evacuation of the wounded. Cpl. Red Cloud's dauntless courage and gallant self-sacrifice reflects the highest credit upon himself and upholds the esteemed traditions of the U.S. Army.

Red Cloud was the son of Mitchell Red Cloud Sr. and his wife, Nellie. She had ancestors who were leaders of the tribe over the decades and longer, all named Chief Winneshiek.

The soldier had one child: Annita, who was born Nov. 25, 1944, in Indiana to a white mother who already had four other children and was working three jobs in order to make ends meet. She says a foster family in Bloomington, Ind., raised her from the age of one week to age 12, then (when her foster mother was diagnosed with tuberculosis), then she was placed with another foster family for a year.

In all of her youth, Annita was raised with the name Wanneta Penrose. This was an era in which white society hid a person's non-white heritage; starting in the 1970s society gradually became more enlightened and began to recognize and honor native American cultures, especially when tribes stepped up for their own cultures. "I just knew I was native and my father was killed in the military," Annita says. She was three weeks short of her 6th birthday when Red Cloud was killed.

At some point, she was allowed to use her real first name, Annita. From age 13 on, she lived at the Indiana Soldiers' and Sailors' Children's Home in Knightstown, which was for destitute children. The home, which had all her records, informed her that real surname was Red Cloud, and that became the name it used for her. She says a social worker informed her that there was a Camp Red Cloud in South Korea, named for her father.

Her birth mother had five more children after Annita.

Twice a year, a generous family picked her up from the state home to take her on trips and vacations; a way of helping its residents while not bringing them into their homes on a permanent basis, which would be a giant commitment. When she was age 17, after four years living at the home, this family took her to meet her Red Cloud relatives in Chicago, who then took her on to Wisconsin to meet Chief John Winneshiek in Wisconsin Rapids. He took her to her grandmother, the soldier's mother. John was some sort of relative in the extended family but not an uncle, Annita says.

Her grandmother was Nellie Winneshiek – "What a remarkable lady," Annita says, "living out there in a little shack in the woods near Hatfield, raising two grandchildren by herself, living off the land. She had lost a leg as a child." She spoke only Winnebago and Annita knew nothing about the language, but learned some by listening closely to the translations.

"She always knew about me. I had never been to WIsconsin before. I would say it was a dream come true. I did want to meet my family."

Her grandmother had hidden the Medal of Honor, fearing that someone would steal it along with any other valuables. She brought it out and "she offered it to me. I said no. It was her connection to her son."

After Nellie died, the medal and others that Red Cloud earned were displayed at the American Legion hall on Ho-Chunk land – the tribe was called Winnebago in that day – and Annita now has donated them to the Wisconsin Veterans Museum in Madison for all to enjoy.

Annita moved from Indiana to Tomah in 2011. In November 2012 she spoke to fifth-grade classes at a Black River Falls school, and was impressed by the amount of what they already had studied about her father's story and legacy. There were two visits with a total of 110 students; maybe 10 percent of them were Ho-Chunk, she says, adding it was good to see so many other young members of the community who were so tuned-in to their area's history.

She shared with them a recording of a 1950s program that was created by Armed Forces Radio, a dramatization starting with young Mitchell Red Cloud learning from his father about courage, being a warrior and what his heritage entailed. The show was entitled, "Honor for the Brave."[4]

---

[4] This was one of 11 half-hour radio dramas about Medal of Honor recipients from Korea that were produced by the Armed Forces Radio Service between 1951 and 1953. The original recordings are kept in the National Archives. They have been remastered by the Pritzker Military Library in Chicago, and are online at http://www.pritzkermilitarylibrary.org/home/the-story.aspx

"He knew it was his responsibility" in life to carry on these traditions, Annita says. "My grandfather had been in World War I."

The program ended with Red Cloud on watch and hearing the voices of his parents to "do the best you can," "fight for your country," "a place of honor," "our heritage" of native Americans in a free and democratic world like everyone else, then firing into the Chinese attacking his position and shouting he was giving them one for his father, "my dead brother" and one "from me."

A historical marker about Red Cloud that is located on Highway 54 about five miles east of Black River Falls says he "was descended from a family of warriors. Chief Winneshiek, his grandfather, with others of his tribe, refused to be resettled in Nebraska and returned to this region."[5] That would have been in the 1800s; Red Cloud was born in 1924. The historical marker is near Red Cloud's birthplace and at the site of Winnebago powwow grounds. A mile or so away is the Indian Mission and Old Decorah Cemetery, where he is buried.[6]

There is a Winneshiek County in Iowa, which was organized in 1847, and named after one of the earlier Chief Winneshieks. The county is in northeastern Iowa along the Minnesota border. In 1830, that area was set as the boundary of the "Neutral Ground" of removals of native Americans from large areas by the federal government to allow white settlement in Wisconsin and other states.[7]

"I heard about Mitchell Red Cloud as a kid and attended observances at his cemetery and at the Indian Mission," says Robert Mann, the Ho-Chunk's director of heritage preservation. "That's how I became familiar with it."

Mann says the soldier is esteemed fully as much as legendary tribal chiefs. "He is held in high honors and always will be. When a warrior gets killed in combat like he did, they're special and their spirit lives on forever, and the others who died in combat as well."

As part of that esteem, the Ho-Chunk nation holds Mitchell Red Cloud Day every July 4. "We put on a little powwow that has singing, dancing and we talk about him. This is our way of honoring one of our own."

---

[5] http://www.wisconsinhistory.org/dictionary/

[6] http://www.waymarking.com/waymarks/WM1K5N_Mitchell_Red_Cloud_Jr_1925_1950_Historical_Marker

[7] There are many references to the Winneshiek chiefs in tribal history at http://www.ho-chunknation.com/?PageId=820

Mann says that after World War II, Winnebago veterans were not allowed in the American Legion, so they set up their own organization, the Wisconsin Winnebago Veterans Association. His father, Ralph, who had been in the Burma-China-India theater, was one of organizers. Later they organized a Legion post on Ho-Chunk grounds, the Andrew Blackhawk Post 129. There also is the Red Cloud American Legion Post 250 at Adams in Adams County, because there are a large number of Ho-Chunk in that area, Mann says.

Outside the tribe, the VFW post in Black River Falls added Red Cloud to its name in 1951 – it is the Thompson-Red Cloud Medal of Honor Post 1959.

Red Cloud also is honored at the National Hall of Fame of Famous American Indians at Anadarko, Okla.[8] His bust is one of more than 40 at the museum, led by elite chiefs such as Sitting Bull, Geronimo and Black Hawk. "His legacy is remembered. He's got quite a story in his military career. It was quite impressive both in World War II and Korea," Mann says.

Red Cloud had been a Marine in World War II in Carlson's Raiders, the 2nd Marine Raider Battalion led by Lt. Col. Evans Carlson. He served first on Guadalcanal, where he was stricken by jungle diseases and could not recover for months, and when he did he fought on Okinawa with the 29th Regiment of the 6th Marine Division. He was wounded in the left shoulder on May 17, 1945, ending the war for him.[9]

Red Cloud left the military but enlisted in the Army in 1948 and arrived in Korea with the 24th Division in July 1950, in the first weeks of the new war. The 24th was in the teeth of the battles, starting with battling to stem the North Korean invasion, the quick turnaround in success and then going far into North Korea.

An article about Red Cloud in Military History magazine [10] tells more of the story of his death:

On the night of Nov. 5, the Chinese (attack) followed field telephone lines that led to C Company of the 19th Infantry. Many of the Americans were caught and killed in their

---

[8] http://www.travelok.com/listings/view.profile/id.5280

[9] http://www.historynet.com/mitchell-red-cloud-jr-korean-war-hero.htm The article was written by Dana Benner and originally published in the June 2006 issue of Military History magazine.

[10] http://www.historynet.com/mitchell-red-cloud-jr-korean-war-hero.htm

sleeping bags. Nearby, entrenched on Hill 123, E Company of the 19th was trying to hold its section of the Chongchon River line. Fortunately for that company, Cpl. Red Cloud had heeded the warnings (about Chinese sneaking in) and stayed awake.

Quietly, about 1,000 infantrymen of the Chinese 355th Regiment infiltrated …. Red Cloud was positioned in a forward observation post at a point immediately in front of the E Company command post. From there, he was able to detect the Chinese when they launched their assault at about 3:20 a.m., under a nearly full moon. As the enemy charged from a brush-covered area, less than 100 feet from him, Red Cloud gave the alarm to his fellow soldiers. Then, grabbing his Browning Automatic Rifle and springing up from his place of concealment, Red Cloud emptied magazine after magazine into the charging Chinese troops at point-blank range. (He was shot twice in the chest and his assistant BAR man was killed.)

Perry Woodley, the 2nd Platoon medic, rushed to Red Cloud's foxhole and applied field dressings to his wounds. As Woodley went off to treat others on the hill, he could hear the bark of a BAR resume behind him. Red Cloud was hit again and called for aid. Woodley found him badly wounded and tried to get him off the hill, but Red Cloud refused further medical help and told Woodley to concentrate on getting the other wounded men to safety.

Under his covering fire, the rest of E Company began a fighting retreat from the hilltop to fortified positions 1,000 yards south of Hill 123. Red Cloud was reportedly struck by as many as eight bullets before dying. When his comrades went to retrieve his body the next day, they found "a string of dead Chinese soldiers" in front of him.

The story of the Chosin disaster is told in many books, including "The Last Stand of Fox Company," published in 2009, and the 1953 book "The River and the Gauntlet: Defeat of the 8th Army by the Chinese Communist Forces November 1950 in the Battle of the Chongchon River."[11]

---

[11] "The Last Stand of Fox Company" is written by Bob Drury and Tom Clavin. "The River" was written by noted military historian S.L.A. Marshall.

The period of late October and early November 1950 was a time when U.S. and United Nations forces had been riding high given their rapid turning of the tide from the Communist invasion of South Korea on June 25 and nearly being pushed off the Korean Peninsula two months later. By November, the U.N. forces were nearing the Chinese border at the Yalu River but began encountering the Chinese, and there were many intelligence reports about their numbers being massive.

An article at the CIA's website criticizes the quality of some of the intelligence, but supports most of it (not a surprise given whose website this is) while saying Army commanders repeatedly fumbled the ball.[12] Because of the dramatic turnaround and stunning losses, and some items on the very day of Red Cloud's death, it is quoted at length here:

> **On 25 October, the first phase of the Chinese offensive began with the South Korean 1st Division in contact with Chinese units. Chinese POWs, interrogated that evening by U.S. 8th Army intelligence officers, told of a sizable Chinese presence. … Yet, on 28 October, the CIA Daily Summary stated that only small, independent Chinese units were fighting in Korea. It totally discounted the possibility that major Chinese forces were present.**
>
> **By 29 October, South Korean units on both coasts captured Chinese from regimental-sized units, and these prisoners convinced X Corps intelligence that the Chinese were being committed to battle as units, rather than as replacements for North Korean losses. That same day, however, the Far Eastern Command Intelligence Summary advised that Chinese forces had little combat potential against a modern army.**
>
> **… On 30 October, MacArthur's G-2, (Maj. Gen. Charles Willoughby, chief of intelligence) flew from Tokyo to X Corps Headquarters to personally interview 16 Chinese POWs. After this session, he pronounced them to be "stragglers" rather than members of an organized unit. That same day, the 8th Army**

---

12 https://www.cia.gov/library/center-for-the-study-of-intelligence/csi-publications/ csi-studies/studies/fall_winter_2001/article06.html Abundant initials such as ROK and PLA have been replaced in this excerpt with words – South Korean forces and Chinese forces.

reported that 10 separate Chinese POWs stated that several Chinese divisions were now in Korea. While reporting this in its Daily Summary, CIA restated its belief that Chinese intervention was unlikely, and that these troops could be protecting the hydroelectric plants essential to the Manchurian economy.

... By early November, field reports from Korea could no longer be ignored in Tokyo and Washington. In addition to POW reporting from both the 8th Army and X Corps, Marine Corps pilots reported massive truck convoys moving from Manchuria into Korea. ... By 4 November, the 1st Cavalry identified five Chinese divisions opposing it, and the 1st Marine Division identified three Chinese divisions operating against it. ... But Willoughby continued to claim these forces did not represent official Chinese intervention. By 3 November, the Far Eastern Command had raised its estimate of Chinese strength in Korea to 34,000, backed by reserves in Manchuria of 498,000 Chinese army soldiers and 370,000 Chinese security troops.

... Finally, on 5 November (the date Red Cloud was killed), Willoughby admitted that Chinese forces in Korea had the potential to conduct a large-scale counteroffensive. Later that day, however, MacArthur advised the Joint Chiefs of Staff (in Washington, D.C.) that he still did not believe the Chinese would enter the war in force. ... Between 4 and 5 November, the Chinese forces broke contact and melted back into the countryside (but Red Cloud's heroism came vs. against a massive force of Chinese). ...

By mid-November, Far Eastern Command reported that 12 (Chinese) divisions had been identified in Korea. On 24 November, however, National Intelligence Estimate 2/1 stated that China had the capability for large-scale offensive operations but that there were no indications such an offensive was in the offing. That same day, the second Chinese offensive started, leaving the 8th Army fighting for its life and most of the 1st Marine Division surrounded and threatened with annihilation.

It took several days for MacArthur and his staff to face the fact that his "end of the war" offensive toward the Yalu (River) was over and victory was not near.

Finally, on Nov. 28, the very day that Hopfensperger was lost, MacArthur said in a report to the Joint Chiefs of Staff that he faced "an entirely new war." The front page headline of the Wisconsin State Journal in Madison that day shouted in two lines of all-capital letters across all eight columns: "Chinese Reds Stab 20 Miles, Threaten Entire Allied Line," with deck headlines of "Flank Drive Perils 2nd, 25th Divisions" and "Facing Disaster, UN Forces Battle to Seal Breach Where South Koreans Collapsed." The story was equally dire.

The day before, the paper's main headline had been "Red Counter-Blow Pierces UN Line" with a deck headline of, "14-Mile Gains Shatter Allied End-War Drive."

MacArthur did not make a public statement until Dec. 2, and the State Journal gave it a more-subdued one-line banner headline and the letters were not in all-caps. But it proclaimed, "Undeclared War Now On, Mac Says," with deck headlines of "Claims Allies Facing 500,000 China Reds" and "UN Forces Far 'Outnumbered; Foe Masses for Drive on Pyongyang," the North Korean capital that the Americans captured only weeks earlier.

The story, written by the United Press at MacArthur's headquarters, began:

> **Tokyo – Gen. Douglas MacArthur said in a special statement today that a "state of undeclared war" exists between the Chinese Communists and United Nations forces.**
>
> **MacArthur said that the immediate Chinese forces now engaged "comprise approximately 500,000 men divided into two great echelons."**
>
> **"A state of undeclared war between the Chinese Communist and the United Nations forces now exists," MacArthur said in the statement which he released to the press.**
>
> **Although he did not disclose his UN forces' strength, MacArthur added that the enemy "overwhelmingly outnumbers our forces."**
>
> **"His forces are throughly equipped with modern and efficient weapons," he said.**

MacArthur said that UN reverses "are due entirely to the overwhelming strength of the enemy who completely outnumbers us on the ground."

Counting remnants of the North Korean forces, he added, the UN forces face an enemy total of about 600,000 men.

The UN commander said he knew of no way in which the Allied reverses could have been avoided "under the conditions which existed."

He denied that his military command ever had exceeded its authority. He said his command "has acted in complete harmony and coordination with higher authority."

He explained that the military only carries out the policies prescribed for it.

MacArthur said he had never recommended or asked for authority to bomb targets north of the Yalu River and had not asked for authority to use the atomic bomb.

The story did not elaborate, but his last comments were rather defensive against the criticism that soon would be flowing hotly. Many historical accounts[13] say MacArthur basically wanted to start World War III by going all the way to the Yalu River – the border between North Korea and China – and bombing installations in China along with bringing in the Nationalist Chinese, who had lost the civil war to Mao Tse-tung in 1949 and fled to Formosa. President Harry Truman, commander in chief, fired MacArthur four months after this disaster, on April 11, 1951, but it easily could have been done in the December debacle or even weeks before that, because the general gave every appearance of running his own show and not being under command of the commander in chief or the Joint Chiefs of Staff. Truman had flown to Wake Island for a summit with MacArthur on Oct. 15 amid such concerns.

---

[13] Such reporting is in many books, but of particular note is "American Caesar: Douglas MacArthur, 1880-1964" by WIlliam Manchester (1978), an in-depth study of the good and odd of MacArthur to the tune of 793 pages. Other fine studies of his role are "The Forgotten War: America in Korea 1950-1953," by Clay Blair (1987) and "The Korean War: The West Confronts Communism," by Michael Hickey (1999). Books about World War II are equally critical of many of MacArthur's methods.

MacArthur, a World War II commander and Medal of Honor recipient, was now age 70. He had brilliantly conceived of the surprise landing at Inchon on Sept. 15, which turned the war around. But, as one account[14] says, problems began to brew

> **with the flamboyant and egotistical General MacArthur .... MacArthur argued for a policy of pushing into North Korea to completely defeat the Communist forces. Truman went along with this plan, but worried that the Communist government of the People's Republic of China might take the invasion as a hostile act and intervene in the conflict.**
>
> **In October 1950, MacArthur met with Truman and assured him that the chances of a Chinese intervention were slim. Then, in November and December 1950, hundreds of thousands of Chinese troops crossed into North Korea and flung themselves against the American lines, driving the U.S. troops back to South Korea.**

During all of this, Hopfensperger was killed.

The Pentagon's announcement of the identification of his remains said elements of the 31st Regimental Combat Team (a collection of units including his battalion), known as Task Force Faith, named for the unit commander, in late November had been "advancing along the eastern banks of the Chosin Reservoir in North Korea. After coming under attack, they began a fighting withdrawal to positions near Hagaru-ri, south of the reservoir. During this withdrawal Hopfensperger went missing."[15]

"Fighting withdrawal" means they were trapped and took severe losses in moving back.

The Pentagon sent Hopfensberger's family a report with further details. "Since there had been little enemy contact for the past couple days, the two infantry battalions (one of which was Hopfenspeger's) established themselves for the night in two mutually unsupported defensive positions about 2½ road miles apart. ... However, late on the evening of 27 November everything changed as the (group) was stunned by a massive Chinese surprise attack. ...

---

14 http://www.history.com/this-day-in-history/truman-relieves-macarthur-of-duties-in-korea

15 http://www.dtic.mil/dpmo/news/news_releases/2012/release_hopfensperger.pdf

The first attack came south along the main road that split the Able Company positions from Charlie Company. Neither Able nor Charlie Company had placed any blocking position on the road and the Chinese swarmed through the perimeter basically unimpeded."

Soon the Chinese were battling Hopfensperger's B (Baker) Company.

"In view of the overwhelming enemy force and the large number of casualties suffered on the two previous nights, it was clear that the (positions) had to be consolidated. To that end, the survivors of (Hopfensperger's 1st Battalion of the 32nd Regiment) made a withdrawal under fire south to join (other units). ... With a limited number of operable vehicles and with the large number of wounded, the bodies of the dead, including Pfc. Hopfensperger, had to be left, either where they fell, or near the location of the ... aid tent where some of the dead had been consolidated."

Sgt. Robert Boulden of Burlington was in this mess as a member of the 5th Regiment of the 1st Marine Division. Hagaru was at the bottom tip of the Chosin Reservoir, where routes branched to the west and the east on either side of frozen waterway. He says mass burials were all that could be done amid the Chinese waves and then the massive U.S. pullout to safer areas, sometimes fighting through a gauntlet in the form of a valley with Chinese firing from above.

"We would scratch a hole in the ground with a bulldozer, lay them in side by side, and cover them over," Boulden says. As space permitted, which was rarely, bodies would be strapped to vehicles. Too often, the vehicles were packed with dying and freezing troops.

"There were hundreds of dead at the Chosin Reservoir. Hundreds," Boulden adds. "I prayed every instant that I could make it. I asked the Good Lord, 'Give me tomorrow.' We had doubts. We didn't know we were going to make it out."[16]

A larger overview[17] of Hopfensperger's group in this period before and after his death (and because of the turbulent period, it is quoted at length here) says:

In a seemingly minor change in plans, Army Gen. Edward Almond, the X Corps commander, ordered the 31st Regimental Combat Team of the 7th Division to relieve the 5th Marine

---

[16] "Heart of the Century," p. 126. The book also has several other quotes from Boulden about Chosin and other news reports from Korea throughout the war.

[17] http://www.history.army.mil/brochures/kw-chinter/chinter.htm

Regiment (Boulden's group) on the east side of the Chosin Reservoir so the Marines could concentrate their forces on the west, reorienting their drive to the north and west of the frozen reservoir. ...

The roads were treacherous, trucks were in short supply, and the different battalions and artillery assets only slowly began to assemble east of the reservoir. Although the unit was called the 31st RCT, the 31st Regiment commander, Col. Allan D. MacLean, was to command the 1st Battalion of the 32d Infantry (this was Hopfensberger's battalion) along with his 2d and 3d Battalions of the 31st Infantry.

The 1st Battalion, 32d Infantry, commanded by Lt. Col. Donald C. Faith Jr., was first to reach the new positions, relieving the Marines on 25 November. Faith's battalion was alone on the east side of the reservoir for a full day before other elements of Task Force MacLean, the 3rd Battalion of the 31st Infantry and two artillery batteries arrived on the 27th.

... Almond's offensive was not to be. Late on 27 November the Chinese struck the U.S. forces on both sides of the Chosin Reservoir nearly simultaneously. Two Chinese Communist Forces divisions, the 79th and 89th, attacked the Marines west of the reservoir in the Yudam-ni area. The Marines killed the Chinese by the hundreds but were in danger of being cut off from the division headquarters at Hagaru-ri ...

In a similar maneuver, the Chinese 80th Division struck the spread-out positions of Task Force MacLean (where Hopfensperger was) while simultaneously moving around its flank to cut it off from the Marines at Hagaru-ri.

... Convinced now that launching any kind of attack (toward China) on the 29th was futile, Col. MacLean abruptly ordered a pullback to form a more consolidated defense. ... However, during the withdrawal operations his troops came under renewed enemy attack, and in the confusion MacLean was captured by the Chinese. With no hope of rescuing his commander, Col. Faith took command of the task force. ...

The epic struggle of Task Force MacLean, now called Task Force Faith, was drawing to a close. Its separated tank company, augmented by a pickup force of Headquarters Company soldiers and clerks, attempted twice to relieve the beleaguered force. However, the tanks foundered on the icy roads, and the attacks were further hindered by misdirected air strikes. ... Faith, unaware of this attempted rescue because of faulty communications, was running short of ammunition and had over 400 wounded on his hands.

... Continued Chinese attacks during the night of the 30th and into the morning of 1 December left Task Force Faith in a dangerous situation with no help in sight. Chinese assaults had almost destroyed the perimeter that night, and the number of wounded went up to nearly 600, virtually one-fourth of the entire formation. Believing that one more Chinese attack would destroy his force, Faith decided to withdraw and run the Chinese gauntlet down the frozen road along the east side of the reservoir in hopes of reaching the Marines at Hagaru-ri.

Faith was killed the next day, Dec. 2, and also became an MIA like Hopfensperger. Faith's remains were identified in April 2013. Col. MacLean, the predecessor of Faith who had been taken prisoner, also is MIA, recorded as assumed dead on Nov. 29.[18]

The Pentagon report that was sent to Hopfensperger's family included maps showing he was killed along the far northeast end of the Chosin (the Korean word was Changjin) Reservoir and said that between 1995 and 2005, its excavations in North Korea "resulted in the recovery and repatriation of remains of over 220 U.S. servicemen." The packet to his family also included a chart of "major remains concentrations in North Korea" with 1,079 at the Chosin Reservor area, 1,559 at Unsan / Chongchon, and other sites of a few hundred.

While relations with North Korea were non-existent for decades after the war, and have been very frosty in recent years, there was a short time of improvement between 1991 and 1994, then 2002 and 2005, and the latter is when remains that proved to be Hopfensperger's were returned to the United States. The Pentagon said more than 7,900 Americans remain unaccounted for

---

[18] http://www.abmc.gov, found via searching for MacLean's name.

[19] http://www.dtic.mil/dpmo/news/news_releases/2012/release_hopfensperger.pdf

from the Korean War.[19]   Several other men lost in the same period as Hopfensperger have been identified in recent months and years.

Elayne Lastofka of Appleton, a cousin of Hopfensperger, says his parents were Ray and Pearl and that he had five siblings. Lastofka submitted her DNA after another cousin received a letter from the Pentagon requesting a DNA sample. The agency had been looking for direct relatives in Appleton after somehow determining what unit these men in a grave likely were from. Still, it took many years between excavation a decade ago and identification.

Hopfensperger was killed Nov. 28, but he also had been wounded on Sept. 23, a week after his 7th Division was part of the surprise landing at Inchon along with the Marines. Hopfensperger was wounded when the division was near the Han River south of Seoul, was out of action for a week and returned to duty on the Oct. 1.[20]

The loss of Arthur was not the first in Korea for the extended Hopfensperger family in Appleton. Sgt. 1st Class Daniel D. Hopfensperger Jr., who was Arthur's second-cousin (their grandfathers were brothers and their fathers were first cousins, Lastofka says) was killed on Sept. 11, 1950, scarcely two weeks before Arthur was wounded and scarcely two months before Arthur was killed.

Daniel was a member of Company E of the 8th Regiment in the 1st Cavalry Division. He was 19.

Besides the bravery of Red Cloud, four other men from Wisconsin received the Medal of Honor in Korea; two before him and two after:[21]

– Army Master Sgt. Melvin Handrich of Manawa (Waupaca County), killed Aug. 26, 1950. He was in the 5th Infantry, 1st Cavalry Divison.[22]

– Marine Pfc. Stanley Christianson of Mindoro (La Crosse County), killed on Sept. 29, 1950; He was in the 1st Regiment, 1st Marine Division.[23]

– Army Cpl. Einar Ingman of Irma (Lincoln County), for actions on Feb. 26, 1951. He survived the war, the only Wisconsin Medal of Honor

---

[20] http://www.abmc.gov/search/detail.php

[21] http://www.wisvetsmuseum.com/researchers/military/Honors_Memorials/?ID=58

[22] http://www.usa-patriotism.com/heroes/moh/kw/handrich.htm

[23] http://www.marinemedals.com/christiansonstanley.htm

[24] http://www.victoryinstitute.net/blogs/utb/1951/02/26/einar-h-ingman-jr-medal-of-honor-citation/

recipient in Korea who was not killed in the action for which he was cited. Ingman was in the 17th Regiment, 7th Infantry Division.[24]

– Army 2nd Lt. Jerome Sudut of Wausau, killed on Sept. 12, 1951. He was in the 27th Regiment of the 25th Infantry Division.[25]

Nationally, Red Cloud was one of four native Americans who earned the Medal of Honor in Korea, and there were a few others in World War II and in the late 1860s and 1870s in what are called the "Indian Wars."[26]

Another honor came in 1957, when the Army established Camp Red Cloud in South Korea. "I was there in 2001 to rededicate it," his daughter Annita says. "The camp is 14 miles from the DMZ and during the war was a MASH camp, for Mobile Army Surgical Hospital. It is the headquarters of the 2nd Infantry Division in Korea and there is a museum there."

It is known today as U.S. Army Garrison – Red Cloud, located in the city of Uijeongbu, about 25 miles north of Seoul. Its website says it "is the 'tip of the spear' for forwardly deployed soldiers serving on the Korean DMZ." There is one other garrison and multiple camps, all part of the Army Installation Management Command Pacific.[27]

Garrison Red Cloud is home to about 15,000 U.S. soldiers, civilians, contractors, Korean soldiers and family members. The 2nd Division has its headquarters there, but a majority of its soldiers are deployed to the north, in Dongducheon City, the garrison says.

Also in 1957, a city park in La Crosse was named for Red Cloud. The park is on the site of what was a tribal village.[28]

In 1999, Annita was invited to San Diego to launch the Navy's USNS Red Cloud, breaking a bottle of champagne over the hull of the cargo ship. The Red Cloud is part of the Military Sealift Command.[29] Its official desig-

---

[25] http://www.usa-patriotism.com/heroes/moh/kw/sudut.htm

[26] http://www.history.army.mil/html/topics/natam/natam-moh.html

[27] http://redcloud.korea.army.mil/ and http://redcloud.korea.army.mil/USAG-Red-Cloud

[28] http://www.cityoflacrosse.org/index.aspx?NID=1711

[29] http://www.msc.navy.mil/inventory/ships.asp?ship=147, http://www.msc.navy.mil/N00p/pressrel/press04/press11.htm Ships that are USNS are those operated with a civilian master and civilian crew by the Military Sealift Command, according to the Navy, at www.navy.mil/navydata/ships/lists/shipalpha.asp

nation is T-AKR 313 and it is one of the command's 19 Large, Medium-Speed Toll-on/Roll-off Ships, so-named for their ability to load and unload cargo.

It is one of 30 ships in what is called the command's Pre-Postioning Program, meaning they are essentially floating warehouses stationed around the world so they can bring massive amounts of cargo much faster than loading and unloading at a domestic port or major U.S. ally. In Operation Iraqi Freedom in 2003, the Red Cloud carried "multiple cargo loads of equipment and supplies from Southwest Asia, Europe and the continental United States to U.S. forces in the Middle East," the Navy says.

For many decades, the Ho-Chunk were called the Winnebago, but the tribe maintained that had derogatory roots and changed the name in 1993. Its history[30] says: "Winnebago was a name given by the Sauk and Fox, who called the people Ouinepegi, or People of the Stinky Waters. … This name was heard as Winnebago by the government agents, and was the name the United States government took for the Ho-Chunk people. This remained the official name of the Nation until the Constitution Reform in 1993, when the Ho-Chunk reclaimed their original name."

---

[30] http://www.ho-chunknation.com/AboutUs.aspx

Chapter 11
The 37 Wisconsin MIAs in Vietnam

Ten of the 37 Wisconsin men missing in action from the Vietnam War have been identified over the years, with partial remains sometimes being repatriated more than four decades after a soldier was killed and then taking several more years to be identified via DNA and other scientific analysis. The latest identification came in 2013, as this book was being finalized.

Detailing the stories of the MIAs is an important part of this book about the Ultimate Sacrifice. It is very difficult to find any list of the Wisconsin men from state government, but Vietnam veterans meticulously keep a record, especially http://www.war-veterans.org/Wi37.htm, the tribute website set up by Jeff Dentice of Muskego. He says wants to ensure they are never forgotten, and that he will keep that pledge "until they all come home."

In the rare times when there is reporting about the 37 MIAs, the information inevitably is alphabetical by name, unit, date of loss, etc. This chapter instead will discuss them all in chronological order, what they were doing and what their unit's mission was; the next chapter will examine some of them closer as people.

As such, this chapter perhaps is the most extensive research on the Badger State MIAs as a group in decades, if not ever.

The youngest Wisconsin MIA was 18; the oldest 42. The earliest MIAs were in 1965; the last man was in 1973, a week after the Paris Peace Accords were signed. They include Navy pilots and crews, Army ground troops and helicopter pilots and their crewmen, Marine ground troops and pilots, and Air Force pilots and crews. Some were in special operations units and on extremely secret missions. Some disappeared in Laos and Cambodia. Three of the MIAs are from a five-day period in January 1968; each was on a separate plane. Then in February of that year, there was a plane crash in which two Wisconsin Navy men were MIA along with several other sailors. And in May of the same year, a pair of Wisconsin Marines were MIA in the same ground battle.

The facts in this chapter are drawn from two sites devoted to the Vietnam Veterans Memorial, http://www.virtualwall.org and http://www.thewall-usa.com; from websites devoted to units that the men were in, and especially from detailed reports posted by the POW Network.[1] Its statement of purpose

Navy Chief Aviation Ordnanceman Donald Louis Gallagher (top) of Sheboygan Falls, and Navy Lt. (j.g.) Roy Arthur Huss of Eau Claire and Abbotsford, were on a Navy patrol plane that crashed off the coast of Vietnam on Feb. 6, 1968, along with 10 other men. They are MIA. Later in 1968, two other Wisconsin MIAs disappeared in a ground battle but their remains were recovered decades later and identified in 2005 – Marine Pfc. Thomas Joseph Blackman of Racine and Marine Lance Cpl. Raymond Thomas Heyne of Mason in Bayfield County.

is, "Since 11/11/89, dedicated to information distribution on our Prisoners of War and Missing in Action Servicemen."

The POW Network draws together information from various agencies and official reports, such as this entry for Marine Capt. Harold John Moe of Eau Claire, MIA since 1967: "Compiled by POW Network from one or more of the following: raw data from U.S. government agency sources, correspondence with POW / MIA families, published sources, interviews and Combined Action Combat Casualty File."

The POW Network questions part or all of some official reports, seeking the possibility that men still may be alive and the government has not tried hard enough to find them or press a nation like Vietnam to fess up. For example, it says this while reporting about one Wisconsin man: "Adding to the torment of nearly 10,000 reports relating to Americans missing in Southeast Asia is the certain knowledge that some Americans who were known to be prisoners of war were not released at the end of the war. Others were suspected to be prisoners, and still others were in radio contact with would-be rescuers when last seen alive. Many were known to have survived their loss incidents, only to disappear without a trace."

For others, though, the POW Network says the serviceman almost certainly was killed but deserves to have his body brought home.

---

[1] http://www.pownetwork.org/

The author of this book has faith in the professionalism of the Defense POW / Missing Personnel Office[2] and its laboratories, which make the identifications only after substantial scientific analysis. However, the author of this book also was age 18 in 1969 and age 21 and a college senior in journalism at the time of the Paris Peace Accords in 1973 and fully agrees that skepticism about the "official government line" in the Vietnam era often was quite justified.

Another group quoted in this chapter is Task Force Omega.[3] It is a POW / MIA "organization dedicated to the full accounting and return of all prisoners of war and those missing in action during the defense of our country. This website contains useful information, historical documents, links to other POW / MIA and military organizations as well as a complete database with the names, biographies, and in many cases pictures and map data with the location of the incident leading to their capture or when they were reported missing in action."

It is a bit less skeptical than the POW Network, but both parties share reports on their respective websites.

Here is the chronological list of Wisconsin MIAs. If a man has been identified, that fact appears in capital letters immediately after his name. The home of record usually is where his family was living at the time; several cases have been found of the veteran graduating from high school in a different city. The rank that is listed is what is on the Wall sites, but in many cases the man had been promoted posthumously.

Air Force Capt. Walter Frank Draeger Jr., Deerfield: He was on a mission over North Vietnam on April 4, 1965, and was shot down while providing cover for a helicopter trying to rescue another pilot. Draeger was age 31 and his death was classified as "hostile, died outright." He was in the 1131st Special Activities Squadron of the 13th Air Force and crashed in the Tonkin Gulf.

Draeger received the Air Force Cross posthumously for

> **extraordinary heroism in connection with military operations against an opposing armed force as pilot of an A-1 Skyraider with Detachment 10, 1131st Special Activities Squadron .... Draeger volunteered to fly as a fighter-adviser**

---

[2] http://www.dtic.mil/dpmo/ There are regular announcements of identifications not only from Vietnam but also the Korean War and World War II.

[3] http://taskforceomegainc.org

with the Vietnamese Air Force into an area of known heavily concentrated antiaircraft artillery. He participated in a highly successful bombing mission of a vital Viet Cong target, contributing materially to its destruction.

On the return flight from the primary target, Captain Draeger's flight leader was shot down by hostile ground fire. Captain Draeger immediately called for search and rescue assistance. Although completely alone and within range of the hostile ground fire, he orbited the area of his downed flight leader until the unarmed search and rescue aircraft arrived in the vicinity.

... The unarmed rescue aircraft requested fire suppression assistance. Captain Draeger commenced a firing pass to allow the rescue aircraft to safely enter the area. With complete disregard for his own personal safety, he made the strafing run into the hostile fire. Ignoring the air bursts from shore batteries, Captain Draeger pressed his attack and, in so doing, sacrificed his own life. Through his extraordinary heroism, superb airmanship, and aggressiveness in the face of hostile forces, Captain Draeger reflected the highest credit upon himself and the United States Air Force.[4]

The target of the raids was the Thanh Hoa Railroad and Highway Bridge.[5] The POW Network says Draeger's plane was an A1-H Douglas Skyraider, "probably an escort for rescue teams, was shot down over the Gulf of Tonkin just northeast of the Dragon that day. Draeger's aircraft was seen to crash in flames, but no parachute was observed."

The work of the Special Activities Squadron is as secret as it sounds. Material at the tribute page to a man killed two months after Draeger says the men were "were commanded directly out of the Pentagon .... One was not just assigned to this detachment, but rather interviewed for it at the Pentagon, so the work was extraordinary even applying Air Commando standards. The aircraft had no standard markings on it, but were painted with a unique camo pattern of low-reflectivity black, green and brown paint. The aircraft

---

4 http://militarytimes.com/citations-medals-awards/recipient.php?recipientid=3554

5 http://www.pownetwork.org/bios/d/d387.htm and http://taskforceomegainc.org/d387.html

was rigged with pylons on it. Runways were often replaced by landing on very wide roads. The 1131st flew only at night. They operated in a shroud of secrecy, no reports, no tail numbers due ... All aircraft were sanitized as well as the nationality and individuality of those on board."[6]

Navy Cmdr. James David La Haye, Green Bay: He was flying from the aircraft carrier USS Midway when he was shot down over the Gulf of Tonkin on May 8, 1965. The pilot was age 41 and flying an F-8D Crusader in Squadron VF-111.

La Haye was lost about 10 miles from shore and 20 miles northeast of the city of Vinh, in Nghe An Province, North Vietnam. The POW Network says: "Accompanying aircraft stated that La Haye's aircraft had been hit and evaded over water for easier possible rescue. La Haye apparently did not eject, as aircraft observed no parachutes. It was felt that Lt.Col. LaHaye was killed when his aircraft went down."[7]

The squadron was known as the Sundowners. The Midway now is a museum in San Diego, and an F-8 is on display. It bears the name of La Haye and its two other men killed in action in 1965: Cmdr. Doyle W. Lynn of Aliquippa, Pa., lost on May 27, and Lt. (j.g.) Gene R. Gollahon of Cincinnati, lost on Aug. 13.[8]

Air Force Capt. Robert Ira Bush, Racine: Bush was a pilot who was shot down over North Vietnam on June 9, 1966, one day after his 28th birthday. He was flying an A-1 Skyraider in the 602nd Fighter Air Commando Squadron, 14th Air Commando Wing.

The 14th was based at Nha Trang Air Base from Feb. 1, 1966, to Dec. 15 of that year, when it was moved to Udorn Air Base, according to Internet information. The Skyraider was a single-seat plane.

The POW Network says only, "No further information available at this time."[9] The Virtual Wall, www.virtualwall.org, says the 602nd Squadron lost another pilot on the same day as Bush – Maj. Theodore J. Shorack of Oregon, and also over North Vietnam.[10]

---

[6] http://airforce.togetherweserved.com/usaf/servlet/tws.webapp.WebApp?cmd =ShadowBoxProfile&type=AssignmentExt&ID=195077

[7] http://www.pownetwork.org/bios/l/l352.htm

[8] www.midwaysaircraft.org/acft/f8.htm Also see http://www.scribd.com/doc/5776 7288/Vought-s-F-8-Crusader-Navy-Fighter-Squadrons

[9] http://www.pownetwork.org/bios/b/b452.htm

Navy Lt. Cmdr. William Tamm Arnold, West Allis: He was lost on Nov. 18, 1966, while flying a mission from the USS Coral Sea. His A-4C Skyhawk crashed in waters off North Vietnam or over the coast. He was 26 at the time and was promoted to lieutenant commander after he became MIA. In 1978, the Pentagon changed his status from missing to "died while missing." Arnold had been wingman to another plane while on a coastal weather reconnaissance mission.

According to an account on a website devoted to the Coral Sea: "Flying beneath the overcast approximately seven miles from the coast, the flight leader determined that the cloud base was of sufficient height to effect a bombing maneuver. The flight leader completed his maneuver, staying beneath the overcast, and was turning east when he heard the transmission, 'I'm in the clouds, coming down.' The leader looked back, but did not see Arnold's aircraft. The flight leader called to Arnold but received no response. He saw no evidence of an ejection nor any debris which would indicate a crash. ...

"It is the assumption of the wingman that Arnold became disoriented in his maneuver and in trying to recover, crashed into the sea. Further, the possibility that he ejected in the proximity of land and was captured was considered very remote. Arnold's last known location, however, was quite near the coast of North Vietnam off Quang Binh Province, just south of the halfway point between the cities of Quang Khe and Dong Hoi. A report was received from the Vietnamese that a pilot parachuted down on shore in the general vicinity of Arnold's disappearance, hit his head on a rock which killed him and was then buried."[11]

Air Force Capt. Roy Robert Kubley, Glidden (Ashland County): He was on the crew of a plane spraying Agent Orange or other pesticides when it was shot down on Jan. 31, 1967, over Laos. He was 27 and in the 12th Air Commando Squadron of the 315th Air Commando Wing. The death is listed as "hostile, died outright."

---

[10] http://www.virtualwall.org/ds/ShorackTJ01a.htm A list of the squadron's men lost in the entire war is at http://skyraider.org/skyassn/menlost.htm The overall story of the Air Command Association is at http://www.specialoperations.net/1SOWWW-77.htm

[11] http://www.usscoralsea.net/pages/pow.php#arnold Also see http://www.pownetwork.org/bios/a/a025.htm

The plane was a UC-123B and Agent Orange was the work of Project Ranch Hand, spraying the jungles to expose the Viet Cong. The pilot this day was Maj. Lloyd Walker of Oregon, and the crew consisted of Kubley and three others.

The POW Network says, "The aircraft had leveled off and started spraying when it suddenly inverted and crashed. Further investigation revealed that hostile fire struck the propeller, causing the crash. The crash occurred about five miles south-southwest of Sepone in Savannakhet Province, Laos. All crew members were eventually determined to have been killed in the crash of the aircraft."[12]

An explanation of the infamous Agent Orange program, which began testing in South Vietnam in 1962, is at http://www.airpower.maxwell.af.mil/airchronicles/aureview/1970/jan-feb/mcconnell.html

Marine Pfc. Duwayne Soulier, Milwaukee: He had been wounded in action and then his medical evacuation helicopter crashed into the sea on May 1, 1967. Soulier was age 20, and died along with five others on the chopper. No bodies were recovered.

Soulier was in Headquarters Company of the 7th Communications Battalion of the 1st Marine Division. The helicopter was a Boeing-Vertol CH-46 Sea Knight.

According to a summary by Task Force Omega,[13] Soulier had been wounded and taken to the hospital at Chu Lai, Quang Tin Province, South Vietnam, for treatment. He and four other wounded Marines were on a medevac flight from Chu Lai to one of the Navy's hospital ships stationed in the South China Sea.

Task Force Omega says: "Just before the aircraft crashed into the water, the pilot made a Mayday call outlining their emergency and giving their position, which was about 12 miles east-northeast of Chu Lai and 57 miles southeast of Da Nang. Search and recovery operations were launched immediately and rescue helicopters were on site within minutes of the loss. They were able to locate and rescue the pilot, co-pilot, crew chief and at least one Navy corpsman assigned to this flight. However, they were unable to find any trace of Soulier, the four other Marines and one of the copter's crew.

---

[12] http://www.pownetwork.org/bios/k/k393.htm

[13] http://www.taskforceomegainc.org/s231.html

"... Under the circumstances, it is highly unlikely the remains of the men killed in this tragic loss at sea can ever be found without a massive underwater salvage / recovery operation being undertaken."

Marine Sgt. James Neil Tycz, Milwaukee REMAINS HAVE BEEN IDENTIFIED: Tycz was the leader of a Marine ground patrol and was lost near Khe Sanh on May 10, 1967, when a North Vietnamese grenade exploded as he tried to throw it out of the way of his men. He received the Navy Cross for this act of heroism. Three other men were killed in the fight, and helicopters evacuated the rest of the force under heavy fire.

Remains were repatriated in 2003 and identified a year later. Tycz, 22, and two of the men he was killed with were buried at Arlington National Cemetery on May 10, 2005. Another who was identified was buried that spring in California.

Tycz and two of the dead were in the 1st Platoon, A Company, 3rd Recon Battalion of the 3rd Marine Division. The fourth was a Navy corpsman; medic to the unit.

The Pentagon announced the identifications on April 25, 2005, and said: "The four men were part of a reconnaissance patrol operating near the U.S. Marine base in Khe Sanh, Quang Tri Province, South Vietnam. They came under enemy attack shortly after midnight ... while occupying a defensive position. During the firefight (the four) were killed. The patrol's surviving members were rescued by helicopter later that morning but the bodies of the four men could not be recovered.

"In the fall of 1991, several Vietnamese citizens visited the U.S. POW / MIA office in Hanoi claiming to have access to the remains of U.S. servicemen. One of the men provided skeletal and teeth fragments. Between 1993 and 2004, eight joint U.S.-Vietnamese teams led by the Joint POW / MIA Accounting Command interviewed witnesses and surveyed the skirmish area. Two other joint teams conducted excavations during which material evidence and remains were recovered."[14]

Here is the Navy Cross citation:[15] "When an enemy hand grenade landed near one of the seriously wounded Marines, Sergeant Tycz courageously and with complete disregard for his own personal safety moved

---

[14] http://www.dtic.mil/dpmo/news/news_releases/2004/documents/Vietnammia 42505.pdf

203

forward, picked up the grenade and attempted to throw it back at the enemy. The grenade exploded after traveling only a short distance, and he fell, critically wounded. Throughout the encounter, Sergeant Tycz set an example of calmness and coolness under fire that was an inspiration to the remainder of his patrol. By his unselfish act of courage, he risked his life to save his comrades from injury and possible loss of life and thereby upheld the highest traditions of the Marine Corps and the United States Naval Service."

Newspaper stories about the comments of Tycz's family are at http://www.arlingtoncemetery.net/jntycz.htm,

Marine Lance Cpl. Merlin Raye Allen, Bayfield REMAINS IDEN-TIFIED IN 2013: The 20-year-old field radio operator in the 3rd Recon Battalion, the same battalion that Tycz was in, was lost June 30, 1967, when the CH-46A Sea Knight helicopter in which he was a passenger went down. The crash occurred in Thua Thien Province in South Vietnam. Four other men on the helicopter also are MIA.

In 2013, the Pentagon listed Allen as "recently accounted-for," but did not issue a full press release about him. The item said Allen "was accounted for on Feb. 16, 2013" and will be buried in Wisconsin with full military honors at the end of June.[16]

The Pentagon commonly issues a full press release just before a funeral.

The POW Network says: "As the helicopter approached the landing zone, it came under enemy small arms fire. The aircraft was hit several times, exploded in midair and crashed. ... Later, a search and recovery team was inserted into the crash site to search the area for possible survivors and to recover the dead. The team found no sign of survivors in or around the area.

"They examined the helicopter's wreckage and successfully recovered several sets of remains ... Later, remains of the Sea Knight's co-pilot and crew

---

[15] http://www.homeofheroes.com/members/02_NX/citations/07_RVN-nc/nc_19rvn_usmcS.html

[16] http://www.dtic.mil/dpmo/accounted_for/ This obscure listing was found by journalist Catherine Breitenbucher of Whitefish Bay while she was double-checking some segments of this book for the author. The POW Network quickly reported a message from Sheila Allen-Kelly that "his remains were recovered in June 2012. POW MIA Organization met with our family to discuss their findings on Feb. 16, 2013." She said the burial will be on York Island at Bayfield.

chief were positively identified along with some members of the reconnaissance team. These remains were returned to their families for burial. Unfortunately, no remains were recovered that could be identified" as belonging to Allen or the four others. ... There appears to be little doubt that (they) died in the crash of the Sea Knight and, under the circumstances of loss, there seems to be little chance that their remains are recoverable."[17]

Army Staff Sgt. James Lee Van Bendegom, Kenosha: He was lost on July 12, 1967, in the Ia Drang Valley of South Vietnam. Van Bendegom and some other soldiers who were in that fighting were taken prisoner; five eventually were released and one is MIA along with the Kenosha soldier.[18]

He was 18 and a member of B Company, 1st Battalion, 12th Regiment of the 4th Infantry Division. Van Bendegom was a private first class and promoted in steps to staff sergeant after being captured.

According to the POW Network, Van Bendegom's group was "on patrol when they engaged a hostile force in the Ia Drang Valley, Pleiku Province. Pfc. Van Bendegom was wounded and treated by a medic. He was left behind when his unit's position was overrun, and he was captured.

"According to other U.S. POWs released during Operation Homecoming (in 1973 after the Paris Peace Accords), it was rumored that Pfc. Van Bendegom was taken from Pleiku Province into Cambodia and was treated at a field hospital. His name did not appear on the ... 'died in captivity' list. He was declared dead / body not recovered in May 1973.

" ... During 1992, U.S. investigators in Vietnam received information describing the death of three Americans in captivity. One death was correlated to Pfc. Van Bendegom," but nothing was decided officially.

James F. Schiele of Utah is the other soldier still missing today, along with Van Bendegom. Like Van Bendegom, he has become a staff sergeant. "Schiele's platoon leader saw him as his unit was forced to withdraw; Schiele had been hit a number of times in the legs and chest by automatic weapons fire and was thought to be dead. Pfc. Van Bendegom had been wounded and treated by a medic. Van Bendegom's status was changed on July 31, 1967,

---

[17] http://www.pownetwork.org/bios/a/a357.htm and http://www.usvetdsp.com/vn_pw_bios/h414.htm

[18] http://www.pownetwork.org/bios/v/v012.htm

from captured to 'died while captured;' Schiele's status was changed on March 27, 1978, from missing to 'died while missing.'"[19]

The POW Network added that Van Bendegom and one other man "were captured by the North Vietnamese, while the others, apparently, were captured by Viet Cong ... One of the released Americans was later told by the commanding North Vietnamese officer at his prison camp in Cambodia that Van Bendegom had died of his wounds."[20]

A total of 35 Americans died in this battle, most of them from Van Bendegom's company.[21]

Navy Lt. Michael John Allard, Schofield REMAINS HAVE BEEN IDENTIFIED: Allard was the pilot of an A-4 Skyhawk Bomber on the aircraft carrier USS Coral Sea when he was shot down over North Vietnam on Aug. 30, 1967, just north of the DMZ. He was 26, and it was only his second attack mission from the carrier.

Remains were repatriated in 1993, and identified as Allard's in the fall of 2000. He was buried at Arlington National Cemetery on March 19, 2001.[22]

The POW Network says very little[23] about his case, and did not update Allard's listing when the identification was made. Task Force Omega has nothing.

Allard was killed nine months after the Coral Sea lost pilot William Tamm Arnold of West Allis, who already has been reported in this chapter. Arnold also was flying a Skyhawk.

Air Force Capt. Donald William Downing, Janesville: Downing was the bombardier / navigator on a mission over North Vietnam in the 557th Squadron, 12th Tactical Fighter Wing, when he was shot down on Sept. 5, 1967. This was only a week after Allard was lost.

---

[19] http://www.virtualwall.org/dv/VanbendegomJL01a.htm

[20] http://www.pownetwork.org/bios/v/v012.htm and http://taskforceomegainc.org/v012.html

[21] The battle is described in full at http://www.virtualwall.org/units/c-1-12in.htm

[22] http://www.arlingtoncemetery.net/mjallard.htm The site also includes newspaper stories about his memorial service. Also http://www.usscoralsea.net/pages/pow.php#allard

[23] http://www.pownetwork.org/bios/a/a356.htm

Downing, 33, was promoted to lieutenant colonel while he was missing and was declared "died while missing" in April 1978. The squadron flew F-4C Phantom fighter-attack jets out of Cam Ranh Bay, Vietnam.[24]

Downing's pilot and fellow MIA was 1st Lt. Paul D. Raymond of Deposit, N.Y. They went down about 10 miles north of the city of Vinh Linh.[25] So did another Phantom, occupied by Thomas P. Hanson of Miami, Fla., and Carl D. Miller of Marshall, Mo., who also are MIA.

"Whether the four airmen ... survived to be captured is not known. Whether they are among those believed to be still alive today is uncertain," the POW Network says.

Marine Capt. Harold John Moe, Eau Claire: Moe was the radar intercept officer aboard an F-4B Phantom jet when it was shot down over Quang Tri Province of South Vietnam on Sept. 26, 1967. He was 29.

One report says he was in Marine Attack Squadron 542, nicknamed the TIgers.[26] But the record at the Virtual Wall, www.virtualwall.org, lists him as a member of Headquarters and Maintenance Squadron 13 in Marine Aircraft Group 13.

Moe's case was declared "hostile, died outright." He was a first lieutenant at the time and was promoted to captain at some point afterwards.

The pilot was Maj. P.M. Cole, who safely ejected along with Moe.[27] The number of their plane was 148422 WH, and the unit was VMF-542 flying out of Chu Lai. The POW Network has "no further information" on Moe's case other than the basics.[28] It has nothing on Cole because he was not killed or taken prisoner, nor is he missing.

Six days after Moe's plane was shot down, the Daily Telegram in Eau Claire reported his case on page 3A, under the headline, "Marine Officer

---

[24] http://airwarvietnam.com/557tfs.htm

[25] http://www.pownetwork.org/bios/d/d037.htm

[26] http://www.ejection-history.org.uk/Aircraft_by_Type/F-4_PHANTOM_USA/f4_phantom_US_1967.htm The squadron history is at http://www.marines.mil/unit/2ndMAW/mag14/vma542/Pages/documents/vma542history.pdf

[27] http://www.ejection-history.org.uk/Aircraft_by_Type/F-4_PHANTOM_USA/f4_phantom_US_1967.htm and http://www.ejection-history.org.uk/project/year_pages/1967.htm#sep

[28] http://www.pownetwork.org/bios/m/m211.htm

Killed in Action in Vietnam." The article, found with the help of the Chippewa Valley Museum in Eau Claire, said Moe's parents first were notified he was missing on Sept. 26, and soon were updated. The pilot "was later recovered but no trace was found of Moe," the story said. "Later word was received by his wife, the former Nancy Neill, Route 1, Eau Claire, that his chute failed to open."

He was born in Strum and was a 1956 graduate of Altoona High School. He was married in 1958 and had six children, including year-old twins. His parents were Mr. and Mrs. Bernard Moe of Eau Claire, and he had three siblings. Moe's memorial service was Oct. 4 at Altoona Methodist Church.

A friend of Moe's from Eau Claire posted a message at www.thewall-usa.com in 2008. Francis (Corky) Coe said: "Harold was a good friend during high school in the 1950s. I remember his pink and white, shoebox custom Ford and his white buck shoes. He was a really cool guy! A recent motorcycle ride in Arizona with the Patriot Guard to welcome home two Marines from Iraq reminded me how poorly the returning troops from Vietnam were treated. We thank you, old buddy, for your extreme sacrifice!"[29]

Marine Gunnery Sgt. Richard William Fischer, Madison REMAINS HAVE BEEN IDENTIFIED: He was a machine gunner in Company M, 3rd Battalion, 5th Marine Regiment, and disappeared on Jan. 8, 1968, in Quang Nam Province, South Vietnam. He was 20.

Bone fragments from Fischer were identified in 2007.[30] The Pentagon said he was in an ambush patrol south of Da Nang, "became separated from his unit and subsequent attempts by his team members to locate him were met with enemy fire. In 1992 and 1993, joint U.S. / Socialist Republic of Vietnam teams, led by the Joint POW / MIA Accounting Command, conducted three investigations and interviewed several Vietnamese citizens. The citizens said that Fischer was killed by Viet Cong and his remains were buried in a nearby cultivated field. In 1994, a joint team excavated the burial site and recovered human remains and other material evidence including uniform buttons," and he was identified via DNA.

The Virtual Wall gives more details: "After daybreak, the ambush position was compromised by the normal movements of the Vietnamese civilians.

---

[29] http://www.thewall-usa.com/guest.asp?recid=35824

[30] http://www.dtic.mil/dpmo/news/news_releases/2007/documents/Fischer.pdf

A number of the civilians greeted or otherwise interacted with the Marines, and two young women (one with a leg amputated below the knee) paid particular attention to … Fischer. Fischer separated himself from his squad and was last seen going with the women toward the amputee's house. When he didn't return the patrol attempted to search the hamlet but was taken under fire by an unknown-size enemy force. After exchanging several hundred rounds, the squad withdrew. A larger force returned later on 08 January and searched the village; searches continued for the next two days but without success. Most villagers denied any knowledge of Fischer's whereabouts but an older local resident did say that an American had been taken prisoner.[31]

Marine Capt. Paul Stuart Gee, Manitowish Waters: He was flight officer and radar observer on a Marine Corps reconnaissance plane that crashed on Jan. 16, 1968, in Quang Nam Province of South Vietnam. He was 24. Gee was declared dead in 1974, having been promoted to captain while he was MIA.

His unit was Marine Composite Reconnaissance Squadron 1, abbreviated VMCJ-1, in Marine Aircraft Group 11. The plane was a two-man Douglas EF-10B SkyKnight, piloted by Maj. William David Moreland of California. Moreland also is MIA.

The aircraft was returning from a mission and within sight of Da Nang, barely over water, the POW Network says in a very brief account for both him and Moreland.[32]

Air Force Col. Robert Frederick Wilke, Milwaukee: This pilot had been decorated twice for protecting a downed pilot and taking heavy fire on a mission, and then his jet was lost over North Vietnam on Jan. 17, 1968. Wilke, 42, a lieutenant colonel at the time, was flying an A1-E Skyraider in the 602nd Fighter Squadron of the 56th Air Commando Wing, based at Udorn Royal Air Base in Thailand. His case was declared in 1978 as "hostile, died while missing."

---

31 http://www.virtualwall.org/df/FischerRW01a.htm A brief history of the 5th Marine Regiment is at http://www.combatwife.net/5thMarines.htm

32 http://www.pownetwork.org/bios/g/g009.htm and http://www.aero-web.org/specs/douglas/ef-10b.htm The history of the squadron is at http://www.mcara.us/VMCJ-1.html

Wilke received the Air Force Cross for the incident in which he was killed, in which he again was protecting downed airmen. He was cited[33] for

extraordinary heroism in connection with military operations against an opposing armed force as an A-1E Skyraider pilot … in action on 16 and 17 January 1968. On these dates, Colonel Wilke participated in the successful combat recovery of two downed aircrew members and commanded an effort to recover two other downed pilots. The latter attempted recovery required a penetration of and flight beneath an extremely low overcast condition.

With complete disregard for his own safety, Colonel Wilke executed a slow spiral maneuver into the cloud formation, broke out beneath the overcast, and initiated his search in mountainous terrain with extremely limited air space. As he was conducting this low-level search in a heavily defended hostile environment, intense ground fire was being directed toward his aircraft and resulted in his being shot down over hostile territory. Through his extraordinary heroism, superb airmanship, and aggressiveness in the face of hostile forces, Colonel Wilke reflected the highest credit upon himself and the United States Air Force.

His previous medals were the Distinguished Flying Cross and Bronze Oak Leaf Cluster for that cross. The first was from Sept. 3, 1967, protecting a downed pilot and, "as the rescue helicopter approached the area, Colonel Wilke's A-1E sustained a direct hit from a 37mm anti-aircraft artillery position. Colonel Wilke, realizing the seriousness of the situation, remained calm and continued to suppress ground fire thereby protecting the unarmed rescue helicopter during its egress from the hostile area," and getting his own stricken plane to safety.

The Bronze Oak Leaf Cluster was for Sept. 21, 1967, when he was part of "a successful large-scale attack against one of the most important and heavily defended targets in Southeast Asia."

Air Force Capt. James Allan Ketterer, Milwaukee: He was on an F-4C Phantom fighter-bomber in the the 389th Squadron, 366th Tactical Fighter Wing, that was lost in a night reconnaissance mission over North

---

[33] http://militarytimes.com/citations-medals-awards/recipient.php?recipientid=3566

Vietnam on Jan. 20, 1968. This was the third MIA loss of a Wisconsin man in only a week and fourth in two weeks.

Ketterer was 25 and was promoted to captain while an MIA; in 1976 his case was classified as "hostile, died while missing."

The 389th was flying out of Da Nang at this time. It had been based there starting in October 1966; previously it flew out of Phan Rang Air Base. Ketterer's pilot was Capt. Tilden Holley of Cameron, Texas. Their plane's call sign was "Outlaw 01."

The POW Network says Ketterer's job was to operate the bombing equipment and other technical gear on the aircraft. "While striking a target near the city of Quang Khe in Quang Binh Province, North Vietnam, flight members (this means Holley's wingman) observed an orange streak of light through the clouds while Holley's aircraft was making passes over the target. A brief beeper was heard after the light was seen, but no radio transmissions were received and no parachutes were observed. Evidently, the aircraft had been hit by enemy fire.

"Even though the Air Force states that no parachutes were seen, and no emergency radio beepers were heard, subsequent information is included in the Defense Department raw data which may reveal the fates of Ketterer and Holley," the POW Nework adds. "The DIA notation on Holley's incident indicates that he successfully ejected from the aircraft, but was killed in a shootout with enemy troops in the area. Ketterer's DIA remarks simply state he is dead, and list the report code numbers."[34]

An account by Task Force Omega says the wingman "observed heavy automatic weapons tracers rising up on their left and 37mm anti-aircraft artillery tracers from the right passing 100 feet below their aircraft."[35]

Navy Chief Aviation Ordnanceman Donald Louis Gallagher, Sheboygan Falls, and Navy Lt. (j.g.) Roy Arthur Huss, Eau Claire: They both were lost on a Navy P-3 Orion patrol plane off the coast of Vietnam on Feb. 6, 1968, along with 10 other men. Gallagher was age 29 and a member of Navy's VP-26 air patrol squadron based in Thailand; Huss was 24 and a flight officer in VP-26, which was part of Task Force 72 of the 7th Fleet.

Their unit was an antisubmarine group based in Brunswick, Maine, but was on "temporary duty" in Vietnam. The plane crashed 50 miles off the

34 http://www.pownetwork.org/bios/k/k013.htm

35 http://taskforceomegainc.org/k013.html

shore of South Vietnam's An Xuyen Province in the Gulf of Thailand; they likely were monitoring sea shipments of goods to the Viet Cong.

One report [36] says

antisubmarine teams were frequently used for search missions. They also sometimes assisted in attacks on small enemy water craft.

Shortly after midnight on Feb. 6, the Orion reported a surface contact. Some two hours later it reported another contact somewhat further east. The last report received from the Orion was after 0300 hours. No subsequent communication was received.

An emergency communication alert for the aircraft was declared shortly after daybreak and a full search and rescue was declared. In the late afternoon of Feb. 6, wreckage and debris were sighted and identified. (After searching for weeks), the investigating officer concluded that the Orion had impacted with the water, and that the aircraft had been completely destroyed, and that all of the crew members had died instantly.

Gallagher's family received a telegram about the crash on Feb. 8, and it was front-page news in The Sheboygan Press the next day, under a two-column headline, "Navy Confirms Death of Chief Gallagher." He was a chief petty officer at the time and the story said he was from Sheboygan Falls. It added that he was the eighth man from Sheboygan County to die in the war; the final total at the Virtual Wall, www.virtualwall.org, is 16 from just the city of Sheboygan. Gallagher was a 1957 graduate of Sheboygan Falls High School, and his parents, Mr. and Mrs. Jack Gallagher, were living in that city. He had been in the Navy for 11 years.

The Eau Claire Leader ran a short Associated Press wire story about Huss on Feb. 10, saying he lived in Abbotsford, which is 64 miles to the east. The story noted that his wife, Judy, and daughter were in Abbotsford, so perhaps she was from that city originally. Nevertheless, Eau Claire was Huss'

---

[36] http://www.vpnavy.org/vp26mem.html Another account is at http://navy.togetherweserved.com/usn/servlet/tws.webapp.WebApp?cmd=ShadowBoxProfile&type=Person&ID=414238 More about VP-26 at http://www.vpnavy. org/vp26_1960.html, http://www.vpnavy.org/vp26.html and http://www.vpnavy. org/vp26_history_unknown.html

home of record. The story also said he enlisted in 1965 and was a graduate of what at the time was Eau Claire State University. The university registrar says Huss received a degree in biology and minored in chemistry.

The AP story reported that the unit of Huss and Gallagher had been sent to the Philippines in November 1967. That article was tracked down by the Chippewa Valley Museum at the request of the author of this book.

While the Wisconsinites are MIA, those whose bodies were recovered were the pilot, Lt. Cmdr. Robert Meglio of Flushing, N.Y., and Aviation Antisubmarine Warfare Technician 1st Class Billy McGhee of Rockwood, Tenn. A memorial site for Lt. (j.g.) Lynn Travis of Arkansas, another man on the plane with Gallagher and Huss, is at http://www.nhsalumni.net/ memorial/travis.html.

A Navy history of the Orion aircraft is at http://www.history.navy.mil/ planes/p3.htm

Navy Aviation Electronics Technician 2nd Class John Francis Hartzheim, Appleton REMAINS HAVE BEEN IDENTIFIED: He was the radioman on a nine-man reconnaissance plane that was shot down over Laos on Feb. 27, 1968. He was 22. Remains were repatriated in 1996 and his identification was announced on Feb. 19, 1999.

The Pentagon statement said: "Hartzheim was on board an OP-2E Neptune flying a reconnaissance mission over Khammouan Province, Laos. While over the target area the aircraft was struck by an enemy 37mm anti-aircraft round, causing the radar well and bomb bay to catch fire. Shrapnel from the explosion struck Hartzheim. He collapsed at the rear of the aircraft during evacuation and was presumed dead.

"The crew parachuted out of the aircraft as it entered a steep climb before crashing. A subsequent search and rescue team succeeded in rescuing only seven of the nine crew members. In January 1985, a unilateral turnover from a Laotian source to the Joint Casualty Resolution Center Liaison Office in Bangkok consisted of several bone fragments, a compass and a plastic E-and-E (Escape and Evasion) map. The source indicated that the items were recovered near a 1968 crash site of an U.S. aircraft in Khammouan Province.

"In October and December 1994 joint U.S. / Lao teams traveled to the Khammouan Province to interview several villagers with information about the crash. While surveying the crash site the team found aircraft wreckage, a fragment of a possible knife sheath and human remains. Successive visits in

1995 and 1996 recovered more remains, life support equipment and other crew-related items."[37]

Marine Pfc. Thomas Joseph Blackman, Racine REMAINS HAVE BEEN IDENTIFIED, and Marine Lance Cpl. Raymond Thomas Heyne, Mason (Bayfield County) REMAINS HAVE BEEN IDENTIFIED: They both were lost on May 10, 1968, in Quang Tin Province of South Vietnam. Blackman was age 19 and a field artillery fire controller in D Battery of the 2nd Battalion, 13th Regiment, 1st Marine Division. Heyne, 20, was in the same battery.

Remains of both were repatriated 31 years later, in September 1999, and identified years after that. The Pentagon announcement on Aug. 10, 2005, dealt with 11 Marines and one Army man in that battle. It said seven men, including Blackman, were being buried as a group in Arlington National Cemetery and that five sets of remains – including Heyne's – were being returned to families for burial. Heyne's family chose Arlington right by his comrades.

The Pentagon[38] reported: "The Marines were part of an artillery platoon airlifted to provide support to the 11th Mobile Strike Force, which was under threat of attack from North Vietnamese forces near Kham Duc in South Vietnam. On May 9, 1968, the Strike Force had been directed to reconnoiter an area known as Little Ngok Tavak Hill near the Laos-Vietnam border, in the Kham Duc Province. Their base came under attack by North Vietnamese Army troops, and after a 10-hour battle, all of the survivors were able to withdraw from the area.

"Six investigations beginning in 1993 and a series of interviews of villagers and former Vietnamese soldiers led U.S. recovery teams in 1994, 1997

---

[37] http://www.dtic.mil/dpmo/news/news_releases/1999/documents/990317_osd_
019m_sea.pdf and http://community.seattletimes.nwsource.com/archive/ ?date=
19990318&slug=2950148

[38] http://www.dtic.mil/dpmo/news/news_releases/2004/documents/12MIA080
905.pdf Also see http://www.arlingtoncemetery.net/vietnam-recoveries-august-
2005.htm for related news coverage. One of the photos shows that the grave of
Wisconsin's James Neil Tycz, from earlier in this chapter, which is in the same area.
A Washington Post story about the Arlington service is at http://www.journaltimes.
com/news/local/racine-soldier-killed-in-vietnam-in-laid-to-rest/article_4766c3e5-
081d-552f-8a6e-b714bd8fe16d.html

and 1998 to specific defensive positions within the large battle site. Additionally, maps provided by American survivors helped to locate some key areas on the battlefield. Three excavations by the Joint POW / MIA Accounting Command in 1998 and 1999 yielded human remains, personal effects and other material evidence."

Army Sgt. Paul Reid Frazier, Milwaukee: He was 19 and a repairman for UH-1 helicopters in the 191st Assault Helicopter Company of the 214th Aviation Battalion when his chopper was shot down on Sept. 3, 1968, in Long An Province, South Vietnam. Frazier was the crew chief of the copter. He is profiled in the next chapter.

Marine Capt. Paul Derby, Menomonie: He was a 25-year-old pilot who was shot down on Nov. 17, 1968, over Quang Ngai Province of South Vietnam while flying a Mach II supersonic Phantom F-4B. He is profiled in the next chapter.

Marine Capt. Edwin James Fickler, Kewaskum: He was a pilot who was shot down on Jan. 17, 1969, over Quang Tin Province in South Vietnam. He was 25 and in Headquarters and Maintenance 11, in Marine Air Group 11, which was based at Da Nang. Five years after his loss, Fickler's status was changed from missing to died while missing. He is profiled in the next chapter.

Army Sgt. William Anthony Evans, Milwaukee: Evans, 20, was killed on a secret mission in Cambodia on March 2, 1969. He was a member of unit B-50 of the Special Forces, part of the Military Assistance Command, Vietnam Studies and Observation Group. Evans received what was described as multiple fragmentation wounds.

The POW Network says Evans was the leader of an 11-man team, with Specialist 4 Michael May of Vassar, Mich., as the No. 2. It says the unit: [39]

> **was a joint service high command unconventional warfare task force engaged in highly classified operations throughout Southeast Asia. ... The teams performed deep-penetration missions of strategic reconnaissance and interdiction which were called, depending on the time frame, "Shining Brass" or "Prairie Fire" missions. ...**
>
> **After being inserted at a landing zone, the team moved toward its objective. As the team approached the wood line,**

---

[39] http://www.pownetwork.org/bios/e/e363.htm

several members of the team heard the sound of rifle safeties being clicked, followed by a blast of weapons fire from the front and left flank. It was later judged that the team had been hit by a battalion-size North Vietnamese Army force from its base camp. The team fell back 60 meters to a mound located in the area. A perimeter was formed, and the enemy closed in on the position.

Gunships were called in to repel the enemy advance, and after they departed the area, at about 1700 hours, the enemy attacked again. Later that day, a projectile thought to be a B-40 rocket exploded directly over the team's position, resulting in wounds to eight of 11 men. Evans at that time sustained a lethal head wound and died shortly thereafter. May received multiple wounds to the head and chest and died 30 minutes later. The surviving members of the team moved about 60 meters from the area, leaving the remains of Evans, May and three (South Vietnamese army) team members behind.

One account of the action states that medical evacuation teams conducted an aerial search during which aerial photos revealed the Americans on the team had all been killed. Another account reports that the nine American members of the team survived.

Both Evans and May were classified as killed / body not recovered.

Army Capt. Richard Lee Bowers, Lake Mills: He was commander of Mobile Advance Team IV-49 when he was lost – apparently he was captured and then tried to escape – on March 24, 1969, in Ba Xugen Province in South Vietnam.

Bowers, 22, was listed as a case of "died while captured," and was declared dead in September 1978, termed a ground casualty. A report on the website of the American Ex-Prisoners of War lists Bowers as captured with another soldier "when their base near Saigon was overrun, escaped day of capture, recaptured later that day. Killed next day in his second escape attempt." The site says the other soldier was Sgt. Gerasimo Arroyo-Baez of Puerto Rico, who "escaped day of capture, recaptured later that day. Died in captivity. North Vietnamese Army's list death as 22 Aug 1972."[40]

---

[40] http://www.axpow.org/vietnamescapes.pdf

Arroyo-Baez's remains were repatriated in 1985 and identified less than a month later, according to Virtual Wall. Bowers still is MIA.

Army Chief Warrant Officer William C. Pierson III, Madison: Pierson was a helicopter co-pilot who was lost in Quang Nam Province in South Vietnam on April 13, 1969. He was age 21; he is MIA, but the body of the copter pilot was found a few days later. Pierson is profiled in the next chapter.

Marine Capt. Norman Karl Billipp, Milwaukee REMAINS HAVE BEEN IDENTIFIED: Billipp was the pilot of OV-10 Bronco fixed-wing observation plane in Marine Observation Squadron 6 (VMO-6) and was shot down on May 6, 1969, over Laos. He was age 24 and promoted soon afterwards.

Remains were repatriated in March 1996 and identified as Billipp in November of that year.[41]

Pentagon announcements usually are made made a few months after identification, once the family has been notified and a service arranged, but Billipp's name is not in anything from 1997. Announcements on the Pentagon website go back only to 1997. There is, however, a statement from Feb. 25, 1997, that says remains of five servicemen had been identified "and are being returned to their families for burial in the United States" and that the names of three of them "are being withheld at the request of their families."[42] The two who were named in that release were the Marine pilot of an A-4E Skyhawk lost in April 1967 and a Navy air crewman killed in November of that year.

A website devoted to VMO-6 says Billipp was the pilot of the OV-10 Bronco and his one passenger was Maj. John Robert Hagan of Georgia.[43]

Hagan was age 23 and "a 6-foot-6 red-haired Marine officer, was known for getting airsick on the dangerous, twice-a-day missions. Few knew he had been awarded a Silver Star, Bronze Star and Purple Heart in the war," according to a buddy who brought his photo to Washington for a history project in 2009.[44] "On May 6, 1969, a group of the planes had gone out but were

---

41 http://www.ov-10bronco.net/usmc-3.cfm

42 http://www.dtic.mil/dpmo/news/news_releases/1997/documents/970225_osd _023m_sea.pdf

43 http://www.popasmoke.com/kia/incidents.php?incident_id=210&conflict_id=24

44 http://www.washingtonpost.com/wp-dyn/content/article/2009/09/16/AR200 9091603361.html

ordered back to base because of bad weather. All returned but Hagan and his pilot, Norman Billipp," the Washington Post reported in a story posted at that site.[45]

The POW Network reports that the "last radio contact said 'do visual recon Highway 9, Ca Lu to Laos Border,' and concludes, "No further information available at this time."[46] Hagan's body was recovered later; it is not clear when or whether he is one of the three unnamed persons in the 1997 statement by the Pentagon.

Navy Aviation Boatswain 3rd Class William Dale Gorsuch, Cambria: He was aboard a C-2A plane carrying 26 men from the Philippines to an aircraft carrier and destroyers in the Gulf of Tonkin on Oct. 2, 1969. The plane went down and all were MIA. Gorsuch was 21, and his death is classified as "non-hostile, died of other causes."

The aircraft was headed for the USS Constellation, but the carrier's radar lost contact with the plane, which was 26 nautical miles away, at 6:55 a.m. This was 68 miles due east of the North Vietnamese coastline.

Reports say an oil slick and debris was quickly spotted. Debris indicated that the plane was "in a relatively high-speed, nose down, right wing down impact with the water, or a possible right wing failure before impact." There were no sign of survivors and no bodies were recovered.[47]

Air Force Staff Sgt. Charles Richard Fellenz, Marshfield REMAINS HAVE BEEN IDENTIFIED: He was lost on Nov. 24, 1969, while on an airdrop mission over Laos with the 41st Squadron, 374th Tactical Airlift Wing. Fellenz, 30, was aboard a C-130A Hercules transport plane. Remains were repatriated in November 1993 and were identified as those of Fellenz in October 1995. The other seven men on the plane also were identified.

Fellenz was promoted to chief master sergeant while an MIA. He was an inventory management specialist.[48]

---

[45] A history of the observation squadron is at http://vmo6rocks.homestead.com/history.html

[46] http://www.pownetwork.org/bios/b/b125.htm

[47] http://www.facesfromthewall.com/1969oct.html Also http://taskforceomegainc.org/g123.html and http://www.pownetwork.org/bios/l/l103.htm

[48] http://airforce.togetherweserved.com/usaf/servlet/tws.webapp.WebApp?cmd=ShadowBoxProfile&type=Person&ID=80150

According to Task Force Omega, he was serving as a flare operator aboard the plane "over the rugged, jungle-covered mountains near the city of Ban Bac, Savannakhet Province, Laos; the C-130A was observed as several rounds of 37mm antiaircraft artillery fire hit it. Other pilots saw the aircraft burst into flames, crash to the ground and explode on impact in an area laced with primary and secondary roads, along with rivers of various sizes. The crash site was located about 29 miles west of the Lao / Vietnamese border, 67 miles west-northwest of Kham Duc and 90 miles west-southwest of Da Nang, South Vietnam."[49]

Another report says: "In January 1993, a team from the Joint Task Force for Full Accounting visited the C-130A crash site for the first time. During that survey and excavation operation, no bone fragments or teeth were found. A full-scale crash site field excavation was conducted from Oct. 21 to Nov. 8, 1993, during which time 649 unidentifiable bone fragments and five teeth were recovered. On Oct. 23, 1995, nearly two years later, the remains were accepted by the United States government as 'positively identified group remains' of all eight crew members." They are buried at Arlington National Cemetery.[50]

Army Maj. Dale Wayne Richardson, Cashton: Richardson was in D Company, 34th Armored Regiment of the 25th Infantry Division, and was lost on May 2, 1970, in Cambodia. Eight men were on a helicopter on a highly secret mission; Richardson and several others were taken prisoner by the Viet Cong. But when some were freed in 1973, he did not appear.

Richardson, who turned age 29 three days after his loss, was aboard a UH-1H helicopter. He was a captain and was promoted to major at some point afterwards; his status was changed in 1979 to "hostile, died while missing."

The copter was shot down was during the controversial "incursion" into that country ordered by President Richard M. Nixon a few days earlier, although there are ample reports from earlier in the war about missions over Cambodia and Laos.

Here is Task Force Omega's report of the loss; the account is detailed because the case involved so many people:[51]

---

49 http://taskforceomegainc.org/f025.html.

50 http://www.findagrave.com/cgi-bin/fg.cgi?page=gr&GRid=22307269

51 http://taskforceomegainc.org/R070.htm

The helicopter departed Tay Ninh, South Vietnam, on a logistics mission to Fire Support Base Bruiser, Kontum Province, South Vietnam, which was located just south of the Vietnamese / Cambodian border. During the flight, it encountered a heavy rainstorm, and while trying to locate the fire support base in the zero visibility caused by the weather conditions, the Huey crossed the border into Cambodia. It was struck by enemy radar-guided .60 caliber anti-aircraft machinegun fire which ignited flammable material in the rear of the aircraft."

(The copter ditched) in a rice paddy near the city of Memot, Cambodia, approximately two miles north of the Vietnamese / Cambodian border and 30 miles due north of Tay Ninh. ...

The crew and passengers exited the aircraft unharmed .... The group decided it was best for them to head for Firebase Bruiser ... , but within 30 to 40 seconds of hitting the ground, Michael Varnado (the pilot) warned the group that the enemy was approaching. They disbursed in different directions in order to find cover in the elephant grass that grew from the edge of the rice paddy to the tree line. As they scattered, the enemy opened fire from all sides.

Pvt. Tony Karreci ran, jumped into a ditch, and hid under a bush. From that vantage point he watched as Michael Varnado disappeared from sight into the elephant grass. Dan Maslowski found shelter in a ditch / depression in the rice paddy near Frederick Crowson and Dale Richardson, where they were pinned down by the enemy. As he fired his .38 caliber pistol at one VC soldier, another one put the muzzle of his gun to Warrant Officer 1st Class (Dan) Maslowski's head and said: "Surrender or die."

The trio surrendered, were searched then led away to an enemy camp located in the tree-line about 25 yards from where the aircraft landed in the rice paddy. ... They were tied and blindfolded, then led through a small village to a larger one, where they were held until dark. From there the captured Americans were marched for about two hours to their first detention camp.

Pvt. Karreci also recounted that after Richardson, Maslowski and Crowson surrendered to the VC, he saw some enemy soldiers go over to a clump of bamboo and begin firing into it. Then they dragged the wounded aircraft pilot out and dragged him in the direction of the rest of the captives. The door gunner also stated that an hour after Warrant Officer 1st Class Varnado was captured, he saw the Communists pull the body of an unconscious or dead "blond, heavyset man" from out of the bamboo and left him out in the open. He was not able to identify that man, but based on intelligence analysis, government personnel believe it was possibly Rodney Griffin.

Varnado joined Capt. Richardson, WO1 Maslowski and Specialist 4 Crowson at the first detention camp. Because of the wounds to his side and leg, Michael Varnado was brought to this camp on a stretcher. The three uninjured POWs were subsequently moved out of this camp while the injured pilot was left behind. Dan Maslowski also stated that while in that first compound, Capt. Richardson was interrogated by their Viet Cong captors about a top secret document they produced. This document was last known to be in Capt. Richardson's possession.

... Only Tony Karreci, the 18-year-old door gunner, successfully evaded capture and made his way back to friendly control on 4 May 1970. The other seven passengers and crew were initially listed missing in action. Once their true status became known to US authorities, (the status of) Dan Maslowski, Frederick Crowson, Michael Varnado, Bunyan Price and Robert Young was immediately changed to prisoner of war. Even though Dale Richardson was known to have been captured, his status, and that of Rodney Griffin, remained missing in action.

Both Frederick Crowson and Dan Maslowski were released by the VC at Loc Ninh, South Vietnam, with 25 other American POWs on 12 February 1973. In their debriefings, they recounted how they survived under extremely primitive conditions filled with malnutrition, dysentery and no medical attention at the hands of the Viet Cong who moved them between jungle camps in both South Vietnam and Cambodia. ...

On 27 April 1989, the Communists returned Michael Varnado's remains to US control. They were positively identified on

1 August 1989. ... For Bunyan Price, Rodney Griffin and Dale Richardson, only unanswered questions remain.
Army Specialist 4 Peter Alden Schmidt, Milwaukee: He was lost on Aug. 15, 1970, in the crash of a UH-1H Iroquois Huey helicopter in Laos during a rescue mission. Schmidt, 20, was its door gunner, and an aircraft maintenance apprentice in the 71st Assault Helicopter Company of the 14th Aviation Battalion.

Task Force Omega[52] says the copter was "on a reconnaissance team extraction mission about four miles from the Lao / Vietnamese border and one mile north of Dokchung, Xekong Province, Laos. Because of the extremely rugged, jungle-covered mountains in the planned extraction area, the reconnaissance team was to be lifted out. The helicopter hovered 50 feet over the pickup zone and dropped a ladder from the right side of the aircraft and the five team members climbed onto it. With the men clinging to the ladder, the helicopter climbed to an altitude of 100 feet before it began receiving enemy small arms fire. The reconnaissance team members were stripped off the ladder by the trees as the helicopter crashed into the jungle."

The pilot ... checked his crew, "and Schmidt was trapped in the right gunnel (gunwale). ... A few minutes later Specialist 4 Michael Crist checked Schmidt. The crew chief noticed that he was breathing in short gasps and was now losing a great deal of blood. Michael Crist had dislocated his collarbone during the crash and Raymond Anderson was equally shaken up in the landing. By working together, they attempted to free Peter Schmidt and James Becker from the wreckage, but were unable to do so.

"Anderson and Crist then made their way to the pickup zone and were extracted by a search and rescue helicopter. Because of the difficult terrain and the enemy presence in the area, no attempts were made to return to recover 1st Lt. Becker and Schmidt. Both men were immediately listed killed in action / body not recovered. ... While the fate of Becker and Schmidt is in little doubt, they have the right to have their remains returned to their families, friends and country."

Schmidt's company was known as the Rattlers and Firebirds.[53]

---

[52] http://taskforceomegainc.org/S365.htm

[53] Its history is at http://rattler-firebird.org/vietnam/unithistory/ The site discusses Aug. 15, without giving names. The 14th Battalion's history is at http://www.1stavnbde.com/14th/14th_Combat_Aviation_Battalion.htm

Army Sgt. 1st Class Randolph Leroy Johnson, Milwaukee: He was a repair mechanic on UH-1 Huey helicopters in the 48th Assault Helicopter Company of the 223rd Aviation Battalion and was killed in Laos on Feb. 20, 1971, along with three others on the bird. Johnson was age 21 and the crew chief; he was promoted in the years while his status was missing. That status was changed to "died while missing" in 1979.

The remains of two soldiers on the helicopter were identified in 1999 – Capt. David May, of Hyattsville, Md.; and Chief Warrant Officer Jon E. Reid, of Phoenix, Ariz. The Pentagon said the copter was "on an emergency resupply mission over Laos when they were hit by enemy ground fire and crashed. A search and rescue mission was repulsed by hostile fire. In 1994, 1996 and 1998, U.S. and Lao investigators interviewed villagers in the area of the crash, then initiated an excavation which recovered human remains as well as portions of an identification tag with the name 'May, David M.'[54]

However, nothing was identified from Johnson or the fourth man – Staff Sgt. Robert Joseph Acalotto of Pennsylvania. Thus there is speculation that Johnson and Acalotto may have made it away from the wreck and somehow were taken captive.[55]

One account is from a fellow pilot and says the copter was Joker 06. Its tail number was 66-00700.[56] The 48th Assault Helicopter unit was named the Bluestars and Jokesters.[57]

Army Specialist 5 Richard Jay Hentz, Oshkosh: He was a voice interpreter in the 138th Aviation Company of the Army Security Agency's 224th Aviation Battalion. He was lost when a surveillance plane was shot down over North Vietnam on a top-secret mission on March 4, 1971. Hentz was 23.

The plane was a JU-21A, a twin-engine turboprop especially designed for ASA intelligence work. A total of five men were aboard; the pilot was Capt. Michael Wayne Marker of Wichita Falls, Texas.

---

[54] http://www.dtic.mil/dpmo/news/news_releases/1999/documents/991209_osd_188m_sea.pdf

[55] Two accounts are at http://army.togetherweserved.com/army/servlet/tws.webapp.WebApp?cmd=ShadowBoxProfile&type=BattleMemoryExt&ID=142380 Another is from the POW Network, http://www.pownetwork.org/bios/j/j035.htm

[56] http://www.48ahc.org/html/we_will_not_forget.htm

[57] http://www.raydon.com/48ahc/ Other links to the unit are at http://www.vhfcn.org/unitlinks.html

An account of the mission [58] says the plane, "number 18-065, call sign 'Vanguard 216,' departed Phu Bai, Republic of Vietnam, on an early-morning combat support mission in the vicinity of the Demilitarized Zone. ...

> **The pilot and crew were assigned to ... 509th RR (Radio Research) Group. ... 'Radio Research' was actually a secret cover designation for certain units operating under the direction of the U.S. Army Security Agency Group, Vietnam. All missions of this agency were highly classified. The 224th Aviation Battalion was referred to as an aviation battalion in Vietnam for security reasons only. The JU-21A aircrew's actual unit designation was 138th ASA Company, 224th ASA Battalion (Aviation), U.S. Army Security Agency Group, Vietnam.**
> **Two hours into the mission, at 0840 hours, radio and radar communication was lost. When the aircraft failed to return from the mission at the appointed time, search efforts were initiated and continued for two days over a 300-mile area, but proved negative. A reliable source indicated that an aerial detonation in the vicinity of the DMZ occurred (the same day) at the same flight altitude and pattern flown by Vanguard 216. Hostile threat in the area precluded any visits to the suspected area of the crash. No trace was ever found of the aircraft or the crew.**

> **While the missing crew members were initially listed as missing In action, a change in status to "killed In action, body not recovered" occurred within 90 days of the incident. Regarding the status change, the families were told that all information pertinent to the incident was classified and would remain classified for 10 years. Since that date, the families have been told that the aircraft was involved in electronic surveillance, and their mission was top secret. The aircraft was hit by enemy artillery and was downed over North Vietnam.**

---

[58] http://army.togetherweserved.com/army/servlet/tws.webapp.WebApp?cmd=ShadowBoxProfile&type=Person&ID=52569 More about the the 224th Aviation Battalion (Radio Research) is at http://www.inscom.army.mil/Insight/2010/10%20May/10May2.html A history of the 509th Group is at http://www.inscom.army.mil/Insight/2010/10%20May/10May2.html and information about the Army Security Agency is at http://www.nasaa-home.org/history/narr.htm

Army Warrant Officer 1 Albert Raymond Trudeau, Milwaukee: He was the co-pilot of a cargo helicopter that crashed in bad weather off the coast of Khanh Hoa Province of South Vietnam on Oct. 26, 1971. Trudeau was 22. He is profiled in the next chapter.

Marine Capt. David Leverett Leet, Kenosha: Leet was a pilot who was lost at sea off of North Vietnam on April 13, 1972, in Marine Composite Reconnaissance Squadron One, VMCJ-I. The EA-6A Intruder plane was returning from a mission and there was no distress call or signal. He was age 25.

Task Force Omega says[59] Leet and his crewman, Capt. John M. Christensen of Ogden, Utah, the electronic countermeasure officer, "departed Da Nang Airbase on a night combat mission deep in North Vietnam. Their target area included the extremely well-defended area of Hanoi / Haiphong Harbor. After completing their mission, (they headed home). Capt. Leet established their last radio contact at 0412 hours.

"At that time there was no indication of trouble with the aircraft and it was approximately 100 miles inland from the coast of North Vietnam, 165 miles south-southwest of Haiphong, 92 miles northeast of Dong Hoi, North Vietnam; and 175 miles north-northwest of Da Nang. When the Intruder failed to return to base, a full scale search and rescue operation was initiated. During the extensive aerial search, no trace of the aircraft or its crew was found."

Air Force Staff Sgt. Todd Michael Melton, Milwaukee REMAINS HAVE BEEN IDENTIFIED: The 37th and final Wisconsin MIA of the war was a radio technician on a communications plane and was lost over Laos on Feb. 5, 1973, a week after the Paris Peace Accords were signed. One report says the crew was flying without dogtags, obviously a very secret mission. Melton was age 23 and serving with the 361st Tactical Electronic Warfare Squadron. He was one of eight people on the plane that was nicknamed the "Flying Pueblo" after the Navy spy ship that had been seized by North Korea in 1968.

Remains were repatriated 20 years later and Melton was identified in 1995.

---

[59] http://taskforceomegainc.org/L067.htm More about the EA-6A is at http://www.mcara.us/VMCJ-1.html

The plane's call sign was Baron 52. Task Force Omega says:[60]

It departed Ubon Airfield, Thailand, on a night intelligence-gathering mission to monitor any enemy traffic flowing down the Ho Chi Minh Trail. Such movement of men and material by the Communists would constitute a direct violation of the Peace Accords on their part.

... At approximately 0125 hours on 5 February 1973, Baron 52 reported to Operational Command that they were observing ground fire directed toward them from the jungle-covered mountains of southern Laos. The last message received ... came five to 10 minutes later when (Capt. George Spitz, the pilot) reported that everything was all right. When the aircraft failed to return to friendly control, the crew was declared missing.

(The wreckage was found two days later, and searchers found the bodies of the pilot and three other men.)

Evidence that the four sergeants (including Melton) bailed out of the aircraft and survived the loss manifested itself in several ways. ...

In 1978, five years later, the mother of one of the "back-enders" heard columnist Jack Anderson, on "Good Morning America" describe a Pathet Lao radio communiqué that described the capture of four "air pirates" on the same day as the EC-47Q carrying her son was shot down. There was no question that this information pertained to that specific crew because it was the only aircraft downed during that time frame. (Task Force Omega does not say whose mother this is, but later it refers to a letter in 1996 from the mother of Sgt. Joseph Matejov.)

In the fall of 1992, the Senate Select Committee on POW / MIA Affairs received sworn testimony from the Defense Intelligence Agency's senior analyst, Robert DeStatte ... that "the intercepted NVA communication that excited US Air Force analysts actually related to the movement of four airmen

---

[60] http://taskforceomegainc.org/m195.html

to the area of the port city of Vinh in the panhandle of North Vietnam and hundreds of kilometers from the site of Baron 52's disappearance. ...

In November 1992, a survey team arrived at the crash site. During its preliminary examination of the area, a team member "looked down and found, lying in plain sight and totally exposed to the elements, a military dogtag in pristine condition with Joe Matejov's name on it." Since this crew was flying "sanitized" – wearing no dogtags and with no insignias or rank on their flight suits, this find was both miraculous and suspicious. Later, the American excavation team recovered 23 bone fragments and half a tooth, a pre-molar reportedly belonging to (Sgt.) Peter Cressman. ...

Task Force Omega continues: "On 27 March 1996, a group burial of 23 bone fragments, half-tooth and dogtag bearing Joseph Matejov's name was conducted at Arlington National Cemetery. The families of all seven men were in attendance; however, the families of the four sergeants were there to honor the (flight) officers who gave their lives providing the men the time needed to jettison their equipment and bail out themselves. ... For the families of the four sergeants, only questions remain."[61]

---

[61] The work and mission of the 6994th Security Squadron is discussed in-depth at its comprehensive website, http://www.6994th.com. A former military colleague wrote a piece about Melton and the incident at http://www.angelfire.com/mn2/aviator9942/my_adopted_powmias3.html

Chapter 12
The lives of 5 who became MIAs in Vietnam

Four decades after he became an MIA in Vietnam, Paul Derby's fraternity brothers established a scholarship in his name at the University of Wisconsin – Stout. And his wife still wears a ring made from a tie tack that the Marine pilot bought just before being shot down in 1968.

As a boy, Jim Fickler went fishing all year round on the Milwaukee River in the heart of Kewaskum, and nearly broke his neck in a swimming accident at a local pond. He recovered well enough to be not only a Marine, but a Marine pilot. He was lost in 1969.

Al Trudeau was a helicopter co-pilot who never has been forgotten by a buddy who had lunch with him only hours before he disappeared in 1971; nor has he been forgotten by a patriotic Fort Atkinson woman who wore his MIA bracelet for more than a quarter-century until it wore out. Trudeau went to high school in West Germany on a U.S. military base, and had started high school in Milwaukee before his Army father was transferred there.

Bill "Biff" Pierson of Madison wanted to fly helicopters, but when he got to Vietnam he instead was made maintenance officer in his copter unit, according to a family friend. One day in 1969, a pilot took him up for a flight – and the copter was shot down.

Paul Frazier spent much of his high school time in Milwaukee hanging out with friends and partying; he soon wound up in Vietnam and so did one of his pals – a medic who long has worked to keep alive the memory of Frazier and others who were declared missing in action. Frazier's helicopter was shot down in 1968.

These five MIAs were from big towns and small towns, all across Wisconsin. They were pilots or co-pilots or crewmen of jets and helicopters when they were lost at ages ranging from 19 to 25.

This chapter takes a closer look at five of the Vietnam War MIAs from the total field of 37 that was examined in detail in the previous chapter.

Marine Capt. Paul Derby was a 25-year-old pilot who was shot down on Nov. 17, 1968. He was flying a supersonic jet, the Mach II Phantom F-4B, when he was lost over Quang Ngai Province of South Vietnam. His crewman's body was recovered; Derby's was not.

Marine Capt. Paul Derby (left) of Menomonie and Marshfield was MIA after his plane was shot down in 1968. Marine Capt. Jim Fickler (center) of Kewaskum, another pilot, was shot down in 1969. Army Warrant Officer 1st Class Al Trudeau of Milwaukee was lost when his helicopter crashed in bad weather off the coast of South Vietnam in 1971.

Derby's home of record was Menomonie, where he attended what now is UW – Stout. But he was from Marshfield, where he had graduated in 1961 from Columbus Catholic High School.

"He was a real fun-loving guy who liked to walk up to someone and give them a bear hug. He was a very athletic, very sports-minded person; always in a rough-housing mode," says Bob Koppes, who was one year behind Derby at Stout and was a housemate in Derby's senior year. Five of the frat brothers from Chi Lambda lived together in a rental house near the city's water tower. It was not a fraternity house per se; but it sure saw a lot of frat-type activities.

When Gerry Tietz joined Chi Lambda, "Paul walked up and asked me, 'Ever play tennis? We'll get a racket and we'll play.' That's the kind of guy he was – he embraced people and become your buddy." So they often played tennis or went skiing.

Tietz and Derby had the same major, industrial tech, and were in the Stout Society of Industrial Technology together. The organization was established in 1963, and Derby was its president in his senior year, 1964 to 1965.

Chi Lambda put together a car for racing in the winter carnival on Lake Menomin. "It was an old beat-up car, a piece of junk," Koppes says. "We painted it in our fraternity colors of light gray and red, and there was no glass and we made it a stock engine."

Dorothy Wormet says it was car No. 5 but that Derby was not allowed to be the driver. "It was such a neat car. I thought they wanted it in one piece when the race was over," she says. Another brother, Dwight Davis, was the driver.

Derby had met Wormet, who was from Wisconsin Dells, in his junior year. They were in the same circle of fraternity-sorority friends, and she was a Tri Sigma. Their first date was going to be the night of Nov. 23, 1963, but a tragic event in Dallas the day before had sent the nation into mourning. "When I heard the news about the president being shot, I wanted to go home, as did most of the students. It was not considered proper for girls to phone boys, back then, but I called Paul to inform him I was going home," says Dorothy, whose last name is Franczyk and who lives in Baraboo. "He always teased me about breaking our first date."

Soon, however, they were an item, and they married in Menomonie in January 1965, between semesters of their senior years. Father Charles A. Blecha officiated, and Franczyk says "Paul hid his car in a physician's parking space at the Red Cedar Clinic across the street from where he was living. He was afraid the car would not withstand any antics the Chi Lambdas might perform!"

On some of their dates, they attended stock car races, not that she was a fan. Derby also loved downhill skiing and waterskiing. Anything with speed seemed to draw his interest. "He told me he had had a desire to fly since he was a small boy. He had already completed one summer of OCS in Quantico, Va., before we met. I am not sure how he decided to become a Marine. But he was so proud to wear that uniform."

Derby went into the Marines immediately after graduating in May 1965 – Franczyk says "it was so important to Paul, but I was getting leery of it," because the war was escalating. He trained at Cherry Point, N.C.

"The squadrons performed an air show," Franczyk says. "Paul was one of the pilots. As the final maneuver of the show, Paul requested the tower to allow him to perform a maximum performance climb. I knew that was Paul's plane and will never forget watching Paul fly out of sight into the clouds. The day Paul left Madison for Vietnam, I, once again, watched his plane until it disappeared into the clouds."

That was in July 1968, the last time she saw him. Their kids were 1 and 2 years old – and his son turned 3 only five days before Paul was MIA.

"Paul flew over 100 missions," Franczyk says. "It was his first tour. He did have the opportunity to go to Hong Kong for a brief R & R. While there, he purchased a pair of black star sapphire earrings in a heart-shaped setting for me. We had an R & R planned for Hawaii in December."

But he was lost on Nov. 17.

The earrings were in Derby's belongings that were shipped home, along with a white-gold tie tack. "I decided to make the tie tack into a ring. I took it to the Twin Cities to have it done. And I wear it every day still." She still has the earrings.

At Stout, Derby had been very interested in taking the Marine flyer's test in the student union and was looking for someone to take it along with him.

"No one else would go with him at the time, so I said, 'I'll go,'" Koppes says. "I regret that to this day, because of his outcome. I almost feel a tremendous sense of guilt. I went to his graduation day (in 1965) and after his walk, the Marines took him away. I never went into the program. He was one special frat brother and one of a kind. I miss him!!!"

Chi Lambda, which is purely a Stout organization, was organized in 1956. Its goals are "To create a strong bond of brotherhood among the members, to foster social competence of the members, to promote high moral and ethical values and to contribute to the wholesome growth of the extracurricular activities of the campus."[1]

Members from the 1960s meet somewhere in Wisconsin every two years, according to Tietz and Koppes, who each live in the Twin Cities area. A few years ago, Tietz had just won money in a drawing and preferred to be a donor to something worthy instead of having to fork a high percentage over to the Internal Revenue Service, so he challenged the frat alums to set up a scholarship of some sort for one current Chi Lambda student.

"It went from an idea to a blaze, instantaneously," Tietz says – Derby's name quickly came up as the possible name for the scholarship and that assent was as fast as his supersonic jet was. The men quickly raised enough to endow the annual award, and have kept the amount going up since then. Tietz and others journey to Stout each fall to present the Chi Lambda / Paul Derby Memorial Scholarship.

---

[1] http://uwstout.orgsync.com/org/chilambda/home

Franczyk is a contributor and a big fan, saying: "Words cannot express my heartfelt thanks toward the Chi Lambda Fraternity and their effort and success in their scholarship endeavor." She has attended two of the scholarship presentations, plus some Chi Lambda reunions that the young recipients have attended.

For the applicant, financial need is important, but there is more beyond that. "The winners strike me as young men that have the same values that we did in the 1960s," Tietz says – honor, loyalty, having a strong bond together and high moral and ethical values. "They're going to be great men and will be great members of Chi Lambda."

Koppes and Tietz graduated from Stout in 1966, one year behind Derby. Beyond the sting of Derby's loss in 1968, Koppes also has a friend from back home in Ohio who wound up as an MIA – Air Force Capt. Alan Robert Trent, a pilot lost over Cambodia a year and a half after Derby.

Derby was in the Marine Fighter Attack Squadron 115, known as VMFA-115, the Able Eagles. Its mission was to "intercept and destroy enemy aircraft and missiles under all weather conditions, and attack and destroy surface targets and conduct other such operations as may be directed."[2] His Phantom F-4B could go twice the speed of sound.

"Even though Paul is listed as MIA, his plane was observed by ground units as having been hit by ground fire, exploded and disintegrated in mid-air," Franczyk says. "The body of his radar intercept officer was recovered. A search followed until I gave direction to allow the search to be discontinued. I am not sure how many days the search went on. ... It was certainly no more than a week. I believed if we could not have all of Paul, I did not need his remains, nor did I want to put others in harm's way in the area of the crash site."

There is very little on Derby's case at http://www.pownetwork. org/bios/d/d373.htm. It merely says, "No further information available at this time." The POW Network is not shy about giving full details about other

---

2   http://lxgjmushroom.tripod.com/miaamericansoldiers/id5.html Its history is at http://www.marines.mil/unit/2ndMAW/mag31/vmfa115/Pages/history.aspx It flew more than 34,000 combat sorties, participating in such battles as the Tet Offensive, Hue City and Khe Sanh. Some of its formal reports are at http://www. recordsofwar.com/vietnam/usmc/VMFA-115.htm

cases and questioning them, so it apparently has little concern about whether Derby could have been captured.

The POW Network does not even give the name of his crewman, but he was Marine 1st Lt. Thomas Alan Reich, 24, of Cleona, Pa.[3]

Ellis Langjahr of Wausau never knew Derby, but his daughter married Chad Derby, the nephew of the pilot. In 2008, Langjahr posted this message on the MIA's page on http://www.thewall-usa.com: "The fight for freedom never ends, the brave among us will defend. The cost of freedom is very high, those with insight can't deny. To settle for peace at any price, defines you, not as man but as mice."

The author of this book saw the posting, which included Langjahr's email address, and sent him a message in what proved to be a day of a striking coincidence. Langjahr reported: "How did it happen that I opened this e-mail when I just got back from looking at the Traveling Wall, and as a retired vet took part in the opening ceremony at the VFW here in Wausau?"

Also eerie, Franczyk says, was that a few years ago, "our daughter, Pam, and her children made a trip to Fort McCoy, Wis., to visit the base military museum. There was a jar on the counter containing POW / MIA bracelets. There were only three left when she reached in and grabbed one. It was Paul's."

Another Marine pilot who would become MIA in Vietnam, and at the same age of 25 as Derby, was Jim Fickler. At Kewaskum High School, Fickler was involved in seemingly nearly every activity. The 1961 yearbook, for his senior year, had a long list of his work: class president for two years, prom royalty, prom committee, dramatics in his sophomore and senior years; Spanish Club, secretary, Variety Show and operetta.

Then there were the athletic things: football for three years, baseball for two, basketball for two, earning letters in his junior and senior years.

"He was pretty well-rounded," says David Oppermann, who was one year behind Fickler and spent many a day with him while growing up.

"We didn't have cars. We spent a ton of time fishing on the Milwaukee River in the center of Kewaskum," Oppermann says. "Jim lived east of the

---

[3] http://lxgjmushroom.tripod.com/miaamericansoldiers/id5.html More on Reich at http://www.myhometown-lebanonpa.com/Thomas%20Allen%20Reich.html and http://www.virtualwall.org/dr/ReichTA01a.htm

river and I lived west. He was pretty outdoors-ish; spearing carp and fishing for northern pike and making rafts. He was a typical boy growing up in a rural environment. He enjoyed life."

He had hopes of becoming a game warden and thus spending his life in the woods and on the water. That field of study became his major at what is now UW – Stevens Point.

Oppermann continues: "They were on my paper route when I was a little 12-year-old," delivering the Milwaukee Sentinel in the morning and the Milwaukee Journal in the afternoon to the home of Ed and Sylvia Fickler at 524 Habeck St.

Fickler did not play football his sophomore year, or do much of anything else. In fact, he was lucky to be alive – he nearly broke his neck when diving off a slide at Lake Seven outside the town.

One of Fickler's three siblings, Nancy Wickert of West Bend, says the slide was about 20 steps high. Going down the slide was not enough fun – kids would climb up it and then "shallow-dive," a kind of near-belly flop into what they knew was water only three feet deep. But one day, Jim's foot slipped on the ladder at exactly the wrong second, and he wound up going straight down, head-first.

This was long before there was anything like dialing 911. The friend he was with somehow got him to the car, laid him in the backseat to stabilize his neck and raced to a doctor. "He spent almost six months in a body cast for a hairline fracture in the neck," Wickert says.

"I have a picture in my mind of Jim in a full body cast, neck to butt," says Frank Schoenbeck, four years younger than Fickler. "It looked most uncomfortable. I was amazed to hear he had become a pilot. I would have thought his injury would prevented that. It is sadly ironic that he healed so well he become a pilot and then got killed in the war."

Later, Jim went to UW – Stevens Point and found he liked being in the mandatory ROTC program, and went into officer's training after graduating. Then he became keenly interested in becoming a pilot – he had not grown up with any particular interest in airplanes or the military or the Marines, Wickert says. He excelled in training in North Carolina, but when he was ready to ship out for Vietnam, a Marine doctor called a halt because of the old injury.

"Jim was very excited about flying. He loved it," Wickert says, and was crestfallen by the rejection. "That is probably the only time in his life that I saw him upset."

Fickler fought to remain a pilot, and after getting three other doctors to sign off, he was allowed to go.

He was within one month of completing his tour when Jan. 17, 1969, came. Paul Derby had been shot down two months earlier.

Fickler was the pilot of an A-6A Intruder that disappeared that day over Quang Tin Province in South Vietnam. He was in Headquarters and Maintenance 11, in Marine Air Group 11, which was based at Da Nang. Five years after his loss, Fickler's status was changed from missing to died while missing.

The POW Network says Fickler's plane:[4]

> **was conducting direct air support and armed reconnaissance missions in the vicinity of the A Shau Valley, Republic of Vietnam.**
>
> **The aircraft departed Da Nang Air Base at 8:43 p.m., and arrived in the A Shau Valley area at approximately 8:50 p.m. ... the bombardier / navigator, Robert Kuhlman, contacted the forward air controller for assignment of missions. At 9:25 p.m. the forward air controller (radioed) a target to the aircraft which appeared in the northern portion of the valley. The controller of the mission attempted to contact the aircraft at 9:45 p.m. to assign another target; this attempt was met with negative results. Further attempts were made to make contact but in each instance the results were negative.**
>
> **...The possibility that the aircraft crashed in the target area can only be presumed. The airborne controller did observe what appeared to be an explosion, which he assumed at that time was a bomb cluster followed by a secondary explosion. It was known that the enemy possessed antiaircraft weapons in the vicinity of the A Shau Valley.**

Kuhlman, the man on the plane with Fickler, was a second lieutenant from Richmond, Ind.

On the page for Fickler at the Virtual Wall[5] are more accounts of this case, including: "Quite simply, the aircraft disappeared, victim to either

---

[4] http://www.pownetwork.org/bios/f/f009.htm

[5] http://www.virtualwall.org/df/FicklerEJ01a.htm

enemy antiaircraft fire or a ground collision. … Both men were classed as missing in action and remained in that status until the secretary of the Navy approved presumptive findings of death, Fickler on 04 Feb 1974 and Kuhlman on 16 June 1978."

Kuhlman was in Marine All-Weather Fighter Attack Squadron 242.

Back home, Oppermann was working at the West Bend Co. and came home one day to hear the entire town talking about his old friend.

"It was pretty shocking," Oppermann says. "He was a well-liked person. This rattled our community. His parents were beside themselves, looking for answers."

"My Mom and Dad never gave up hope," Wickert says. "They were very active in the MIA organizations and went to Washington all the time. They were in the centerspread of one issue of Life magazine" in a story about MIAs. … (Decades later) they did not want to move from their house, in case he would come home and come there."[6]

The work of Marine pilots like Derby and Fickler, and helicopter pilots like the next ones in this chapter, was invaluable to the grunts.

Chuck Dziedzic, a Marine mortarman who was in Vietnam in 1967, 1968 and 1969, salutes the pilots, along with the artillery. "Any help that you could get from the air or artillery, we felt that they saved our ass," he says.

Dziedzic also salutes copter pilots for getting them in and getting them out, not without physical difficulties en route. "We didn't like humpin' but we didn't like riding in copters, either. It was the worst roller coaster ride you could take, and so noisy."

One such helicopter man was Albert Raymond Trudeau, 22, an Army warrant officer first class. On Oct. 26, 1971, Trudeau had lunch with buddies Leonard Maquiling and John Shelton, colleagues in the Army's 68th Assault Helicopter Company.

It was a day like any other in Vietnam; full of prepping before a mission but also full of joshing at lunch and looking forward to poker games.

But hours later, Trudeau, Maquiling and all eight other men aboard a CH-47B cargo helicopter were lost. The chopper, flown by Maquiling and

---

[6] Kewaskum's only other loss in Vietnam would come two years after Fickler. On March 21, 1971, Warrant Officer James Walter Manthei, 20, was killed when his Army helicopter was shot down over Laos.

co-piloted by Trudeau, was on a supply mission and crashed off the coast of South Vietnam because of bad weather; Trudeau and five others are MIA but the bodies of Maquiling and three other men were recovered.[7]

Shelton, of Marietta, Ga., posted a memorial on Trudeau's page at http://www.thewall-usa.com in 2011: "Had lunch that day with Al and Leonard at the Air Force Officer's Club at Tuy Hoa. Just hours later learned that their aircraft was missing. Al was a great guy and liked by all in the unit. Still hard to believe."

Shelton was contacted by the author of this book in 2012 and said: "Al Trudeau was a really great guy. Everyone in the unit would agree. He was fun-loving, always with a twinkle in his eye. He seemed to always have his camera slung over his shoulder ready to snap photos. He also often played poker at our company officers' evening game.

"He was one of several young Warrant Officer 1's in the unit, having just turned 22. I was old for my first tour, being 25 at the time." Maquiling was 23.

Not long before his disappearance, Trudeau had called home. His oldest sister, Barbara Connolly, who goes by her family nickname of Bobbie, said the family always had him make a collect call, meaning it paid the bill and thus he would not have to worry about using his soldier pay to handle it. His call this time was that "he was thinking of buying Christmas presents and asked what would people want," Bobbie says. He also mentioned an upcoming copter mission.

She remembers the phone ringing again the next day: The military informing the family that Trudeau was MIA.

"I said, 'I just spoke with him last night,'" Bobbie reports. "It can't be him. ... Everybody in the family said that can't be possible, because everyone in my family who was in World War II came home – my father and his six brothers." Plus, their father was in the Army himself as a major in the Army's Criminal Investigation Division or the Counterintelligence Corps.

Bobbie, the first child, says "Alby" Trudeau was the fourth of nine kids in the family. The mother was Ruth and the father was Francis. All the kids

---

[7] http://www.virtualwall.org/dl/LautzenheiserMx01a.htm The flight engineer of the copter was Specialist 5 Michael Lautzenheiser of Muncie, Ind., who like Trudeau is MIA.

went by nicknames or shortened versions of their formal names. These included John being Jet, Robert Michael being Mikey or Mouse, daughter Frances being Sissy and Catherine being Taffy.

The Trudeau clan lived in many states because Maj. Trudeau frequently was transferred. It had lived in France and West Germany, and Al was born in New Jersey; the family came to Milwaukee from Louisiana when Bobbie was 18 and Alby was 12 or so. It lived at North 34th Street and West State Street, near the headquarters of Harley-Davidson and Miller Brewing Co., and the kids always enjoyed the area playground between the two companies and watching motorcycles in action at the plant. Al and the other kids attended St. Rose School a few blocks east of their home. "Milwaukee was a nice, friendly, family-type city," says Bobbie, who spent a quarter-century in Virginia and now lives in Little Chute, Wis.

Al had just started at West Division High School when his father was transferred again, back to West Germany, and so the rest of his high school years were in that country. Bobbie already was married and had two kids of her own, and would have two more before Alby was lost in Vietnam.

Richard Elias had posted a remembrance message on Trudeau's Vietnam Wall page in 2004. Elias said in an interview for this book that his classmate at the Ludwigsburg American High School was one year younger but in the same Class of 1967. This was at a U.S. Army base named Pattonville, outside Ludwigsburg, which is northwest of Stuttgart. Elias' father was an Army financial officer. They were neighborhood buddies because "our front window and their front window lined up, in opposite buildings," Elias says, and they hung out together in all sorts of things.

Elias says the students were more intent on studying the fine points of German beer and other partying than they were on being serious in school. "Al Trudeau was a super-nice guy and was on the cross country team," says Elias, now of Lexington, Va. "We skipped school as much as we could. We partied a lot, played and worked on our cars. There was no drinking age in Europe. We consumed copious amounts. We did several Oktoberfests."

During the Cold War, tens of thousands of American troops were based in then-West Germany in order to protect it against any Soviet invasion from East Germany. It often was thought that World War III would begin in that region; the boys graduated only six years after the Communists built the Berlin Wall.

After graduation from high school, Al Trudeau came back to Milwaukee and lived with Bobbie and her own clan at 35th and Highland Boulevard, very close to where the Trudeaus originally had lived, until joining the Army.

Bobbie says she does not remember how Alby wound up as a helicopter pilot, but that he always seemed to have an interest in old cars. Plus, "he was one of those people who liked and appreciated rules. He said they're not strict enough about obeying rules."

In his calls and letters home from Southeast Asia, he said Vietnam was a beautiful place, scenery-wise, and "it was a shame there was war there."

In the spring of 2013, Bobbie's son Tim Connolly, of Ruther Glen, Va., which is near Fredericksburg, visited the Vietnam Wall website of http://www.vvmf.org/thewall/Wall_Id_No=52656 and found it had a photo of Trudeau – the one that Elias had provided to the author of this book, and which Tom Mueller then posted on the Wall when it was updating its pages and soliciting photos. Connolly wrote to Mueller to express appreciation, and that led to contacts with Bobbie.

The Class of 1967 had about 165 students, Elias says, adding that the light-hearted comment at graduation was "See you in Vietnam." The last time he saw his friend Trudeau was in July 1967, one month after graduation, when the Elias family moved back to Virginia. The school chums fell out of contact.

Elias did indeed go to Vietnam, as a Marine sniper from April 1968 to October 1968. He was wounded five times and came home long before Trudeau arrived in Vietnam in February 1971. Years later, Elias became active in Rolling Thunder groups coming from all over America to the Vietnam Wall, which opened in 1982 in Washington, D.C. Elias often searched for the names of some of his Marine buddies and regularly helped other vets find their pals on the Wall.

One day in the 1990s, he was helping a vet find a lot of friends on the Wall. "He was crying and shaking, and I was holding him but still looking around. That's how I saw Al's name," with just an idle glance at other names but then a thunderbolt of recognition – his friend from Germany did indeed go to Vietnam, and did not come back.

"I saw his name by accident. I was just wandering around, looking at names of people I served with, but they are at one far end of the wall; Al Trudeau's was more toward the apex, pretty low on the panel" Some of the panels in the center are 10 feet high, and Trudeau's panel is the second one west of the center.[7] It was quite remarkable to find that one name amid the more than 58,000 on the Wall.

Trudeau's copter crashed off the coast of Khanh Hoa Province of South Vietnam. The Virtual Wall says:[8]

> **A CH-47B helicopter (tail number 66-19143) of the 68th Assault Support Helicopter Company was tasked with a resupply mission originating from Camp Holloway in Pleiku. After several stops, the helicopter arrived at Tuy Hoa at 1115, departing at 1350 hours with an expected arrival at Cam Ranh Bay at 1420. There were 10 men aboard the aircraft at that point; five crewmen and five passengers.**
>
> **The helicopter (call sign Warrior 143) was sighted by another CH-47 near Nha Trang, headed south into bad weather; it did not arrive at Cam Ranh Bay. Search and rescue was initiated at 1555 hours. Between 27 October and 01 November, debris identified as being from Warrior 143 washed ashore on Hon Tre island, just offshore from Nha Trang. The condition of the debris recovered indicated that the aircraft had struck the water at high speed.**
>
> **Search and rescue efforts did recover the remains of four men. Underwater search efforts in October 1974, based on a reported sighting of the aircraft wreckage, were not successful."**

Until April 1971, Trudeau's unit was named Company C, 228th Aviation Battalion, 1st Cavalry Division. When the 1st Cav left Vietnam, Company C

---

[8] http://www.VirtualWall.org/iPanels/iPanelsL2.htm explains The Wall "has the names listed in the order of the date of death or when the person became missing. The earliest casualties are named on line 1 of panel 1 East, at the center of the Wall. The list of names goes down panel 1 East, then to the right to line 1 of panel 2 East. That sequence moves to the right to panel 70 East, at the east end of the Wall, which has one row of names of those killed on May 25, 1968. That date continues at the opposite end of the Wall, on panel 70 West. The names then continue to the right to panel 1 West, which is adjacent to panel 1 East." Trudeau's 1971 loss thus is on the next-to-last panel chronologically. He is on panel 2W, Row 52.

[8] http://www.virtualwall.org/dl/LautzenheiserMx01a.htm A similar account is at http://www.pownetwork.org/bios/t/t394.htm

was redesignated as the 68th Assault Helicopter Company and remained in Vietnam for another year.

Two and a half years before Trudeau was MIA in a helicopter crash, another Army helicopter co-pilot from Wisconsin had become an MIA: William C. Pierson III, age 21.[9] His helicopter on April 13, 1969, was an AH-1G Cobra gunship. Pierson was in B Troop, 2nd Squadron, 17th Cavalry, 101st Airborne Division. He was a warrant officer first class, and promoted to chief warrant officer before his status was changed in 1978 to "hostile, died while missing."

Pierson's home of record was Madison, but his mother's boss in offices at Rayovac, the battery-maker that is a longtime big employer in that city, says he had gone to high school in Oshkosh.

Jerry Garren, now of Los Osos, Calif., posted a tribute to Pierson on www.thewall-usa.com in 2012: "I knew him as 'Biff'. He wanted to serve his country. He did serve it and he died for it. I remember him with great respect. He was a man of great courage and purpose. He loved his country and his family."

Garren told the author of this book: "I was pleased to receive your email. A person who cares. People who give a damn are in sort supply in our country."

He said he did not know where the nickname "Biff" came from, but told this story: "I worked at Rayovac with Biff's grandfather, William Goff. His grandfather was a sort of a mentor to me. Biff's mother, Shirley Pierson, moved to Madison from Oshkosh to be near her parents. She was divorced. Biff's two sisters (both younger) moved with her. Shirley was my secretary for many years."

When Shirley Pierson moved to Madison, "Biff was already in the Army. Biff's dream was to fly a helicopter and he worked very hard to do so. When he graduated and finished additional training his unit was sent to Nam."

Garren then tells of a fateful circumstance in which Pierson was not allowed to fly, but wound up going on a fateful ride: "He was disappointed

---

[9] Another Wisconsin man killed in Vietnam was William Edwin Pierson, a Marine lance corporal from Brookfield. He was killed on Dec. 15, 1967, and his body was recovered.

when on arrival there the pilots drew lots to select a maintenance officer. To his chagrin Biff 'won'. He did not normally fly combat missions. An officer pilot friend offered to take him for a joy ride. The aircraft was shot down. It broke apart in the air. It crashed in enemy territory."

The copter crashed in Quang Nam Province in South Vietnam. Pierson was MIA, but the body of the pilot, Capt. Alvie J. Ledford Jr., of Afton, Okla., was found a few days later.[10]

The POW Network says Ledford and Pierson were on[11]

a visual reconnaissance ... . Their area of operation was covered in jungle with several rivers running through it and scattered clearings used for growing rice.

The pilot of an OH-6A light observation helicopter (a second bird), nicknamed 'Loach,' reported seeing enemy activity on the ground and requested the AH-1G to attack the target. When the Cobra gunship was about 500 feet into its dive, the crew of the Loach saw flames spurting from one side of the aircraft that appeared to come from below and behind the pilot's compartment.

They then saw the pilot compartment separate from the aircraft and disintegrate in the air as it fell to the ground approximately 41 miles east of the Lao / Thai border, 73 miles west of South Vietnamese / Lao border and 104 miles west of Kham Duc, South Vietnam.

At 1400 hours on the same day, while conducting an aerial search of the area for survivors, the Loach pilot saw what he believed to be human remains located in a stream southeast of the main aircraft wreckage. At 1530 hours, a recovery team was inserted into the area. The next morning the Loach pilot who participated in the initial operation returned to the area and observed the six-man Ranger team as they searched the area.

---

[10] Veterans of B Troop are organized at http://www.vietnamproject. ttu.edu/banshee/M_Assoc.html. Many pictures of its service are posted. The group honors Pierson and its other KIAs of B Troop at http://www.vietnamproject.ttu.edu/banshee/kia.html

[11] http://www.pownetwork.org/bios/p/p079.htm

The team inspected the wreckage and surrounding area, and noted no signs of blood, flesh or personal belongings, but did not find the remains of either crewman.

A week later, on 20 April, the Loach pilot again returned to the loss area and relocated the remains which he had seen in the stream shortly after the gunship was shot down. Those remains were subsequently recovered and identified as belonging to Capt. Alvie J. Ledford Jr. He continued an aerial search for WO1 Pierson, but again found no trace of him. At that time William C Pierson III was listed missing in action.

In another helicopter several months before the loss of Pierson, a crewman was Army Sgt. Paul Reid Frazier, 19, only a year out of Custer High School in Milwaukee. He was the crew chief on a UH-1 helicopter when it was shot down on Sept. 3, 1968. The bodies of the pilot and co-pilot were recovered, but not Frazier. There were no passengers.

Frazier was in the 191st Assault Helicopter Company of the 214th Aviation Battalion. Here is the story told by Task Force Omega:[12]

As the Huey flew low over the hotly contested countryside, it was struck by hostile ground fire, crashed and exploded on impact about five miles north of Can Duoc and 10 miles south of Saigon...

Numerous hamlets and villages of various sizes surrounded the area of loss. It was also laced with rivers, canals, waterways and rice fields. ...Search and recovery operations were immediately initiated and American ground forces inspected the crash site within four to eight hours of the crash. With the exception of Sgt. Frazier, the remains of the rest of the personnel aboard the Huey were recovered. ...

The crash site was inspected thoroughly on 7 and 8 May 1973 (the Paris Peace Accords had been signed Jan. 27) by a Graves Registration team from the Joint Casualty Resolution Center who confirmed the identification of this helicopter as being

---

12 http://taskforceomegainc.org/f365.html The site has a map that comes up when clicking the coordinates, and it shows the site was just south of Saigon. The POW Network does not give a location other than the same coordinates, 103441N 1063728E. That is at http://www.pownetwork.org/bios/f/f365.htm

Sgt. Frazier's aircraft. No remains were found in or around the crash site during this search. ...

Over the years several reports have been received by US government agencies pertaining to the location of remains that might relate to Sgt. Frazier; but to date no positive correlation has been made. Likewise, no remains have been recovered or identified as his. There is no doubt Paul Frazier died in the loss of his Huey. However, by (the center's) evaluation of his record there is a good possibility that his body was removed from the wreckage by either local villagers or Communist forces and buried.

The pilot of the copter was Warrant Officer Ronald Michael Cederlund of Illinois (Chicago, according to postings on his page at http://www.thewall-usa.com), and the co-pilot was Capt. David Carroll Burch of North Carolina.

The copter likely was helping the 9th Infantry Division, because four members died as ground casualties in hostile in Long An Province that day, along with an Army reservist. This was found via using the search for dates at http://www.thewall-usa.com/search.asp. All their bodies were recovered.

Frazier's 191st Assault Helicopter Company was known as the Boomerangs and Bounty Hunters. A total of 46 members died in the war.[13]

Jeff Dentice of Muskego had known Frazier well at Custer High in Milwaukee. Dentice was one year ahead of him, leaving in 1966, and served in Vietnam from June 1967 to June 1968 as an Army medic with the 25th Division. He departed three months before Frazier was lost.

Dentice says there were two kinds of students at Custer – "the hoods and the collegiate groups," and that he and Frazier were part of the first. "A bunch of us were hoods. We would attend dances, parties and hang out drinking on Villard Avenue, six-packs and whiskey. We partied hard, we drank hard and chased the girls around. We were not into the school s——"

Dentice adds, however, that the boys definitely WERE into any kind of dance, such as those held by the Catholic Youth Organization or any other

---

13 http://www.191ahc.org/honor.htm The battalion's website is http://www.1stavnbde.com/214th/214th_Combat_Aviation_Battalion.htm and includes some magazine-style articles from that era. A story about Frazier's and other Army helicopter companies in Vietnam is at http://www.vietnamexp.com/DATA/organizational.htm It says this is from the 1991 book "Vietnam: The Helicopter War" by Philip D. Chinney.

organization. They were not interested in the religious aspects, however. "We all wore black trenchcoats so we could hide whiskey bottles inside."

As a Vietnam veteran, he was volunteering at the Traveling Wall in Racine or Kenosha one day in the early 1990s, helping people find someone's name and assisting them in making a rubbing of it. One man showed up and it was Frazier's brother, and they talked, but in the rush Dentice neglected to get his contact information.

Years of passion for MIAs

Dentice (a.k.a. Doc), Roger Boeker and Charlene Klemp each has a deep passion for remembering those who are MIA.

Dentice, who got his nickname as an Army medic in Vietnam, has worked on behalf of his fellow vets for years, particularly his organization of the Wisconsin POW / MIA National Balloon Launch[14] on Memorial Day at Wind Lake, next door to his home of Muskego. The 16th anniversary was in 2013.

Roger Boeker of Madison for many years wore the bracelet of a fellow Marine, Capt. David Leverett Leet of Kenosha, a pilot who was lost at sea off of North Vietnam on April 13, 1972. Boeker served in Vietnam from 1966 to 1967.

And for more than a quarter-century, Klemp, of Fort Atkinson, wore an MIA bracelet with the name of Albert Raymond Trudeau, who readers met earlier in this chapter. She wore it until the bracelet wore out. But until being contacted about this book, she had never seen his picture.

Trudeau's "stick buddy" in Vietnam, John Shelton, dug a photo out of his war memorabilia sent it to author Tom Mueller, who forwarded it to Klemp and to Dentice's extensive website that pays tribute to the MIAs, http://www.war-veterans.org/Wi37.htm Trudeau and a group of soldiers were sitting around in lawn chairs at their helicopter base. Trudeau's high school classmate in Germany, Richard Elias, later dug up a formal photo from their 1967 yearbook.

---

[14] http://www.war-veterans.org/Wlaunch.htm

"I was really glad you sent the photos," Klemp enthused. "I had no idea what he looked like."

She got the red MIA bracelet honoring Trudeau at a fund-raising event in the early 1980s; Wisconsin men were the focus of the sale. Klemp wore it until 2011; "I took it off because it was so faded."

One of her daughters had a bracelet memorializing Marine Pfc. Thomas Joseph Blackman of Racine, an MIA since 1968 whose identification in 2005 was discussed in the previous chapter of this book.

No such announcement has ever come for Trudeau, and given the fact that his helicopter crashed in the sea, it is not likely. "It just is sad that he seems to be forgotten," Klemp says.

She left messages on his page at http://www.thewall-usa.com in 1999 and 2007. The first one said, "Dear Albert, I have worn your MIA bracelet for about 15 yrs. now and I think of you every day. Thank you for the greatest sacrifice that anyone can give so that I can remain free. Since putting on this bracelet, I have never removed it but once. God speed and may you find eternal peace with Him who gave us our lives. Rest in Peace in His loving arms."

Klemp said in an interview, "Everybody deserves something. Gone but not forgotten."

"Forgotten" is one of the words that Dentice also uses.

He says: "Forgotten is the word of these heroes from all wars. He appreciates identification work on MIAs by the Pentagon, but pledges to stand guard "until they all come home."

A quarter century ago, Dentice launched a program called "to bring the holidays to these men and women who served proudly. They cannot be home with their families, so what better way, then to bring the Christmas spirit to our wounded warriors and veterans."

He adds: "Someone has to do the work and take the time to make sure our veterans are never forgotten. It's a blessing for me to do so," but also notes, "It's also been a healing experience and therapy of sorts from my time in Nam."

Boeker wore Leet's bracelet for many years, but after a chance encounter, gave it to someone who deserved it more: Leet's high school baseball teammate.

"In the course of my work, I met the vet benefit coordinator at Gateway Technical College in Kenosha," Boeker says. "He asked about the band and I told him – I bought it the Vietnam Memorial because he was a Marine and from Wisconsin. The fellow from Kenosha had been half of the high school baseball pitching team and Maj. Leet's best friend.

"A few weeks later I attended the man's retirement and gave him the bracelet as he was much closer to Leet – it felt like a piece of Leet had come home."

Chapter 13:
Sharp increase in women KIAs

Until 2003, only two Wisconsin women had ever been killed by enemy fire in America's foreign wars: an Army nurse at Anzio in 1944 and a helicopter mechanic at the end of the Persian Gulf War in 1991 who was filling in as a gunner.

But that history has been greatly rewritten in the last decade, with a total of seven Wisconsin women killed in Iraq and Afghanistan.

And many, many more were in harm's way in those wars amid the increasing role of women in combat zones in the military. At the time, women still were officially banned by Pentagon policy from "direct combat," basically meaning offensive attacks. But the wars in Iraq and Afghanistan showed that hostile fire could come at any time in the form of improvised explosive devices, insurgent mortars, suicide bombers and turncoat attacks by people the U.S. forces were training to fight.

A total of 152 women had been killed in Iraq and Afghanistan as of January 2013, when Defense Secretary Leon Panetta and Gen. Martin Dempsey, chairman of the Joint Chiefs of Staff, signed an order opening combat positions to service members regardless of gender.

The landmark order instructed the military services to begin a sweeping review of the physical requirements of the jobs. Women currently make up about 14 percent of the 1.4 million active U.S. military personnel. "Not everyone is going to be able to be a combat soldier. But everyone is entitled to a chance," Panetta said.[1]

So very soon, women will be in even more combat than they were in during the Iraq and Afghanistan wars.

Soldiers who have served alongside women greatly admire their ability and dedication.

"No one could say she didn't deserve to be there or was of any less ability than one of the guys,"[2] one soldier said of 2nd Lt. Tracy Alger, one of the Wisconsinites who made the Ultimate Sacrifice in Iraq.

---

[1] Associated Press story in Milwaukee Journal Sentinel, p. 5A, Jan. 25, 2013.

[2] http://www.ourfallensoldier.com/AlgerTracy_MemorialPage.html

Army Pfc. Rachel Bosveld (left), was killed in Iraq in 2003; Army Reserve Pfc. Nichole Frye (center), KIA in Iraq, 2004; and Army National Guard Specialist Michelle Witmer, KIA in Iraq, 2004.

Navy Reserve Petty Officer 2nd Class Jaime Jaenke was killed in Iraq in 2006, and Army Reserve Sgt. 1st Class Merideth Howard (far right), KIA in Afghanistan, 2006.

Army Reserve Cpl. Rachael Hugo was killed in Iraq in 2007, as was Army 2nd Lt. Tracy Alger (far right).

Alger, 30, of New Auburn in northwestern Wisconsin, was killed in 2007 by a roadside bomb. The tribute was posted by Sgt. Wally Holt, who called her "a female in foreign land – being forward support for best infantry the Army has to offer."

Waylon Gross, now of Menomonee Falls, who served two tours in Iraq, the second as a captain, said the female medics who occasionally were attached to his unit "were extremely proficient and highly adaptive, highly skilled professionals. I don't see the difference between the male medic and the female medic. Male or female, it didn't matter. They were soldiers and they performed a soldier's job."

Gross' unit was a security detachment, and he also says: "A lot of the supply truck drivers were female. The females would be in just as much danger as the men."

In this new, bloody era of females coming under fire, the first Wisconsin death came in 2003 in Iraq; the most recent[3] came four years later in the same country.

Six of the seven Wisconsin women who were killed were victims of ambushes or improvised explosive devices being used against their vehicles while in convoys or patrols.

Army Reserve Sgt. 1st Class Deanna Czarnecki of Jackson, Wis., said that when she was in Afghanistan from 2009 to 2010, the Army was relying on the Mine-Resistant Ambush Protected vehicle, known as an MRAP, instead of the less-well- armored Humvees first used in Iraq. The MRAP is made by Oshkosh Corp. and formally called the MRAP All-Terrain Vehicle, or M-ATV.[4] The company says, "It's proven for harsh terrains, proven to save lives, proven to accomplish missions ...."

Czarnecki's work took her from her Sharana Forward Operating Base in troublesome Paktika province to some others. She usually was taken by air; going only once on the ground – a 25-mile ride in an MRAP.

She says the Army "learned from Iraq," where many deaths, including some of the Wisconsin women in this chapter, came in Humvees. "The MRAPs were a lot safer. They saved a lot of lives," Czarnecki says. "Those Humvees would be ripped to shreds. The Army had to adapt to the war. The war is so different from 2003," in Iraq. Still, the MRAP crews were vulnerable to snipers.

For example, Gross says the MRAP has a V-shaped hull rather than the Humvee's flat bottom. "The V shape has a better chance of deflecting directional blasts from the ground up from a land mine or similar explosive device. Another advantage offered by the MRAP was that troops are seated at different heights

---

[3] This book was finished in spring 2013, and final editing of proofs lasted into the summer.

[4] http://www.oshkoshdefense.com/products/5/m-atv

than the Humvee – meaning a directional blast had to have a penetrating punch and be accurately aimed. ... the MRAP was developed with these battlefield learnings in mind and was started with a more substantial platform."[5]

The seven Wisconsin women who were killed in Iraq and Afghanistan were regular Army, Army Reserves, Navy Reserves and Wisconsin National Guard – three were in military police companies and two were in civil affairs groups. Two were medics. Their ages ranged from 19 to 52.

Here is the chronological roll call of the seven Wisconsin female heroes. This was developed starting with a list of basic facts and photos meticulously kept for all the fallen in Iraq and Afghanistan by the Wisconsin Department of Veterans Affairs.[6] The research for this book also checked news reports, along with memorial sites and other items and in one case came across a book that frequently mentioned one of the women.

Army Pfc. Rachel K. Bosveld, 19, of Waupun: She was killed Oct. 26, 2003, in Abu Ghraib, Iraq, when U.S. forces at an Iraqi police station were attacked with mortars. Bosveld was in the 527th Military Police Company, V Corps, which had been based in Giessen, Germany. She had arrived in Germany in the fall of 2002 and within a few months was at war in the Iraqi desert.

The war had begun March 19, and on May 1 President George W. Bush had given a triumphant speech under a "Mission Accomplished" sign on the aircraft carrier USS Abraham Lincoln off of San Diego. The carrier had sent out air strikes in the first weeks of the war. But victory quickly turned ugly when insurgent attacks began, and they remained that way for years.

Abu Ghraib is about 20 miles west of the center of Baghdad. It was just another Iraqi town name at the time, but starting in April 2004 it became infamous – when it was revealed that multiple low-ranking members of a different U.S. military police company, the 372nd, had been systematically abusing and humiliating prisoners at the jail in that town. That abuse began in late 2003.

---

[5] Czarnecki says that in Afghanistan, the 4,700 Army engineers and Navy Seabees who were under the administration of her Headquarters Company had 35 teams of road-clearance soldiers, using things like mine rollers, robotic systems and interrogator arm devices. "Our troops were out there and busy all the time," she says, and four were killed and 138 wounded in her time there.

[6] http://dva.state.wi.us/PA-Heroes.asp

Bosveld frequently is mentioned in a book about a gruesome murder committed in New Orleans in 2006 by a member of her MP company, Zack Bowen. Bosveld was in a close circle of soldier colleagues with Bowen, and the book, "Shake the Devil Off,"[7] is about how he murdered his girlfriend and dismembered her body, cooking her head in a pot and other parts in the oven, then committed suicide by jumping from a hotel rooftop after leaving a bizarre note about the corpse. The book also is a thorough case study of post-traumatic stress disorder based on the many tense situations that the 527th had encountered, including Bosveld's death.

The book says that in Germany, Bowen entertained the company by playing the drums and guitar, and Bosveld would jam with him on the violin and viola, plus was skilled in drawing intricate tattoo designs in a notebook.[8]

Once the unit got to Baghdad, though, the daily dangers and tedium of war began to mount. In Abu Ghraib, the 527th "soon discovered that the city's (Iraqi) law enforcement was far more dysfunctional than they had believed it to be. Many of the cops in Baghdad were inept, corrupt, and all too willing to provide insurgents with intelligence about the Americans for a little cash." The city and its main marketplace also were rife with criminals because Saddam Hussein had emptied the prisons months before the U.S. invasion. "The freed prisoners had access to looted weaponry, readily available in the black markets that filled Abu Ghraib." One soldier said, "We'd head out on patrols and get into constant firefights."[9] The unit faced small-arms fire, rocket-propelled grenades, roadside bombs, explosives in Coke cans, other IEDs and mortar attacks.

Army Specialist Todd Ranch, quoted often in the book, was severely wounded in August and evacuated to Germany and then to Walter Reed National Military Medical Center in Washington, D.C.

On Sept. 12, 2003, Bosveld's Humvee was hit by a rocket-propelled grenade near a police station, and was engulfed in flames because the RPG hit the fuel line. The door jammed and she was lucky to escape, and only by

---

[7] "Shake the Devil Off: A True Story of the Murder that Rocked New Orleans," by Ethan Brown (2009).

[8] "Shake the Devil Off," p. 49.

[9] "Shake the Devil Off," p. 66, 67, 72, 73.

repeatedly slamming herself against the door. She was not physically hurt but had persistent headaches from the blast and was suffering from stress.[10]

She had seen enough. "More and more people want us to go home," she wrote in a letter to her father, Marvin. "Believe me, we want to go home."[11]

Bosveld was not so fortunate on Oct. 26. She and other MPs pulled into the parking lot in front of the police station and were talking in their Humvees. A mortar round landed landed between her Humvee and another one. Two MPs lost all or part of a leg, and "a pin-size piece of shrapnel struck Rachel's heart. ... she lay pale and lifeless in the Humvee's front seat." She was the first female MP to die in Iraq and also the first member of the 527th to be killed.[12]

Colleagues, friends and others have made memorial comments about Bosveld.[13] There are similar places for comment for most of the other women in this chapter, although some have many more comments than others. This is a citizen website and is not affiliated with any group, but its collection of tributes and comments about those who made the Ultimate Sacrifice is impressive.

"I can't forget her, ever," wrote Matthew Coffield of Eunice, N.M., who was a sergeant in the 527th. "I used to pass by coming in from being outside the wire, and she would ask me how I was doing. I always gave her a 'thumbs-up' even if I didn't really feel that way, and ask her how she was. She was always 'doing good, sergeant,' and that was good to hear. I was utterly shocked when I found out she had fallen. My squad had been dispatched to the scene of the attack on her squad a month before, and remembering that night made me even more heart-broken, because she had survived that, and now she's gone. I was sad, angry, and frustrated. I know that an incredibly beautiful light was removed from our world, and that light won't be forgotten, ever. Until we meet again, Thumbs-Up to you, Rachel."

Bosveld had attended Waupun High School for her final two years, having started at Oshkosh West, according to local media stories at the time of her death.[14]

---

[10] "Shake the Devil Off," p. 82-83.

[11] http://militarytimes.com/valor/army-pfc-rachel-k-bosveld/256864

[12] "Shake the Devil Off," p. 83-84.

[13] http://www.fallenheroesmemorial.com/oif/profiles/bosveldrachelk.html

[14] http://militarytimes.com/valor/army-pfc-rachel-k-bosveld/256864

Army Reserve Pfc. Nichole M. Frye, 19, of Lena in Oconto County: Frye died Feb. 16, 2004, when an IED was set off near her convoy in Baqubah, about 30 miles northeast of Baghdad. She was in Company A, 415th Civil Affairs Battalion, U.S. Army Reserve, Kalamazoo, Mich.

Over the years, several soldiers have posted messages about Frye's death and about her time in Iraq.[15]

Staff Sgt. Jimmy Struckhoff of another civil affairs battalion, the 418th, was in the ill-fated convoy.

> **We, members of the 418th and 415th Civil Affairs Battalions, were getting ready to return to Tikrit at 0830 hours when at the last minute, a group from the 415th and the 422nd decided to piggyback with us out to Warhorse (a camp).**
>
> **Pfc. Frye was requesting that she be allowed to go along. Someone from the 415th told her she could. She was willing and eager to get out of the wire (the camp) that morning. She had a serious demeanor and yet was all smiles.**
>
> **We headed out at 0930 hours after a short delay. Pfc. Frye was driving the trail HMMWV (Humvee). It had recently been up-armored (reinforcing its weak areas, which soldiers had started doing when realizing how vulnerable the vehicles were).**
>
> **Shortly down the road the inevitable happened. Myself and Sgt. Nathan Craft were in the vehicle ahead of hers and were the first on the scene. ...**
>
> **I just wanted you to know that she was doing what she wanted to do and what she loved to do. Serving her country to the fullest of her potential. She was ambitious and extremely strong-willed. She truly will be missed by everyone who knew her.**

Another soldier, colleague Bruce Moore of Peachtree, Ga., posted this message about Frye:

> **My observations of Nicky, in the short time she was with us, were mostly of her working on her vehicle. She was the driver of a "gun-Hummer", which is short for "High-Mobility**

---

[15] http://www.fallenheroesmemorial.com/oif/profiles/fryenicholem.html

Multi-purpose Wheeled Vehicle." I'd spent some time in the military, and so I guess I noticed things about soldiers that old soldiers notice. Nicky was always in a proper uniform; she kept her vehicle well-maintained; and she had a good attitude. A soldier's lot in a war zone is anything but fun, but I only remember seeing her one time when she wasn't smiling. And that was on the morning she died.

It was a beautiful morning. I was out early to oversee the delivery of some 7,000 space heaters to a camp of refugees ("displaced persons", in Army lingo), who camped in some ruins outside of town. When we arrived back at the compound, our two vehicles had to be searched for any explosives which might have been attached to them while we were out. Since this normally took some time, and since it was a nice day, I told the drivers that I would walk in, and that I'd see them inside.

As I walked through the security zone of concrete blast walls, I noticed that an Army patrol of three or four Hummers was formed up and waiting for my vehicles to finish being searched, so that they could depart. My path took me alongside the out-going patrol's vehicles, and in the passenger side of the second Hummer, I saw the 415th CA's battalion commander, a young major whom I had met just days before. I stopped to say hello, but he was busy talking on the radio, so after a short pause I continued on my way. I remember thinking, as I walked away, how the major's driver wasn't smiling today. It was Nicky Frye. She wasn't smiling. She appeared determined, confident, and focused. If she was afraid, I saw no sign of it. She was ready. ...'

Not long after the column moved out, we heard an explosion off in the distance. Since this was not an unusual occurrence in Baqubah, we went on about our work, until we got a report that our patrol had been hit by an IED, a roadside bomb, and that a female soldier had been killed. As the morning wore on, we learned that the same blast had seriously wounded the major and two other soldiers. We also learned that, on my mission just minutes earlier, my two vehicles had rolled past the same IED twice. Perhaps the insurgents decided we were moving too fast. Perhaps they simply preferred to wait for an Army vehicle.

Army National Guard Specialist Michelle M. Witmer, 20, of New Berlin: Less than two months after Frye's death, Witmer was killed April 9, 2004, when a convoy was attacked in Baghdad. She was the gunner, in the turret of a Humvee with an M-249 machine gun. Witmer was in the Wisconsin Army National Guard's 32nd Military Police Company, Milwaukee.

Her father, John Witmer, wrote in his book, "Sisters in Arms," about what happened:[16]

> **Six vehicles exited the Green Zone through Assassin's Gate; one squad turned right, across the Tigress River toward al Al A'zamiyah; the other continued north. Just minutes later, high-caliber bullets rained down on the northbound convoy. An RPG (rocket-propelled grenade) landed on the curb as an explosion crippled the lead vehicle. The lead vehicle swerved hard to the right. ...**
>
> **Tracer bullets flecked the night sky. The lieutenant looked up through the hatch; his gunner, a bright young woman, with so much to live for, was slumped forward, looking down. He took her in his arms, placed her across the back seat, and began CPR as the convoy pushed through the three-block-long ambush. ...**
>
> **The lieutenant was puzzled. She had been wounded in the shoulder; there was very little bleeding, but she was not breathing. But then the saw the blood around her mouth. They continued CPR as they struggled to understand her injuries. ... Hospital personnel continued to try and revive her, but it was hopeless. The bullet, which hit her in the shoulder, passed through her heart, stopping it almost instantly.**

Witmer's sister Rachel was in the same 32nd Military Police Company, also as a Humvee gunner, and had seen Michelle in the gunner's seat as the Humvees were lined up to embark. Their sister Charity was in the Wisconsin National Guard's 118th Medical Battalion about 14 miles away.[17]

---

[16] "Sisters in Arms: A Father Remembers," by John Witmer (2010). p. 64-66.

[17] "Sisters in Arms," p. 64, 69.

Sgt. Nate Olson was in the Humvee with Witmer and his report in her father's book says there was an explosion, then the RPG hit. Heavy gunfire "was coming from everywhere, ground-level, second-story windows, roofs, etc. Most of the gunfire was directed at our vehicle. This was a well-planned ambush, and their intention was to render our middle vehicle inoperable, causing us to stop. Michelle was hit as she attempted to engage the targets. She did everything right. Unfortunately, the gunfire was too heavy, and concentrated on our vehicle."[18]

Dozens of tributes to Michelle Witmer from colleagues and those who did not know her are posted at http://www.fallenheroesmemorial.com/oif/profiles/witmermichellem.html

One, posted in all capital letters, is from someone identified only as Raasch of Milwaukee: "I had the honor and privilege to serve in Iraq with this special person. Her spirit set the standard for positiveness and she was one hell of a soldier. Thank you for giving me the opportunity to get to know you and for making me a better person and soldier because of it."

Another, from Sgt. Darrell Huber of Ohio, said: "I was in Iraq in 2009-2010 and was treated at Witmer TMC (troop medical clinic at Camp Liberty) several times for injuries and read the picture and how the TMC came to be named Witmer and was very moved. I am sorry for your loss and will always remember being there and the care that was given to me and others knowing that an Army Angel such as your daughter was still looking out for us!"

Naval Reserve Petty Officer 2nd Class Jaime S. Jaenke, 29, of Bay City in Pierce County: She died June 5, 2006, when her Humvee was struck by an IED in Al Anbar province in western Iraq. She was a hospital corpsman assigned to Naval Mobile Construction Battalion 25, Fort McCoy, Wis. That is a Seabee unit (Seabees build airstrips, housing and the like); a corpsman is a person working as a pharmacist or hospital assistant.

Jaenke and Petty Officer 1st Class Gary Rovinski, 44, were killed in the blast.[19]

---

[18] "Sisters in Arms," p. 100.

[19] http://www.iraqwarheroes.org/rovinski.htm and http://www.iraqwarheroes.org/rovinski.htm

Media reports at the time said Jaenke had completed 25 missions in Iraq, safely escorting 375 personnel.[20] The news coverage said Jaenke had been living in Ellsworth, in Pierce County, but had moved to Iowa Falls, Iowa. She had been volunteering as an emergency medical technician in Ellsworth and helping run the family's horse training facility. She also enrolled in the nursing program at Ellsworth Community College in Iowa Falls.[21]

A colleague writing to a memorial page described Jaenke was as "caring and giving. Those are the type of people you want to be around you," said Petty Officer 3rd Class Esteban Burgoa. "If there is someone you want to be friends with in life, she's it." Recalling how Jaenke once treated his injured hand, Burgoa said: "Gosh, she's just like an angel."

Al Anbar province included such infamous cities as Ramadi and Fallujah, which often were in the news during the time of Jaenke's death.

Army Reserve Sgt. 1st Class Merideth Howard, 52, of Waukesha: She was killed in Kabul, Afghanistan, on Sept. 8, 2006, when a suicide car bomber raced alongside her Humvee and detonated his vehicle.

Howard was the oldest American woman killed by enemy fire and was in the Army Reserve's 405th Civil Affairs Battalion, Fort Bragg, N.C. She was from Texas and had lived in Alameda, Calif., and many other cities. She had moved to Waukesha when her husband took work there.

The Chicago Tribune reported about her case in a long story two weeks after her death[22], datelined Mehtarlam, Afghanistan. It is quoted here at length because of the portrait that it paints and how someone in a civil affairs battalion wound up as a gunner on a Humvee and being ambushed.

Her last night here, Howard and Staff Sgt. Robert Paul sat on the back stoop of their barracks with the base cook, as usual.

[20] http://militarytimes.com/valor/navy-hospital-corpsman-2nd-class-jaime-s-jaenke/ 1861359. More material is at http://navy.togetherweserved.com/usn/servlet/ tws.webapp.WebApp?cmd=ShadowBoxProfile&type=TributeExt&ID=1274 and at http://www.fallenheroesmemorial.com/oif/profiles/jaenkejaimes.html

[21] http://militarytimes.com/valor/navy-hospital-corpsman-2nd-class-jaime-s-jaenke/ 1861359

[22] http://www.iraqwarheroes.org/howardm.htm

"We started talking about the time she got shot at," said Air Force Tech. Sgt. Marlin McDaniel, 42, the cook. "I said I'd probably duck. I wouldn't know what to do. But they both basically said at the same time, 'When it's your time to go, it's your time to go.'"

The next day, Howard and Paul (age 43) made a supply run to a U.S. military base near the Afghan capital. They never made it back, dying in a fiery suicide bombing in Kabul on Sept. 8.

At 52, Howard … became the oldest known American woman to die in combat.

The fact that she was even here, serving as a gunner on a Humvee, shows the drain that two wars have put on an all-volunteer military. She was the new face of the military's civil affairs units, which do reconstruction and relief work. Constant deployments have tapped out the regular Army Reservists who most often filled those jobs in Iraq and Afghanistan.

Howard never had been deployed before, not since joining the Reserves on a whim in 1988. After her medical unit was disbanded in 1996, she was assigned to the Individual Ready Reserves, for soldiers without a unit. She still went to monthly drills but mainly handled paperwork, biding her time, putting in her 20 years before earning retirement benefits.

But as a stopgap – and in a first for the U.S. military – provincial reconstruction teams in Afghanistan were being filled by a mix of Navy, Air Force, Army, National Guard and Reserve soldiers. And many in the Reserves were like Howard, in the Individual Ready Reserves, home also to retired soldiers who had recently left the Army. A few regular reservists, such as Paul, volunteered for civil affairs. The rest, such as Howard, were called up last December (that was 2005).

… In 1991, Howard started dating Hugh Hvolboll, who made fireworks for a living. … In 2004 the couple moved to Waukesha for his job. They never felt the need to get married, not until she was called up in December. Slightly nervous, Howard wanted to make their relationship official.

"As a boyfriend, I would have no status with the Army," Hvolboll said. "As a husband, I did."

The Tribune story then described how two vehicles came up behind a convoy and each maneuvered until a fiery blast was set off:[23]

A Lexus SUV pulled up behind the third Humvee. A blue Toyota Corolla followed the Lexus. Witnesses said the Corolla tried to pass the Lexus on the left. But the Lexus blocked the Corolla and started trying to pass the convoy on the left.

The gunner on the third Humvee told soldiers after the attack that he was focused on the Lexus, warning it to stop.

But at the same time, the blue Corolla moved up on the right. One soldier in the third Humvee saw the back of the driver's head, his blue shirt. Another soldier noticed the brake lights.

And they all watched as the car swerved into the second Humvee (on which Howard was the gunner), bounced off, and then swerved in again. Everything seemed slow, the soldiers said, slow enough to notice the driver's face as he pulled in the last time – his mustache, no beard. And then a loud explosion, and a flash, and everything was on fire. The blast left a 6-foot-wide crater in the road ....

Howard was the only Wisconsin woman killed in Afghanistan. Robert Paul, the soldier killed with Howard, was from Oregon.[24]

Army Reserve Cpl. Rachael L. Hugo, 24, of Madison: Hugo was killed Oct. 5, 2007, in Bayji, Iraq, when insurgents attacked her unit using an IED and small-arms fire. She was a medic with the 303rd Military Police Company, 97th Military Police Battalion, 89th Military Police Brigade, U.S. Army Reserve, of Jackson, Mich. That unit provided security for convoys.

Bayji is in northern Iraq, about 130 miles north of Baghdad.

Hugo was the third Wisconsin woman – Bosveld and Witmer were the others – who was killed while serving in an MP company. An Associated Press story at the time said that in an e-mail to her parents from Iraq, she wrote: "Being a medic is what I live to do."

---

[23] http://www.iraqwarheroes.org/howardm.htm

[24] http://www.soc.mil/Memorial%20Wall/Bios/Paul_Robert.pdf and http://oregon atwar.oregonlive.com/iraq/bios/bio.php?/91

"She was always very adamant about volunteering and going out on missions with her guys," her father, Kermit Hugo, said in the story. "She told us countless times that she needed to be out there with them. If somebody got hurt or something and they didn't have a medic, she was beside herself." He said his daughter was credited with saving the life of a sergeant who was badly wounded by a roadside bomb about three months into her tour. She was in the back of the convoy when the bomb exploded and jumped into action even though gunfire was going off, he said.[25]

Hugo had been working on a bachelor's degree in nursing at Viterbo University in La Crosse before she was deployed to Iraq a little more than a year before her death, former co-worker Juanita Davis said. The two were classmates and worked as home health aides for the La Crosse County Health Department. Hugo also was employed by Meriter Hospital in Madison as a nursing assistant in the hospital's mobile unit, said Sue Simo, one of her supervisors.[26]

Army 2nd Lt. Tracy L. Alger, 30, of New Auburn: Less than a month after Hugo was killed, Alger died Nov. 1, 2007, in Shubayshen, just south of Baghdad, when an IED detonated near her Humvee. She was in the 3rd Battalion, 187th Infantry Regiment, 3rd Brigade Combat Team, 101st Airborne Division (Air Assault), of Fort Campbell, Ky.

Alger grew up in New Auburn, went to Chetek High School and studied graphic design at the University of Wisconsin – River Falls. "Serving her country was what she wanted," her mother, Pauline Knutson, said in news coverage of the death. "We had a conversation before she left that she might not be coming back, so we spent as much time together as we could."[27]

Alger was in charge of convoys that transported supplies, her mother said. "She didn't have to go on a lot of the convoys, but she wanted to serve alongside her people. She was not a stay-back-at-camp kind of person."

The story said Alger had spent many years barrel-racing, a rodeo-like event in which horse and rider are timed as they maneuver around large barrels. Her

---

25 http://militarytimes.com/valor/army-cpl-rachael-l-hugo/3096622 and http://www.jsonline.com/news/wisconsin/29290889.html

26 http://www.flickr.com/photos/52961928@N00/1714914418/ Some coverage and memorial comments also are at http://northshorejournal.org/spc-rachael-l-hugo

27 http://militarytimes.com/valor/solider/3161816/

horse was named Tango. She was on the rodeo team at River Falls, and had been president of the Wisconsin Girls Barrel Racing Association, Knutson said.

Several tributes to Alger are posted at http://www.ourfallen soldier.com/,[28] including this from Staff Sgt. Derek R. James: "It seems like yesterday you asked me if I would supply the chips for our meeting which we had every day. I must say that you was one hell of a leader and FRIEND!!! In the worst of times you SMILED, and made your soldiers feel better. I am retired now and times have been a little rough, but when I think of you I always seem to pick myself up and move on with life. Just what you would have told me, LT!!!! You will always be LOVED and MISSED Ma'am." He ended his message with his call-sign, "Nomad 8 Out."

Sgt. Wally Holt, quoted earlier in this chapter, posted his message on the third anniversary of Alger's loss. He added: "I was her enlisted right-hand man and her gunner. She was one hell of a leader. She was an officer who was willing to learn what she might not already have known, if it meant making her and her soldiers better for the task or mission at hand."

Losses before Iraq and Afghanistan

The only two Wisconsin predecessors of these seven woman killed in Iraq and Afghanistan died at Anzio, Italy, in 1944 and in the Persian Gulf War in 1991.

Army 2nd Lt. Ellen G. Ainsworth was a nurse with the 56th Evacuation Hospital and died Feb. 16, 1944, four days after being wounded in a German bombing of her hospital at Anzio, where the Allies invaded but did not get very far off the beachhead for months. The beachhead was almost constantly under fire from huge German artillery guns such as Anzio Annie and from Luftwaffe attacks, and patients said they felt safer at the front than in the hospital.

Ainsworth, 24, was from Glenwood City in St. Croix County in northwestern Wisconsin, and is buried in Italy.[29]

---

[28] http://www.ourfallensoldier.com/AlgerTracy_MemorialPage.html

[29] Ainsworth was the topic of Tom Mueller's Memorial Day story in 1986 in The Milwaukee Sentinel, at which time his research determined her unique status in Wisconsin history. The story was updated and appeared as Chapter 8 of Mueller's 2009 book "The Wisconsin 3,800."

Ainsworth's loss has appeared in multiple books, one of which says she "refused to use the air raid shelter (during the many raids and shellings), for reasons of her own. When (fellow nurse) Avis Dagit mentioned the shelter at breakfast one morning, Ellen answered insouciantly, 'I'm not going to use it. Everyone would be killed if a bomb hit that shelter. I'll take my chances elsewhere.'"[30]

On Feb. 10, Ainsworth had led efforts to protect patients at the 56th Evac amid an extremely heavy artillery barrage that left some of the unit's tents in tatters. She would be awarded the Silver Star for gallantry for her work on that day, but did not live to receive it and probably never even knew about it because she had only a few days to live. The citation for the medal honored Ainsworth for "calmly directing the placing of surgical patients on the ground to lessen the danger of further injury during the enemy shelling of the hospital. By her disregard for her own safety and her calm assurance, she instilled confidence in her assistants and her patients, thereby preventing serious panic and injury."[31]

Ainsworth's sister, Lyda, said in 1986 that other nurses told her family the method was to put the patients on the ground and put the beds over them.

The bombing raid on Feb. 12 in which she was severely injured did not last as long as the artillery barrage had lasted and only slightly damaged the hospital. When the all-clear sounded, Ainsworth "dared leave for a minute, to run back to her hut and get something," Lyda reported. But just as she got there, another bomb fell, and the fluke scored a direct hit on her tent.

Another version tells that at 18:30, German planes waged an attack on the harbor that lasted about 90 minutes, during which time a bomb fell into the officers' living area of the 56th Evac, and Ainsworth was struck by fragments in the chest and abdomen. She had a tear in her left lung, lacerations of the right side of the diaphragm and spleen, and a stomach wound.[32]

"But the doctors and nurses held high hopes for her recovery. While carried to the operating room, it was rumored, Ellen had taken her own blood

---

[30] "They Fought at Anzio," by John S. Eisenhower (2007), p. 202.

[31] "And If I Perish: Frontline U.S. Army Nurses in World War II," by Evelyn M. Monahan and Rosemary Neidel-Greenlee (2003), p. 272.

[32] "And If I Perish," p. 274-275)

pressure, reporting it as 130 / 80." Ainsworth asked Dagit "if anyone else had been hurt in the raid. On being assured they had not, she whispered, 'Oh thank God.'" [33]

But Ainsworth grew weaker and weaker and died four days later. She was one of six nurses killed at Anzio.[34]

No other Wisconsin woman was killed by enemy fire in a war for nearly a half-century, until the very end of the Persian Gulf War in 1991. Helicopter technician Sgt. Cheryl La Beau O'Brien of Caledonia in Racine County volunteered to be the door gunner on a helicopter flight from her base in Kuwait into Iraq to pick up the bodies of American soldiers who had been killed in the crash of a medical evacuation helicopter.[35]

O'Brien, 24, of the Army's 1st Aviation Battalion, was killed along with all eight other soldiers on the UH-1H helicopter on Feb. 27, 1991. The very next day, President George H.W. Bush told the nation that the war was over, 100 hours after the ground invasion had begun.

"She volunteered to fly that mission. That was like her," her husband, Michael O'Brien, 32, who was an aviation mechanic, told the Chicago Tribune. "She was the door gunner, returning fire. But they were shot down by enemy fire."[36]

La Beau O'Brien first had trained as a mechanic in aviation electronics and stayed in the Army until her discharge in 1990. She soon rejoined the Army with the proviso that she be stationed with her husband at Fort Riley, Kan., O'Brien said. She deployed with him on Jan. 11. Operation Desert Storm began Jan. 17 with air attacks, followed by the ground war on Feb. 24.

The pilot apparently was Army Warrant Officer John K. Morgan of Bellevue, Wash. News coverage in Seattle[37] at the time – this was a few years

---

[33] "They Fought at Anzio," p. 203.

[34] http://www.history.army.mil/books/wwii/72-14/72-14.HTM

[35] http://www.journaltimes.com/news/local/a-day-to-remember/article_6410c676-a0c0-540b-ae32-654193df894d.html

[36] http://articles.chicagotribune.com/1991-05-22/news/9102150711_1_saudi-arabia-army-eight-other-soldiers

[37] http://community.seattletimes.nwsource.com/archive/?date=19910313&slug=1271422

before the rise of the Internet and it is not easy to find a lot now – said he was the pilot of a copter and was killed along with eight other people. Morgan was 28. The story also said another passenger was Sgt. Lee Belas, 22, of Port Orchard, Wash.

The helicopter website of http://armyaircrews.com/blackhawk.html says the chopper was picking up the crew of another helicopter that had crashed. O'Brien's chopper was #78-23015 and was shot down in Iraq, it says, giving this crew list (the pilot usually is listed first, but in this case Morgan does not come until later):

WO1 George R. Swartzendruber [PC]

WO1 David G. Plasch [PI]

SGT Lee A. Belas

SGT Jason C. Carr

SSG Jonathan H. Kamm

WO1 John K. Morgan

SGT Cheryl LaBeau-O'Brien

SFC Gary E. Streeter

1LT Donaldson Tillar III

The website says the first chopper was #64-14273 and "was on a medevac mission … when AAA fire hit the T/R causing aircraft to enter an uncontrollable spin."

A total of 147 Americans were killed by hostile fire in the Gulf War, and the Wisconsin toll was 11, including O'Brien.[38]

---

[38] www.history.navy.mil/library/online/american%20war%20casualty.htm#t8 and http://legis.wisconsin.gov/lrb/bb/11bb/Stats_Military.pdf

Chapter 14
Recent losses in Afghanistan

Andrew and Laura Johnson of Mayville and Greg and Barb Gassen of Beaver Dam have formed a friendship based on the worst days of their lives.

They are there for each other and to listen to each other and to cry with each other on significant dates and birthdays and anniversaries, or when someone just needs to talk on the phone or in person.

The firstborn son of the Johnsons made the Ultimate Sacrifice in Afghanistan in 2012; the Gassens lost their eldest son in the same country 14 months earlier.

Army Pfc. Jacob A. Gassen, 21, of Beaver Dam, was killed Nov. 29, 2010, when an Afghani border policeman being trained by the Americans attacked his teachers with small arms fire, killing six of them. Gassen was a medic in the 1st Squadron, 61st Cavalry Regiment, 4th Brigade Combat Team, 101st Airborne Division (Air Assault), Fort Campbell, Ky. He was killed in Nangarhar province in eastern Afghanistan along the Pakistani border. The capital of that province is Jalalabad, which often is in the news.

Army 1st Lt. David A. Johnson, 24, of Mayville, died Jan. 25, 2012, when an improvised explosive device in the form of a boobytrap went off while he was leading a raid against a hut where intelligence had reported IEDs were being made. Johnson was in the 5th Battalion, 20th Infantry Regiment, 3rd Stryker Brigade Combat Team, 2nd Infantry Division, based out of Joint Base Lewis-McChord in Washington state. He was killed in Kandahar province in southern Afghanistan, along the Pakistani border.

The Gassens quickly reached out to the Johnsons after hearing news that was hauntingly familiar.

"We're all part of that unfortunate family, the Gold Star families," Greg Gassen says. "It's not normal to bury your child. I describe it as 'somebody hit me with a 2-by-4 and I went down so hard I couldn't get up off the ground.'"

The Gassens had not gotten involved with the families of other fallen soldiers from Wisconsin – their mourning over Jake's death was just too difficult, Greg says – until the ultra-bad news came to the Johnsons: the loss of a another Dodge County soldier / neighbor / son.

Army Pfc. Jake Gassen (top of page) of Beaver Dam took this photo of a large bird in Afghanistan, moments before he was killed in 2010. This was the final photo on his camera. Gassen was a medic whose Army unit was conducting an artillery training session for Afghan forces; a border policeman at the training killed six Americans. Army 1st Lt. David Johnson (bottom photo) of Mayville was killed in Afghanistan in 2012.

"I saw on Facebook that someone was saying a Mayville guy had died in Afghanistan," Barb Gassen says. "I sent a message of sympathy to Laura Johnson and said that if you want to talk, just call or send a message back."

The Gassens traveled the 16 miles to David Johnson's wake at Mayville High School. They stood in the long line of mourners – as so many others had waited to console them over Jake – and introduced themselves to the Johnsons. "He knew who I was, right away," Greg says of Andrew Johnson. "I said, 'I kind of got an idea of what you're going through.' It was emotional for us, too. And we just started to talk over the months."

They also quickly found that David Johnson's final birthday had been Nov. 28, which was one day before the first anniversary of Jake Gassen's death.

Barb says: "They're a really nice family and I wish I had known them for other reasons." Both sets of parents are "strong-willed, independent persons whose brains got scrambled" by the horrible news from the war zone, she adds.

The Johnsons own the Dodge County Pionier weekly newspaper in Mayville; Andrew is the publisher. Laura Johnson is a CPA who does private work. Greg Gassen is a court reporter for various judges, while Barb Gassen works for the state Department of Transportation, and "I ran construction. We're all used to taking care of things," she says.

Knowing each other has helped the Gassens and Johnsons tremendously. They meet frequently for dinner and talk on the phone more often than that. In 2013, they started a grief counseling group along with a few other local parents who have lost young men for reasons other than war.

Jacob Gassen; Afghanistan 2010

The soldier's little black camera was returned home as part of his personal effects. Greg Gassen says there were 544 photos and short video clips on its memory card, painting a comprehensive portrait of his son's final weeks, days ... and even minutes.

The last three frames on the camera were of a large bird, likely one of the many kinds of eagles found in Afghanistan,[1] such as the Greater Spotted Eagle, Steppe Eagle and Booted Eagle, to name only a few. It got closer and closer and the last frame is an excellent photo in and of itself; the bird with wings fully spread and gliding in a peaceful, perfect, heavenly blue sky.

The automatic time stamp by the camera shows Jake took it at 4:16 a.m. Beaver Dam time, which Greg Gassen says was only a few minutes before Jake was killed. Anyone seeing this photo no doubt will think of the hymn "On Eagle's Wings," and its soaring refrain of:

And He will raise you up on eagle's wings,

Bear you on the breath of dawn,

Make you to shine like the sun,

And hold you in the palm of His Hand.

Only one day earlier, father and son had talked for about 15 minutes via satellite phone. This was just a few days after Jake's 21st birthday. "I was up north for the last day of deer-hunting season, Greg says. He said, 'I'm kind of homesick, Dad. I can't wait to get home to see you on the 15th of January.'" He had been in Afghanistan since August and was going to come home on a

---

[1] A long list of eagles in Asia, and photos of many of them in flight, has been compiled at http://en.wikipedia.org/wiki/List_of_birds_of_Afghanistan More descriptions are at http://avibase.bsc-eoc.org/species.jsp?avibaseid=05F1144132A7E4FF

30-day leave, a break that each soldier gets at some point, in order to help his family move from Beaver Dam Lake into its newly built home in Beaver Dam. It was starting a new chapter.

Then Jake went on a supposedly simple "training mission," as he had said to his father. The unit was training Afghan soldiers on how to shoot 155mm artillery. As a medic, Gassen had little to do on a training mission, but had to be there. Everyone was watching where the shells were landing. "When the first boom went off, this guy stood up with an AK-47 five feet away and shot them in the back of the head," Greg says.

Jake Gassen and five other American soldiers died, and the action quickly was national news.[2]

"I was coming home from Madison and I heard on the news that six soldiers got killed by an Afghan border guard," Greg says. "I said, 'I hope that isn't Jake,' but he said he was on (just) a training mission.

"When I got home that day, I was cooking chili and there was a knock on the door. I saw the captain and the chaplain."

In some of its last frames before the shots of the bird, Jake's Canon Power Shot camera has photos of Afghani guards sitting along a wall waiting for the artillery firing to begin. Greg has not been able to determine whether one of them was his son's killer.

Also on the camera were videos of birthday "spankings" of one playful swat with a cricket bat. Greg says "these guys are family," laughing and at ease in a fortified bunker. Jake was spanked on his birthday, which was Nov. 19, just 10 days before he was killed. Sgt. 1st Class Barry Jarvis got the same swat on his 36th birthday Nov. 24, only five days before he also was killed. Other men who soon would be killed are visible in the video.

The sergeant, a rank usually known as a hard-ass in basic training, must have had an extremely strong gluteus maximus, because he hardly winced from the blow or the stinging of the next few seconds. The same could not be said for Gassen.

Another swatee was Sgt. Tyson Hegel, whose birthday was the same day as Jarvis. Hegel, in fact, had wielded the cricket bat on Jake Gassen's behind, and soon would deliver the eulogy for the Wisconsinite at the unit's memorial ceremony in Afghanistan.

---

[2] http://www.nytimes.com/2010/11/30/world/asia/30afghan.html?_r=0

As to what he was doing in combat, Jake had not told his parents much, but did say he had earned a combat medic pin. Some guys were injured "but I glued them up," he modestly and tersely reported. Others have reported that Jake "could put in an IV with night vision goggles," Barb says, with Greg adding, "The other medics were saying he was a really good medic."

Greg calls the anniversary of his son's death the "Angel-versary." They often have seen things they consider to mean that "Jake is still with us."

For example, a couple months after his death they were moving boxes to their new home in Beaver Dam. Jake had been scheduled to come home on leave in order to help them. "The mailman delivered a box of Jake's personal effects that were on his body when he was killed." It made him feel that Jake was moving boxes of stuff along with the rest of the family, Greg says. These items included the camera with all those photos and the videos, and Jake's military dogtags, which the father now wears every day.

Another omen came when Greg joined a motorcycle ride of the nationofpatriots.org from Oconomowoc to Woodstock, Ill., on Memorial Day weekend of 2011, and was told there were 101 motorcycles; he considered that a sign from above because Jake was in the 101st Airborne.

At the end of the ride he met Sgt. Jacob Hoelscher of Jake's unit, and he "wanted me to know personally that he was the one who killed the Afghan" who had killed Jake and the other soldiers. "Hoelscher was shaking and said he had survivor's guilt."

Hoelscher reported that the shooter had been with Americans for two or three years, and "just that day seemed upset. He got a phone call just before starting to shoot," Greg says, evidently his final orders to turn against the teachers.

Two weeks before the first anniversary of the incident, the Gassens traveled to Kentucky for a ceremony at Fort Campbell, home of the 101st Airborne, in which Jarvis – the man being spanked in one of the birthday videos – was awarded a posthumous Silver Star for valor. He had shoved the platoon leader, 1st Lt. Will Janotka, out of the way of the gunman's fire and then was gunned down.

The citation[3] said that as

Jarvis came into view of the scene, he realized that both he and the platoon leader were in the gunman's line of fire. Sgt. 1st Class Jarvis immediately pushed 1st Lt. Janotka out of the

---

[3] http://militarytimes.com/citations-medals-awards/recipient.php?recipientid=53888

line of fire, and in doing so, knowingly placed himself in harm's way to prevent his platoon leader from being engaged.

As Sgt. 1st Class Jarvis was turning to engage the gunman, he was mortally wounded. Sgt. 1st Class Jarvis' courage under fire, selfless service and total disregard for his own safety are in keeping with the finest traditions of military service and reflect great credit upon himself, 1st Squadron, 61st Cavalry Regiment, 101st Airborne Division and the United States Army.

The Army Times interviewed Janotka after the Silver Star ceremony. He said the platoon had made three previous visits to the observation post at which the incident occurred; the most recent visit was a week earlier. Its story also said: [4]

When the soldiers arrived, seven of them — including Janotka and Jarvis, the platoon sergeant — trekked 500 feet to 600 feet up a hill to the highest point of the OP.

"As soon as the first (rocket) round impacted, the guy started shooting," Janotka said. "He started shooting and Sgt. Jarvis yells, 'We've got to move.' "

It was over in a flash, no more than 30 or 45 seconds, Janotka said. "When the rounds ceased, I looked down and (Jarvis) had been fatally wounded in the chest."

The shooter, whom the soldiers had seen on previous visits to the OP, was 10 feet away from the soldiers. "He shot five of my soldiers in the head," plus Jarvis, Janotka said.

Killed with Gassen and Jarvis, of Tell City, Ind., were Pvt. Buddy W. McLain, 24, of Mexico, Maine; Pvt. Austin G. Staggs, 19, of Senoia, Ga.; Spec. Matthew W. Ramsey, 20, of Quartz Hill, Calif., and Staff Sgt. Curtis A. Oakes, 29, of Athens, Ohio.[5]

---

[4] http://www.armytimes.com/news/2011/11/army-soldier-posthumously-awarded-for-saving-lieutenant-112611w

[5] This was one of the largest groups of soldiers to die in recent years, except in plane crashes. Their array of photos is striking. See them at http://www.sunjournal.com/national/story/951399 This is a newspaper in Maine, where McLain was from. The original Associated Press story also is there. Accessed January 2013.

The Gassens met their families, other members of the platoon, Hoelscher and Janotka at the event and shared their tears and hugs.

Father and son spent considerable time together while Jake was growing up.

"Jake was my waterskiing buddy on Beaver Dam Lake," says Greg, who when interviewed was about ready to sell the prized 20.5-foot Crown Line boat that the two used. Greg and Barb had bought it in 2004. There are two younger sons in the family, but they never had warmed up to the water fun like Greg and Jake did, and so use of the boat had fallen way off. Simply put, it reminded Greg too much about Jake. The father managed to use it only twice in 2011 and once in 2012. "It's just a shame. It just sits there," he says.

Jake was "a real intelligent guy but not real motivated in school," Greg says, other than in sciences like biology, and perhaps was headed toward a career in physical therapy – he "liked to make people happy and maybe he could help people be well."

He played the viola in the school orchestra and was on the golf team. Jake trained himself on the lead guitar and piano. "He was everyone's buddy, a fun-loving guy, and he worked out and would not wear a shirt," preferring to show off his physique, Barb says. Jake worked on the farm of her brother Dan Luck starting at age 12 or 13, "getting dirty and yelled at occasionally. The Army honestly wasn't that new to him" in that sense of physical work and sweating. Still, "Jake is the last guy I thought would ever turn into a soldier, where you follow all these rules and follow orders," his mother says.

He graduated from Beaver Dam High School in 2008 and went to UW – Oshkosh for a year, and "succeeded in having a really good time" and a low GPA, Greg says. Two members of his fraternity had been in the Army, and Jake took note and eventually reported home: "I'm going to go in a different direction, Dad, and join the Army," be a medic, serve for four years, and then go to college to be a nurse.

Greg adds: "He would have made a good nurse. He cared about people, and he'd light up a room when he came into it. His buddies say Jake could make everyone smile."

Greg says Jake was one of the top five medics in his class of study – Jake and another were killed in action, while two committed suicide after coming home, Greg says.

Suicides are a huge problem for the military. The Pentagon said a record 349 service members around the world killed themselves in 2012, far exceeding

American combat deaths in Afghanistan (295) for that year. That number is the highest since the Pentagon began tracking them carefully in 2001, and does not include people who killed themselves after being discharged.[6]

Gassen is buried in Annunciation Cemetery in Randolph in Dodge County, in a plot with other relatives.

Beaver Dam has renamed short streets around the high school for Gassen – Jacob Gassen's Way – and its two graduates who died in Iraq – Marine Pfc. Ryan Cantafio in 2004 and Marine Sgt. Kirk Allen Straseskie in 2003. Straseskie was the very first Wisconsinite to die in Iraq.

Similarly, David Johnson was not the first from Mayville High School to fall. Army National Guard Specialist Michael Jacob Wendling was killed in Iraq in 2005.

David Johnson; Afghanistan 2012

In 2011, Johnson was the star of the Veterans Day observance at his alma mater of Evangel University in Springfield, Mo. He was back to visit the school, teachers and friends before going off to war in Afghanistan.

One year later, he was memorialized at the same event.

Johnson was an Evangel graduate of 2010, and one of only two ROTC grads at the school that year. He was a member of Bear Battalion, which was drawn from students at Evangel, Missouri State University in same community and other local schools. So before going to Afghanistan, "David made a special trip to Missouri for that Veterans Day event and to see people," says his father, Andrew.

Only six weeks after arriving in Afghanistan, Johnson was killed by a boobytrap while the platoon he led was tracking down places – his father calls them "factories" – that were making improvised explosive devices. The news spread quickly at Evangel and students gathered to pray for the soldier they had celebrated less than three months earlier.

Then at the 2012 Veterans Day event, 1,200 people gathered to pay tribute to Johnson and comfort his parents. "His company commander from

---

[6] Associated Press story from Jan. 14, 2013; at http://bigstory.ap.org/article/2012-military-suicides-hit-record-high-349

Afghanistan, Capt. Nathan Smith, was there. His classmate graduates who survived Afghanistan were there. They wanted to do something special for David," Andrew says.

The event provided some continuing support for the Johnsons in their grieving, the latest of a months-long flood of emails, Facebook messages, calls, visits and hometown support since the tragic events of the preceding January, when they received the same shocking knock on the door that the Gassens had received.

They were taken from Wisconsin to meet the plane that brought David's body to the U.S. Air Force base at Dover, Del. He then was flown to Milwaukee and taken to Mayville via a motorcade. "Schools closed for the motorcade, as did the John Deere factory in Horicon," Andrew says. "They came out to the road. There were thousands and thousands of people. I couldn't believe it." Mayville's population is about 5,000.

There was a massive community visitation on Saturday and a memorial service Sunday that filled the high school gym. His casket then was carried over the Rock River to the city's new war memorial for a service that featured a gun salute, a flyby from a Blackhawk helicopter like David had used, and the solemn folding of the flag from his casket.

His body then was flown to Washington, D.C., and he was buried in Arlington National Cemetery on Feb. 22, three weeks later, with the casket borne on a horse-drawn caisson accompanied by an Army band. He received a 21-gun salute and is buried in Section 60, Site 9947.

Andrew says his son lived for the Army through and through, and that is why the family decided he should be buried amid so many colleagues in that national shrine instead of in Mayville. "He belongs there. His friends said he would have wanted to be there," Andrew says. The Johnsons were awed by the massive size of Section 60. "It's kind of spooky. When your son is there, you realize every gravestone has a story like yours. You are overwhelmed by the great sadness of these stories."

David was a lieutenant and leader of men, a natural extension of his life from back home in Mayville.

"David was a natural leader from the time he was a little boy," his father says. "He was a high achiever and had 43 merit badges as a Boy Scout," double the amount needed to get into the Eagle Scout program, in which he built benches for Dodge County's Ledge Park.

"He was always interested in the Army and enlisted in the Army Reserves right out of high school," Andrew says. He was age 14 on Sept. 11, 2001, but "I don't recollect anything special as that day pointing to the Army," or that the immense national tragedy would reach into the Johnson family in barely more than a decade.

Laura Johnson says David always was a whirlwind of activity. He ran the high school greenhouse as a senior, as part of the Future Farmers of America. He was in the men's choir, and played one of the townsmen in the school play, "Beauty and the Beast." He played a bit of football but was far from a star.

"He was friends with everyone," transcending the usual cliques in a high school. Andrew adds, "Relationships were always the most important thing to David. There were three bands at his graduation party, which was at our house outside of town." He would meet people who were in bands, and invited them and they gladly accepted. Hundreds of friends attended.

He did his Army basic training between high school graduation in 2006 and entering college that fall. After his freshman year, he took Army Chaplain Assistant training at Fort Jackson, S.C. In 2010, he graduated from the ROTC program, was commissioned as a second lieutenant, and from Evangel with a bachelor of science degree. Then it was on to more officer leadership training and assignment to Joint Base Lewis-McChord at Tacoma, Wash.

In Afghanistan, David was commander of the 1st Platoon of his unit at a firebase. "He also had a platoon of Afghani forces," Andrew says. The Johnsons do not know what part of Kandahar province this was in, or whether it was near any village with an actual name. But the soldiers were busy – "the captain told us they were attacked every day," Andrew says. "Their mission was to provide stability to little villages."

Laura says "the entire firebase was the size of two football fields," and the villagers appreciated what the troops were doing, especially in terms of building schools. Villagers called Johnson "the man with the big smile," and his men called him "Big Dave." Johnson was 225 pounds and 6 feet tall.

On the fateful day, the team was on a foot patrol. The Army had gotten reports that insurgents were making improvised explosive devices in a structure with a walled courtyard. David volunteered to lead the mission. Six men went into the structure and turned left. David and one other man turned right. Each group had a bomb-sniffing device.

"As David stepped in, the IED was inside the door. It did not go off when he went in, but it did when he went out," Andrew says.

It was a boobytrapped door, with a pressure plate that made it go off. The soldier with Johnson was injured, but not seriously. But Johnson had extensive wounds and was flown out on a helicopter, dying en route.

The soldiers with David reported to the Johnson family that "after he was hit, he did not think of himself, even though he was in great pain," Andrew says. "He said, 'Don't despair. Don't despair. Tell my Mom and Dad I love them.'" Those were his only words.

Andrew proudly notes that because of David leading this mission, two other IED "factories" in that area were destroyed, thus saving several lives.

Laura Johnson shared a message from a soldier in another platoon in David's company that said: "David was too good for this world and I know he is smiling down on us now as we honor his name. I was with him the night before he died and I want you to know he was his happy, optimistic self. Never looking back, never questioning who he was or what he was doing. Just gliding through life with love and perspective. He was thinking of you guys." This message was from 1st Lt. Benjamin Westman.

"David WANTED to go to Afghanistan. He had other opportunities," Andrew says. "He volunteered to take the firebase position. He was so concerned that he would be a good enough leader for his men. We were told David always listened to his men."

Andrew also says: "We never worried about David," even though he was in a war. "We didn't know how much danger he was in. He was always smart on his feet."

And he adds: "We're very proud of David. He had a very purpose-driven life. He wanted to make a difference. We have no regrets about his service. He was where he wanted to be."

Laura Johnson says her son's life mission was to "instill character and Godly values. We wanted him to do that."

The Johnson family is a longtime member of Christian Life Fellowship, whose mission is to reach all people in Mayville "and the world with the hope of Jesus Christ." Two of David's younger siblings also have attended Evangel; one (Michael) graduated after David and another (Matthew) was a student in 2013. It has about 2,000 students and its motto is "Boldly Christian, Unquestionably Academic," and it explains, "from our deep integration of faith into campus life to our challenging yet rewarding academic focus, Evangel University does more than prepare you to live life – we prepare you to live a life that matters."

David was the second soldier from Evangel University to die, the first happening in Iraq in 2009.

A classmate of David's in chaplain assistant training was Sgt. Jeffrey M. Phail II, who said in a message to the family, and shared by Laura Johnson, that "we instantly became friends even before we got there once we discovered we were both Christians" who also had been through a previous Army course. The Army says a chaplain assistant's main purpose is support for the unit ministry team programs and worship services.[7]

Phail continued: "There are not many people that you just click with and become deep friends with. David was one of those friends to me. When I received a message from (another buddy) today that David had been KIA, I was in complete disbelief. My heart hurts so deeply to know that David is no longer here to help us with our mission of spreading the love of Christ.

"Your son was the man that God had called him to be, through and through. He ran the race hard and he never quit on his God. I thank you for raising such an amazing example for the rest of us. Your son motivated me not just as a soldier, but as a follower of Christ. I pray that I can take the torch from him and continue the race for our God."

Families unite

The friendship of the Gassens and Johnsons extends to and from other people whose sons and daughters made the Ultimate Sacrifice in Iraq and in Afghanistan.

Being There, Reaching Out is an organization for Wisconsin families that lost a son or daughter or other loved one in Iraq and Afghanistan. The Gassens and the Johnsons are members and are comforted by spending time with others who have been through similar horrid news.

Judith Singer of Wauwatosa established the group in 2005. She sends an introduction letter about the group a couple months after a death is

---

[7] http://www.goarmy.com/careers-and-jobs/browse-career-and-job-categories/administrative-support/chaplain-assistant.html

announced, waiting until after the funeral and the many details have been taken care of. The Johnsons and Gassens immediately responded to her communication.

Among other things, the group holds a three-day weekend retreat once a year, with an overall gathering and breakout sessions for parents, siblings and children. "Getting together at our gatherings is like a shot in the arm to allow them to go on," Singer says. So is participation in the Milwaukee Veterans Day parade, which included a float and some vehicles that had been owned by fallen soldiers. She says 60 families were represented in the parade in 2012.

Its website of http://www.beingtherereachingout.org/ has spots for families to post photos, family updates and to cheer each other on.

Eligibility has been expanded in recent years to family members of those lost in suicides and accidents after military service, because of the strong likelihood that post-traumatic stress disorder was involved.

Singer says she has been involved in Gold Star issues since the death of her "first love" in Vietnam – Army 1st Lt. Thomas Francis Shaw of Fond du Lac was pilot of a helicopter that crashed in a mountainous area of South Vietnam on April 27, 1972. He was 24. Singer, who grew up in Green Bay, had met Shaw while he was attending St. Norbert College in De Pere, but each had moved on and she says that by 1972, Shaw was married and had a child.

Chapter 15
What the veterans did, and when

No matter what the era, most of those fighting the nation's wars were ages 18 to 25. And no matter what the era, they toiled daily amid rotating circumstances of hardship, boredom, danger and loneliness.

Here are comments by more than three dozen veterans of the nation's wars spanning from World War II to Korea to Vietnam to Kuwait to Iraq to Afghanistan. They were obtained in a mixture of emails, written letters, phone interviews and in-person interviews.

This is not intended to be a perfect examination of a group of those who served in any particular war. But the reader will see that the ages, duties, sights, sounds and smells of war are universal no matter what the era or the country. For that reason, the wars of these men and women are interspersed in this chapter.

The reader also will see that many veterans had intricate jobs that are not commonly heard about when talking about soldiers, sailors, airmen and Marines – including aircraft repair work on a ship that was a floating garage in World War II, being engineer of a train in India in World War II, work on a submarine in Vietnam, repairing and prepping most parts of an airplane in Korea, etc.

In this chapter and the next chapter, most of the Vietnam veterans bring up the spiteful reception they received from people when returning home, and a few of them also discussed how older veterans looked down on them. Korean War vets have said that about their predecessor veterans, too.

Jeff "Doc" Dentice, Muskego, Army in Vietnam: Dentice was a specialist 5 in the 25th Medical Battalion of the 25th Infantry Division. He had just turned 18 when he arrived in Vietnam, and was there from 1967 to 1968, based at Cu Chi, about 20 miles northwest of Saigon.

Dentice's first impression of Vietnam was "hot, wet, humid, dead soldiers and war." His best period of the war was any day he "saved the life of a soldier. Many, many times. Many wounded. The officers at the medical battalion were doctors. Great guys. Saved lives." His worst period was "dead soldiers, body bags, rockets and mortars."

Dentice put the story of one day on one of his many websites that honor veterans, MIAs, etc.:[1]

Thanking you for your efforts in saving the lives of those I knew after the rocket attack at Cu Chi, Vietnam, at the 125th Signal Co. in early 1968 on the perimeter. You were the only medic that came from the 25th Medical Battalion after the call for help. You treated the badly wounded, and there were many, and you evacuated them all to the 12th Evac Hospital down the road. They had sucking chest wounds, shrapnel wounds, broken legs and burns, and you treated them all. You ran right into the bunker that was hit by a 122 rocket and saw death and smelled flesh burning, and did all you could to save the lives of my friends.

You did this all while we were still under attack and receiving incoming rounds. You should, in my opinion have received the Medal of Honor. It's a shame you were not put in for it. Many men from the 125th Signal Battalion owe you their life, and they and the officers, should have submitted your name for the Medal of Honor.

Herb Mueller

25th Infantry Division Vietnam

125th Signal

Henry Ratenski, Brookfield, Army Air Forces, World War II: When President Harry Truman announced Japan's surrender, Ratenski's 315th Bomb Wing still was flying back to Guam from the war's last mission, bombing oil refineries in far northern Japan. That mission took nearly 17 hours.

Ratenski, 20, was based at Northwest Field on Guam. The wing flew the B-29B bomber. He was the radar bombing and navigation officer, with 15 missions overall – his first coming on June 26, 1945. All of them targeted oil refineries and all were at night because of a sophisticated new radar system.

The book "The Last Mission: The Secret Story of World War II's Final Battle"[2] superimposes the raid by 132 B-29Bs from Ratenski's bomb wing over other research about young officers attempting to stage a coup against

---

[1] http://www.war-veterans.org/Awards.htm

[2] The book is by Jim B. Smith and Malcolm McConnell (2002). Smith was the radio operator on one of the bombers.

Emperor Hirohito and then continuing the war. They unsuccessfully searched for the message of surrender that Hirohito had recorded before its scheduled broadcast at noon Aug. 15 Japan time, which was Aug. 14 in the United States. Because of the air raid, Tokyo was blacked out, hindering the efforts by the coup planners, the book says.

Japan had sent peace feelers soon after the second atomic bombing, at Nagasaki on Aug. 9. But it wanted caveats to the Allied demand of unconditional surrender, and on Aug. 13 in Washington (Aug. 14 Japan time), Truman had ordered the Air Forces to keep bombing, "go ahead with everything we've got."

Ratenski was part of that. He was in the 15th Squadron of the 16th Bomb Group in the 315th Wing. It was ready for takeoff Aug. 14 Japan time when a rumor spread about the war ending. The planes were told to turn off their engines. Everyone was happy. Then they were told to get back into action; that nothing had been announced.

His group took off and got to its target about 2 a.m. Aug. 15 Japan time and dropped its bombs. When Truman announced the surrender, it was 8 a.m. Japan time, with Ratenski's B-29Bs still a long way from home. They learned of the surrender while returning to Guam – "we had big smiles," Ratenski says – and arrived there shortly before noon; some planes had to land on Iwo Jima for fuel and others had to sweat out their landings as tanks were running very low.[3] Ratenski says his plane had a normal landing.

The last mission and his others were essentially "to establish a line in the sand" to the Russians, meaning they should not touch the northernmost Japanese island of Honshu, Ratenski says. Oil facilities at Tsuchinzaki, Japan, were the target of the last mission. His wing also had a mission Aug. 9-10, hours after Nagasaki. Ratenski and author Smith note that most of the world seems to think everything stopped after Hiroshima and especially after Nagasaki, but they say that was not true – plenty of B-29s went into harm's way.

The B-29B had a new, secret radar, the AN / APQ-7 Eagle system for precision radar-bombing.[4] "I happened to be in the first class trained in that. We flew only at night with this precision radar," Ratenski says.

---

[3] "The Last Mission: The Secret Story of World War II's Final Battle," p. 241-244, 266 and 267-272.

[4] The system is detailed at http://www.vectorsite.net/ttwiz_06.html#m2

His pilot in the last mission was Capt. Harold W. Wynn. There were eight other crewmen besides the pilot and Ratenski.

Roger Boeker, Madison, Marine in Vietnam: Boeker (pronounced Baker) went into the Marine Corps after graduating form college and was in Vietnam from 1966 to August 1967, arriving when he was 23 and a private first class. He made corporal three months later. Boeker served in Headquarters Company of the 3rd Marine Division as education NCO – an administrator and tutor of the GED, the high-school equivalency test, given to hundreds of Marines in order to prepare them for their post-war years.

Overall, "I was an enlisted man with a college degree," he says, adding that his officers wondered, "what the hell are you?" given that someone with a degree should be an officer. His degree was in political science from what is now the University of Wisconsin – Madison, in 1965.

"I administered and proctored hundreds of tests. Many servicemen passed the tests, but I do not know the percentage. Others took the test to break up the between-battle boredom or avoid tedious additional duties such as KP, guard duty, latrine cleaning, etc." Boeker would travel out to a unit, "approach the company-level commanding officer or executive officer and ask if he could spare off-duty troops that lacked a high school diploma to give them a GED exam. Sometimes in front-line outfits tests were given open-air and subject to combat interruptions." Upon request, he also would "make a trip to counsel troops, review elements of the weak areas of knowledge, and / or administer another test of the failed portions. If contacted by a person that passed, I would discuss post-military occupational preparation, even college, all in line with the aptitudes and interests of the individual."

The testing "was in addition to what I call adventures on the side," such as dropping propaganda leaflets over North Vietnam, participating in ambushes, roadblocks and guard duty.

One of his greatest joys in handling the GED program was a Marine from Ohio who had failed, got Boeker's tutoring and then passed on the second try. "He had the biggest, brightest smile you ever saw," Boeker says, "an LED smile – very easy to recall and remember. … unforgettable." Boeker says this all "gave me a feeling that I was worthwhile."

But Boeker chokes up when he tells the rest of the story: A couple years after he came home to Madison, he was reading Leatherneck magazine, and saw the same Marine – in a photo spread of those who received the Medal of Honor, posthumously in this case.

Pfc. Douglas Eugene Dickey, age 20, of the 4th Regiment in the 3rd Marine Division, had been killed on March 26, 1967, when he threw himself on a Viet Cong grenade in order to save his buddies. Boeker does not recall when his tutoring was of Dickey was, but Boeker remained in Vietnam until August 1967 and so it likely was only weeks or a couple months after the tutoring.

"I pray for him and my two other close friends every week before Communion," Boeker says.

John Scocos, Army Reservist in Iraq, and now in his second stint as Wisconsin secretary of veterans affairs: Scocos was an Army Reservist who was called up in 2007 and again in 2008-2009. In the second deployment, he was a colonel and director of the Commercial Logistics Distribution Agency, Multi-National Force Iraq, Unified Command Executing Operation Iraqi Freedom. He ran the unit "in support of Iraq reconstruction efforts via port reception, movement (travel, rail and private security), and the security of $12 billion in assets." He also "directed operations of the Logistics Movement Coordination Center and the AB4 Ghraib and Umm Warehouses. Oversaw a joint service workforce of 1,500 personnel which includes active and reserve military components, contractors and local materials."

It was located "in Baghdad and various locations in theatre. Unit took numerous casualties, especially during the surge of 2007."

In his first tour in Iraq, Scocos was deputy director and chief of staff "for Reconstruction Logistics Directorate, Gulf Region Division, U.S. Army Corps of Engineers, Baghdad."

Deanna Czarnecki, Jackson, Army in Afghanistan: Czarnecki was from Grafton and is an Army Reservist who deployed to Afghanistan from October 2009 to September 2010 with a Minnesota Reserve unit, the 372nd Engineer Brigade. She was a single parent at the time, and sent her two daughters back to Grafton to be with her mother. She had moved to Minnesota in 2003 "when I went AGR (Active Guard / Reserve)."

Czarnecki was a sergeant first class and was based at the forward operating base at Sharana, in Paktika Province in southeastern Afghanistan along the Pakistani border. She was age 30 when she arrived. "I traveled to forward operating bases at Orgun-E and Salerno, and Bagram Airfield" on occasion.

"My unit was commanded by a one-star general. We had five battalions under us: two active component, two National Guard and one Navy Seabees.

There were a total of 4,700 engineers and Seabees. Many of our battalions had multiple route clearance teams who drove on hundreds of miles of roads throughout Afghanistan, working to clear IEDs and make the roads safe." In all, her brigade conducted 2,500 patrol missions and found 880 IEDs while clearing 200,000 kilometers of roads.

"We also had construction units that were responsible for building up forward operating bases. Sharana was expanded from 700 acres to more than 4,000. Our unit was there in 2009 during the big surge of troops and we needed extra space for them."

Czarnecki was one of eight women out of 138 people in the headquarters unit, and had two jobs. "My main job was the non-commissioned officer in charge of the personnel section of the brigade. I was in charge of seven soldiers in the section. ...

"My second job was the equal opportunity adviser. I taught a week-long class to train equal opportunity leaders for various units within theater. I handled various cases of discrimination and sexual harassment. ... Various assaults happened on different bases all over Afghanistan. Some were Afghan locals assaulting our soldiers. But others were our soldiers assaulting other soldiers. Those were the cases I dealt with."

In guard towers at the base, there was one American and one Afghan. Did she and other troops trust the Afghans? "No, not at all. You always had to be very careful. You always had to keep one eye on them. Some of them were great but I still don't know if I would trust them." One time, there was a report of a vehicle-borne IED, and the Afghan in the tower ran away, Czarnecki says.

"Near FOB Sharana, in the town of Sharana, the province governor's compound often saw attacks from the Afghans. A firefight could sometimes be seen from our FOB when the Afghans would attack the governor's compound. Unfortunately, we had several American soldiers on that compound. They were responsible for training up Afghan police and soldiers."

Waylon Gross, Menomonee Falls, Army in Iraq: Gross served two tours in Iraq – the first as a 23-year-old in 2004 to 2005 (by the time he went home he was a first lieutenant) and the second as a captain from 2006 to 2008. The first was with the 282nd Field Artillery in the 1st Cavalry Division. He says there was not a large need for field artillery and so in the second tour, he was in the 215th Brigade Support Battalion, doing recon and security. In the first tour he was based in Baghdad; in the second he was about 30 miles away at Baqubah.

"We transformed into a motorized infantry unit, escorting people in the Green Zone in Baghdad to where they were going elsewhere in the country," Gross says. The vehicles were Humvees and gun trucks.

The war began in 2003, so when Gross arrived it was only a year old and with the insurgency gaining strength. "We knew we were going into an escalating situation. You could see the insurgents learning as they went along. There were crude IEDs (improvised explosive devices) at the start, but they became more and more lethal. ... At the start, we were doing missions with doors completely off and guys hanging out of them. Then we started putting armored doors on" as things got more and more dangerous. "From day one to the day we left, there was quite a bit of change."

More specifically, "I'd say the size of the IED's varied; medium to very large – I doubt you'd find many guys who've been hit by an IED call them 'small'. But they were somewhat ineffective. The insurgents were still learning how to effectively employ these weapons, so oftentimes the explosives would be buried too deep under-ground or too far away from the intended target. In general the IED's in use at this time were non-directional and big-blast, but not much armor-penetrating power.

In his first tour, his own vehicle was hit by IEDs on 13 occasions, and Gross says he was lucky not to be wounded. "I personally didn't get hit by any IEDs on the second tour, although the unit I commanded, Recon and Security Detachment, had roughly 20 situations involving IEDs. In general it seemed like there were less IED strikes, but they were more effective – directional blasts were becoming more common.

As more and more losses came in Humvees, the soldiers looked in trash heaps for items to weld to their vehicles to protect them better. In December 2004, a National Guardsman from Tennessee pointedly questioned the visiting Defense Secretary Donald Rumsfeld about soldiers "up-armoring."[5]

Gross says: "More armor was bolted on, leading to the need for more powerful engines. More powerful engines needed better cooling systems in an already hot environment. All of these needs made the Humvee heavier and it needed a more robust suspension system. During this evolution, you were continually trading capabilities – more armor equals less power, bigger engine equals much higher cab temps, etc."

---

[5] http://www.nytimes.com/2004/12/08/international/middleeast/08cnd-rumsfeld.html?_r=0

Tightening up the Humvees meant lack of air circulation, and wearing full body armor made things even tougher physically. "The water bottles would be hot to the touch" inside the Humvees, where temperatures would reach 130 degrees, he says.

Doug Miller, New Berlin, Navy in Vietnam: "I was a gunfire control technician on the USS Iredell County (LST-839), an old World War II landing ship, and was in Vietnam from November 1969 to June 1970. We then sailed back across the Pacific to San Diego and proceeded to turn the ship over to the Indonesian Navy in July 1970.

"We had a crew of 70 to 80. Our job was to supply patrol boat units on the Mekong River with ammo of all kinds, such as artillery shells in cases that were stacked 15 feet high, supplies, etc. Sometimes we would come ashore at a base, sometimes smaller boats would come out to us" to load up.

But first came training in the United States. "We had 14 shots before getting on the plane to go overseas. I was trained to repair computers and hydraulics in the gunfire system, but instead (when he got on the ship) I was put on the fire team for a .50-caliber machine gun.

"We got to Vietnam at night, and you could see a lot of flares going off. We talked to people while the ship was being loaded (for its first supply run). Then we suddenly were ordered to back the LST off the dock unannounced at 2 a.m., and the beach was rocketed at 5 a.m. It would have looked like the Pearl Harbor blast if we had gotten hit (with all the ammo on board). A lot of the loaders that I had talked to on the beach the day before were killed in that shelling. I asked myself, 'I've got a year of this left?'"

His "best period was getting off that ship. The worst period was when we were on General Quarters all the time, on the west side of Vietnam in the Gulf of Thailand. And dealing with 18-year-olds who didn't want to be there at all." Miller was three to four years older.

Of combat, Miller says: "You just didn't see the enemy at all – just their tracers. You had to be on guard against any swimmers coming in to attack the ship, and all night long you would hear concussion grenades that we threw in periodically in order to guard the ship from the swimmers."

His ship once ran aground "on a sandbar 30 miles off the coast of Vietnam. This was on Dec. 19, 1969. It was unbelievable. When the tide went out, it looked like the Mojave Desert. The captain later was removed from duty. We got off the sandbar on Christmas Day with the help of a rescue tug" and a lot of other work. "We had damaged the screws and they had to be replaced, and the new ones were put on at a wrong angle, so to go straight, the tiller had to be at a 15-degree angle" for the rest of the time he was in the war.

Julia Lannin, West Allis, Army nurse in World War II: She was a first lieutenant in the Army Nurse Corps and served with the 33rd General Hospital in Bizerte in Tunisia, and then in Rome, for 30 months.

Lannin worked in neurosurgery, specifically brain and spinal cord injuries. "The critically wounded patients came straight from the front lines," rather than via an Evac Hospital, she says. One case is very memorable – an 18-year-old private named Ryan, whose first name she does not recall. "He had a bullet in the brain, but walked out of the hospital months later. "Before he went into surgery, he went into bad seizures. I held him down on the bed and called for help."

After the surgery, "I asked him when he had written to his mother. And I helped him do it. It was the greatest thing I could have done. I said, 'You dictate and I'll write.' His sister wrote to us six months later and said he was going downhill and what should she do? He wound up in the VA hospital in Philadelphia."

The hospital lost one nurse, and she is buried in Italy, Lannin says. The cemetery website www.abmc.gov shows that was 2nd Lt. Sara B. Vance, from West Virginia. She died of non-battle injuries on Oct. 22, 1944, and is buried in the Sicily-Rome American Cemetery at Nettuno.

Lannin's nursing degree is from Mercy Hospital School of Nursing in Charlotte, N.C. She was a native of Cateechee, S.C.

When she came home, it was aboard the SS Randolph. There was one Italian passenger, a boy of 5 or 6 named Murto, and he was a darling on a ship full of soldiers and nurses. She often has wondered what happened to him.

Roger Merkel, Wauwatosa, Army in Korea: He was 18 and in the 27th Regiment of the 25th Infantry Division, based near Osaka, Japan. One day in 1950, when the unit was on maneuvers on Mount Fuji, suddenly "we were told we were going to Korea real fast. I got there July 9 and was in an advance party for the regiment." North Korea had invaded the south on June 25.

Merkel was in Korea[6] for a year, participating in advances and setbacks in the war, but says the closest he came to getting killed was in the early days – "I got strafed when we were unloading a boxcar of ammo in the middle of nowhere in some little village. There were ground markers out identifying us as friendly," but the American planes strafed them anyway.

"We were called the 'fire brigade.' We were on the move all the time. We had just a few understrength battalions" that needed the fire brigade to help out, Merkel says with understatement.

Martin Berndt, Cudahy, Army Air Forces in World War II: Berndt was in a little-known but vital unit in the Philippines: the 6th Aircraft Repair Unit Floating, which was a giant machine shop on a ship that repaired airplane parts like the hydraulics, wheels, instruments, generators, wing parts, bomb sights and on and on. It was a secret operation, named Ivory Soap.[7]

These parts were for P-38 Lightning and P-51 Mustang fighter planes and B-17 and other bombers in the 5th and 20th Air Forces. Three helicopters – yes, helicopters were in World War II – ferried the problem parts out to the Liberty ship SS Alfred J. Lyon; Berndt and other welders and repairmen – about 250 in all – did their job and the copters ferried them back to land.

"Anything they could bring out to the ship, we could fix," Berndt says. There were about 20 Navy gunners on board to protect the ship.

Berndt was a staff sergeant; he had begun the war as a truck driver in an antiaircraft artillery battalion, which had .90mm guns to protect Hawaii from any future Japanese attack, but he switched to the repair unit in 1943. His ship spent most of its time off the Philippine islands of Palawan and Leyte.

At one point, he was able to go ashore, but "the mud was ankle-deep and we were damn glad to go back on the ship."

Tom Schmidt, Oak Creek, Army in Vietnam: Schmidt was age 20 when he arrived in Vietnam July 1967, and stayed to February 1969. He was

---

[6] A total of 15 other Korean War veterans were interviewed for author Tom Mueller's book "Heart of the Century: 1949 to 1951," published in 2010. Some of them discussed being sneered at when trying to join the VFW or American Legion; being told they were not in a real war and that they lost it. The book also featured six men killed in Korea; some of them at the time that Merkel was there.

[7] http://www.usmm.org/felknorivory.html

a specialist fifth class in the 8th Radio Research Group of the Army Security Agency and was based in Phu Bai, two miles outside Hue.

The unit's job was to monitor enemy radio frequencies. Reports and transcripts would be typed up, and then soldiers like Schmidt would analyze them. "I had a top secret crypto," he says, and from his level it would go up the ladder to further analysis and then communication to U.S. troops. For example, by locating where enemy troops were, which units were which, tracking what they were saying directly or indirectly, and his work could inform American units "we're going to get hit tonight."

His facility plus a Marine base all were surrounded by a fence, with a minefield between his team and the Marines. "Tet was the scariest time when I was there. They were a half-hour from us, and we were ordered to destroy our records. We piled them up. But then the commander said, "Now, put it back" – it had gotten down to the last minutes before a final order to destroy.

Fresh on everyone's mind was the North Korean capture of the spy ship USS Pueblo on Jan. 23, 1968, and how the Communists were able to seize substantial amounts of secret equipment and documents.

Jerome Zelenka, Milwaukee, Army Air Forces in World War II in China-Burma-India theater: Zelenka was a sergeant who was based in India in 1945 and 1946, in Delhi, Karachi (which now is Pakistan, which became independent in 1947) and Calcutta. He was age 19 or 20 and worked in the Army Airways Communications System.

The unit's job was to help guide and track supply flights by cargo planes over "the Hump," the route through the Himalayas from India through Burma and on to bases in China.

"It was a long mission," Zelenka says of the flights. "When you landed, you got unloaded and got the hell out of there in a hurry. It wasn't safe in China. The word was, 'You never go out by yourself anyplace.' They would even go after the gold in your teeth."

He had graduated from North Division High School in Milwaukee before going into the Army. The rumor in his unit was that it was headed for Alaska; it wound up going to Australia and then on to steamy India. Quite a difference.

"We lost a lot of planes even though we had direction-finding stations and equipment on the planes. We had 40 transmitters that we had to maintain – a triangulation system to track the planes."

Jim Blankenheim, Madison, Marine in Vietnam: Blankenheim was a sergeant in the 3rd Battalion of the 5th Marine Regiment and was in Vietnam from February 1968 to March 1969. He turned 19 soon after arriving there. Now he is state president of Wisconsin Vietnam Veterans Inc.

His unit's work ranged "from blocking outside Hue for Tet 1968 (the Communist offensive) all the way down to An Hoa for Tet 1969." He was a forward air controller attached to H&S, M, I, and K companies. "My job was to save Marine lives either by medevacing the wounded or bombing the enemy (by calling in air strikes). I wish I could have saved more."

Blankenheim also says: "In May 1968, M Company, 82 of us, went up into the mountains near Hai Van Pass just north of Da Nang and accidentally walked into an North Vietnamese Army base camp with an estimated 800 to 1,000 soldiers in it.

"For five days we hung on for dear life fighting attack after attack by the NVA. We lay next to our dead and wounded each day in 100-plus degree weather doing our best. On the last day help arrived and broke us free. A total of 38 of us walked off that hill, walking wounded included. We found six mess halls that could seat 100 men each in a base camp that was over a quarter of a mile long, with running water and electricity. Of the survivors, more died in the following battles."

Edward Heffner, Milwaukee, Navy in World War II: Heffner enlisted at the age of 17 in August 1941 because he could see that war was coming in Europe. He was in the Navy until 1947, so he was there on multiple kinds of ships before it started, when it started, during its worst days, in its days of hard-earned American advances, and past the very end.

Heffner was on the troop ship USS Edward Rutledge in the invasion of Morocco in November 1942. It was torpedoed by a U-boat and sank in little more than an hour. "We lost 13 in the engine room, and if I had been able to get to my battle station, I would have been No. 14," says Heffner, who was a fireman second class. The overall toll on the ship was 15.

Then Heffner was on the aircraft carrier USS Intrepid in the invasion of Kwajalein in early 1944. "Our ship sent up three planes but didn't find anything. As they were coming back to the ship in the dark, four planes were in the pattern. One was a Jap. The first plane was waved off, so was the second, but the third one, the Jap one, headed off to the starboard side and came around and dropped a torpedo at us, causing damage to our starboard side and putting us out of action."

The Intrepid was sent to California for repairs (it now is a museum in New York City) and Heffner was put on the destroyer USS Hyman. Heffner's destroyer escorted troop ships carrying Marines to Iwo Jima in February 1945.

"We did picket duty until a request came for a destroyer volunteer. The Hyman was one of the first to volunteer. They wanted to replace the battleship USS Pennsylvania that was shelling Mount Suribachi. We were to seal up the ports that the Japanese were shooting out of, by using our five-inch guns. We could see the Marines on the beach; that's how close we were. Later we were told to lay to near the shoreline, and using our search light, and our guns, we were to give support to the Marines to get to the top of Suribachi." About 4 a.m., the Hyman had to leave to replenish its ammunition, "and when we returned to the island and picket duty, you could see the flag that the Marines had put up," the one in the famous photo.

The Hyman was in the invasion of Okinawa a month later, and was attacked by kamikazes. "Our gun crews did a good job and shot down four of them, but the last one had a wing shot off by our gunners and crashed between our stacks, into our main torpedo mounts there," says Heffner, who at this time was a machinist's mate second class. "There was an explosion, and the center of the ship blew up, and all that was on the main deck disappeared, and there was a hole in the main deck above the forward engine room. Even then our gunners helped shoot down three more planes, and we kept the ship afloat." A dozen sailors were killed and more than 40 injured.[8]

David Schmid, Oak Creek, Navy in Vietnam: Schmid joined the Navy right after graduating from St. Francis High School in 1967 and became a sonar technician. His most vivid experiences in Vietnam involved not being shot at, but some decisions by those in charge of his destroyer and then his auxiliary destroyer tender; one of them a la Capt. Queeg of "The Caine Mutiny." Those decisions put the ships and crews in acute danger, Schmid says.

In one such case, his destroyer ran aground in the Mekong Delta and tore off the sonar dome, which was under the keel. The crippled ship could not turn around and for a time, the captain ordered it lit up at night, for no evident reason, and "we were sitting there like a Christmas tree," Schmid says. He and some other senior crew soon got this order reversed.

---

[8] http://www.history.navy.mil/danfs/h10/hyman.htm

"I do not regret any of my six years in the Navy," Schmid says. "The thing I do regret is that there was no welcome home. I got spit upon. I had cabs refusing to take me from the Milwaukee airport to my folks' home in St. Francis. And while job-hunting, there was "no thank you, no nothing. The places that I applied to for jobs didn't care that I was a veteran. It still hurts me to this day." He wound up working at the county House of Correction in Franklin.

He is now the 4th District (Milwaukee) commander of the VFW. But when he tried to join it right after coming home, "they said, 'you lost the war.'" Things were warmer a few years later when his first son was playing in a VFW baseball league, and that is when he started getting involved.

Jack Adams, La Crosse, Marine in Korea: Adams was a corporal in the 1st Tank Battalion of the 5th Regiment of the 1st Marine Division and was in the war from February 1952 to March 1953. He was in Marine boot camp six weeks after graduating from Aquinas High School in La Crosse in 1951, and when he got to Korea he was age 19.

He went through Seoul upon arrival, and that was the largest city he saw until the day he left. He was 50 to 90 miles north of Seoul, north of today's Armistice Line, the 38th Parallel. The war halted four months after he left Korea.

Adams was a tank mechanic; "I had five tanks that I had to keep going." They would have trouble with carburetors, cooling fans, and, of course, combat damage, particularly having their tracks blown by large mines and enemy fire. "We would have to get a retriever up there" to pull the tank away or to put the tracks back where they were supposed to be.

Adams also served as the assistant driver and front machine gunner on tanks.

"We would go up and down valleys and reclaim them. We went wherever the infantry went. They'd follow our tracks because we would blow up mines," Adams says. Often the tanks would plow right through minefields, detonating the mines, and the ground forces would follow in their tracks, for safety. But that was for small mines. Larger ones would stop the tanks, but Adams says such mines were relatively rare.

One day, he got a radio call to go back to the headquarters of his tank group. He asked why, and said "we are very busy up here." The answer was, "Don't you want to go home?" Adams had been so occupied that he was not counting down the days.

"It was the most exciting year of my life," Adams says. He is president of the west central Wisconsin chapter of the Korean War Veterans Association, No. 275.

Chuck Dziedzic, Racine, Marine in Vietnam: Dziedzic, originally of Oak Creek, was in Vietnam in 1967, 1968 and 1969. He came home on bereavement leave after his brother Mark, a fellow Marine, was killed in March 1968. Then he had other duties stateside before opting for another tour in Vietnam.

Chuck was in the 5th Regiment of the 1st Marine Division, and when he returned to Vietnam was in another battalion of the same regiment. He was a lance corporal in the first tour; later a sergeant.

He was the gunner in a unit that fired 81mm mortars, the largest size; he says the man carrying the base plate had the toughest job, lugging around a 24-pound piece while "humpin'" in the jungles and rice paddies. The gunner is the one who sets the sights and drops the mortar shell into the tube. On his second tour, Dziedzic was with 60mm mortars, which he says were much more manageable.

For a time, Chuck belonged to the Oak Creek VFW Post that was named for his brother Mark and another KIA, James Meyer (they were profiled earlier in this book). He tells of meeting of the post in which he wanted to speak in support of President Jimmy Carter's 1977 granting of unconditional pardons to hundreds of thousands of men who had evaded the draft during Vietnam by fleeing the country or by failing to register. Carter had pledged in the presidential campaign to do this immediately after inauguration as a way of putting the war and the bitter divisions it caused firmly in the past.[9]

The VFW members were bitterly opposed to amnesty, and even more so when Dziedzic – a Marine veteran, not some outsider, and the brother of a city native who had made the Ultimate Sacrifice – tried to speak in support of the new president's move. They cut off the meeting so that there would be no remarks in the record, Dziedzic says. In short, there was no freedom of speech among a group that had fought hard for freedom

"I left and never came back," he says. People like him served in Vietnam "because the country said we need to do this." But with revelations about the

---

[9] http://www.history.com/this-day-in-history/president-carter-pardons-draft-dodgers

Gulf of Tonkin incident that the U.S. used as justification to enter the war, "I question it all the time. We definitely were not told the whole truth." Dziedzic says.

He adds, "People had a right to protest," but his wife, Barbara, quickly interjects, "but not to call people 'baby killers.'"

Seth Joppe, of Sobieski in Oconto County, Marine in Afghanistan: Joppe served three tours in Afghanistan, in 2008 – arriving there at the age of 21 – then in 2009, and again in 2010, when he was a lance corporal and was with Task Force Gulf 25, a NATO mission, located in north-central Afghanistan at Mezar-e-sharif.

Joppe left the Marines in April 2011 and was interviewed for this book while doing work-study at the Vet Center of the U.S. Department of Veterans Affairs in Green Bay and attending the University of Wisconsin there.

In his first tour, Joppe was the ammo man for a machine gun team, and says the duties included carrying the "A-bag," for accessory bag, of cleaning utensils and extra parts, "the brunt of ammo for the gun" and providing rear security for it. In the second tour, he was the machine gun team leader – the team was supposed to be three people total, but "we were undermanned, so there were only two of us." On the NATO mission, he was fire team leader, in charge of four to six other men, "looking out for their safety" and carrying extra medical gear.

Duane Sanborn, La Crosse, Army in Korea: Sanborn was a private first class in Headquarters Company of the 3rd Battalion, 5th Regiment, 1st Cavalry Division. He was 19 when he arrived in Korea in August 1950, less than two months after the North Koreans invaded the South, and served there until June 1951.

In his time, the Allied forces were pushed far to the south, then battled back and recaptured Seoul, and went far into North Korea – Sanborn says that for a time he was 20 miles south of the Yalu River, which was the border between North Korea and China. His regiment was on the west side of the Korean Peninsula, and "was on the road to a reserve area just before the Chinese hit;" it had been replaced by the 24th Division, "which took a major beating."

"When things would get a little bit scary, I'd end up on guard" for a time, says Sanborn who originally was from near Mankato, Minn. Otherwise, his work was as an armorer in the supply room, which he says meant he was a "gopher for the supply sergeant."

When the war began, he was in training at Fort Carson, Colo. He originally had enlisted for one year, then to serve as a Reservist. "I was in Korea when my enlistment would have been up. I was classified as a 'recalled reservist,'" Sanborn chuckles.

Michael Ogrodowski, Milwaukee, Army in Vietnam: "I served in the 25th Infantry Division as a combat engineer with rank of specialist 5. I was in country for two years starting in 1967, all of 1968 and part of 1969. I worked and served in the city of Saigon and the towns of Tay Ninh, Dau Tieng, Cu Chi, Bien Hoa and others."

On Ogrodowski's first night in Vietnam, the barracks "received a direct hit and my best friend from Milwaukee in the Army was injured. I had been inducted into the Army with him. Months later, my mother wrote me a note and said that Frank was home. That was the first I knew he wasn't killed that night."

Ogrodowski continues: "The 25th Infantry Division built temporary firebases and bridges in the countryside as needed by the military commanders. I started driving five-ton dump trucks filled with rocks or dirt between Saigon and the boonies. It was hard work with long days in dangerous country areas. As my skills improved I progressed to road-grading equipment, which was easier duty always protected with military escort.

One night, the base at Cu Chi was attacked by Viet Cong sappers who threw themselves on top of Chinook helicopters, and about 20 were destroyed. "We all had to go on the front line and fight. I was not wounded that night or otherwise. I was very lucky."

In his last month or so, he was rotated to easier duty, driving a jeep for visiting stars and high military officers. "I picked up Ann-Margret at the airport and drove her around base to visit the wounded soldiers and then to the amphitheater were she appeared with Bob Hope. She was pretty tired from the trip but she was very nice, very young, very pretty, very thin and very vivacious. She was really at ease and wanted to stop the jeep to pet one of the monkeys that soldiers kept as pets." She sat behind him; the jeep had a turret and machine gun.

Far from being dressed like the "plain Jane" mode that she wore upon her arrival, in the show Ann-Margret wore the tightest possible black leotard, which Ogrodowski and the thousands of other servicemen found "very sexy. Bob Hope was good, but Ann-Margret was absolutely the blockbuster of the night. It was incredible."[10]

---

[10] See more about her USO tours at http://www.ann-margret.com/uso.html.

Ogrodowski has "visited the Vietnam War Memorial in Washington twice and reacted with strong emotion both times" because of the sheer numbers of people on it, and in particular for the years he was there. He regrets not attending the dedication of the Wall, to which he had been invited.

Kris Stolpa, Green Bay, Marine in Vietnam and Army during Iraq War: Stolpa was on "a normal overseas tour" and stationed on Okinawa, but was sent to Vietnam in early 1975, not long before the sudden Communist advances (Vietnam would surrender April 30) and the American evacuation of Saigon via helicopters to Navy ships at Cam Ranh Bay, the port where he was based. The mission was called Operation Frequent Wind. He was a sergeant in the 1st Battalion, 4th Marine Regiment, and his job was ammo tech, meaning he supplied it.

In the evacuation, he was on two ships, the Duluth and Dubuque, called LPDs (amphibious transport dock), searching the evacuees to be sure they were not Viet Cong agents who had smuggled bombs and other explosives aboard. The command ship was the helicopter carrier USS Blue Ridge. Helicopters had to be pushed over the side of the Duluth and other ships to make room for more arriving copters. These were dramatic photos that epitomized the chaotic finish. Stolpa said he spent 45 days in Vietnam.

Thirty years later, he was back in a war, stationed in Kuwait at Camp Arifjan, supplying troops going into Iraq and de-supplying those leaving that country plus repairing and refurbishing that gear. Stolpa was a major in the 32nd Infantry Brigade – he had retired from the Marine Corps a few years after Vietnam, but now was in the Wisconsin National Guard and was called up for the Iraq war.

Stolpa ran the 377nd Theater Support Command, responsible for gear like big vehicles and body armor all the way down to toilet paper. "We were like a Motel 6 – we left the light on for you." He had gone to Officer Candidate School as a Guardsman at the age of 32: "Learning the Army was like a foreign language, compared to the Marine Corps."

Jeff Dziedzic, Allenton, Marine in Vietnam: Dziedzic is the older brother of Chuck Dziedzic from earlier in this chapter and the younger brother of Mark Dziedzic, who was in the chapter on Oak Creek men killed in wars.

Like many, Jeff enlisted because he would have been drafted otherwise. He was a full corporal and a forward artillery observer assigned to F Company, 7th

Marine Regiment, and was in Vietnam for a year beginning in September 1966. Mark Dziedzic was killed six months after Jeff went home.

Jeff was based around Da Nang and Chu Lai, about 55 miles to the southeast. He had a minor shrapnel wound in the left hand and received a Purple Heart.

Bernard Perszyk, Milwaukee, Army in World War II: Perszyk was a corporal who landed on Utah Beach on D-Day with the 508th Engineer Light Ponton Company. It built floating bridges across streams and rivers; longer bridges and those that could carry heavier vehicles were built by heavy ponton companies.

"We were taking lots of prisoners," Perszyk says. "Jawohl, jawohl, they were saying." That is the word for yes, indeed.

His company was in the 1111th Engineer Group along with the 296th Combat Engineer Battalion, the 291st and the 51st, according to the extensive planning document for D-Day, code-named Operation Neptune.[11] Various other ponton units and combat engineer battalions were in the 1103rd Group, the 1105th, 1109th and 1128th.

The plan for the 1111th said, "upon arrival will support the XIX Corps Engineer operations by execution of engineer work in the forward zone of the Army area immediately in rear of XIX Corps."

Paul Manderle, Oak Creek, Navy in World War II: He was an electrician's mate third class on a troop transport ship, the USS Gen. John Pope. Its hull number was AP 110. Manderle had joined the Navy in March 1945 at age 17, and when the Pope left San Francisco at the end of August, the war had just ended but the September signing ceremony in Tokyo had not yet been held.

"They said submarines were out there," so the Pope had destroyer escorts, Manderle says. Fresh on everyone's mind was the sinking of the cruiser USS Indianapolis on July 30 after it had delivered parts for the atomic bombs to the island of Tinian. Nearly 900 crewmen were killed in the torpedoing or in following days, when the Navy was not yet searching for survivors, in what became a major scandal. Instead of standard zigzagging, the Indianapolis had been traveling in a straight line, acting as if the war were over.

---

[11] http://www.american-divisions.com/unit.asp See pages 24-26.

The Pope carried 5,000 troops to Japan – they had thought they were preparing for the invasion of Japan, which was not to happen so they became occupation troops. "We took them to the Caroline Islands instead, then to Yokohama, Japan. The minesweepers swept the bay. We dropped off 5,000, and then picked up 5,000 to come home," Manderle says.

The Pope would make five more trips like it.

David Howard, Oak Creek, Army Reserves in Vietnam era: "I was a veteran in the Vietnam era, but not in Vietnam. I was in Company D, 1st Battalion, 84th Regiment, 4th Training Brigade, at 5236 W. Silver Spring Drive in Milwaukee. I was in from 1959 to 1965," Howard says.

"In time of war, we were to train troops to take all the positions that a company and / or regiment needs to function as a fighting unit. Not basic training, but the next step up. These were jobs such as clerk, supply sergeant, armorer, truck driver, cook, field cook, communications clerk, maintenance mechanic, etc.

"We went to the Training Unit one night a week. Every month we had to be there for a two-day weekend. Once a year we went for a two-week camp at Camp McCoy, Wis., or Fort Jackson, S.C. Going to Fort Jackson was the first time I had flown in a Constellation aircraft, a 'Big Connie.'" He never considered himself a Vietnam veteran until being told at a history event that he was; that his time ended during the Vietnam era.

Bill Moore, St. Francis, Navy in Vietnam: Moore served on the submarine USS Perch as an electronics technician and petty officer second class. Moore was in the Navy from 1961 to 1967 and then served in the Wisconsin Air National Guard.

"We did about 32 war patrols over in 'Nam – our job, being very covert, was to sneak special forces into certain areas of South and North Vietnam, on the surface or underwater. We did get two VC prisoners and evacuated a village and saved many South Vietnamese lives. We also used our 40mm deck guns and .50-caliber machine guns many times during our missions. The Special Forces were Marine underwater demolition teams, Seals, frogmen, and Republic of Korea Special Forces, to name a few.

"I was an electronics tech, so I stood radar and sonar watches. I was also qualified on many other jobs – escape trunk operator, bridge phone talker, trim manifold operator and a qualified quartermaster (navigation) and a qualified still operator (making fresh water for the sub and crew).

"When maneuvering watch was set, I was bridge phone talker. During time at sea, I stood radar watches; when submerged, sonar watches. When battle stations were set, I was either on sonar, or operating our escape trunk, depending upon our mission at the time."

Art Gale, Onalaska, Air Force in Korea: Gale arrived as a private first class one week before his 21st birthday in November 1951, and was there for a year. He was a fighter jet technician on F-84 Thunderjets in the 49th Fighter Bomber Wing. He became a crew chief, responsible for the airplane being ready in every regard except for its many armaments and its radar system.

He was based at Taegu south of Seoul. The planes' missions were over "pretty much all of North Korea," and sometimes there were four missions by the plane per day with different pilots, each mission lasting about two hours.

"The F-86s got all the glory, but our F-84s got all the work," Gale says – the F-86 Sabre engaged in dogfights with Soviet-built MIGs, while Gale's F-84s were the Air Force's workhorse. A plane that he serviced for several months was No. 537, which had named Yaddti Yaddti, which meant "Hot to Go."

At full strength, each of the three squadrons had 25 F-84 jets. But because of extensive losses, a squadron sometimes was down to only five planes.

The airbase at Taegu – the town was the scene of early ground battles in the war – was not really attacked in Gale's time, but he did spend five days in Seoul and there was visited by Bed-Check Charlie. "That bastard always flew over. It was a little biplane, and he would throw hand grenades out. The only place I could run was a ditch full of water," and he did.[12]

Bob Menefee, Milwaukee, Army in Vietnam: "I was the Radar O'Reilly" of the Army's 345th Aviation Detachment, serving as the office clerk at Can Tho, a little airstrip 55 miles southwest of Saigon in the center of the Mekong Delta. It was being turned into an infantry support base when he was in Vietnam from February 1967 to February 1968.

Menefee was 19 when he arrived, "a greenhorn southwestern Iowa farm boy;" a private at the start and a specialist 5 at the end.

---

[12] More of Gale's war service appears in "Wisconsin Korean War Stories," by Sarah A. Larsen and Jennifer M. Miller (2008).

Most of those at the airfield in his time were refuelers, maintenance, motor pool and supply personnel. The base had Huey helicopters at the start, followed later by Cobra gunships. There also were single-engine airplanes and visits from what the soldiers were told was a Vietnamese plane company but actually was CIA. More and more personnel of the 9th Infantry Division began arriving during his service.

Danny Harmann, Waukesha, Army in Vietnam: Harmann was a 20-year-old corporal in the 9th Infantry Division in the Mekong Delta in 1968 and 1969. This was the division that was coming in as Menefee was leaving. "I was there for both Tet offensives," he says, and he likes to note that his tour was one day longer than a year because "1968 was a Leap Year and I arrived in February," before the 29th.

His infantry unit was attached to mobile artillery the entire time, so he was "airlifted and set up fire support bases and then would get water and supplies." It also was "pulling perimeter guard and fighting your ass off when you had to."

On more than a few days, the soldiers passed time by smoking marijuana, Harmann says, and relations with commanders often were nonexistent as soldiers neared the end of their tours.

Andy Harmann, New Berlin, Army in Afghanistan: Harmann was age 20 when he arrived in Afghanistan in February 2005, and was there for a year with the 173rd Airborne Infantry, in Company C of the 505th Regiment. His rank at the end of his tour was specialist.

His unit was based in Paktika Province, which borders Pakistan and is in eastern Afghanistan. The provinces on either side of Paktika were far worse in terms of fighting, he notes, but Paktika "saw a considerable amount of action."

Harmann was in a weapons squad and his job was to run an M-60 machine gun, along with an assistant gunner and an ammunition bearer. He also was an ammo carrier for the M-240 machine gun. The weapons squad took no losses during his time, but some in the platoon were wounded, and there were about seven deaths in his larger 1st Battalion, he says.

A weapons squad consisted of six to nine men and was part of an infantry platoon of 36 soldiers. "I had enlisted because of 9-11, but I had always wanted to do this, and probably would have done it anyway" even if the terrorist attacks had not occurred, Harmann says. Some who served with him have gone back for a second or even third tour, but he was not nearly so tempted and left the Army after three years.

Bob Boulden, Burlington, Marine in Korea: Boulden was a rifleman, then a wireman in the Signal Battalion of the 5th Regiment in the 1st Marine Division. He arrived in the surprise invasion at Inchon in September 1950, was in the disaster at the Chosin Reservoir, the pullout via the port of Hungnam in North Korea that then was destroyed by the Americans rather than let it fall into Chinese hands, and sailed to Pusan for regrouping of severely depleted forces. He wound up in the Iron Triangle, which is north of today's DMZ, and left Korea in August 1951.

Boulden was quoted in the Korean War chapter of this book. He stayed in the Marines for one more year, and applied to go back to Korea but was not sent there.

"When we got rotated, we met some Army guys going on R & R," Boulden says, referring to rest and recreation. "We said, 'What is R & R? In the Marine Corps, we never heard of R & R.'" An even odder thing to him was that his initial job specification after his first training was "baking," which confused him. "My captain said, "Don't worry. Where you're going, there ain't going to be any baking.""

William McManus, Shorewood, Army in China-Burma-India theater in World War II: McManus had been a fireman on the Milwaukee Road railroad, and his wartime duty was to be a train engineer in India. He was in the Army's 745th Railway Operating Battalion, on the 111-mile segment from Lumding to Mariani, a leg on the Bengal-Assam Railway. This was in Assam state in far northeastern India. His area was a small part of a giant pipeline of supplies headed into Burma and then onto the Ledo Road painstakingly built through the Himalayas en route to U.S.-supported forces in China. He shipped all sorts of cargo, ammunition and forces with a four-man crew – himself as engineer, a conductor and two Indian firemen (coal handlers).

When he arrived, McManus was a corporal and was 21 and more than 10,000 miles from home; he went there via the West Coast and came home two years later via New York City, so "I've been around the world."

The trains usually were 40 cars, and departed at any time the Army had them loaded. Until a second track was built, McManus sometimes would have to pull over to let another train go past. The route itself took six to eight hours unless there were stops like that, although sometimes the speed was only 10 m.p.h. and there seemingly always was heavy rainfall and extreme heat.

He had a .45 sidearm and a carbine in the cab, but never had to use them; the biggest obstacles were elephants or tigers that did not want to leave the tracks. There were no Japanese air attacks on the trains or their bridges, but "sometimes we could hear ground battles going on. ... We were very fortunate to be away from fighting. I don't think anybody in our camp ever had to fire a shot at anybody," McManus says.

When supplies arrived in India, they were put onto boxcars on a regular railway, called standard gauge. They then reached a point where the railroad bed became a narrower gauge (width), and everything had to be unloaded and put onto the new cars. Then they traveled to a new point where the gauge became narrower again, about 400 miles west of Lumding, which was where McManus' leg was. "That's what took the damndest time – to unload the car and reload it back on the next gauge." The locomotives, however, were built in America, so they were not ancient or hard to understand.

Carolyn Morgan, Madison, Air Force in Persian Gulf War: Morgan joined the Air National Guard in 1980 at Truax Field in her hometown of Madison, then went on active duty in the Air Force from 1985 to 1993 before coming back to the Guard for three years. She served in the United Arab Emirates during the Persian Gulf War – Operations Desert Shield and Desert Storm – as a senior airman with MWR Services, which means Morale, Welfare and Recreation. The unit offered everything from aerobics to beer tents for various Guard units in the Air Force's 20th Fighter Wing. Alcohol was forbidden in Saudi Arabia and Kuwait so as not to offend those host nations, but R & R in the UAE meant there was beer.

Not that this was just a picnic: Morgan was sent overseas on Aug. 10, 1990, eight days after Saddam Hussein's invasion of Kuwait, which put the vital oilfields of Saudi Arabia in acute risk. "I put my six-month-old baby boy to bed and the phone rang. There was no preparing like there is now," she says. Her base, Shaw Air Force Base in South Carolina, was sent with its F-16 fighters and all support units, including the hospital unit. She flew to the UAE on a C-5 transport along with firetrucks and ambulances.

The war was quickly won after a lengthy buildup of U.S. and allied forces, but coming home in March 1991 posed another challenge. "My son didn't have any idea who I was. He was scared of me," says Morgan, noting that this was long before email and Skype made it far easier to stay connected. "It was hard to transition to being a Mom and wife again."

Morgan now works in the Wisconsin Department of Veterans Affairs as the outreach coordinator for women veterans, helping the vets have a smoother transition coming home, obtaining help finding a job, getting services and benefits, and organizing events around the state including a summit about women's issues.

Bill Weber, Oak Creek, Navy in Vietnam: Weber was a hull technician repairman second class on the destroyer USS Shelton and made two trips to Vietnam from the West Coast in the late 1960s and early 1970s. His job was to repair metal, piping, plumbing, carpentry and the like.

Weber says the Shelton once escorted a Chinese freighter through a minefield – he does not remember, but thinks it was at the port of Haiphong, because the Chinese were carrying medical supplies to North Vietnam. But after escorting, his ship then shot at the North Vietnamese vessels that came out to unload the same freighter. "Why did we mine this harbor?" Weber wondered. President Richard M. Nixon's trip to China came in February 1972, and had been announced in July 1971, so the warming relationships may have led to this thaw. However, Nixon also ordered the the Haiphong harbor mined in May 1972.

The Shelton's job also was to rescue downed American pilots, and Weber says they were frustrated not only at losing their planes but also at not being allowed to bomb certain targets that were declared off-limits. They considered it micromanaging and not being allowed to really win a war.

The Shelton was part of a force with the USS Constellation on one of Weber's periods in the war zone.

"We also went up the Mekong River a ways to support the river patrol boats with our .50-caliber machine guns and help with casualties," Weber says.

"My job was down in the boat, but you could hear the shrapnel hitting the hull and the ship. To this day, I don't watch the fireworks on the Fourth of July, even with my grandchildren, because they remind me of star shells and things blowing up and the smell of burning flesh."

John Woolley, Sturtevant, Marine in World War II: "I served in the 5th Marine Division in the United States and trained in the 5th Joint Assault Signal Company. This unit was to be the shore-to-ship communications for an invasion in the South Pacific area and would go ashore before the first wave.

"Then I got lucky and was transferred to the 6th Joint Assault Signal Company, which was training on Guadalcanal (My original unit wound up going ashore on Iwo Jima after training in Hawaii). I was later transferred to the 6th Division Headquarters Company, Signal Platoon.

"I went ashore on Okinawa on April 1, the first day of the invasion. April 1 was Easter Sunday and April Fools' Day!!! The first day we were way ahead of schedule due to the fact that the Japanese did not defend the beach that day. The Marines were under the command of the 10th Army until Army Lt. Gen. Simon Bolivar Buckner was killed (on June 18, 1945) and a Marine general took over."

Robert Dempsey, Onalaska, Marine in Korea: Dempsey was 19 when he arrived in Korea in February 1953 (five months before the war halted), and served until March 1954 with a supply depot for the 1st Marine Division, specifically responsible for the needs of the 11th Marine Regiment, an artillery unit.[13]

Dempsey originally was from Fennimore. The depot was just below the MLR, the main line of resistance.

The supply depot provided "basic needs such as clothing, toiletries, sometimes the C-rations," but the regiment's ammunition came from elsewhere, Dempsey says. "They would send their dirty uniforms back and we'd see that they would get cleaned at a central laundry by Korean labor and repaired."

Dempsey's duty was to check stuff going in or out, and at night to pull guard duty "to keep away the people who wanted to pilfer our depot."

Norbert Herrick, Milwaukee, Marine in World War II: "I was in the Marines from 1942 to 1945. I was a sergeant in VMF 324, a fighter squadron. We had Corsair fighter-bombers, the F-4U1 and the FG-1."[14]

VMF-324 was activated on Oct. 1, 1943, and served until Oct. 15, 1945.[15] It served mostly on Midway.

"My best period of the war was the day of discharge. My worst period of the war? Arriving in boot camp," Herrick says.

---

[13] The history of the artillery group in Korea is at http://www.au.af.mil/au/awc/ awc-gate/usmchist/11thmar.txt

[14] http://militaryhistory.about.com/od/worldwariiaircraft/p/f4ucorsair.htm

[15] http://www.alternatewars.com/BBOW/Organization/USMC_Squadrons_WW2.htm

Chapter 16
What the vets want us to remember

The more than three dozen veterans who were interviewed were asked what all the rest of us always should remember about their time in war. They were free to answer that question on the basis of complex geopolitics, their own work, their unit's job, their own time in the war, or anything else.

The result is a blend of viewpoints, each worth consideration from the standpoint of any vet of World War II, Korea, Vietnam, Iraq or Afghanistan, or any combination thereof. What one person said about one war could well apply to another in another war.

Very few of the 11 World War II vets who were interviewed wished to deal with the question. Perhaps they considered it a bit too obvious, when the entire nation was galvanized in a fight against fascism that lasted only a few years, or perhaps it was a bit too "heavy" to consider the overall meaning of their work when it was far easier just to talk about what their unit was and where they were, and when.

Seth Joppe, of Sobieski in Oconto County, Marine in Afghanistan: He laments that over the years, as the war dragged on and on to become the longest in American history, the troops became "an afterthought, on the back burner. The war claimed a lot of lives, and forever changed many people such as myself. There is lot more going on behind the scenes than is reported on the news."

Joppe, who was not physically wounded, continues: "A lot of people returned with post-traumatic stress and depression. You don't deal with things the same way you did before."

Jeff Dziedzic, Allenton, Marine in Vietnam: "I was pretty optimistic that we were doing the right thing and serving our country. But I became opposed to the war about halfway through my tour. The villagers pretty much wanted to be left alone. They didn't care about having to pay a rice tax to someone (the Viet Cong). And they were getting maimed, exposed to Agent Orange" and the like.

His vehicle displays a bumper sticker that says, "Support the warrior not the war." Dziedzic adds: "I support all of our veterans and I always have. But if we had a draft, we never would have been in Iraq" because there would have been a citizen outcry by conscripting young people to go there and be there for so long.

Like his brother Chuck (from the previous chapter), he belonged to the local VFW for a time, "primarily because it had my brother's name on it." That was Mark Dziedzic, killed in Vietnam in March 1968. But he says the older veterans, who fought in a different war with a more clear-cut mission, strategy and results, had a "philosophy different than mine. I didn't blame people for going to Canada (to evade the draft). I might have done the same thing," had he been a little younger and based on what he saw in Vietnam.

Doug Miller, New Berlin, Navy in Vietnam: "We were there to help a small country that asked for our help from being overtaken by Communists, who were supported by China. However, it was a war that was difficult to win ... there were too many restrictions placed on us, political and others, that made it frustrating for those fighting the battles. We had the capability to win the war but for whatever reason chose not to do so.

"I am glad to see that the attitudes and support towards military personnel from the general public, media and government has improved greatly as compared to the Vietnam era."

John Scocos, Army Reservist in Iraq, and now Wisconsin secretary of veterans affairs: Scocos tells families of the fallen: "Service of their loved ones will not be forgotten by the state and nation."

And he says the nation should "ensure that the contributions of the men and women who served in Iraq and Afghanistan are indeed honored and remembered. I believe those who distinguished themselves on the battlefield, on the seas, and in the air did not seek glory any more than they sought the horror of war. All they ask is that their contributions are remembered."

The Wisconsin Department of Veterans Affairs is the chief advocate for more than 400,000 veterans of all wars, Scocos notes. "As an agency we were very proud of Wisconsin GI Bill—allowing veterans the opportunity to audit or organize up to a doctorate degree. This also includes a section for the spouses and children of veterans. We also are proud of our extensive work with Legislature to grant licenses and credit for military service.

"The department needs to assist our returning service personnel with employment opportunities. The department and the state need to realize that all veteran-related programs should be consolidated into WDVA. This would provide us with one-stop shop concept (employment, training, benefits). This would include families of veterans also."

Deanna Czarnecki, Jackson, Army in Afghanistan: "Six months later, I had an opportunity to go back for another deployment. If it weren't for my two young daughters, I would have been glad to go again. I love what I do, and I'm very thankful for the opportunities that I've had."

Czarnecki laments "a year of being gone from family," but says the work of the individual soldier and her unit "impacts things far greater than we can imagine" in the world and for U.S. security.

"I believe we are setting up for the next generation of Americans to continue our strong stature in the world as the leading country. We won't change the attitude in Afghanistan. They are a country built upon very old traditions and an old way of life. It's something that will take an incredibly long time to change. However, in our efforts to assist, hopefully we were able to catch the eye of some of the younger-generation Afghans. Hopefully they know our intentions were good ones and that there is a possibility for a better, safer way of life. But what we think is 'better' may not seem better to all Afghans."

The American people have so many things that others in the world do not have, Czarnecki says, including simple things like "the ability to drive to the store on a road that actually exists, to sign my daughters up for a Christian school and not to be told by anybody where to send them."

Roger Merkel, Wauwatosa, Army in Korea: "The only reason we were given for why we were there was to kick the North Koreans back to where they belong," which American forces did in only a few months, Merkel notes. Some commentators "say we lost. That irritates anyone who was there and fired a rifle." He also is irritated that even the VFW and American Legion referred to the war as a "police action" for many years, and he reports the World War II vets looked down on the new vets.

"I was one of the lucky ones" who came home, Merkel says. "I never look back. I did talk to my children, but not about the gory part."

Tom Schmidt, Oak Creek, Army in Vietnam: "I don't know if a lot of us understood the big picture – why we were there. And there was frustration at never being able to cross into North Vietnam. We were in the service, but I don't know think many of us knew the true politics of it. We were just fighting for our friends and buddies, trying to save their lives."

David Schmid, Oak Creek, Navy in Vietnam: "The world was different then. It's different now," says Schmid, who regularly volunteers at the Clement J. Zablocki VA Medical Center near Miller Park, particularly those with drug and alcohol issues. And when he sees people "with arms and legs gone, I realize they are so worse off than me (when coming home). Help those combat veterans."

Duane Sanborn, La Crosse, Army in Korea: "We went over there to a place none of us heard of before. We went through some pretty rough times. The end was not a smashing success. But we did stop Communist aggression from taking over more countries in the Far East region. And South Korea as a country is a major success. North Korea is a vast wasteland. Just look at a nighttime picture from outer space," where the South is all lit up and the North has wide areas of darkness because of energy shortages.

Michael Ogrodowski, Milwaukee, Army in Vietnam: He came home from Vietnam in 1969. "None of us felt like a hero. You did not come back with any pride. My parents put up a sign outside their house that said 'Welcome Back, Soldier,' but I asked them to take it down right away."

Kris Stolpa, Green Bay, Marine in Vietnam and Army during Iraq War: "There is a total contrast between the two periods that I served. The first time, you come home and are proud of your service, but a friend told me, 'You may want to take that uniform off.'" The bitterness of the 1960s had not gone away in the mid-1970s, when he returned a few months after South Vietnam surrendered.

"The second time, how people treated me showed how the world had changed. It was rough to be a serviceman in the 1970s. People treated you like dirt, even the people I grew up with. You did your job, but people really trashed you. Coming home from Iraq, I am glad the country appreciates their soldiers even if they disagree with the war."

Bob Menefee, Milwaukee, Army in Vietnam: Soon after returning home in 1968, he realized the transition he had gone through since going off to war: "It had been a time of concern about the spread of Communism. But it spanned to a time where we said 'this war isn't working. It's not the domino theory,'" which had been espoused in Washington – that if one country in Southeast Asia fell to Communism, so would another and another. "I lived both of those emotions. I could see this was a war we had to end."

Art Gale, Onalaska, Air Force in Korea: Although the war saw major U.S. and U.N. troop advances and setbacks over the entire peninsula from 1950 to 1951, from that year to the armistice in 1953 it by and large was in trenches along the 38th Parallel, with only slight movement – on the ground. But Gale wants people to know the air war continued strongly – "A lot of guys died in foxholes, but we lost a LOT of pilots. And the F-84 squadrons (like his) lost far, far more than the F-86s, probably a margin of 20 to 1. ... We hit everything from bridges to railroads to highways. We lost airplanes there and everywhere."

Danny Harmann, Waukesha, Army in Vietnam: "I'm proud to be a Vietnam veteran. But we got spit upon. I couldn't even date a girl because her parents thought I was wild," having been in Vietnam.

From what he went through, Harmann fully understands anyone snapping under the stress of combat in any war. "You are trained to hate and kill beginning in basic training. ... You distrust anything that happens" involving the enemy.

But Harmann also says being in the military taught him organization and planning. "I would never, ever, ever give up that life experience. It helped me in running a business. I really learned a lot about life from it."

He is an active member of Chapter 425 of Vietnam Veterans of America in Waukesha. His son Andy enlisted in the Army and served in Afghanistan in 2005. "How do you protect a man from himself? I didn't want him to go in," Harmann says.

Andy Harmann, New Berlin, Army in Afghanistan (son of Danny Harmann): "We felt we were doing the right thing, and I still feel that way. It has given the United States the opportunity to take the fight to the terrorists. But I don't think the people of Afghanistan care either way – the effect of the Taliban was not big out where I was (in Paktika province). Some of the people were so rural that they didn't even know the Russians invaded," which was in 1979. The Soviets found Afghanistan to be a disastrous quagmire fighting some of the same tribal clans the Americans have faced, and finally pulled out in in 1989.

Bob Boulden, Burlington, Marine in Korea: He returned to South Korea and Seoul in 1995 and 2001 and was proud. "The streets of Seoul were so clean you almost could eat off of them." Overall, "Had the United States not been there, Communism would have taken over the world entirely. We believed we stopped Communism in its tracks."

Waylon Gross, Menomonee Falls, Army in Iraq: "When a military unit is functioning well, there is a great deal of camaraderie, a really strong bond. There's nothing really like it. That's what I miss now that I'm in the civilian sector," says Gross, who left the Army after his second tour in Iraq because of many factors, including the likelihood of a third tour. Gross is part of the Combat Veterans Motorcycle Association (http://www.combatvet.

org/), which puts veterans of many wars in outings and in projects, some of which help other veterans who are in need. It's all about "getting that camaraderie back," he says.

William McManus, Shorewood, Army in China-Burma-India theater in World War II: "Our biggest contribution was hauling all the supplies as far as we could to help with the fighting in China. At the time, we didn't think much of it, but we hauled a lot of tanks, too. We never realized how big our effort was." Nor does the world, he adds, given that the China-Burma-India Theater is seldom written about, compared to the ETO and major points in the Pacific.

Robert Dempsey, Onalaska, Marine in Korea: Koreans in America and in South Korea are thankful for their freedom, he says. "The entire Korean population here in La Crosse had a picnic for us. We made quite a few friendships. The kimchi was not too bad. They had it mild for us."

Appendix 1
Research example involving Tony Bennett

Some of the content of this book was developed from only a few words in some other book about some other subject; words that sent alarm bells of curiosity ringing loudly.

That is great advice to anyone with a historical question: Keep your eyes open. Be curious. Follow the smallest clue. Information is out there, just waiting for you to develop it.

Here is a non-Wisconsin example of how the compelling story of a typical G.I. infantry private was tracked down. Readers are encouraged to use this as inspiration in discovering and preserving the story of a relative of their own. This can range from something you always heard relatives talking about (but nobody ever bothered to start compiling) to piecing together someone's untold record from various components.

Anthony Benedetto of the 63rd Infantry Regiment was an 18-year-old private from Queens, N.Y., in the final months of World War II. He was one of the millions of Allied soldiers in Europe.

Benedetto arrived in the 63rd from the repple depot in February 1945 and was shocked by stories he heard from his new colleagues about those who had been killed just before he arrived, shocked by his own close calls as a newbie – and soon would by especially shocked by the concentration camps at Landsberg, Germany. They were 35 miles west of Dachau.[1]

Benedetto was just an anonymous young face, like every other GI. But he has been known for decades since as singer Tony Bennett.

A reader seeing that in Bennett's book could take the entertainer's comments and research what the Landsberg concentration camps were all about.

In author Tom Mueller's case, he already had researched Landsberg because his father, Tech Sgt. Wilferd (Bill) Mueller of the 286th Combat Engineer Battalion, had been at that very camp system, possibly on the same day as Bennett. The revelation about Bennett was news to the author.

---

[1] There were 11 small concentration camps around the city of Landsberg to supply slave labor for weapons producers. They were known as the Kaufering camps, named for another town in the area, according to the United States Holocaust Memorial Museum in Washington, D.C. at www.ushmm.org/wlc/en/article.php?ModuleId=10006171

Tom Mueller plugged Bennett into what he previously developed about his father and other members of the 286th, which he compiled in "Building the Bridges to Victory," a book that came out in 2011. Mueller wrote that book because that was his father's engineer unit, whose speciality was constructing floating bridges and the portable Bailey Bridge, and its history had never been written until he got involved with its veterans.[2]

The 286th was attached to Bennett's 63rd Division during large parts of February, March and April 1945, with the engineers doing the infantry's heavier tasks in minefields, at obstacles and building bridges for the dogfaces to advance. Basically, any infantry division had a combat engineer company or battalion (a battalion had engineer Companies A, B and C) attached to it.

After publishing the engineer book, Tom Mueller kept poking around the Internet, and found a note in which author Michael Hirsh was seeking members of the 255th Infantry Regiment, part of the 63rd Infantry, to interview a few years ago.

Hirsh's book was "The Liberators: America's Witnesses to the Holocaust" and came out in 2010.[3] Tom Mueller found it has a full chapter about Landsberg, quoting 11 soldiers, including six from the 63rd, plus an inmate. It would have been a great source to quote in Mueller's book had he come across it several months earlier. Alas.

In a segment on Bernard Schutz of the 20th Special Services (which put on entertainment shows for GIs) seeing the Landsberg camps, author Hirsh dropped this research bombshell: "For a short time Tony Bennett, a member of the 63rd Infantry Division, was their vocalist."[4]

Author Mueller quickly researched whether Bennett had ever discussed Landsberg, and he had, in precisely two pages in his 1998 autobiography, "The Good Life."[5]

Bennett said liberation of the camp was "the last official mission of the 255th Regiment" and that others can speak more eloquently, but that he would "never forget the desperate faces and empty stares of the prisoners as

---

[2] This book is from Eau Claire, Wis.: Holtz Creative Enterprises.

[3] The book is published by Bantam Books, New York.

[4] "The Liberators," p. 183.

[5] This book was written with Will Friedwald. The material about Landsberg is on pages 60-61.

they wandered aimlessly around the camp grounds. Once we took possession of the camp, we immediately got food and water to the survivors, but they had been brutalized for so long that at first they couldn't believe we were there to help them and not to kill them."

Bennett also said: "The whole thing was beyond comprehension. After seeing such horrors with my very own eyes, it angers me that some people insist there were no concentration camps."

Bennett does not give a date for when he was there. Bill Mueller of the 286th Engineers encountered Landsberg on April 30, and a paratrooper in the 101st Airborne was there one day earlier. Hirsh's book has segments dated April 25, 27 and 28 for being in the area or actually at the camps.

Mueller was the senior noncommissioned officer in the Recon and Intelligence section of the 286th Engineers and was on a recon mission when he encountered "the stench that haunted me for 50 years," as he once put it in a short letter to his son.[6]

In 1985, when President Ronald Reagan ignited a world uproar by joining West German Chancellor Helmut Kohl in visiting a cemetery in Bitburg that included the graves of SS men, he said in a letter to Tom: "All the talk this past week of Nazi concentration camps has stirred up memories that have lain dormant for years. We were told there were 5,000 at Landsberg perhaps when at capacity. Some left just before we entered but most were incapable of going far. ... The one (Croatian) I helped out the gate never made it any farther. The train-car loads of dead were for real – two I saw, another I didn't look in. But they were there just to work until death by starvation."

Mueller also gave a few other details in another brief handwritten account: "The live inmates I spoke to were Balkan Jews for the most part. There were three boxcars in the southern end of the camp – two I looked in were full of bodies to be shipped to the Dachau crematoria. The third I didn't look in. The man I helped leave the camp was a Croatian – he died just outside the gate."

Winton Petersen of A Company of the 286th Engineers, in the extensive oral history that he recorded for the Veterans History Project at the Library of Congress,[7] said he saw that:

---

[6] "Building the Bridges to Victory," p. 74.

[7] http://lcweb2.loc.gov/cocoon/vhp/story/loc.natlib.afc2001001.00138/transcript?ID=sr0001. This account is quoted at greater length in "Building the Bridges to Victory."

Hundreds of inmates had been frantically machine-gunned and feeble attempts were made to burn the bodies. They were interlaced with wood and set on fire to destroy the evidence. Whether it was a fast advance of the American troops or the fact that they just did not have time to get the fire started, they failed. Many of the corpses had their hair singed. Others were half in and half out of the mass grave as if they were attempting to crawl out of the death trap when they died.

Scattered over four or five acres were bodies that had been shot or clubbed and left where they fell. Possibly the most repulsive and emotional site of all was in the woods near the camp where small children were literally cut in half by machine gun bullets. The condition of the bodies indicated how they had suffered, as most appeared as skeletons with skin over the bones from a long period of starvation. Decomposition had not yet begun, so the murders had to be committed very recently.

... Farther down toward town, we came across several boxcars on a railroad siding, and again the refugees kept pointing to them and tried to explain to us that we should look inside the cars. We expected to find ammunition or foodstuffs, so we shot open the doors only to find that they were piled to the roof with dead bodies.

The Holocaust Museum says "inmates provided the labor necessary to build subterranean facilities for fighter aircraft production in the Landsberg area. The region was chosen in part because of its favorable geological composition for the construction of mammoth underground installations, which were to be insulated by 9- to 15-foot-thick concrete walls. To house the concentration camp prisoners, the SS created camps near the proposed industrial sites."[8]

While the Landsberg camps sometimes are mentioned in books and the national press, the city of Landsberg is far better known for being the place where Adolf Hitler was imprisoned in 1924 and wrote "Mein Kampf" in his cell.

The camps housed a total of about 30,000 Jews and other people, and about 14,000 had died by the time of liberation, according to a New York

---

[8] www.ushmm.org/wlc/en/article.php?ModuleId=10006171

Times story that Tom Mueller found in 1989, one year after passing through the area, and sent to his father.[9]

Another account, which also was found by keeping one's eyes open for mentions of Landsberg when reading other books, is from Paratrooper Donald Burgett. He said his 101st Airborne Division found one Landsberg camp on April 29, one day before Bill Mueller of the 286th Engineers was there or at others.

Burgett, who thought he had seen almost everything in months of combat in Normandy, Holland and then in Germany, devotes a 20-page chapter to Landsberg in his book, "Beyond the Rhine: A Screaming Eagle in Germany."[10]

Behind the fence was a sight that I will never forget: bodies upon bodies of starved, skeletal human beings. They were piled about three feet or higher in a mass that seemed to cover the largest part of this side of the compound. Living skeletons dressed in blue-and-white-striped uniforms wandered about in the streets and within the compound; others just wandered inside the wire enclosure like zombies ...

A few who were in slightly better condition than the others came stumbling, holding their arms out to us, wanting to embrace, to thank us for their liberation. As much compassion as we felt for them we just couldn't bring ourselves to accept their hugs, for they looked near death, had dysentery caked down their legs, large open sores on their arms and legs, and they looked as though they might have had lice and other vermin. ...

A few in critical condition were made to lie on the ground

---

[9] Schemann, Serge (1989). Bavarian Town Chases Away Prostitutes, Ghosts of Nazism. New York Times story in Milwaukee Journal, July 9, p. 2J.

[10] Published in 2001 by Presidio Press of Novato, Calif. The excerpts quoted are from pages 102 and 105, but there are many more notable passages and the book is strongly recommended. The 2001 HBO series "Band of Brothers" dealt with other men in the 101st Airborne coming across this camp. See its home page at http://www.hbo.com/band-of-brothers/index.html

where they were, to be made as comfortable as possible with blankets in their last moments of life. Many smiled as they passed on, knowing they had died in freedom. ...

Bernard Schutz of the 20th Special Services tells this story in Hirsh's book: "recently freed prisoners lynched one of their former guards while his cries for help were spurned by an American captain who said, 'They knew what they're doing, leave them alone.'"[11]

The Holocaust Museum in Washington, D.C., honors six Army divisions for liberating Landsberg or the Kaufering camps. Two of those divisions are the 36th Infantry, to which the 286th Engineers were attached at the time, and Bennett's 63rd Infantry, to which which the engineer battalion had been attached at various other times. Specifically, on April 27, the after-action report of the 286th Engineers says: "The 63rd Division, which the battalion was supporting, was relieved by the 36th Division. However, the battalion continued operations" in the same area with the replacement division.

The Holocaust Museum lists Bennett's 63rd Division as being at Landsberg on April 29-30 and the 36th as there on April 30 (which jibes with Bill Mueller's account that he was there on April 30). The other four divisions that the museum honors as Liberators of the Kaufering camps, and what the museum says are their dates, are the 103rd Infantry (April 27), 12th Armored (April 27), 10th Armored (April 27) and 101st Airborne (April 28).[12]

To summarize, the point of this appendix is that the reader should always keep her or his eyes open for details that will further develop a story or can develop a story in the first place. Sometimes that is in only a few words, as the Benedetto / Bennett example is.

---

[11] "The Liberators," p. 183.

[12] The title of Liberator is given only to full divisions – the museum says that under guidelines formulated by the Army, "Recognition will go to the parent division of the respective lower-echelon unit (regiment, battalion, company or platoon)." Thus, Tony Bennett is an official Holocaust Liberator. But because that status goes ONLY to full divisions, not smaller units, the 286th Combat Engineer Battalion is NOT an official Holocaust Liberator. The museum / Army guidelines also say, "Recognition will not be limited to only the first division to reach a camp, but will include divisions that arrived at the same camp or camp complex within 48 hours of the initial division."

Then those few words can be taken to the Internet and to the library to flesh out the details, as was done for every chapter in this book and for Bennett in this appendix. Sometimes those searches can be done via broad category; sometimes they can be done by searching for particular accounts within some history of an Army division; sometimes they show up after your initial searches.

The result of this diligence is excellent history for your family.

Appendix 2
How to help

These groups have been a great help to the research that went into this book – either directly or via intricately detailed, searchable databases of information – and thus are recommended for your donations and support in the future.

Wisconsin Historical Society
> www.wisconsinhistory.org/

Vietnam Veterans Memorial Fund
> www.vvmf.org

The Virtual Wall Vietnam Veterans Memorial
> www.virtualwall.org/

Memorial Day MIA Balloon Launch, Muskego, Wis.
> www.war-veterans.org/Wi37.htm

American Battle Monuments Commission (overseas cemeteries)
> www.abmc.gov

Chippewa Valley Museum, Eau Claire, Wis.
> www.cvmuseum.com/

Oak Creek Historical Society
> http://ochistorical.freeservers.com/

South Milwaukee Historical Society
> www.southmilwaukee.org/historical_society/

Your own local and / or county historical societies

Your own library

Sons of Union Veterans of the Civil War
> www.suvcw-wi.org/

Civil War Trust (battlefield preservation group)
> www.civilwar.org/

Bibliography

Ambrose, Stephen E. (1997). Citizen Soldiers: The U.S. Army From the Normandy Beaches to the Bulge to the Surrender of Germany. New York, N.Y.: Simon & Schuster.

Bearss, Edwin C., with Hills, J. Parker. Receding Tide: Vicksburg and Gettysburg, the Campaigns that Changed the Civil War. Washington, D.C.: National Geographic Society.

Beaudot, William J.K. (2003). The 24th Wisconsin Infantry in the Civil War: The Biography of a Regiment. Mechanicsburg, Pa.: Stackpole Books.

Bennett, Tony, with Friedwald, Will (1998). The Good Life. New York: Pocket Books.

Blakeley, H.W., Maj. Gen. (1957). 32nd Infantry Division in World War II. Madison, Wis.: 32nd Infantry Division History Commission, State of Wisconsin.

Bradley, James (2000). Flags of Our Fathers. New York: Bantam Books.

Brown, Ethan (2009). Shake the Devil Off: A True Story of the Murder that Rocked New Orleans. New York: St. Martin's Paperbacks edition.

Buenker, John D. (1998). The History of Wisconsin: Volume IV. Madison: State Historical Society of Wisconsin.

Burgett, Donald R. (2001). Beyond the Rhine: A Screaming Eagle in Germany. Novato, Calif.: Presidio Press.

China-Burma-India Hump Pilots Association (1992; third volume of information compiled from and for the association members). Paducah, Ky.: Turner Publishing Co.

Cole, Hugh M. (undated). The Ardennes: Battle of the Bulge. Old Saybrook, Conn.: Konecky & Konecky.

Cozzens, Peter (1990). No Better Place to Die: The Battle of Stones River. Urbana, Ill: University of Illinois Press.

Current, Richard N. (1976). The History of WIsconsin: Volume II. Madison: State Historical Society of WIsconsin.

Currey, Cecil B. (1984). Follow Me and Die: The Destruction of an American Division in World War II. Briarcliff Manor, N.Y.: Stein and Day.

D'Este, Carlo (1991). Fatal Decision: Anzio and the Battle for Rome. New York, N.Y. HarperCollins Publishers.

Dugan, James, and Stewart, Carroll (1962, 1998). Ploesti: The Great Ground-Air Battle of 1 August 1943. New York, N.Y.: Random House.

Eisenhower, John S. (2007). They Fought at Anzio. Columbia, Mo.: University of Missouri Press.

Gaff, Alan D. (1991). If This Is War: A History of the Campaign of Bull's Run by the Wisconsin Regiment Thereafter Known as the Ragged Ass Second. Dayton, Ohio: Morningside House Inc.

Garrison, Webb (1992). 2,000 Questions and Answers About the Civil War. New York: Gramercy Books.

Glusman, John A. (2005). Conduct Under Fire: Four American Doctors and Their Fight for Life as Prisoners of the Japanese. New York: Penguin Group.

Groves, Leslie (1962). Now It Can Be told: The Story of the Manhattan Project. New York: Harper & Brothers.

Gurda, John (1999). The Making of Milwaukee. Milwaukee, Wis.: Milwaukee County Historical Society.

Halliday, E.M. (2000). When Hell Froze Over: The Secret War Between the U.S. and Russia at the Top of the World!" New York: ibooks.

Hanson, Neil (2005). Unknown Soldiers: The Story of the Missing of the First World War. New York: Alfred A. Knopf.

Heckscher, August (1991). Woodrow Wilson. New York: Collier Books, Macmillan Publishing Co.

Herdegen, Lance J. (2008). Those Damned Black Hats!" The Iron Brigade in the Gettysburg Campaign. New York, N.Y. Savas Beatie LLC.

Hornfischer, James D. (2011). Neptune's Inferno: The U.S. Navy at Guadalcanal. New York, N.Y. Bantam Books.

Hoyt, Edwin P. (1972). Leyte Gulf: The Death of the Princeton. New York, N.Y.: Avon Books.

Hirsh, Michael (2010): The Liberators: America's Witnesses to the Holocaust. New York: Bantam Books.

Hunt, Gaillard (compiler) (1925). Israel, Elihu and Cadwallader Washburn: A Chapter in America Biography. New York: The Macmillan Co.

Hurst, Jack (1993). Nathan Bedford Forrest: A Biography. New York: Vintage Books.

Jeffers, H. Paul (2000). An Honest President: The Life and Presidencies of Grover Cleveland. William Morrow.

Klement, Frank (1997, 2001). Wisconsin in the Civil War: The Home Front and the Battle Front. Madison: The State Historical Society of Wisconsin.

Larsen, Sarah A., and Miller, Jennifer M. (2010). Wisconsin Vietnam War Stories: Our Veterans Remember. Madison: Wisconsin Historical Society Press.

Larsen, Sarah A., and Miller, Jennifer M. (2008). Wisconsin Korean War Stories: Veterans Tell Their Stories From the Forgotten War. Madison, Wis.: Wisconsin Historical Society Press.

Lukacs, John D. (2010). Escape From Davao: The Forgotten Story of the Most Daring Prison Break of the Pacific War. New York, N.Y.: Simon & Schuster.

MacDonald, Charles B. (1985). A Time for Trumpets: the Untold Story of the Battle of the Bulge. New York: William Morrow and Co. Inc.

MacDonald, Charles B. (1973, 2007). Victory in Europe, 1945: The Last Offensive of World War II. Mineola, N.Y.: Dover Publications Inc.

Martin, Michael (2006). A History of the 4th Wisconsin Infantry and Cavalry in the Civil War. New York : Savas Beatie.

Mead, Gary (2000). The Doughboys: America and the First World War. New York: Overlook Press.

Michno, Gregory (2001). Death on the Hellships: Prisoners at Sea in the Pacific War. Annapolis, Md.: Naval Institute Press.

Miller, Francis Trevelyan (1957). The Cavalry: The Photographic History of the Civil War. New York: Castle Books.

Monahan, Evelyn M., and Neidel-Greenlee, Rosemary (2003). And If I Perish: Frontline U.S. Army Nurses in World War II. New York: Alfred A. Knopf.

Moser, Don (1978). China-Burma-India. Alexandria, Va.: Time-Life Books.

Mueller, Tom (2011): Building the Bridges to Victory: The Story of One Army Combat Engineer Battalion From France to Germany to a Concentration Camp. Eau Claire, Wis.: Holtz Creative Enterprises.

Mueller, Tom (2010). Heart of the Century 1949 to 1951. Indianapolis, Ind.: Dog Ear Publishing.

Mueller, Tom (2009). The Wisconsin 3,800: Our Men and Women Buried or MIA in the Lands They Liberated in World War II. Indianapolis, Ind.: Dog Ear Publishing.

Nesbit, Richard C. (1985). The History of Wisconsin: Volume III. Madison: State Historical Society of Wisconsin.

Peck, George W. (1958). Peck's Bad Boy and His Pa. Introduction by E.F. Bleiler. New York, N.Y.: Dover Publications. The earliest copy in the Milwaukee County library system is from 1893.

Peck, George W. (1887). How Private George W. Peck Put Down the Rebellion, or the Funny Experiences of a Raw Recruit. Chicago and New York: Bedford, Clarke & Co. Republished in 2002 by Faded Banner Publications of Bryan, Ohio.

Ross, Bill D. (1985). Iwo Jima: Legacy of Valor. New York, N.Y.: Vanguard Press Inc.

Ross, Sam (1964). The Empty Sleeve: A Biography of Lucius Fairchild. Madison, Wis.: The State Historical Society of Wisconsin.

Sears, Stephen W. (ed.) (1991). Eyewitness to World War II. Boston, Mass.: Houghton Mifflin Co.

Smith, Jim B., and McConnell, Malcolm (2002): The Last Mission: The Secret Story of World War II's Final Battle. New York: Broadway Books.

Sulzberger, C.J. (1966). The American Heritage Picture History of World War II, Heritage Publishing Co. Inc.

Symonds, Craig L. (2011). The Battle of Midway. New York, N.Y.: Oxford University Press.

Wisconsin War History Commission (1920). The 32nd Division in the World War, 1917-1919. Madison, Wis.

Witmer, John (2010). Sisters in Arms: A Father Remembers. New Berlin, Wis.: John Witmer.

———— Wisconsin's Gold Star List; Soldiers, Sailors, Marines, and Nurses from the Badger State Who Died in the Federal Service During the World War (1925). Prepared by John G. Gregory. Madison, Wis.: The Society.

CPSIA information can be obtained at www.ICGtesting.com
Printed in the USA
LVOW01s1140100913

351728LV00002B/58/P